NOAM CHOMSKY

Consensus and Controversy

Essays in Honour of Noam Chomsky

Falmer International Master-Minds Challenged

Psychology Series Editors: Drs Sohan and Celia Modgil

NOAM CHOMSKY

Consensus and Controversy

EDITED BY

Sohan Modgil, Ph.D.

Reader in Educational Research and Development
Brighton Polytechnic

AND

Celia Modgil, Ph.D.

Senior Lecturer in Educational Psychology
London University

The Falmer Press
(A member of the Taylor & Francis Group)
New York, Philadelphia and London

USA   The Falmer Press, Taylor & Francis Inc., 242 Cherry Street, Philadelphia, PA 19106-1906

UK   The Falmer Press, Falmer House, Barcombe, Lewes, East Sussex, BN8 5DL

First published in 1987

Library of Congress Cataloging in Publication Data

Main entry under title:
Noam Chomsky: consensus and controversy.

  (Falmer international masterminds challenge)
    1. Chomsky, Noam. 2. Linguistics. 3. Psychology.
4. Anthropology. I. Modgil, Sohan. II. Modgil, Celia.
III. Series.
P85.C47N63 1986   410   86-13385
ISBN 1-85000-022-0

Jacket design by Caroline Archer

Typeset in 10/12 Times
by Imago Publishing Ltd., Thame, Oxon.

*Printed in Great Britain by Taylor & Francis (Printers) Ltd,
Rankine Road, Basingstoke, Hants.*

Contributors

Dr Sohan Modgil   and   Dr Celia Modgil
Brighton Polytechnic   *University of London*

Dr Terence Moore and Christine Carling
*Clare College, University of Cambridge and
formerly at University of Manchester
Institute of Science and Technology, currently freelance writer*

Professor Antoine Danchin
Institut Pasteur, Paris

Professor John Marshall
Radcliffe Infirmary, University of Oxford

Professor Neil Smith
University College, London

Dr David Kilby
University of Essex

Dr Margaret Deuchar
University of Sussex

Jean Aitchison
University of London

Dr Raphael Salkie
Brighton Polytechnic

Dr David Gil
Tel Aviv University

Professor P.N. Johnson-Laird
*Medical Research Council
Applied Psychology Unit, Cambridge*

Professor Thomas Roeper
University of Massachusetts, Amherst

Professor Hermina Sinclair
University of Geneva

Dr Colin Biggs
University of Reading

Professor Yorick Wilks
New Mexico State University

Dr Philip Carr
University of Newcastle-upon-Tyne

Dr James Russell
University of Liverpool

Professor Thomas de Zengotita
New York University

Professor Scott Atran
Columbia University

Dr Clive Criper
University of Edinburgh

Dr Christopher Coker
University of London

Acknowledgments

The undertaking of this 'Falmer International Master-Minds Challenged' Psychology Series was only possible in collaboration with the numerous distinguished contributors herein. We are greatly indebted to them for demonstrating their trust by accepting our invitation to join forces to provide statements of how Chomsky's theory is seen in relation to particular disciplines.

We are further grateful to Falmer Press, a member of the Taylor & Francis group. We express our very sincere gratitude to Malcolm Clarkson, Managing Director, Falmer Press.

Sohan and Celia Modgil
December 1985

Contents

In loving memory of
Lilian and Victor

I: Introduction

1. Noam Chomsky: The Continuing Debate

SOHAN AND CELIA MODGIL

INTRODUCTION

During the last thirty years, Noam Chomsky's brilliant contribution to knowledge has been well known world-wide. From the early transmission, his work has not been without its critics. Naturally, criticisms persist, although his work continues to be acknowledged frequently with great admiration in psychology. Given his prolific work, it would seem justified to consider the discrepancies, the omissions, together with the various interpretations which have been and are currently being highlighted.

Among recent significant attempts to evaluate Chomsky's theory is Chomsky's (1980) dialogue with Piaget, the founder of genetic epistemology, which involved considerations of the aspects of cognition that are innate, the developmental relationship between language and cognition, together with a range of related issues. With the support of a group of anthropologists, biologists, mathematicians, philosophers, psychologists and leading behavioural scientists, this debate made a significant contribution regarding the relevance of the two great masters (cf. Atran; Bischof; Cellerier; Changeux; Duting; Fodor; Mehler; Papert; Petitot; Premack; Putnam).

More recently, the publication of Terence Moore and Christine Carling's (1982) book, *Understanding Language: Towards a Post-Chomskyan Linguistics*, has provided an excellent forerunner to a wider, directed analysis of Chomsky's work and its place in the evolution of psychology. The authors examine Chomsky's contribution to the study of language and argue that his model of explanation is insufficient. They maintain that Chomsky's work was believed by many

to be one of the most technically sophisticated of the human sciences, throwing new light on fundamental issues in the related fields of psychology and philosophy. Yet today theoretical linguistics is deeply divided with little agreement on goals, problems and methods of investigation, and with few of its findings not in dispute ... Paradoxically under Chomsky's influence linguistics turn out to have been moving not closer to but further away from the fundamental issues in language acquisition, understanding and production they initially appeared to be confronting ... Chomsky's own attempt to turn linguistics into a '*hard*' science was itself a reaction to the view prevailing when he entered the field of what a scientific linguistics should be.

However, Sampson (1983) argues that 'to say that a discipline deals with issues that many people find uninspiring is not to say that the discipline is invalid in its own terms.' Moore and Carling's account of the recent history of linguistics is not persuasive. 'Moore and Carling say many perceptive things about the unsatisfactory current state of linguistics. But the trouble with the method they ascribe to Chomsky is the same as the trouble with Christianity: it hasn't been tried' (p. 17).

The following quotation from *Dialogues on the Psychology of Language and Thought* (Rieber and Voyat, 1983) encapsulates Noam Chomsky's contribution to psychology, and indicates the basis of his objectives together with his general approach and attitude to theory development and research:

> The particular domain into which I put most of my energies, the structure of language, seems to me to have been a very exciting one just in the last seven or eight years. I don't pretend to speak for any consensus in the field here, in fact, I'm in a very small minority in the field in this respect, but I believe it's been possible in the past few years to develop a theory of languages with a degree of deductive structure that provides a kind of unification and explanatory power going well beyond anything that would have been imagined even a decade ago. Again, I don't think many linguists agree with me about this—but that's the way it looks to me. Let me stress again, so there is no confusion about it, that with regard to what I just said, I suppose I'm in a very small minority in the field today. But then, that has always been the case. With regard to me, it doesn't seem very different now from what it was ten or twenty years ago. But my own views are not what they were then, and I hope they will not be the same ten years from now. Any person who hopes to be part of an active growing field will take that for granted. (p. 63)

CONTINUING THE DEBATE: THE STRATEGY OF THE BOOK

The book has as its objective the evaluation of elements of Chomsky's work from the perspectives of a range of areas: neurobiology; universals and typology; pidgins and creoles; core grammar and periphery; syntax, semantics and psychology of language; innatism *vs* constructivism; artificial intelligence; epistemology; anthropological linguistics; and politics. The aim is to provide in one single source the most recent 'crosscurrents and crossfire', to begin to clarify the contribution of Chomsky to the evolution of the understanding of human behaviour.

The volume attempts to provide theoretical analysis supported by research on aspects of Chomsky's work, presented predominantly either positively or negatively by *pairs* of distinguished academics representing particular areas of knowledge. The *paired* contributions have been exchanged, through the editors, to provide an opportunity for both parties to refute the 'heart' of the opposing paper. In exceptional contexts, single contributions supplement the 'paired' debates. This would perhaps go some way towards the prescription that what the study of human behaviour needs at this stage of its own development is a wide-ranging approach to the facts. It is hoped that this growth will continue so as to include an openness to the evidence outside Chomsky's own framework.

Although axiomatic, it would be expedient to emphasize that the labelling 'predominantly positive' or 'predominantly negative' implies that the writer of the predominantly 'positive' chapter agrees in the *main* with the theory but is not in *entire* agreement, therefore being allowed some latitude towards disagreement. Likewise, 'negative' chapters mean that contributors *predominantly* but not *entirely* disagree with the theory, therefore permitting some latitude towards agreement. The interchange of chapters therefore produces points of consensus and points of controversy.

The difficulties in this ambitious debate project are not minimized. Although every attempt has been made to achieve precision matching of pairs, in exceptional cases, one of the contributors within a matched pair has followed a 'middle course'. This established itself as a 'contrasting' enough pair to lend itself to the debate format of the book.

Although the editors dictated the generic topics to be debated, the contributors were free to focus on any inherent aspect or specialization of their own. Again, however, the consequent interchange of the chapters allows formulation of points of consensus and of controversy, therefore retaining the thrust of the debate.

The choice of the contributors was restricted to those who are objectively critical and who are knowledgeable about the theory. Some of the most publicized critics tend to have non-scientific axes to grind and their views and their polemics are well known. The scholarly value of the book could be damaged seriously unless the contributors have the desire and the capacity for the kind of intellectual honesty needed to come to grips seriously with the scientific, psychological and social issues raised by the theory.

CONTENTS OF EACH CONTRIBUTION

Terence Moore and Christine Carling's chapter provides initiation, and their introductory comments are designed to stimulate and provoke the reader to engage in the debate. The Introduction provides a critical overview of Chomsky's work, charting in particular the shifts in aims and direction. A major shift has been in the justification of generative grammars—the move from seeing generative grammars as accounting for 'the creative aspect of language use' to claiming that this style of grammar throws light on the problem of how a child acquires knowledge of the grammar of his own language. Moore and Carling maintain that this shift in the direction of Chomsky's theories from creativity to innateness via universal grammar has raised major areas of controversy, three of which are discussed in some detail in the Introduction: (i) the problem of confirmation/falsification—how are the theories tested? (ii) the problem of correspondence—what are the theories tested against? (iii) the problem of 'psychological reality'—exactly what are the theories theories of? None of these questions has been satisfactorily resolved in the course of Chomsky's work. Moore and Carling assert that Chomsky is further seen as posing severe difficulties of interpretation on occasion because of his versatile use of key terms such as 'language' and 'grammar'.

Neurobiology

Together with an emphasis on the link between meaning and structure, Antoine Danchin considers it unreasonable to support the Chomskyan view of inborn brain structures underlying universal syntactic structures without giving some hint about a neuronal organization that would explain at least some of the language features. The model proposed is far from explaining all of the syntactic structures but it demonstrates that it is not absurd to conceive the question of language-related neuronal circuitry in the terms proposed by Chomsky. Syntactic structures are therefore universals, but tongue and culture are brought into the centre of brain organization of perception. Marshall considers the extent to which Chomsky's work can be responsible for the changes in approach to infants' language as revealed in the changing terminology: language *learning*, language *acquisition* and language *growth*. The hypothesis that language is learned, in the sense that it is taught by 'pedagogically-sophisticated' adult users has fared badly in recent years. Further, attempts to account for the course of language acquisition in terms of environmental contingencies that an all-purpose learning device could respond to have not met with much success. Marshall concludes that if the development of current linguistic theory succeeds in explaining the course of language growth, it will reveal wider areas of ignorance about how to relate 'abstract conditions' to their biological realization.

Universals and Typology

With reference to universals and typology, Neil Smith outlines the effect on linguistic theory of Chomsky's concentration on explanation rather than description. It illustrates the progression from a preoccupation with data via a concentration on analyses to the attempt to deal with universal principles of grammar. This development is then generalized from the construction of linguistic theory to the treatment of language typology. Smith presents a critique of non-generative typology of the kind associated with Greenberg (1963) and Comrie (1981), followed by a discussion of *parametric variation*: the attempt within generative grammar to account for differences among languages on the basis of the choice of particular values for universally determined variables. Specifically, different instantiations of the universal principle of subjacency are illustrated by reference to English and the Philippine language Hiligaynon. Smith pleads for the cessation of hostilities between traditional typology and generative theory so that each can benefit from the insights of the other. David Kilby presents a contrast between the essentially comparative work on language universals in the Greenberg (*op. cit.*) tradition and the Chomskyan approach to universals where they are interpreted psychologically, and are argued for on the basis of just a small range of languages. Just as the Greenbergian tradition has found it more fruitful to move in the direction of implicational universals and typology, so in recent years has the Chomskyan trend moved towards typology. The thrust of Kilby's paper is that the general orientation of the Chomskyan tradition tends to ensure that typology in that framework is inadequate in various ways, and that inconvenient data can be disposed of with too many special considerations: the notion of 'markedness' is singled out here. Much of the criticism is based on the 'Prodrop' phenomenon in a range of languages.

Pidgins and Creoles

Within the context of language universals: pidgins and creoles, Margaret Deuchar aims to demonstrate how Chomsky's work on language universals has proved of considerable benefit for research in pidgins and creoles. She maintains that a psycho-biological view of universals has made it possible to account for the similarities in pidgins and creoles without assuming a genealogical model of language evolution. The same theoretical perspective has made it possible to account for similarities among historically unrelated sign languages, which Deuchar argues are a type of creole. Deuchar continues that sign language research has not only benefitted theoretically from a Chomskyan view of language universals, but has also provided empirical support for Chomsky's view of the relation between universal grammar and language learning, by providing a unique test case for the 'poverty of the stimulus' argument. Jean Aitchison, however, suggests that Chomsky's view of language universals is somewhat narrow. Chomsky's emphasis on their biological necessity leads to the conclusion that language structure is arbitrary and unmotivated. She argues that 'functional' or 'external' explanations are at least as important and interesting as 'internal' or 'innatist' ones: it is possible that a number of principles of universal grammar fall out naturally because they are the most likely solution to a particular set of problems. This can be illustrated by looking at pidgins and creoles. These are simpler than full languages, yet utilize similar linguistic processes. They therefore provide a microcosm for studying the 'natural' developmental course of language. Aitchison continues, that an examination of focusing devices used in the early stages of Tok Pisin (Papua New Guinea) leads to the conclusion that leftward movement rules are considerably more likely to develop than rightward movement ones. This in turn may shed light on the fact that in languages in general, leftward movement rules tend to be unbounded, whereas rightward ones are severely constrained.

Core Grammar and Periphery

In consideration of the Chomskyan distinction between core grammar and periphery, Raphael Salkie argues that the distinction is a virtually inevitable consequence of Chomsky's basic aim in studying languages: to apply the approach of the natural sciences—what he calls the 'Galilean style'—to the study of language. The distinction is one of a number of idealizations and simplifications which Chomsky says are necessary if language is to be studied in this way. Salkie presents and discusses some recent work in generative grammar which assumes the core-periphery distinction. The distinction is evaluated in two ways: first within Chomsky's general framework of assumptions, accepting his basic aim and looking at how the core-periphery distinction helps him to achieve it; and secondly, from a broader perspective, looking at how Chomsky's work connects with empirical research into language acquisition. David Gil points to the three central characteristics of Chomsky's mentalist linguistics: the autonomy thesis, the distinction between language and grammar, and the view that language is a joint product of a number of mental faculties—of which grammar is but one. Gil in his paper suggests that these three characteristics, when followed through to their logical conclusions, lead to a theory of grammar substantially different from most current models—a theory of considerably narrower scope. A wide variety of phenomena in language and elsewhere is shown to instantiate a general principle of linearization whereby small precedes large; this principle is accounted for within a theory of man's prosodic faculty. The linguistic phenomena upholding this principle—pertaining, *inter alia*, to syllable structure, case and agreement morphology, and word order—are consequently argued to fall outside the scope of grammatical theory. The methodological moral is that the study of grammar can only proceed hand in hand with the study of other mental faculties such as prosody, vision and mathematical reasoning.

Syntax, Semantics and Psychology of Language

Johnson-Laird's chapter analyzes and attempts to reassess Chomsky's conception of the psychology of language. Chomsky argues that linguistics forms part of cognitive psychology, and that its initial goal is to construct a descriptively adequate grammar, which corresponds to the mental representation of linguistic competence. Its major goal, however, is to develop an explanatorily adequate theory, which accounts for how children acquire grammar from a corpus of utterances. Johnson-Laird continues, that whilst accepting many aspects of Chomsky's programme, the chapter proposes that there is a more appropriate division of labour: linguistics should characterize the functions that the mind computes in understanding of producing sentences, whereas psycholinguistics should discover the mental mechanisms underlying the computation of these functions. This account makes sense of the contributions of both disciplines, but it also leaves open the possibility of a unified psychology of language.

Innatism vs Constructivism

In the paper entitled 'The Modularity of Meaning in Language Acquisition', Thomas Roeper raises the questions: What do the old debates on language acquisition look like in a modern light? What is the innateness claim? Roeper maintains that Chomsky's earliest notions of an innate transformation were barely more constrained than the notion of 'rule' itself. There was very little that a transformation could not do (i.e., copy, delete, move, permute) and its domain of application was not even limited to sentences (i.e., generalized transformations). In retrospect Chomsky's position might seem nearly as abstract and unconstrained as Skinner's notions of stimulus and response or Piaget's use of 'general cognition'. However, there was and is a fundamental conceptual difference: the notion that language capability was genetically *constrained* in ways that 'general' cognition was not. The constraints themselves, Chomsky argues, have a character at once so abstract and so subtle that there is no conceivable avenue to learning them. Roeper attempts to explicate and buttress this argument. Hermina Sinclair acknowledges the strong and salutary impact of Chomsky's work on philosophy and psychology. Sinclair acknowledges the insights Chomsky's work has afforded her and she shares his anti-empiricist views, but she does not share his modular view of the human mind nor his genetic determinism of language. Sinclair continues that Chomsky analyzes sentence-types, notes adults' knowledge of sentence-meanings, and concludes to the implausibility of this knowledge being acquired by cognitive mechanisms such as induction from data; he thence concludes that the linguistic theory that accounts for the structures reflects intrinsic properties of the human mind. A constructivist psycholinguist analyzes the way children gradually build up a mastery of the interpretation and production of sentences, and concludes that the developmental patterns can be accounted for by general cognitive processes such as those postulated by Piaget, while the patterns appear incompatible with the unfolding of a genetically determined universal grammar. New evidence from neuro-biology may help to clarify the matter further.

Artificial Intelligence

Colin Biggs begins by establishing some of the central tenets of Chomsky's 'scientific study of language' (to echo a phrase of Dresher and Hornstein, 1976). Biggs argues that the most important of these is the competence/performance distinction, and four distinct responses to this distinction are identified in the artificial intelligence literature, two of them involving the notion of 'psychological reality'. Chomsky's recent views on 'psychological reality' are discussed and it is suggested that they form the basis for a research programme which would be of value to artificial intelligence. In considering the extent to which it is possible to establish relevant theoretical links between the work of Chomsky in theoretical linguistics and the field of artificial intelligence, Biggs concludes that Chomsky's influence on artificial intelligence has, as a matter of fact, been considerably less than his influence on other areas identified in this volume, and yet that there is a clear sense in which artificial intelligence can now benefit, both in practical and theoretical ways, by drawing far more on the work of linguistics, and (in particular) by incorporating the methodological insights and explanatory goals of current competence-based grammatical theories. Yorick Wilks is confident that one cannot take up the subject of Chomsky and artificial intelligence with much optimism that any intellectual exchange will take place. Wilks argues that Chomsky's adoption of a range of inappropriate metaphors, with which he has tried to support a particular view of linguistic methodology opposed to all empirical concerns, has been at the heart of the controversies and misunderstandings between artificial intelligence workers and Chomsky and his supporters. Recent developments in linguistics, free of the competence/performance distinction, show that there are at bottom no insuperable barriers between the two disciplines.

Epistemology

A fundamental assumption in Chomsky's (1966, 1968, 1976, 1980) work is the notion that the object of linguistic inquiry should be taken to be a speaker-internal, psychological entity. Philip Carr maintains that this assumption has been fairly widely accepted in the past, and with it the view that linguistics is therefore a branch of cognitive psychology. However, Carr continues that this conception of the ontological status of linguistic structure has been challenged in the past ten years by a gradually increasing number of workers, both in the field of the philosophy of linguistics and within theoretical linguistics itself. Principal among these are Itkonen (1974, 1976, 1978) and Katz (1981), both of whom take the object of linguistic inquiry to be non-psychological, and both of whom establish a philosophical basis for an autonomous theoretical linguistics, distinct from either psycholinguistics or sociolinguistics. Carr surveys these proposals and suggests an alternative to them, interactionism, which acts as the basis for an autonomous theoretical linguistics, but which nonetheless allows for fruitful interdisciplinary work on the relationship between, on the one hand, linguistic structure per se, and on the other, social, psychological and neurological factors. James Russell argues that Chomsky's insistence that linguistic competence consists in *sui generis* linguistic rules and representations makes speech production, comprehension and acquisition very difficult to conceptualize. Russell asserts that the basic problem is that of how an 'interaction' is supposed to take place between a conceptual and a formal-computational component. This difficulty carries over into the way in which Chomsky regards the scientific status of this theoretical psychology. Chomsky feels able to justify paying scant attention to the extra-linguistic determinants of language competence.

Anthropological Linguistics

Maintaining that Kant's *Critique of Pure Reason* once established the limits of natural science and provided eighteenth and nineteenth-century cultural and historical studies with an opportunity to justify themselves philosophically on their own terms, Thomas de Zengotita argues that Chomskyan linguistics, in setting the substantive and methodological standard for sciences of human nature, now provides a similar opportunity. Post-Chomskyan human sciences must follow the example of generative grammar; they must be logically explicit theories of naturally definable domains of cognition, perception and behaviour which are uniquely characteristic of our species and they must entail empirical consequences for testing in that domain. This situation confronts anthropologists with a clear choice. Their traditional subject matter cannot meet the substantive standard set by Chomskyan linguistics; de Zengotita continues that method cannot produce a science when its object does not exist. Politics, religion and kinship are not faculties of our nature like language and vision. They are aspects of a total social performance constituted by all the human faculties in particular historical contexts. If there can be no science of language performance we cannot expect a science of social performance. Anthropologists wishing to be scientists should give up their traditional subject matter for the study of brain organization. Anthropologists wishing to retain that subject matter should find an appropriate way to approach it.

There are striking cross-cultural uniformities in the structure of folkbiological classification. Scott Atran argues that such uniform taxonomic knowledge, under socio-cultural learning situations so diverse, results from certain regular and domain-specific processes of human cognition, though local circumstances undoubtedly trigger and condition the stable forms of knowledge attained. Meaning for living kind terms is analyzed as essentially distinct from the semantics of other object domains (e.g., artifacts). This owes to a living kind being conceived as a physical sort whose intrinsic 'nature' is presumed, even if unknown; that is the semantically typical properties which the definition of a living kind term describes are necessary—not merely possible—in virtue of the presumed underlying nature of that kind. That is why, e.g., a legless tiger can still be classed with animals considered to be quadrupeds 'by nature'. It is this presumption of underlying nature, Atran argues, which underpins the taxonomic stability of such phenomenal kinds. Atran continues that ordinary commitment to phenomenally typical properties precludes construing the bond between a phenomenal type and its underlying nature simply as a causal tie between a provisionally useful stereotype and some nomic essence which experts tell us our stereotype must really stand for (or, barring likely discovery of a nomic essence, stand for nothing at all). Commonsense meaning may thus be logically independent of scientific reference: e.g., trees and sparrows remain American folk kinds, with presumed natures, even though they are not scientific (phyletic) kinds. Likewise, trying to assess the influence of Chomsky's work on anthropology, Clive Criper thinks that one is faced with the recognition either that similar intellectual influences have been at work in both linguistics and anthropology or that, as is likely, his influence on anthropology has come through his influence on this general intellectual climate. Criper asserts that Chomsky's direct contribution or influence is minimal and he would be the first to say so. His position has always been that human linguistic knowledge is different in kind from other types of knowledge requiring special programming and special principles. So it does not seem profitable to expect that the study of the non-linguistic systems constructed and used by humans can be carried out in the same way as the study of structures and transformations; semantic rules are not likely to illuminate our study of social institutions or even other aspects of cognition.

Politics

A discussion of Chomsky's contribution to political science from his works during the Vietnam War to the present period is presented by Christopher Coker. The paper looks first at the extent to which Chomsky's study of linguistics has influenced his analysis of political affairs. The discussion continues on a number of prominent features of Chomsky's political writings. Foremost amongst these is his definition and discussion of the semantics of terror and the systemic violence which he claims to be part of the American imperium. From there it goes on to provide a critical analysis of his discussion before concluding by looking at his anarchistic critique. The paper concludes by assessing Chomsky's impact on the academic community and the extent to which the ideas Chomsky first propagated in the sixties and which have been refined ever since are still of major importance.

A tabulated summary of the various debates, arranged in accordance with the areas of knowledge which the debators represent, has been provided at the end of the book.

REFERENCES

Chomsky, N. (1966) *Cartesian Linguistics*, London, Harper and Row.
Chomsky, N. (1968) *Language and Mind*, New York, Harcourt Brace Jovanovich.
Chomsky, N. (1976) *Reflections on Language*, London, Temple Smith.
Chomsky, N. (1980) *Rules and Representations*, New York, Columbia University Press.
Comrie, B. (1981) *Language Universals and Linguistic Typology*, Oxford, Blackwell.
Dresher, E. and Hornstein, N. (1976) 'On some supposed contributions of artificial intelligenc to the scientific study of language', *Cognition*, **4**, pp. 321–98.
Greenberg, J. (1963) 'Some universals of grammar with particular reference to the order of meaningful elements', in Greenberg, J. (Ed.), *Universals of Language*, MIT Press.
Itkonen, E. (1974) *Linguistics and Metascience*, Studia Philosophica Turkuensia II.
Itkonen, E. (1976) 'Linguistics and empiricalness: Answers to criticisms', papers in *Linguistics* 4, University of Helsinki Linguistics Department.
Itkonen, E. (1978) *Grammatical Theory and Metascience*, Amsterdam, Benjamins.
Katz, J. J. (1981) *Language and Other Abstract Objects*, Oxford, Blackwell.
Moore, T. and Carling, C. (1982) *Understanding Language: Towards a Post-Chomskyan Linguistics*, London, Macmillan Press.

Piattelli-Palmarini, M. (Ed.) (1980) *Language and Learning: The Debate between Jean Piaget and Noam Chomsky*, Cambridge, Mass., Harvard University Press.

Rieber, R. W. and Voyat, G. (1983) *Dialogues on the Psychology of Language and Thought: Conversations with Noam Chomsky, Charles Osgood, Jean Piaget, Ulric Neisser and Marcel Kinsbourne*, New York and London, Plenum Press.

Sampson, G. (1983) 'Meaning to say: Saying to mean', review of Moore, T. and Carling, C. (1982) *Understanding Language: Towards a Post-Chomskyan Linguistics*, London Macmillan Press, in *The Times Higher Education Supplement*, 4 February, p. 17.

II: Part One: Introductory Chapter

2. Chomsky: Consensus and Controversy—Introduction

TERENCE MOORE AND CHRISTINE CARLING

Noam Chomsky has a natural place in a series with the theme: consensus and controversy. Widely accepted as the most influential linguist of the past twenty-five years, his work has never, in the whole of that period, been free from strong and sometimes bitter challenge. His own writings chart the course of the disputes and debates which have marked his career. Nor does his vigour in responding to challenge lessen over the years. The lectures which make up one of his later works, *Rules and Representations*, fairly bristle with the names of opponents—Searle, Dummett, Lewis, and many others. Chomsky, it appears, thrives on challenge. So much so that one characteristic of his work is that he is likely to assume with very little question that his arguments against those who disagree with him must at the same time be arguments in support of his own views and theories. Yet there is no natural progression from proving someone wrong about *X* to proving you are right about *Y*: to proving someone wrongheaded in his understanding of, say, idealization, to proving your idealizations are the productive ones.

Before exploring some of the areas of consensus and controversy within Chomsky's work we want to introduce a word of caution to those who approach his work expecting to find a clear and straightforward exposition of his views. Chomsky is genuinely difficult to interpret at times because of the way he uses language and, in particular, technical terms. The result is that consciously or unconsciously he lays traps for unwary critics and opponents. 'Language', 'grammar', 'sentence', for example, are all on occasion difficult Chomskyan terms. In some discussions he uses 'language' in a technical sense to refer to the set of expressions strongly generated by a deductive rule system i.e. his generative grammar. In others he uses it in something much closer to the layman's sense of 'what we speak', while in some recent publications he has made claims of the type: '. . . language is a derivative and perhaps not very interesting concept' (Chomsky, 1980, p. 90), a claim on the face of it puzzling coming as it does from an eminent linguist. The claim becomes less puzzling once we recognize that in Chomsky's view 'the fundamental concepts are *grammar* and *knowing a grammar*, and that *language* and *knowing a language* are derivative' (Chomsky, 1980, p. 126). But if 'language' derives from 'grammar', a further difficulty of exegesis lies in the fact that 'grammar' itself is not for Chomsky a clearcut term. He uses it with what he has referred to as a 'systematic ambiguity' between the linguist's formal grammar and the 'mental' grammar allegedly constructed by the child learning language. This deliberately ambiguous use of 'grammar' he himself acknowledges 'may lead to confusion unless care is taken' (Chomsky, 1980, p. 220).

This versatile use of key terms is characteristically Chomskyan.[1] It makes him difficult to argue with at times, and may have contributed to some of the controversy his ideas have invoked. If there is a lesson to be learnt it is that Chomsky's writings need to be approached with a measure of caution.

One of the reasons Chomsky's use of key terms such as 'grammar' and 'language' is sometimes difficult to interpret lies in the shifts which have taken place in his own thinking about the direction of his work. Taking 'language' in the technical sense of the product or output of a generative grammar, then very broadly Chomsky's interest in grammar has waxed as his interest in language has waned. Taking language in the non-technical, everyday sense of 'what people speak', Chomsky has become firmer in his conviction that 'what is loosely called "knowledge of language"' is usefully elucidated through the investigation of 'knowledge of grammar'.

To the question of *why* Chomsky should have come to accord such prominence to knowledge of grammar 'now analyzed in terms of a certain structure of rules, principles and representations in the mind', there is no simple, clearcut answer. Yet the question is an important one, bearing as it does on the justification for Chomsky's theories and the direction of his work. All we have space to do here is to bring out some of the main shifts of emphasis, which may provide the seeds of an explanation, before going on to examine more closely the concept 'knowledge of grammar'.

Among the most striking of these shifts has been the rise and fall of Chomsky's concern with 'creativity'. In the early days Chomsky's formal model, his generative grammar—a deductive rule system initially devised to give a firmer theoretical basis to the work of his early contemporaries, the North American descriptivists—was said to model the tacit linguistic knowledge of an ideal native speaker in a homogeneous speech community, and was justified, in part at least, because it appeared to give some account of the 'creative' aspect of language use. The following observations are characteristic of Chomsky's earlier period:

> The central fact to which any significant linguistic theory must address itself is this: a mature speaker can produce a new sentence of his language on the appropriate occasion, and other speakers can understand it immediately, though it is equally new to them.

and:

> ... it is clear that a theory of language that neglects the 'creative' aspect of language is of only marginal interest. (Chomsky, 1964, p. 51)

At that time Chomsky's emphasis on creativity was one of the important differences between him and his contemporaries whose grammars, apart from the occasional reference to the role of analogy, had no way of accounting for this facet of language.

The reason Chomsky saw his theory as giving some account of creativity in his special sense of a speaker's ability to produce and understand novel sentences never encountered before appeared to lie in the fact that it incorporated recursive processes as part of its formal apparatus. Passages like the following certainly suggest that at least at one time Chomsky saw a parallel between recursion and creativity:

> Although it was well understood that linguistic processes are in some sense 'creative', the technical devices for expressing a system of recursive processes were simply not available until much more recently. In fact, a real understanding of how a language can (in Humboldt's words) 'make infinite use of finite means' has developed only within the last thirty years, in the course of studies in the foundations of mathematics. Now that these insights are readily available it is possible to return to the problems that were raised, but not solved, in traditional linguistic theory and to attempt an explicit formulation of the 'creative' processes of language. There is, in short, no longer a technical barrier to the full-scale study of generative grammars. (Chomsky, 1965, p. 8)

That he later came to recognize the barrenness of the analogy emerges perhaps most clearly from an exchange with Herman Parret. In the course of a dialogue with Chomsky, Parret asked: 'Does your notion of "creativity" cover more than just "generativity?"' (Parret, 1974, p. 28). Chomsky replied:

> There has been an unfortunate tendency to confuse what I have called 'the creative aspect of language use' with something quite different, namely, the recursive property of grammars. This is a conceptual confusion, a confusion of competence and performance.... The recursive property of generative grammars provides the means for the creative aspect of language use, but it is a gross error to confuse the two, as some linguists do. (Parret, 1974, p. 28)

When historians of linguistic thought come to ask the natural question: what happened to creativity?—the answer will be disappointing. Chomsky, it appears, came to realize he had nothing to contribute to its understanding. In his later works he has in fact taken to distinguishing between problems—amenable to investigation—and mysteries. Creativity passed from being a problem—a central problem—to being a mystery: '... the creative use of language is a mystery that eludes our intellectual grasp' (Chomsky, 1980, p. 222); '... "the creative aspect of language use" remains as much a mystery to us as it was to the Cartesians...' (Chomsky, 1976, p. 138).

But how was it that creativity was able to disappear with so little trace without this having a profound effect on Chomskyan linguistics? Primarily because in the meantime Chomsky had evolved a fresh justification for his style of grammar. This new justification brought a different problem to the centre of the stage: broadly, language acquisition: 'The fundamental problem in the study of language, it seems to me, is to explain how it is possible for a person to attain knowledge of a language, knowledge that is far underdetermined by experience' (Chomsky, 1977, p. 18). The fundamental problem expressed there as 'knowledge of a language' was in later work more often expressed as 'knowledge of a grammar': 'the fundamental cognitive relation is knowing a grammar; knowing the language determined by it is derivative' (Chomsky, 1980, p. 70). Thus one answer to the question of why Chomsky should have come to accord such prominence to 'knowledge of a grammar' is that he came to believe it sheds light on what he had now come to see as the 'fundamental problem'— that of how a person attains knowledge of a language. Whether or not he is right in this belief is one of the areas of controversy which surrounds his later work.

What is significant for our present task of providing an overview of Chomsky's views and theories is that as language acquisition (and with it universal grammar) became more central, other, related themes became more clearly defined. Important among these has been Chomsky's insistence that knowledge of language—and more particularly knowledge of grammar—is not a skill, but a *state*, a state of knowledge represented in the mind.

This is probably one of the areas of greatest controversy and of greatest misunderstanding which has surrounded Chomsky's work. Though the distinction between language viewed as a skill or activity, and language viewed as a state of knowledge can be traced to an early distinction Chomsky used to make between competence and performance, there was in the original 'competence' an element of ability or capacity to use language. This in turn may have been linked to the prominence of 'creativity' at that time, often construed as the *ability* to produce and understand novel utterances. The current emphasis has none of this: it is firmly epistemological. Chomsky's grammar, he has repeated with what now seems like heroic consistency, is *not* an account of how we use language, not an account of the workings of language in use, not an account of how we talk—his grammar is an account of a state of knowledge.

Chomskyan linguistics has thus become more closely linked to philosophy, or rather that branch of philosophy that deals with theories of knowledge: epistemology. Some philosophers have even seen Chomsky's work as an attempt to reduce epistemic notions first to syntactic and ultimately to bio-chemical ones.

KNOWLEDGE OF GRAMMAR

It is essential then, in order to follow the controversies surrounding Chomsky's work, to get to grips with what Chomsky intends us to understand by the expression 'knowledge of grammar'. Take first 'knowledge' itself. In an attempt to avoid the morass of problems associated since Aristotle with the term 'knowledge', Chomsky at times has used the expression 'grammatical competence' in place of 'knowledge of grammar'. However, he has found, doubtless not to his surprise, that 'competence' no less than 'knowledge' is subject to different interpretations, some of them misleading. More recently, therefore, in another attempt to avoid being misunderstood he has suggested using the verb 'cognize' in place of 'know'. We thus, he says, 'cognize the grammar of a language'.

But what is the nature of this grammar that we have competence in, or know, or cognize if we are in a state of 'knowing a language'?—in Chomsky's own work the language is almost invariably English. Chomsky would argue that what we know can be modelled in terms of a deductive system of rules and principles (i.e. a generative grammar) from which sentences with complex properties can be derived. Evidence that the rules and principles of his style of generative grammar constitute a valid model of our 'knowledge of grammar' comes in Chomsky's view from the judgments we are purported to make on pairs of sentences of which the following are typical:

1 (a) The candidates wanted each other to win.
   (b) The candidates wanted me to vote for each other.
2 (a) People who go to MIT who like maths will get jobs.
   (b) John, who goes to MIT, who likes maths, will get a job.

Chomsky says that we 'know' or 'cognize' that (1a) is well-formed with the meaning each candidate wanted the other to win, and that (1b) is not well-formed with the meaning that each candidate wanted me to vote for the other.[2] Similarly Chomsky believes that (2a) is a well-formed example of a stacked restrictive relative; stacked restrictive relatives progressively define their head noun, so that in (2a) the people who will get jobs are not the intersection of those who go to MIT and like maths, but a subset of those who go to MIT. (2b) on the other hand Chomsky judges we know is not well-formed, because we cognize (know) that non-restrictive relatives do not stack.

Suppose we accept the validity of these judgments of what is well-formed and what is ill-formed in English. Chomsky would argue that these are judgments predicted by his model, which in turn constitutes evidence that the system of abstract rules and principles of the model must somehow be represented in the minds of the language users. Thus, for him, what we know or cognize is a system of mentally represented rules and principles of a type which a formal generative grammar seeks to characterize. He has then gone further: what each of us cognizes is a particular grammar of a specific language. But this particular grammar is derived from, Chomsky would say explained by, its relation to a more abstract object, a universal grammar. A universal grammar, for Chomsky, is 'a unified system of principles with a fairly rich deductive structure and some open parameters to be set by experience.' Universal grammar provides the basis from which knowledge of a specific grammar develops. It is, Chomsky writes, a characterization not of human language but of 'the nature of the language faculty' (Chomsky, 1980, p. 29). It is with this universal grammar that Chomsky claims we are biologically endowed. Universal grammar, he argues, is 'an element of the human genotype'. Chomsky's concern with a universal grammar so conceived explains why for him: 'Ultimately the study of language is part of human biology' (Chomsky, 1980, p. 226).

It explains too how it is that Chomsky has come to see his theories as shedding light on child language acquisition. His picture of the 'fundamental problem' of how language is acquired is something like the following: the language the child is exposed to is not sufficiently rich, even in conjunction with processes of induction, classification, generalization and abstraction, to yield knowledge of the complex properties of natural language that constitute its grammar. Thus in order to acquire knowledge of the systems of rules and principles, the grammar, underlying his use of language the child acquiring language must be biologically endowed with certain innate properties. The abstract principles which constitute universal grammar are candidates for being the innate properties which narrow the range of possible grammars consistent with the data the child is exposed to.

Support for these claims is characteristically drawn from negative instances of data, which is arguably challengeable. Chomsky gives as a clear, canonical case, the child's knowing that: 'the candidates thought each other would win', meaning 'each of the candidates thought the other would win'—is not well-formed.

He argues:

> ... it can hardly be maintained that children learning English receive specific instruction about these matters (the antecedents of anaphoric expressions), or even that they are provided with relevant experience that informs them they should not make the obvious inductive generalization, say, that 'each other' takes some plural antecedent that precedes it.... Relevant experience is never presented for most speakers of English, just as no pedagogic or traditional grammar, however compendious, would point out these facts. Somehow, this is information that children themselves bring to the process of language acquisition, as part of their mode of cognition. (Chomsky, 1980, pp. 43–4)

To explain the knowledge of such a complex property as the binding of reciprocal expressions that children attain, the argument runs, we need to assume that the child's initial state consists of an innate, intricate and highly restrictive schematism of some sort. A universal grammar is Chomsky's attempt to spell out in some detail the nature of this innate mechanism. If anything is to be described as the 'essence of language' for Chomsky, it is the properties and principles that constitute universal grammar.

The universal grammar's deductive structure is conceived as permitting the derivation, from some simple the quite natural principles, of a finite range of possible grammars, thereby providing derivatively a definition of possible language. Note though that Chomsky is under no illusion that particular versions of universal grammar currently being proposed by him or his co-workers will turn out to be on the right track: 'No-one, surely, expects that any of them are correct as they stand' (Chomsky, 1980, p. 142). Such modesty can easily be disarming. Behind it however is a point he insists upon—the promise the approach nevertheless holds for the future: 'Perhaps for the first time in the long and fruitful history of enquiry into language, it begins to provide a glimpse of the kind of theory that might account for crucial aspects of human knowledge ...' (Chomsky, 1980, p. 142). Certainly Chomsky appears in no doubt that: 'To determine these principles [of universal grammar] is the deepest problem of contemporary linguistic study' (Chomsky, 1980, p. 232).

This has been of necessity a highly condensed summary of Chomsky's concerns. What we want to bring out are the main areas of controversy Chomsky's theories and related claims have given rise to. In our view these are primarily three:

(i)   *How is the theory tested?*—the problem of confirmation/falsification, the nature and validity of the evidence supporting Chomsky's theories. Chomsky frequently draws parallels between theory-construction in linguistics and theory-construction in the physical sciences, notably physics. Yet there is, and always has been, an important difference. Mathematical models in physics require an interpretation by reference to observed physical phenomena. They are testable, under obvious qualifications, in a person-independent and time-independent way. Chomsky's linguistic model on the other hand is interpreted by reference to judgments made on the well-formedness or otherwise of isolated sentences by individual native speakers—who may, and often do, disagree with each other. Thus one unresolved controversy surrounding Chomsky's work is the status of a theory about which there is no general agreement on adequate procedures for testing the output of its model.

(ii) *What is the theory tested against?*—the problem of correspondence. Chomsky has constructed a formal model, a 'mathematical' grammar which generates linguistic expressions or 'sentences'. But what is the relation of these linguistic expressions or 'sentences' to our everyday notion of sentence? To avoid a confusion pervasive in the Chomskyan literature between 'sentences' that are the output of the formal grammar and the ordinary everyday notion of sentence, we shall refer to the linguistic expressions the grammar outputs as sentoids. Giving examples of sentences in English (unspecified as to dialect), Chomsky argues that sentoids that the grammar would mark as ill-formed correspond to sentences also judged as ill-formed by English speakers. Sentoids the grammar would specify as well-formed correspond to sentences judged as well-formed also by English speakers. In so doing he puts a natural language—English—on a par with the set of sentoids derived from a formalized system. The question this raises which is not satisfactorily answered in Chomsky's writings is this: in what sense does the formal language—the sentoids generated by the grammar—actually correspond to the sentences of a human language? More briefly, what is the relation between sentoid and sentence?

(iii) *Finally, what is the theory a theory of?*—the problem of psychological reality. Perhaps the greatest controversy Chomsky's work raises is over the question: in what sense can the formal grammar, articulated, modified and refined by the linguist, generating necessarily a formal language, be usefully said to shed explanatory light on an 'unknown'—what it is in our heads that enables us to acquire, produce and understand language?

THE PROBLEM OF CONFIRMATION/FALSIFICATION

On the question of how satisfactory is the evidence for Chomsky's theories, there has never been any real consensus. Theories are, in part at least, justified by relating them to data. A linguistic theory must be readily relatable to some aspect of language. A theory of Chomsky's type, a theory of linguistic structure, a grammar, is minimally justified if it can be shown that the sentoids generated by the grammar meet what Chomsky himself has usually referred to as 'certain external conditions of adequacy'. Fundamental among these is the requirement that the properties the grammar assigns to its sentoids match the properties that would be assigned by native speakers to the corresponding sentences. This basic requirement Chomsky has noted: '. . . cannot be eliminated, or there are no constraints whatsoever on grammar construction' (Chomsky, 1975, p. 81). On the face of it this seems reasonable enough. We need to be able to test the output of the grammar for whatever properties—originally 'grammaticality', later the broader 'well-formedness'—it is claimed to have. Yet in practice there has never been any agreement among theoretical linguists working within the Chomskyan tradition as to what constitutes an adequate set of procedures for testing whether the properties of the sentoids match the properties native speakers would assign to the corresponding sentences. Testing has always depended essentially on intuition.

Naturally Chomsky has been aware that relying on intuition for the testing of a theory is highly unsatisfactory. 'Intuition', he once wrote himself, 'is an extremely weak support' (Chomsky, 1975, p. 101). Not surprisingly, therefore, in *Syntactic Structures* he considered whether it was possible to establish public, person-independent tests for what he was interested in at that time: grammaticality. However he concluded, and this is surprising for one who has always seen linguistics as an empirical science, that there were no adequate tests. His next move at that time was simply to set the problem aside. Chapter 3 of *Syntactic Structures* begins: 'Assuming the set of grammatical sentences of English to be given, we now ask what sort of device can produce this set . . .' (Chomsky, 1957, p. 18).

There is a sense in which Chomsky has continued to set aside—it is difficult not to feel, brush aside—the problem of providing a satisfactory empirical base for his theories. Over the years the model has been considerably changed and elaborated to include phonology, a lexicon, limited aspects of meaning. Over the same period Chomsky has become concerned with far-reaching implications of his theory, with universal grammar, with establishing 'abstract conditions that unknown mechanisms must meet'. Yet underlying this great theoretical edifice that Chomskyan linguistics has become remains an insecure foundation. The data the formal model has to be interpreted in relation to are still person-dependent judgments on the properties of sentences. The rules and principles said to constitute our knowledge of grammar are still argued as being justified because they predict judgments of ill- or well-formedness said then to be borne out by actual native speaker judgments.

Chomsky is quite aware that his methods are open to a charge of circularity.

'Some linguists,' he says, when discussing the indeterminacy of judgments on data, 'have been bemused by the fact that the conditions that test the test are themselves subject to doubt and revision, believing that they have discovered some hidden paradox or circularity of reasoning' (Chomsky, 1980, p. 198). His response—and this is characteristically Chomskyan—is to shift the argument to a broader, more abstract level:

> In fact, they have simply rediscovered the fact that linguistics is not mathematics but rather a branch of empirical inquiry. Even if we were to grant that there is some set of observation sentences that constitute the bedrock of inquiry and are immune to challenge, it nevertheless remains true that theory must be invoked to determine to what, if anything, these pure and perfect observations attest, and here there is no Cartesian ground of certainty. (Chomsky, 1980, p. 198)

What this style of response provides no help with whatsoever is a quite legitimate question regarding the judgments that are so crucial to Chomsky's theories: how is one to resolve differences of judgment between native speakers? These can of course easily be brushed off as differences of dialect, or as idiosyncratic variations in the particular, or final steady state grammar which each person has acquired. Yet if speakers disagree on crucial data, then surely this must have *some* bearing on the rules and principles of both the steady state and the universal grammar. If the rules and principles are justified because they accord with speaker judgments, but if some speakers make different judgments, what does this say about the rules and principles of the grammar?

The difficulty here of course is to identify data which would be widely enough accepted as crucial. It is more than useless to raise objections to a judgement on a set of sentences that have only a marginal status within Chomsky's theory. Fortunately however there are data that run like a bright thread from the first to the last chapter of *Rules and Representations*, and furthermore are relevant to Chomsky's recent work on Government and Binding theory, concerned as that is in large part with the relationship of anaphoric expressions to their antecedents. These data involve what Chomsky believes we know or cognize about the reciprocal expression *each other*.

Chomsky's discussion of these data provides an excellent paradigm of his style of enquiry. He typically starts with the observation of some complex property of pairs of sentences, frequently in his judgment an occurring and a non-occurring form. Then characteristically the observation is used as a springboard to move to a much higher, more abstract level of discussion that calls on a quite complex theoretical apparatus invoked, often quite tentatively, as an explanation of the complex property.

Consider, for example, the following sentences taken from *Rules and Representations:*

(i)   The men saw each other.
(ii)   The candidates wanted each other to win.
(iii) The candidates wanted me to vote for each other.
(iv)   The candidates thought each other would win.
(v)   The candidates hurled insults at each other.

Chomsky makes what he presumably believes are widely acceptable, uncontroversial judgments on the well- or ill-formedness of these sentences, judgments which conform with the prediction of his formal grammar:

(i)   and (ii) are well-formed.
(iii) and (iv) are ill-formed.
(v)   is well-formed.

He then observes that it would be improbable to maintain that children learning English receive specific instructions about the relation of reciprocal expressions to antecedents, neither are they provided, he claims, with relevant experience to guide them not to make the 'obvious inductive generalization that "each other" takes some plural antecedent that precedes it' (Chomsky, 1980, p. 43).

Somehow, Chomsky believes, children know/cognize that (ii), for example, is well-formed and (iii) is not, and here comes the leap, this is knowledge '. . . that children themselves bring to the process of language acquisition, as part of their mode of cognition' (Chomsky, 1980, p. 44). Chomsky supposes that some general principle of grammar, interacting with the knowledge that 'each other' is a reciprocal expression—a category Chomsky believes to be 'innately given'—permits the child to make the proper choice of antecedent. The general innate principle, at the time he was particularly concerned with these examples, was the opacity principle—a principle setting restrictions on variable-like elements in certain opaque domains.

It seems evident that in this case which Chomsky has used to justify a move into deep, complex and far-reaching explanation involving innate faculties, the soundness of the judgments matters. If his theoretical model, formulated in terms of the control and command of bound and free variables makes a prediction of well-/ill-formedness, and that prediction does not correspond to the judgments of a native speaker, then the consequences for the model need to be made clear.

Suppose we look a little more closely at the data. Setting aside the special problem of what we can safely suppose children know, consider the judgments of two native speakers on these data, in particular the pair (ii) and (iii):

(ii)   The candidates wanted each other to win.
(iii)   The candidates wanted me to vote for each other.

For Chomsky, and for us, (ii) is well-formed. For Chomsky, but not for us, (iii) is ill-formed with the reading each candidate wanted me to vote for the other.

What we see as significant is not so much the fact that we differ in judgment from Chomsky, though this *is* important, but the reason we differ. In making a judgment what we did was to set aside electoral systems such as those of the USA and the UK where the candidate first past the post is the winner, and instead consider electoral systems involving a slate of candidates and some version of proportional representation. (iii) then appears perfectly well-formed in the sense Chomsky rejects since it would be quite reasonable for one candidate to encourage a voter to put another, particular, candidate on his list *in addition to himself.* Two friendly candidates on the same list might well want me 'to vote for each other' without specifying order—on the hope presumably that they both got in.

There are several points about these observations. What is not especially interesting to us is to observe a difference in judgment. While you cannot overthrow a theory through rejecting one piece of data—however paradigmatic you may believe it to be—neither can you establish a theory soundly on the basis of a few relatively unexplored pieces of data. Data for theorists are a very mixed blessing. What is important, however, is that a more careful look at the evidence for Chomsky's final steady state grammar shows that it is not sound evidence at all since the 'facts' are not as described. What we have suggested is that a judgment about sentences depends upon beliefs about the world. In this case, modify the beliefs and the judgment can change. Chomsky too is perfectly aware that: '. . . a deeper understanding of given evidence . . . may also lead to a change in theory . . .' (Chomsky, 1980, p. 109). But the consequences may be more grave. A deeper understanding of this particular evidence seems to us to call into question a fundamental presupposition of Chomsky's theories, the autonomy of syntax, or the independence of form and meaning.

What is not in doubt is that these data, like a great deal of the data Chomsky discusses, raise interesting problems. However, it is far less obvious to us than it seems it is to Chomsky exactly what the nature of the problem is. Our strong impression after some years of looking at Chomsky's data is that differences in judgment on crucial cases relate to differences in the beliefs, knowledge, experience and expectations tapped by the words in the constructions. This suggests that Chomsky may have carved up his subject matter in a way that is turning out to be unproductive.

Chomsky is able to set factors such as beliefs, expectations, experience aside—not because he believes they are unimportant, but because his own particular version of modularity allows him to separate them from 'knowledge of grammar' and concentrate on the latter. While he has on occasion acknowledged that '. . . it may well be impossible to distinguish linguistic and non-linguistic components of knowledge and belief' (Chomsky, 1976, p. 43), he continues for the most part to maintain that the implications of such a distinction are nevertheless worth pursuing.

As a further illustration of the kind of evidence Chomsky presents to support his theories, take another familiar case in the literature: the pair of verbs *promise* and *persuade*. Chomsky regularly uses them to make an observation about a complex property of certain constructions. For example:

(i)   Mark promised Bill to leave.
(ii)   Mark persuaded Bill to leave.

The subject of leave in (i) is argued to be *Mark* (*Mark* leave), and in (ii) *Bill* (*Bill* leave). This is usually described nowadays in control theory (Chomsky, 1982, p. 6) in terms of *promise* being a subject control verb, and *persuade* an object control verb. However suppose we try changing the words in the construction in order to explore how much the control is exercised by the verb and how much depends on beliefs, knowledge, experience and expectations tapped by the words. Consider:

I promised the kids to go to the pantomime on Boxing Day.

Now, who is likely to be going to the pantomime? Me alone? Possibly but unlikely, so what has happened to subject control? The kids alone? Possibly—is this an object control verb after all? Or all of us? Is *promise* then a subject-and-object simultaneously verb? Or are we asking the wrong question? Does it depend less on structure than on what we are talking about and its plausibility? And if it does what are the implications for Chomsky's approach?[3]

The quality and reliability of the evidence for Chomsky's theories thus remain open to debate and dispute.[4] Nor is it clear that the data to which the theories are related are explored in anything like sufficient depth. Chomsky typically makes a rather restricted range of observations on a few sentences—and from there makes a massive leap into universals and, via innateness, to neuro-biology. The result is that relevant data are likely to be left out of the initial analysis of the problem. Consider the discussion of the reciprocal expression *each other*. A related problem also involving linking anaphors to antecedents is provided by those anaphoric expressions that express converse relations, expressions such as *otherwise, vice versa, the opposite*. Here however what is critical, we suspect, is not constituent structure, or notions of constituents commanding constituents, but the sense tapped by the words. This type of anaphoric data which lends itself much more obviously to semantic rather than syntactic analysis has not generally been explored.

THE PROBLEM OF CORRESPONDENCE

We noted at the beginning of this overview of Chomsky's work that his use of the key term 'language' sometimes causes confusion. The nub of the correspondence problem lies in the uncertain relation between what Chomsky understands by language in a technical sense and ordinary natural language. For Chomsky as a working linguist, a language is the set of sentences described by a formal grammar: a deductive rule system. A little more technically:

> ... a grammar 'generates' the sentences it describes and their structural descriptions; the grammar is said to 'weakly generate' the sentences of the language and to 'strongly generate' the structural description of these sentences. When we speak of a linguist's grammar as a 'generative grammar', we mean only that it is sufficiently explicit to determine how sentences of the language are in fact characterised by the grammar. (Chomsky, 1980, p. 220)

As one example of the kind of confusion that can easily arise, note the particular way 'language' needs to be construed in the last sentence of the quotation. To make sense it must be read as the grammar is sufficiently explicit to determine how the sentences, or strictly sentoids, of the language *it generates* are in fact characterized by the grammar. Read unsuspectingly, sentences of the language might readily be taken to refer to sentences of English. It was for this reason that earlier we proposed a distinction between sentoids of the grammar and sentences of English. We continue to make the distinction in an attempt, probably doomed to failure, to make it clear that the language Chomsky is describing is a set of linguistic expressions strongly generated by a deductive rule system.

When Chomsky claims—as he did with the *each other* examples—that his grammar gives an account of some complex property of sets of sentences, he justifies the claim by showing the property to be derivable economically from a deductive rule system (his generative grammar) and an associated set of conditions and principles. For this to be illuminating about ordinary natural language there has of course to be a clear correspondence between the sentoids generated by the formal grammar and the sentences of natural language. Without this correspondence the explanatory power of the grammar is rendered vacuous. Yet such a correspondence has never satisfactorily been established. The question of what precisely are the set of sentences of natural language to which the output of a generative grammar corresponds is another of the outstanding controversies to surround Chomsky's work.

The closest parallel ordinary human language appears to offer to a set of sentences resembling those a generative grammar might produce is written texts. Setting aside obvious exceptions—poetry and experimental novels—nearly all written prose consists of sets of sentences. The obvious place to look for a correspondence between a set of sentoids of a formal language and a set of sentences in a human language is in the written form of a human language.

Does this mean that Chomsky's grammars can be put in correspondence with, or are relevant only to, written and not spoken language? This is not an easy question to answer. Certainly the data that Chomsky cites are almost invariably data that look either constructed—Chomsky uses the term 'self-elicited'—or as if they were drawn from the written language. However, Chomsky never says he is concerned only or even primarily with written language, nor does he discuss the difficult question of what the differences between spoken and written language are. Yet he would be unlikely to deny that there are significant differences between the two forms. One fundamental characteristic of the spoken language is that, unlike the 'visual' form, it has an impermanent and transitory nature. The visual form enables us, as Goody pointed out:

> ... to escape from the problem of the succession of events in time, by backtracking, skipping, looking to see who-done-it before we know what it is they did. Who, except the most obsessive academic, reads a book as he hears a speech? Who, except the most avant-garde of modern dramatists, attempts to write as they speak?' (Goody, 1977, p. 124)

Not surprisingly, the correlates of these differences show up in the spoken and written forms:[5] the basic unit of analysis, for spoken language, for example, unless we are to invoke the concept 'incomplete sentence', is not at all obviously the sentence, but tentatively, the phrase in a Topic-Comment relationship (see Givon, 1979).

We raise the question of the spoken/written language distinction primarily to illustrate the way that Chomsky leaves crucial issues unresolved. If his formal grammar is to be acknowledged as throwing light on human language—which it must to have any point at all—then it must be clear how its output corresponds to ordinary language. If the particular grammar in its final, steady state, derived from its initial, universal schematism, is restricted to describing sentoids, how can we confidently suppose that it provides an explanatory account of the structure and content of the utterances, phrases, expressions, non-sentences, of human spoken language?

One answer, to make the question non-rhetorical, is that we might assume that there is no great problem in devising an additional set of principles, a third grammar, that converts the set of sentoids of the formal language into the utterances of human language. Given the deep differences between the two modes of language, this would be a rash assumption. It is, however, one that Chomsky seems close to making:

> A sentence that is incomprehensible in speech may be intelligible if repeated several times or presented on the written page, where memory limitations are less severe. But we do not have to extend our knowledge of language to be able to deal with repeated or written sentences that are far more complex than those of normal spoken discourse. Rather, the same knowledge can be applied with fewer extrinsic constraints. (Chomsky, 1980, p. 221)[6]

This suggests Chomsky's view of the written language as in some ways a more complex form of the spoken and likely to be closer to its essence because of the absence of 'extrinsic constraints'.

Given the overriding importance Chomsky attaches to understanding the innate language faculty, the issue of what the linguistic theory addresses itself to explaining—complex properties of spoken or written language—is not trivial. It is obvious that across the world it is the spoken not the written form that is the primary mode of language activity. Consequently, if it is the genetically-determined, biologically, not logically, necessary properties of human language that Chomsky is seeking insight into, then the spoken language would seem the proper point of departure. Subsequently when we had useful accounts of what underlies spoken language, we might look at the problems, and they are considerable, of moving from acquisition of spoken language to acquisition of writing. But, pathological cases aside, the mechanisms underlying spoken language are, if anything, the universal mechanisms.

Furthermore, if Chomsky's claims that his work throws light on language acquisition are to be taken seriously, then clearly he must of necessity be primarily concerned with spoken language—yet the problem of establishing a correspondence between spoken language and the sentoids of Chomsky's type of formal language is quite unresolved.

THE PSYCHOLOGICAL REALITY PROBLEM

One of the most controversial areas of Chomsky's work is the claim he has made that his grammars—primarily now his, admittedly tentative, universal grammar—bear on the organization of the language faculty in the minds of speakers: Chomsky's innatism. For just as often as Chomsky has propounded some version of the innateness hypothesis, he has been attacked from all sides—by philosophers, psychologists, linguists—for maintaining it. *Reflections on Language* and *Rules and Representations* are to a large extent a defence of his realist and innatist position.

Over the years Chomsky has consistently taken a realist view of the status of the grammars, both initial and steady state, he has proposed. By a realist view we mean— it is tempting to write, simply, but nothing is simple in this domain—that Chomsky imputes existence to his theoretical constructions: ' . . . the grammar represented in the mind is a "real object"' (Chomsky, 1980, p. 120). For Chomsky, as we understand him, this conviction about the psychological reality of grammars, their mental representations somewhere in the mind, is at base a claim about the truth of his linguistic theory. He recognizes (see especially discussion of Dummett in Chomsky, 1980, p. 109) an alternative position, the instrumentalist view of theories as convenient fictions, but firmly rejects it. In arguing his rejection he appeals to the practice in the natural sciences where, he points out, we are quite prepared to accept the physical reality of the theories—though presumably only because they make testable predictions. Chomsky is well aware of the considerable differences between the nature of the evidence and explanatory power of theories in physics compared to theories in linguistics. He writes: 'Of course, there are differences; the physicist is actually postulating physical entities and processes, while we are keeping to abstract conditions that unknown mechanisms must meet' (Chomsky, 1980 p. 197). But despite the differences Chomsky insists: ' . . . in essence the problems are the same, and the question of psychological reality is no more and no less sensible in principle than the question of the physical reality of the physicist's theoretical constructions' (Chomsky, 1980, pp. 191–2).

But is Chomsky's analogy with physics really valid? Among the natural sciences deductively formulated theories in physics have been particularly impressive partly because of their spectacular success in achieving accurate and reliable predictions; and partly, at a higher level, because they have allowed for the formulation of interconnections among apparently disparate fields in a way that suggests fresh lines of research. We note in an attempt to keep our feet on the ground that while deductively formulated theories are productive in some of the physical sciences, there are nevertheless a large number of others in which they play no part (see Suppe, 1977, p. 65).

The pertinent question is not a general but a specific one: how does deductively formulated theory in linguistics stand? Is it on a par with deductively formulated theory in physics? Or is linguistics currently in a state more akin to those natural sciences where it would be, in Suppe's words, 'premature' and 'fruitless' to try to introduce it?

Questions of this sort are easier to ask than answer. If the physical reality of physicists' theories is in part acceptable because of the validity of their predictions, we can ask what predictions does Chomsky's deductively formulated linguistic theory make, and how accurate, reliable and truthful are they? Are they generally sufficient to give confidence to a belief in their psychological reality?

In an earlier section we tried to show for particular cases that Chomsky's current theories were not convincing because they were not making the right predictions for reciprocal expressions. Whether this is a trivial or profound problem depends on the status Chomsky accords to these data. Our assumption was that it was critical. The more general point is that a great deal of the data involving judgments of well-formedness in crucial cases needs a considerably more detailed analysis. In particular we need controlled and detailed studies of the effects on judgments speakers make of varying the lexical items in identical constructions.

Setting aside the problem of the predictive power of Chomsky's grammars, consider the equally challenging question of their plausibility as a model of the innate mechanisms Chomsky believes humans are endowed with. One difficulty with grappling with this issue is that Chomsky consistently fails to draw an important distinction between two related, but separate questions:

(i)   Are we innately programmed to acquire language?
(ii) Are his own initial universal and final steady state grammars plausible models of that innate programming?

Chomsky appears to assume that objections to the second of these questions automatically entail objections to the first. Yet there is no need for this to be the case at all. It is perfectly possible to agree with Chomsky in general terms that human beings are likely to have some innate language processing strategies—we certainly do—yet entirely reject his own proposed model as unilluminating.

The question of why it is likely to be unilluminating is answered in part by an argument which Chomsky used in his own early work against an eminent North American descriptivist, Charles Hockett. Chomsky once severely criticized Hockett for suggesting that the procedures of the North American descriptivists should parallel the processes the child undergoes in acquiring the language. In particular, the methodological principle known as the 'separation of levels'—a cornerstone of the North American descriptivists' methodology—was quite rightly dismissed as inappropriate. 'But clearly the child does not master the phonology before proceeding to the syntax, . . . there is no possible justification of the principle of separation of levels from considerations of this sort' (Chomsky, 1964, p. 108). More generally Chomsky was insisting that the methodological requirements the North American descriptivist placed upon himself could not be justified as being in some way parallel to those of the child acquiring the language. Yet the way in which Chomsky invests his linguistic theory with psychological significance seems to us an equally unwarranted extrapolation. Consider its history.

At the outset Chomsky's commitment to a 'Galilean style' of enquiry,[7] the making of abstract models of an assumed set of known grammatical sentences, was part of his attempt to capture essential ideas of traditional and descriptivist theories of categories and constituents within the new framework of generative grammar. When writing *The Logical Structure of Linguistic Theory*, Chomsky saw the principal task for linguistic theory as that of developing a general theory of linguistic structure. This general theory was to be an abstract formal system and each grammar for a language a particular example of it. At this stage there is no discussion of a 'psychological analogue' to the problem of constructing a general linguistic theory.[8]

What Chomsky is attempting, as *The Logical Structure of Linguistic Theory* makes clear, is an axiomatization of linguistic theory. It is this axiomatized general theory of linguistic structure or, as it came to be more generally known, universal grammar, that Chomsky has right from the start regarded as the definition of 'language' (see Chomsky, 1975, p. 81). The important question this approach raises in Chomsky's case is not a general one of whether linguistic theories can or cannot be axiomatized, but whether his particular axiomatization is likely to lead to insights into what Chomsky currently conceives as 'the fundamental problem', namely how does a child acquire a knowledge of the grammar of their language.

A commonsense way to tackle this problem is of course to patiently and systematically investigate, in the light of tentative hypotheses, the various ways in which the child's mastery of language emerges from adult-child and child-child interactions. The singularity of Chomsky's work is that he approaches the problem in an entirely different way, not from a psychological but from a logical perspective. He assumes that an ever deeper investigation into the logical properties of universal grammar will shed light on the child's achievement in acquiring a knowledge of language. 'It seems not unlikely that the organism brings, as its contribution to the acquisition of a particular language, a highly restrictive characterization of a class of generative systems (potential theories) from which the grammar of its language is selected on the basis of the presented linguistic data' (Chomsky, 1964, p. 113). While a theoretical linguist may believe that his task is to characterize a class of potential theories and devise an evaluation measure for selecting one member of that class as correct for a given language, this does not give us the slightest inkling about how a child acquires their native language. To believe that it does is to be misled by a metaphor. The metaphor that appears to have been misleading is an analogy that Chomsky quite regularly draws between the task of the linguist and the task of the child:

> The construction of a grammar of a language by a linguist is in some respects analogous to the acquisition of language by the child. The linguist has a corpus of data; the child is presented with unanalysed data of language use. The linguist tries to formulate the rules of the language; the child constructs a mental representation of the language. The linguist applies certain principles and assumptions to select a grammar among the many possible candidates compatible with his data; the child must also select among the grammars compatible with the data. (Chomsky, 1975, p. 11)

But the task of the linguist and the task of the child are quite different. The task of the linguist is to lay out a logical order holding among the components of his theory. In Chomsky's case, for example, the claim is made that the semantic and phonological components are interpretive of the syntactic component. There is in his theory a logical, but not a psychological or temporal, priority to syntax. As he has from time to time rightly insisted, there is 'no general notion, "direction of mapping", or "order of steps of generation"' (Chomsky, 1971, p. 188) in his theory. But in a psychological account of a child's mastery of his language, there is a necessary directionality—the process is inescapably temporal. Though at present we know very little about the steps in that process, we can be confident that there will be an order of discovery. By contrast there is no such temporal or psychological priority in the order that Chomsky is seeking to establish between his initial and final steady state grammars;

only the logical order needed to mark out the ways in which some concepts serve as support for other concepts, logically.

Psychological order and logical order are beasts of different species and there can be no necessary justification for any version of universal grammar from considerations of how a child acquires a knowledge of the grammar of his language. In brief the view that universal grammar is capable of shedding light on the character of a learning organism has all the appearance of a category confusion. The often noted systematically ambiguous use of the term 'grammar' in Chomsky's writings may well have contributed to this confusion (Chomsky, 1965, p. 25).[9]

Why should this confusion, if it is a confusion, have occurred? Because, we suspect, of a long and heroic drive by Chomsky for an explanatory linguistics. In Chomsky's view a native speaker's mastery of his language is in part explained by his knowledge of the rules and principles of the grammar of that language. But what explains the rules and principles of that grammar? Chomsky's answer is that they are derived from the deeper, more abstract rules and principles of universal grammar. It is universal grammar that provides for Chomsky real linguistic explanatory force. But what explains universal grammar? Here, unless there is to be an infinite regress to more meta-meta-grammars, a line must be drawn—a limit to linguistic explanation. The line is drawn by the innateness hypothesis, Chomsky's 'psychological analogue'. The universal grammar is of the form it is because of the nature of our genetic endowment. Innateness offers the ultimate explanation.

In seeking a general, unified and universal account of the ideal speaker/hearer's knowledge of grammar, Chomsky appears to stand on one side of what Isaiah Berlin once described as a great chasm separating different kinds of thinkers. In a long and brilliant essay on Tolstoy and historical determinism, *The Hedgehog and the Fox*, Berlin begins by quoting a line from a fragment of a lost poem by the seventh century Greek poet Archilocus. The line runs:

The fox knows many things, but the hedgehog knows one big thing.

Berlin construes this rather arcane observation as a characterization of a major distinction between the world's thinkers, between the world's poets, between the world's writers. Berlin holds that:

... there exists a great chasm between those, on the one side, who relate everything to a single central vision, one system, more or less coherent or articulate, in terms of which they understand, think and feel—a single universal organising principle in terms of which all that they are and say has significance, and, on the other side, those who pursue many ends, often unrelated and even contradictory, connected if at all only in some de facto way, for some psychological or physiological cause, related by no single moral or aesthetic principle ... (Berlin, 1967, p. 1)

Before considering on which side of this chasm Tolstoy stands, Berlin lists some representative foxes and hedgehogs. Shakespeare seems clearly a fox, as does Montaigne, Cervantes, Swift. Dante seems a clear hedgehog, as do, in varying degrees, Plato, Pascal, Hegel, Dostoevsky. Berlin concludes that the subject of his essay, Tolstoy, was by nature a fox but had a hedgehog's longings.

If we consider our own field, it seems to us that Chomsky is an innate hedgehog with a hedgehog's longings. For useful work in coming to understand the workings of language, we feel that the hedgehog will have to lie down with the fox—an uncomfortable but necessary conclusion

NOTES

1   Consider as an example the problem of exegesis posed by the following:

> Here some care is necessary. If by a 'grammar' we mean simply a system of rules that generates an infinite set of expressions in some alphabet or an infinite set of sound-meaning pairings, then for any such set ('a language') there will be infinitely many grammars. If by a 'grammar', however, we mean one of the systems provided by a given linguistic theory, then for some languages there may be no grammars at all, and for others there may be only finitely many (or perhaps only one) grammar. It is entirely possible that the correct linguistic theory provides only finitely many grammars for possible human languages (and no grammars for infinitely many languages), and even that the correct linguistic theory provides no grammars for the systems loosely called 'languages', for reasons already briefly noted, and for other reasons to which I will return in the next lecture. In more realistic terms, the correct linguistic theory—the theory that gives a correct account of the innate language faculty—may provide only finitely many grammars (or perhaps only one grammar) associated by the principles of language development with a collection of data sufficient for language acquisition. (Chomsky, 1980, p. 268)

Even if one exercises considerable care it is not easy to keep the senses of 'grammar' and 'language' in this passage clearly distinct.

2   We shall return to these data later.

3   A further difficulty with *promise* playing a key position in Chomsky's syntactic theories arises from its atypical nature. A careful run through Roget's thesaurus shows that the verb *promise* is not at all typical of the class of verbs to which it naturally belongs.

4   Chomsky has taken up this question on a number of occasions (see especially Chomsky, 1980, pp. 197–9). His natural inclination however appears to be to turn rapidly from the question of the soundness of the data to the 'intellectually far more interesting' question of the validity of the proposed grammars. The moot question is whether in linguistics the time is ripe for such a move.

5   Brown and Yule lay out some of the basic differences in Chapter 1 of their book, *Discourse Analysis*.

6   A representative example of a linguistic expression that is incomprehensible in speech but may, Chomsky would hold, be intelligible if repeated several times or presented on the written page is a self-embedded sentoid such as: 'the rabbit the girl the cat ignored pursued dropped a glove.' Self-embedded sentoids of even the most elementary sort highlight the sharp difference between what is a natural output of a Chomsky grammar and what is a possible sentence of English. The point could easily be made at greater length by using the recursive devices of the grammar to multiply the degrees of self-embedding.

7   At times Chomsky shows a rather narrow view of what is to count as possible scientific approaches to the study of language. Unfortunately he appears to believe quite firmly that 'the only alternative' to the 'Galilean' style for linguistics is: '... a form of natural history tabulation and arrangement of facts, hardly a very serious pursuit...' (Chomsky, 1980, p. 269).

8   In an introduction to *The Logical Structure of Linguistic Theory*, written twenty years after the text, Chomsky points out that even at that time a 'psychological analogue' lay in the immediate background of his thinking. Yet to raise the issue seemed to him then 'too audacious'.

9   In *Aspects* Chomsky proposed using the term 'grammar' with a 'systematic ambiguity'. It was 'to refer, first, to the native speaker's internally represented "theory of his language" and, secondly, to the linguist's account of this, ...' (Chomsky, 1965, p. 25). This further versatile use of the term has not made it easy to keep the psychological and logical categories distinct.

REFERENCES

Berlin, I. (1967) *The Hedgehog and the Fox*, London, Weidenfeld and Nicolson.

Brown, G. and Yule, G. (1983) *Discourse Analysis*, Cambridge University Press.

Chomsky, N. (1955) 'Semantic considerations in grammar', Monograph No. 8, Georgetown Monograph Series.

Chomsky, N. (1957) *Syntactic Structures*, The Hague, Mouton.

Chomsky, N. (1964) 'Current issues in linguistic theory', in Fodor, J. and Katz, J. (Eds), *The Structure of*

Language, Englewood Cliffs, N.J., Prentice-Hall.

Chomsky, N. (1965) *Aspects of the Theory of Syntax*, MIT Press.

Chomsky, N. (1971) 'Deep structure, surface structure and semantic interpretation', in Steinberg, D. D. and Jakobovits, L. A. (Eds), *Semantics*, Cambridge University Press.

Chomsky, N. (1975) *The Logical Structure of Linguistic Theory*, New York, Plenum Press.

Chomsky, N. (1976) *Reflections on Language*, London, Maurice Temple Smith.

Chomsky, N. (1977) *Essays on Form and Interpretation*, Amsterdam, North Holland Publishing Company.

Chomsky, N. (1980) *Rules and Representations*, Oxford, Blackwell.

Chomsky, N. (1982) *Some Concepts and Consequences of the Theory of Government and Binding*, MIT Press.

Givon, T. (1979) 'From discourse to syntax: Grammar as a processing strategy', in Givon, T. (Ed.), *Syntax and Semantics Vol. 12: Discourse and Syntax*, New York, Academic Press.

Goody, J. (1977) *The Domestication of the Savage Mind*, Cambridge University Press.

Parret, H. (1974) *Discussing Language*, The Hague, Mouton.

Suppe, F. (Ed.) (1977) *The Structure of Scientific Theories*, Chicago, Ill., University of Illinois Press.

III: Part Two: Linguistic Universals
Neurobiology

3. Biological Foundations of Language: A Comment on Noam Chomsky's Approach of Syntactic Structures

ANTOINE DANCHIN

Many paradoxes are associated with knowledge creation. Those which are related to language are probably the most difficult, but also the most interesting. Indeed, human knowledge is organized *de facto* by linguistic competence through language performance, and our exploration of reality is always mediated by language. We possess an 'intuitive' knowledge, which we have in common with most higher vertebrates, but such knowledge is the result of the slow evolution of the species, or phylogenesis. Contrariwise, the knowledge we create through language allows us, within the short period of a single generation, to produce models of reality which become more and more adequate,[1] thanks to a self-referent loop that permits us to take ourselves as objects under study. This unique path from subject to object, common to all humans, suggests that there exists a *universal* feature of language. Thus a major question about the biological foundations of language is the roots of such universality.

There are two main approaches to this question. They are formally analogous to attitudes which always precede study of phenomena where learning is, at least in part, involved: how is language placed with respect to the major duality underlying biological phenomena, heredity and development, phenotype and genotype, or innate and acquired structures and functions. We must, however, immediately emphasize that these pairs are always impossible to tell apart. They are consequences of the eternal question of being and becoming, of synchrony and diachrony. The question which must be raised is therefore one of *development*, of *actualization*. Asked otherwise, the question is not to find out whether language is innate—it certainly is

29

simple network bears some analogy with the simplest elements of syntactic structures: all afferent *pathways* (but not cells) are built according to the same overall pattern, but differ in the elements of the input environment they refer to; they carry *meaning*, so that they can be interpreted as standing for noun phrase (with all the semantic content brought about by modifications in input connections along each pathway), and the output cell (or group of cells), which integrates and commands the motor output, stands for verb phrase (with implications for action commands, but also for semantic content of the input pathways, because of the feedback mechanism).

It is impossible to provide details here of this simple illustration, but a few of its properties may be emphasized. At the *macroscopic* level one can visualize the system as a stack of cell layers having similar formal properties according to their relative positions (in particular the input and output layers), a pattern somewhat similar to the layers and columns found in the visual cortex of mammals.[20] The microscopic organization will reveal an interaction between adjacent pathways decreasing in intensity with distance: if the pathways carry meaning this implies a kind of 'geographical' organization of meaning, and will lead to a sequential activation of pathways standing for sentences linked in a semantic way. But the most remarkable feature comes from the 'propagated' activation pattern caused by the *imbalance* existing between two pathways leading to the same 'verb' output cell.[21] Conflict between two interfering inputs at the sensory level (or further downstream, due to a pathway recently activated) will activate a 'verb' cell until it corrects by feedback the origin of the conflict (and, by so doing, starts another conflict on neighbouring pathways), and so on. Thus one has a continuous activation of syntactic structures, semantically linked. Such semantic neighbourhood will only be disrupted when an external event (or internal, but controlled by a neuronal structure, e.g., hunger) becomes strong enough to initiate elsewhere the sweeping process.

Continually stimulated by senses, and by internal neuronal controls, the brain, seat of language, tries constantly to recover equilibrium (i.e., absence of activation of 'verb cells'). It is the organization of the neuronal structure, *independent of meaning*, which explains the universality of syntactic structures, superimposing a sweeping process, which would play the role of explorer of the brain state. The stabilization function of language would thus be particularly emphasized, substantiating the Chomskyan hypothesis of a 'language-organ'.

PROSPECTS

I thought that it would have been quite unreasonable to support the Chomskyan view of inborn brain structures underlying universal syntactic structures without giving some hint about a neuronal organization that would explain at least some of the language features. But I am certainly not naive enough to think that I might have guessed the intrinsic nature of the real world. I am an experimentalist, and I know how many surprises can come from the study of reality. The model proposed is far from explaining all syntactic structures, and it cannot be reconciled easily with the formal properties of transformation grammar. The model can, nevertheless, show a path for investigating neuronal structures, and it demonstrates that, contrary to some opinion, it is not absurd to conceive the question of language-related neuronal circuitry in the terms proposed by Chomsky. Better, perhaps, the neuronal structure pictured above indicates the difficulties to be met in neurolinguistic research.

The neuronal organization described above possesses many *macroscopic* features analogous to those found in the neuronal structure underlying the learning and processing of visual information. In particular the area comprising 'verb' cells might be organized in a way similar to that of the columnar organization of area 17 in the visual cortex of the cat. This implies that it would be extremely difficult to investigate the corresponding organization after the study of lesions or genetic defects: indeed local lesions should not destroy syntax (unless the *whole* structure is destroyed), they would only result in defects similar to 'scotoma', blind spots, or areas which sometimes occur after local lesions in the visual cortex. Such lesions would lead to *semantic* alterations rather than syntactic modifications. In particular 'semantic fields' upstream of certain verbs might be altered, whereas the bulk of meaning would remain unaffected. Performance would look more like the result of a memory 'hole' than a syntactic deficiency. Study of such lesions would only yield some features of the 'geographical' organization of meaning for a given individual, and show the borders of the 'envelope' containing all neurones involved in language and meaning. This is what one observes experimentally.

With respect to genetic defects things are more complex: whole classes of neurones or synapses might be missing. But this time all or most linguistic competence should be affected. It would be interesting (but probably extremely difficult) to study the brain organization of individuals with macroscopic brain structure looking normal, but unable to use language properly. It should be remembered that, because similar structures are present in both hemispheres, only one of which is occupied by linguistic structures, a whole series of non-linguistic competences should also be missing (including face memorization). Finally, by analogy with what is observed in certain cerebellum mutants, one might expect to discover hereditary anomalies in the coordination between substructures in syntactic structures. Dyslexy might be an example. Here again genetic analysis of language is likely to be disappointing.

One area for investigation remains: electrophysiological analysis of the *local* organization of neuronal networks, in the case of the functionally deprived individual. However, because language is unique to man, there is an obvious ethical limitation in experimenting. The only studies which can be (and have been[18]) performed deal with neurolinguistic analyses performed in parallel with neurosurgery in the case of brain damage due to accidents or tumors. A prediction of the model is that electrical stimulation of the upstream cell pathway will produce a disequilibrium which triggers a sequential burst of linguistic performance, linked by semantic relationship. This fits well with observations such as those made by Pribram.[23] The most interesting answer would come from the response triggered by the stimulation of what I called 'verb' cells. Two behaviours should be observed: an action (often a motor action) and a cascade of oral performance *preceding* perception of the corresponding meaning, associated with the odd feeling of being acted on rather than acting. If also the 'verb' cells were to respond to specific neurotransmitters, differing from those used in upstream pathways, one could assume drugs would have this same effect. This might fit well with what is usually described as hallucinated or prophetic behaviour.

The model is still much too imprecise to allow convincing experimental protocols. It only suggests a few lines for further investigation. The separation between performance and competence is analogous to the separation between phenotype and genotype. The description of tongues made by Chomsky tries to uncover *generative* syntactic structures, within a set of rules, a programme (a synchronous corpus) that permits each of individual actualization through a specific diachronous unfolding. The dispute between Chomskyan innatism and Piagetian constructivism is the result of a wrongly asked question, and of the confusion by imitators (or predecessors in linguistics) of Piaget, between a programme and its actualization. This mistake, unfortunately common, is followed by a mistake in the method of looking for neuronal structures underlying linguistic structures, as postulated by Chomsky. There are no neurones corresponding to names, but a neuronal organization corresponding to syntax. On this organization unique and universal (with respect to its rules of connectivity, synaptic stability and evolution, and electrophysiological functioning), is superimposed an *individual* evolution in the connectivity which links a definite pathway to words. The number of such pathways is in practice unlimited because of the large number of connections which can be associated with each individual neurone (10,000 synapses as a mean). What limits word use is the time required to *access* the appropriate pathway (and this time is indeed very limited). Therefore it seems quite reasonable to accept the hypothesis of the existence of the inborn S_0^b structure which allows, before a *critical time*, acquisition of a given semantic content (this would correspond to acquisition of the mother tongue). During this acquisition a significant *loss* of features present in the competence existing at birth will derive from regression of some of the initial connectivity as what is *semantically* relevant is stabilized. Besides, because language functioning is required for the selective stabilization of central brain areas, the relationship between language and sense organs is firmly established. Syntactic structures are therefore universals, but tongue and culture are brought into the centre of brain organization of perception. It is then that ideology appears.

NOTES

1   Adequate, not *true*. We are only *part* of reality, and this prevents us from being able to give a *complete* description of the world. See Danchin, A. (1980) 'Comment peut-on parler de l'automate cérébral aujourd'hui?' *Revue Philosophique*, 105, 3, pp. 287–304.
2   For a detailed analysis see Piattelli-Palmarini, M. (Ed.) (1980) *Language and Learning. The Debate between Jean Piaget and Noam Chomsky*, Cambridge, Mass., Harvard University Press.
3   Sebeok, T. (Ed.) (1977) *How Animals Communicate*, Bloomington, Ind., Indiana University Press;

Brown, C. H. and Petersen, M. R. (1982) *Primate Communication*, Cambridge, Cambridge University Press.

4   Brain dissymmetry does seem to have an impact on specific linguistic abilities. Experiments, mainly of the Geschwind group, tend to prove that dyslexy might be related to dissymmetric brain construction mediated by testosterone. But this only indicates that some interaction between normal, but dissymmetric hemispheres, might interfere with correct processing of language-related data. It does not prove by any means that language is the result of some kind of cooperation between hemispheres. Geschwind, N. (1970) 'The organization of language and the brain', *Science*, 170, pp. 940–4; Eidelberg, D. and Galaburda, A. M. (1982) 'Symmetry and asymmetry in the human posterior thalamus. I. Cytoarchitectonic analysis in normal persons', *Archives of Neurology*, 39, pp. 325–32; Galaburda, A. M. and Eidelberg, D. (1982) 'II. Thalamic lesions in a case of developmental dyslexy', *Archives of Neurology*, 39, pp. 333–6.

5   As is homogeneity. This accounts for the very many errors which led to the identification of homogeneity with disorder (more stable...) and allowed superficial thinkers to make a formal analogy between entropy and disorder. This happened mainly in Europe for cultural reasons which might be interesting to study.

6   The so-called 'minor' hemisphere is as highly organized as the 'major': perception of the three-dimensional world, identification of faces and landscapes, etc. Hécaen, H. (Ed.) (1978) *La Dominance Cérébrale: Une Anthologie* Paris and The Hague, Mouton.

7   Lenneberg, E. E. (1967) *Biological Foundations of Language*, New York, Wiley; Report of the MIT group in the biology of language (1976) *Explorations in the Biology of Language*, Cambridge, Mass., MIT.

8   For instance, the error which corresponds to treating irregular verbs as if they were regular.

9   For instance, the normal position of the adjective with respect to the noun: 'la rouge tasse' analogous to 'the red cup.'

10 Instructive theories, because they are not sensitive to Occam's razor, ought to be put aside from scientific methodology, at least during the implementation phase. During the exploration phase a finalistic approach can have—and has—some usefulness. However, it is necessary to depart rapidly from the 'why?' of childhood if one does not want to be caught in the trap of irrefutability.

11 One frequently observes such a displacement of the relevant questions e.g., Crick or Hoyle, in the question of the origin of life displace the origin from earth to stars, but this does not answer the question at all!

12 Goldin-Meadow, S. and Mylander, C. (1983) 'Gestual communication in deaf children: Non effect of parental input on language development', *Science*, 221, pp. 372–4.

13 Serazin, M-J. (1982) 'La surdi-mutité en Afrique au sud du Sahara: Essai comparé avec la surdité en Occident', Thèse de Spécialité, Paris V.

14 For a review see Wiesel, T. (1982) 'The postnatal development of the visual cortex and the influence of environment', *Biological Reports*, 2, pp. 351–77.

15 Changeux, J–P. and Danchin, A. (1976) 'Selective stabilisation of developing synapses as a mechanism for the specification of neuronal networks', *Nature*, 246, pp. 705–12.

16 Schmalhausen, I. I. (1969) *Problemyia Darwinisma*, Leningrad, Academia Nauk SSSR.

17 Proceedings of MIT's Endicott House Meeting (1975) in Archives du Centre Royaumont pour une Science de l'Homme, unpublished.

18 Changeux, J–P., Courrège, P. and Danchin, A. (1973) 'A theory of the epigenesis of neuronal networks by selective stabilization of synapses', *Proceedings of the National Academy of Sciences (Washington)*, 70, pp. 2974–8.

19 Danchin, A. (1977) 'Stabilisation fonctionnelle et épigénèse: Une approche biologique de l'identité individuelle', in Benoist, J–M. (Ed.) *L'Identité*, Paris, Grasset.

20 Frégnac, Y. and Imbert, M. (1984) 'Development of neuronal selectivity in primary visual cortex of cat', *Physiological Reviews*, 64, pp. 325–434.

21 Such an imbalance would be at the basis of the 'sweeping' we perceive in the kind of inside voice which haunts us all the time we are awake. This might account for what we call consciousness, which behaves as a *deus ex machina* (see Popper and Eccles for a typical dualistic description of the brain: Popper, K. and Eccles, J. (1977) *The Self and Its Brain*, Berlin, Heidelberg, London and New York, Springer.)

22 Penfield, W. (1967) *The Excitable Cortex in Conscious Man*, Liverpool, Liverpool University Press.

23 Pribram. K. H. (1971) *Languages of the Brain: Experimental Paradoxes and Principles in Neuropsychology*, Englewood Cliffs, N.J., Prentice-Hall.

4. Language Learning, Language Acquisition, or Language Growth?

JOHN C. MARSHALL

Human infants (as their very name suggests) are not born speaking a human tongue; neither do they, in the absence of appropriate stimulation, spontaneously reinvent Phrygian, Lallans, or Hebrew. Yet within the space of a few years' exposure, they do acquire a basic mastery of the language of their environment, be it spoken Japanese or American sign language. Clearly, something changes with age and exposure. What shall we call this process of change, this development over time?

When I was a student in the late 1950s, the lecture course in which this progression was reputedly explicated was entitled *Language Learning*; when I started to give lectures on the same topic in the early 1960s, the name of the course had changed to *Language Acquisition*; by the mid-1970s everyone changed the name yet again, the term *Language Growth* being then (and now) the preferred designation. What's in a name? Why these changes of nomenclature? Mere fashion? The recycling of old metaphors? Or a reflection of genuine scientific advance? Whatever the explanation, the writings of Professor Noam Chomsky must bear a very considerable responsibility for the changes.

LANGUAGE LEARNING

If language were learnt (in any significant sense of that term), this would not, of course, imply that there was no important biological base on which the learning was founded. And much of that base would be innate. As the English empiricist John Hughlings Jackson (1872) wrote: 'No child would ever talk unless he were taught; and no child could be taught unless he already possessed, by inheritance, a particular series of nervous arrangements ready for training.'

The first of Chomsky's achievements that is relevant to this claim was simply to point out that if one employs the terms 'teaching' and 'training' one had better (on pain of vacuity) take them seriously. Thus, in his critical review of Skinner's *Verbal Behavior*, Chomsky (1959) noted (among other lacunae) that there was no evidence to suggest that 'teaching' played any major role in the development of language in the child. One hardly needs an argument that exposure is necessary (children brought up in a monolingual English environment acquire English, in a monolingual Turkish environment Turkish); neither would one be surprised to hear that general parental encouragement was a good idea. But none of this can be seriously claimed as 'teaching'. As Chomsky then wrote (1959): '. . . there is neither empirical evidence nor any known argument to support any *specific* claim about the relative importance of "feedback" from the environment and the "independent contribution of the organism" in the process of language acquisition.' Eventually Chomsky's scepticism about the contribution of a pedagogically-tuned environment did provoke psychologists who believed in language learning to look at the nature of the linguistic input to which the child was exposed. The upshot of this was the purported discovery of a specialized teaching-language, 'motherese', whose properties were tailored to the child's learning needs. Many psychologists interpreted 'motherese' as the driving force behind the child's progress in language, and concluded that the specific properties of this linguistic environment were of supreme importance in the eventual acquisition of adult fluency. *Contra* Chomsky, language *learning* was apparently vindicated. Such an interpretation, it transpires, was premature. Although many of the basic facts about 'motherese' are not in dispute, the conclusions drawn from them were often in error.

Some caretakers undoubtedly speak 'baby talk' to their infants and young children. Brown (1977) lists over 100 ways in which this 'motherese' differs from adult language. For example: mean utterance length is very low, and many of the recursive devices made available by universal grammar are not used; proper nouns are produced where pronouns would be more appropriate, and plural pronouns are used to refer to single individuals; independent pronouns are deleted in non-pro-drop languages; fundamental frequency is raised, simple sentences may be assigned more than one primary stress, and falling pitch terminals may be converted into rises. These observations seem fairly reliable and we may take it that some children are indeed exposed to 'simplified' or deviant linguistic input. But this fact does not in itself show that 'simplified' input has any effect (good or bad) upon the course of language acquisition. When studies of the consequences of 'motherese' input have been undertaken (Newport, Gleitman and Gleitman, 1977), it has proved remarkably difficult to demonstrate the effectiveness of many aspects of 'motherese' *qua* teaching aid (Newport, 1977). Most attempts to predict the child's rate of language acquisition from the properties of different maternal speech styles have failed once baseline differences between children have been partialled out. Similarly the extent to which 'motherese' input is maximally simple and clear may have been grossly overstated. Primary active declaratives are not noticeably frequent in the speech addressed to young children; rather imperatives and questions predominate. Neither do mothers materially reduce the number of possible form-function pairings in the questions they direct toward children at early developmental states (Shatz, 1979).

One might nonetheless expect that speech addressed to the 'learner' would at least be more clean and perspicuous acoustically than that intended for the sophisticated user. Yet even this assumption would appear to be false. Shockey and Bond (1980) found that British mothers use phonological reduction rules more frequently when speaking to children than to adults. The mothers no doubt felt that the speech style they adopted toward the young was more informal and intimate, but its effect is to reduce the intelligibility of individual word tokens *qua* acoustic objects. Bard and Anderson (1983) have confirmed and extended this finding in a remarkable series of experiments. They demonstrated conclusively that words taken from parents' speech to children (between the ages of 1, 10 and 3, 0) were significantly less intelligible than the same words as spoken to adults. The effect arises because speakers play off clarity of articulation against the predictability (redundancy) of words in sentential contexts (Lieberman, 1963). The content words in the sentences spoken to children were highly predictable (for *adults*), and parents accordingly reduced the acoustic intelligibility of these words. The trade-off makes perfectly good sense in the context of exchanges between linguistically-fluent adults. But, as Bard and Anderson (1983) point out, 'it makes very little sense when the listener does not have a full command of the language.' Their finding 'directly contradicts the general characterization of motherese as a register which is well "tailored" to the linguistic sophistication of the child.'

In short, the hypothesis that language is learned (in the sense that it is taught by pedagogically-sophisticated adult users) has fared rather badly in recent years. Insofar as caretakers do modify their speech to children, those changes may be more harmful than helpful, and we are thrown back even more upon Chomsky's stress on the child's own 'biological' contribution to language acquisition.

LANGUAGE ACQUISITION

It is, of course, somewhat peculiar even to broach the topic of language learning without some prior characterization of 'what is learnt'. Yet prior to the publication of *Syntactic Structures* (1957), it did seem (almost) possible to sidestep this issue. The reason can perhaps be traced to the structuralist claim summed up in Joos' (1957) now notorious remark: 'Languages differ from each other without limit and in unpredictable ways.' If this were indeed the case there would be little point in attempting to discover the properties of a 'language acquisition device' in the sense of a mental organ specifically committed to language learning. If there were no language universals to which the child's mind was pre-adapted, then the learning of language would simply consist in the application of generalized principle of learning to linguistic data. Such an all-purpose learning device would indiscriminately 'pick up' the structure of whatever stimulus domain it was exposed to. This view seemed to comport well with empiricist hypotheses in psychology, as expressed by Broadbent (1973): '. . . the brain is remarkable in its ability to adjust to different experiences, rather than being remarkable by having an inherent structure through which it is able to handle the world.'

Taken at face value, the quotations from Joos and Broadbent are misguided on any coherent account of learning processes. If, as Joos suggests, absolutely 'anything goes' as a possible linguistic structure, then *no* learning device will be able to acquire each and every language to which it is exposed. If, as Broadbent seems to imply, the brain has no built-in inductive principles, then no learning of any sort will be possible. As Chomsky has repeatedly stressed, no empiricist (from Locke to Goodman, Quine, or Popper) has ever seriously doubted that, if anything is to be learnt, there must be axioms of organization, themselves unlearnt, which (partially) determine the cognitive outcomes of exposure to an environment (Chomsky, 1965, 1980). These principles may (as empiricists have claimed) be small in number, simple in operation and general in application; or the opposite (as rationalists have argued).

Chomsky's analogy between the linguist who attempts to discover 'a function that maps a set of observed utterances into the formalized grammar of the language of which they are a sample' (Chomsky, 1962) and the child who performs (albeit tacitly) the same task, thus provides a neutral characterization of the acquisition problem. The mechanism that effects the function can be called a 'language acquisition device' (LAD), and 'a description of this device would therefore represent a hypothesis about the innate intellectual equipment that a child brings to bear in language learning' (Chomsky, 1962). It now becomes fairly obvious that '. . . the problem of constructing a universal language-learning device cannot be stated clearly until we determine the properties of the formalized grammar that is to be its output' (Chomsky, 1962).

This way of looking at the problem directed attention to the formal power of the grammars that were required to generate (and assign correct structural descriptions to) all and only the sentences of a natural language (Chomsky, 1963). The application to language acquisition takes place in the following fashion. Once formalized, a grammar for a language can be placed within the so-called 'Chomsky-hierarchy' (that is, the hierarchy of increasing generative power from grammars for finite languages to unrestricted rewriting systems). It is then possible to prove whether particular classes of language (generated by grammars of different power) are, in principle, 'learnable' (in the sense of 'identifiable in the limit'), and, if so, by what class of acquisition device. That is, one can show whether or not an arbitrary target grammar selected from the class can be induced from a sample of sentences of the target language.

Important positive and negative conclusions have been reached. Negatively, Suppes (1969) provided an explicit general purpose learning model (derived from statistical sampling theory) that could be applied to language acquisition. However, the system could acquire (in the limit) only finite-state Markovian grammars that are known to be inadequate for the representation of language structure (see Chomsky, 1957). Although the claim continues to be made that *some* all-purpose learning strategy suffices for language acquisition (see Putnam, 1980), all recent requests to demonstrate such a device have been met with a resounding silence. Contrariwise, it has been shown that restricted transformational grammars can (in principle) be learned, given particular (innate) constraints on the operation of transformational rules. Thus Wexler and Culicover (1980) have proved 'degree-2 learnability' for transformational grammars. From a corpus of structures no more embedded *than sentences that contain sentences that contain sentences*, the correct set of transformations can be acquired. If the corpus is more restricted than this, the task is logically impossible for the learning device that Wexler and Culicover (1980) specify. One amusing outcome of this work has been the demonstration that as innate constraints on grammatical rules and structures are lifted, the more complex the input sentences must be if acquisition of the adult language is to be achieved. A simplified ('motherese') input serves to make the task of acquisition harder not easier (Gleitman and Wanner, 1982). The trade-off between innate constraints on acquisition and the properties of the ('teaching') environment turns out to be exactly the opposite of what empiricists had hoped (Wexler, 1982).

One might nonetheless attempt to argue that the developmental course of language acquisition could be traced via a series of grammars of increasing power (from finite-state systems through phrase-structure grammars to transformational grammars). Simplified input might then somehow aid the acquisition of immature grammatical systems, even if access to a wider range of structures were (eventually) required to achieve full adult competence. Much descriptive work in the 1960s seems to have been guided by the feeling that it was appropriate to write finite-state or phrase-structure grammars for the early 'stages' of language acquisition. But this stratagem, it seems, does not at all help in removing the necessity for rich innate constraints upon the language acquisition device.

As Fodor (1975) points out, the only accounts of learning ever developed are variants of the theory of inductive inference. A hypothesis (e.g., canonical word order in English is SVO) is projected, and if confirmed (= not disconfirmed) by the evidence, belief is fixed. The theory entails that 'the concepts that figure in the hypotheses that you come to accept are not only potentially accessible to you, but are *actually exploited to mediate the learning.*' Inductive inference is normally thought of as the cornerstone of empiricist theories of learning, but, as Fodor concludes, the model 'assumes the most radical possible nativism: namely, that any engagement of the organism with its environment has to be mediated by the availability of any concept that can eventually turn up in the organism's beliefs' (Fodor, 1980). Linguistic *development*, the acquisition of qualitatively more powerful grammars, is not ruled out by Fodor's account, but it must arise from maturation, not learning (in the sense of inductive inference). If it were true that grammars for children at different developmental stages could be ordered in the Chomsky-hierarchy, this would not show that the stages were related to each other by learning. Thus whatever the environmental impact of 'motherese' upon early grammars, the acquisition of a low-level grammar would not serve to render unnecessary the innate constraints that make later, more mature grammars learnable.

LANGUAGE GROWTH

Attempts to account for the course of language acquisition (or the final state attained) in terms of environmental contingencies that an all-purpose learning device could respond to have not met with much success. There is, however, another, quite distinct way of looking at the interaction between innate structure and environmental conditions. The phenomenon of biological *growth* is an example of such interaction that is not dependent upon the direct determination of form and function by the external environment. The nineteenth century theoretical psychologist George Henry Lewes (1879) phrases the matter most elegantly:

> Different seeds and different soils yield different plants, but all have the same fundamental substance and the same constituent forms. A speculative botanist extracting these common forms may present them as *a priori* conditions and call them Nature's innate ideas; following thus in the track of speculative psychologists. The psychologist admits that all knowledge arises *in* experience, though not *out* of it. The botanist admits that all plants arise in earth or air, but not all out of them. There are conditions and pre-conditions of experience, as there are conditions and pre-conditions of plant life.

As Chomsky (1980) writes:

> ...we take it for granted that the organism does not learn to grow arms or to reach puberty—to mention an example of genetically-determined maturation that takes place long after birth. Rather,

these developments are determined by the genetic endowment, though the precise manner in which the genetic plan is realized depends in part on external factors, both triggering and shaping. For example, nutritional level can apparently affect the time of onset of puberty over a considerable range. As the biological plan unfolds, a system of interacting organs and structures matures—the heart, the visual system, and so on, each with its specific structures and functions, interacting in largely predetermined ways.

Would it be plausible, then, to regard 'the growth of language as analogous to the development of a bodily organ' (Chomsky, 1976)? This shift in perspective suggests a radically different view of the role of experience in language acquisition (Chomsky, 1980):

> My own suspicion is that a central part of what we call 'learning' is actually better understood as the growth of cognitive structures along an internally directed course under the triggering and partially shaping effect of the environment. In the case of human language, there evidently is a shaping effect; people speak different languages which reflect differences in their verbal environment. But it remains to be seen in what respects the system that develops is actually shaped by experience, or rather reflects intrinsic processes and structures triggered by experience.

The crucial new idea is the notion of 'triggering', and more than ever before linguistic theory (i.e., the theory of universal grammar) becomes identified with the problem of language development.

The principles of universal grammar severely constrain the space wherein natural languages may vary. These constraints on rules and representations allow for limited parametric variation. The parameterized principles of UG are attributed to the child's initial state; they form boundary conditions within which the 'learner' attempts to locate the specific grammar of the particular language to which he is exposed. The function of exposure to a particular linguistic environment is to set the parameters left open in UG; does the language have structure-dependent movement rules (English) or not (Japanese)? Is the order of base elements subject-verb-object (English) or subject-object-verb (German)? Can tensed sentences be overtly subjectless (Italian) or not (English)? Once the value of a parameter has been fixed, the relevant structures then interact with universal principles so that a range of other properties of the language follows deductively. It is in this sense that the linguistic environment exerts a triggering effect, causing the child to come to know more than he experiences. Chomsky (1982) accordingly sums up the goal of current research as follows:

> We hope that it will ultimately be possible to derive complex properties of particular natural languages, and even to determine the full core grammar of a language with all of its empirical consequences, by setting the parameters of general linguistic theory (universal grammar, UG) in one of the permissible ways.

As an example of recent work on language acquisition motivated by such a research programme we can look at how the child comes to interpret relative clauses in English. It is well-known that young children frequently misinterpret object relatives as subject relatives. Given, for example, the sentence, 'The rat hit the cat that jumped over the pig', they assign *rat* as the subject of both *hit* and *jump*. The second assignment is clearly in error. Contrariwise, when the noun in the relative clause is a subject, children interpret the structure correctly. Thus in 'The rat hit the cat that the pig jumped over', *cat* is chosen as the object of both *hit* and *jump*. One account of this pattern of results invokes the 'parallel-function strategy'. The child is conjectured to apply the parsing strategy: If the missing NP of S_2 is a subject, assign the subject of S_1 as its antecedent; if the missing NP of S_2 is an object, assign the object of S_1 as its antecedent. The hypothesis is neat and *descriptively* correct. But the account has two fatal weaknesses: it is ad hoc and provides no hint as to how the child eventually comes to interpret object relatives correctly.

Roeper (1982) accordingly takes a very different tack. His argument is built upon three lines of evidence: first, a principle of universal grammar—a missing NP cannot be higher on the phrase structure tree than the NP that is its antecedent; second, a typological difference between languages—in some languages relatives can attach to both the topmost S and to NP while in others only topmost S attachment is allowed; third, a learning principle—assume the most restricted grammar unless and until evidence to the contrary is obtained. Roeper shows that from these facts and (independently motivated) principles, the child's initially erroneous and later correct interpretation of object relatives follows deductively. The full interpretation of relative clause structure is triggered when the child hears a subject relative (e.g., *The person that I saw is here*). This information enables the child to 'choose' the grammar S → NP + VP (S); NP → NP (S) as appropriate to English, and serves to distinguish subject from object relatives. The role of experience is thus to trigger the rule NP → NP (S) that is made available by 'marked' parametric variation in universal grammar. In the absence of unambiguous evidence for subject relatives, the relevant part of the grammar would remain restricted to S → NP + VP (S). It is appropriate to note, once again, that restricting the child's access to complex sentences can only have the effect of slowing the acquisition of language.

This emphasis upon selective rather than instructional mechanisms in language growth meshes well with current biological thinking in areas as (superficially) distinct as immunology (Jerne, 1967) and developmental neuroanatomy (Purves and Lichtman, 1980). The plausibility of selective theories of language growth has steadily increased ever since Chomsky (1965) pointed out that position within the Chomsky-hierarchy may well *not* correspond with '... the empirically most significant dimension of increasing power of linguistic theory.' The acquisition problem concerns attainment of a *particular* grammar, not attainment of any arbitrary member of a class of grammars. If very severe restrictions can be placed upon universal grammar (such that, for example, only a finite number of 'widely-spaced' core grammars are possible candidates), then acquisition of a particular language will be possible despite the fact that its grammar falls *within*, say, the class of unrestricted rewriting systems (Chomsky, 1981).

More generally, Chomsky's image of a 'language organ' (analogous to the organs and organ systems of the body) that develops under strong, discrete genetic and epigenetic constraints finds ample *general* confirmation from the now overwhelming evidence for the 'modularity of mind' (and brain). Current neuropsychology leaves little doubt but that different domain-specific faculties of mind can be selectively impaired after brain-damage in the adult and can selectively fail to develop in the child (Marshall, 1984). Yet, although no trace of dualism can be found in Chomsky's work, it is clear that his 'biologism' does not deal *directly* with the neuronal substrate for language capacity. The research programme rather attempts to specify '... abstract conditions that unknown mechanisms must meet' (Chomsky, 1978). But this, of course, leaves open the question of how the principles of language growth are physically instantiated in neuronal hardware. As Chomsky (1982b) phrases the question:

> What do we mean for example when we say that the brain really does have rules of grammar in it. We do not know exactly what we mean when we say that. We do not think there is a neuron that corresponds to 'move alpha'. So we are talking somehow about general structural properties of the

brain, and there are real nontrivial questions about what it means to say that the brain, or any system, has general properties.

If the development of current linguistic theory succeeds in explaining the course of language growth, it will reveal wider areas of ignorance about how to relate 'abstract conditions' to their biological realization.

REFERENCES

Bard, E. G. and Anderson, A. H. (1983) 'The unintelligibility of speech to children', *Journal of Child Language*, **10**, pp. 265–92.

Broadbent, D. E. (1973) *In Defence of Empirical Psychology*, London, Methuen.

Brown, R. (1977) 'Introduction', in Snow, C. E. and Ferguson, C. A. (Eds), *Talking to Children: Language Input and Acquisition*, Cambridge, Cambridge University Press.

Chomsky, N. (1957) *Syntactic Structures*, The Hague, Mouton.

Chomsky, N. (1959) A review of B. F. Skinner's *Verbal Behavior*, *Language*, **35**, pp. 26–58.

Chomsky, N. (1962) 'Explanatory models in linguistics', in Nagel, E., Suppes, P. and Tarski, A. (Eds), *Logic, Methodology and Philosophy of Science*, Stanford, Calif., Stanford University Press.

Chomsky, N. (1963) 'Formal properties of grammars', in Luce, R. D., Bush, R. R. and Galanter, E. (Eds), *Handbook of Mathematical Psychology*, Vol. 2, New York, John Wiley.

Chomsky, N. (1965) *Aspects of the Theory of Syntax*, Cambridge, Mass., MIT Press.

Chomsky, N. (1976) *Reflections on Language*, London, Temple Smith.

Chomsky, N. (1978) 'On the biological basis of language capacities', in Miller, G. A. and Lenneberg, E. (Eds), *Psychology and Biology of Language and Thought: Essays in Honour of Eric Lenneberg*, New York, Academic Press.

Chomsky, N. (1980) *Rules and Representations*, New York, Columbia University Press.

Chomsky, N. (1981) *Lectures on Government and Binding*, Dordrecht, Foris Publications.

Chomsky, N. (1982a) *Some Concepts and Consequences of the Theory of Government and Binding*, Cambridge, Mass., MIT Press.

Chomsky, N. (1982b) *The Generative Enterprise*, Dordrecht, Foris Publications.

Fodor, J. A. (1975) *The Language of Thought*, New York, Crowell.

Fodor, J. A. (1980) 'On the impossibility of acquiring "more powerful" structures', in Piatelli-Palmarines, M. (Ed.), *Language and Learning: The Debate between Jean Piaget and Noam Chomsky*, London Routledge and Kegan Paul.

Gleitman, L. R. and Wanner, E. (1982) 'Language acquisition: The state of the state of the art', in Wanner, E. and Gleitman, L. R. (Eds), *Language Acquisition: The State of the Art*, Cambridge, Cambridge University Press.

Jackson, J. H. (1872) 'Case of disease of the brain—left hemiplegia—mental affection', *Medical Times and Gazette*, **1**, pp. 513–14.

Jerne, N. K. (1967) 'Antibodies and learning: Selection versus instruction', in Quarton, G. C., Melnechuk, T. and Schmitt, F. O. (Eds), *The Neurosciences: A Study Program*, New York, The Rockefeller University Press.

Joos, M. (Ed.) (1957) *Readings in Linguistics*, New York, American Council of Learned Societies.

Lewes, G. H. (1879) *The Study of Psychology*, Cambridge, Mass., Riverside Press.

Lieberman, P. (1963) 'Some effects of semantic and grammatical context on the production and perception of speech', *Language and Speech* **6**, pp. 172–5.

Marshall, J. C. (1984) 'Multiple perspectives on modularity'. *Cognition*, **17**, pp. 209–42.

Newport, E. L. (1977) 'Motherese: The speech of mothers to young children', in Castellan, N., Pisoni, D. and Potts, G. (Eds), *Cognitive Theory*, Vol. 2, Hillsdale, N.J., Erlbaum.

Newport, E. L., Gleitman, H. and Gleitman, L. R. (1977) 'Mother I'd rather do it myself: Some effects and non-effects of maternal speech style', in Snow, C. E. and Ferguson, C. A. (Eds), *Talking to Children: Language Input and Acquisition*, Cambridge, Cambridge University Press.

Purves, D. and Lichtman, J. W. (1980) 'Elimination of synapses in the developing nervous system', *Science*, **210**, pp. 153–7.

Putnam, H. (1980) 'What is innate and why: Comments on the debate', in Piatelli-Palmarini, M. (Ed.), *Language and Learning: The Debate between Jean Piaget and Noam Chomsky*, London, Routledge and Kegan Paul.

Roeper, T. (1982) 'On the importance of syntax and the logical use of evidence in language acquisition', in Kuczaj, S. A. II (ed.), *Language Development*, Vol. 1, Hillsdale. N.J., Erlbaum.

Shatz, M. (1979) 'How to do things by asking: Form-function pairings in mothers' questions and their relation to children's response', *Child Development*, **50,** pp. 1093–9.

Shockey, L. and Bond, Z. S. (1980) 'Phonological processes in speech addressed to children', *Phonetica*, **37,** pp. 267–74.

Suppes, P. (1969) 'Stimulus-response theory of finite automata', *Journal of Mathematical Psychology*, **6,** pp. 327–55.

Wexler, K. (1982) 'A principle theory for language acquisition', in Wanner, E. and Gleitman, L. R. (Eds), *Language Acquisition: The State of the Art*, Cambridge, Cambridge University Press.

Wexler, K. and Culicover, P. (1980) *Formal Principles of Language Acquisition*, Cambridge, Mass., MIT Press.

Interchange

DANCHIN REPLIES TO MARSHALL

As clearly stated by Professor Marshall, a fundamental change in attitude has followed the course of Noam Chomsky's writings. There is, nowadays, a general consensus about the gene determined prerequisites for language building, even though there remains a major conflict between those who, like Piaget, favour the 'instructivist' approach, implying that data are structured, and imprinted together with their structure in the developing infant's brain, and those who, after Chomsky, favour the 'selectivist' approach, assuming that plastic preorganized brain structures are shaped to their final form after a proper interaction with the environment (see Piattelli-Palmarini, 1980, for a state of the debate).

Both attitudes, however, are faced with the same difficulty, namely that it seems as yet very difficult to reconcile linguistic structures, be they learned *de novo* or resulting from an appropriate selective stabilization process (Schmalghausen, 1969; Jacobson, 1969; Changeux *et al*, 1973; Changeux and Danchin, 1976), acting on the organization of actual neuronal networks.

In my paper I have tried to face this challenge, knowing however that my answer would be both primitive and incomplete: I do not think that I shall be able, during my lifetime, to understand the actual neuronal basis of language. Despite this rather negative feeling I do think that progress will be made that will enable us to have a fair estimation of the nature of the biological constraints underlying language. Reading the text of Professor Marshall I find that the distance between us is not so large, and that even this would correspond to an attitude which is not very far from the present day attitude of Noam Chomsky himself. Thus, it seems to me more appropriate to add a few comments to the hypothesis I have made in my article than to start an argument with Marshall on points that would be, finally, of minor importance.

My main point will be to try and connect my hypothesis with what is presently known on the brain structure underlying language, mainly from analysis of brain injuries. My principal source will be the work of A. R. Luria who has collected an immense set of data after the study of hundreds of cases of brain damage. In his book *Visshie Korkovie Funkcii Tcheloveka*, Luria presents a synthesis of all his studies, involving lesions in all parts of the brain. Localized lesions have permitted to detail the interacting parts of the brain when special performances are analyzed. In the case of language it appears clearly that the left hemisphere (in the majority of right handers), around the auditory temporal area, is of particular importance. This fact, known from Broca's time, is modulated, in Luria's thesis, by analysis of interaction with cortical as well as central areas, of the specialized 'language' region. For Luria, as for myself, language results from brain properties that are not, in themselves, different from properties of networks involved in other tasks. Luria's thinking is derived from the school of I. P. Pavlov: a central concept of this school is the concept of interactive feedback processes that modify the central processing unit under study. In the case of higher brain functions this means that one has to divide brain into a set of 'analyzers'. An analyzer is comprised of an input, composed of both sensory interfaces and central (e.g. limbic) interfaces, with the central processing unit (usually located cortically), and a motor output, that *feedbacks* onto the input, thus creating a higher order structure. In the case of language, the relevant analyzer is the auditive analyzer, but inputs from the visual analyzer are also important in the understanding of written language (as well as some aspects of oral language, at least during dialogues). A major feature of Luria's interpretation of medical data is the feedback of motor centres connected to speech production to the input of the auditory analyzer: audition related to language understanding requires a kind of 'palpation' of auditory stimuli, in order to be efficiently processed. Several deficits in language use are related to inability of persons having lesions to have this kind of motor feedback. Clearly, this interpretation of experimental data substantiates the hypothesis I have made on the structure of simple neuronal networks underlying language.

The organization of the 'semantic' domain of neurones that would correspond to 'noun phrase' is certainly not yet known in sufficient detail to permit investigation into whether it is split into two pathways, as I have postulated, but there is a clear separation between the two categories, verb phrase and noun phrase, as observed in some deficiencies where the patient can only speak as a series of substantives, interconnected by hesitations and interjections. Moreover the organization of the motor and premotor areas imposes a control on the smooth course of the linguistic performance, due to appropriate feedback: any alteration of these areas results in perseveration of the linguistic tasks (multiple and inavoidable repetitions).

A final aspect of language, that I did not consider in my article, is the voluntary or intentional control of speech content and performance: this special feature, which is not directly related to linguistic competence, but, rather, to the social function of language, seems to be under the control of the frontal cortical areas. People who have been injured in frontal areas usually do not show deficits in the structure of the language they use, but they can no longer use language on purpose, at least on some occasions, thus showing a deficit that is usually interpreted by their environment as a change in character. Such control, obviously related to what we used to name consciousness, can easily be framed into the picture I have proposed. The overall organization of brain areas involved in language organization and production would thus be as shown in Figure 1.

It is certainly much too soon to derive actual networks from the rather scarce data we have on the neuronal organization of human brain (at the microscopic level, if not at the macroscopic level). But it seems to me that the challenge offered to neurophysiologists, as is demonstrated by the content of Marshall's article, does not forbid conjectures, but should, rather, stimulate their production. My hope is that the lines I have proposed will stimulate other proposals, thus showing that the field will be sooner ripe for new types of investigations.

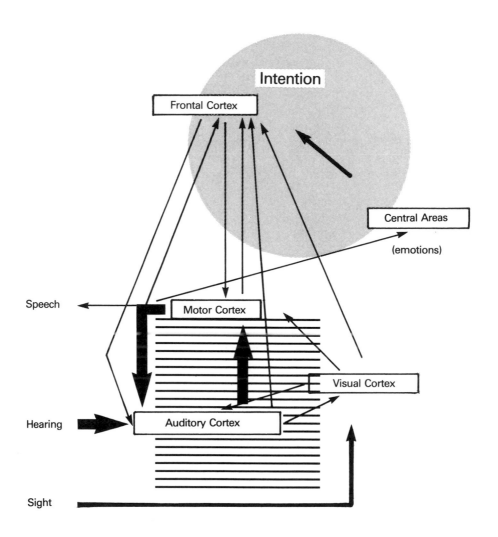

REFERENCES

Changeux, J. P., Courrège, P. and Danchin, A. (1973) *Proc Natl Acad Sci* **70** p. 2974.
Changeux, J. P. and Danchin, A. (1976) *Nature* **264** p. 705.
Jacobson, M. (1969) *Science* **163** p. 543.
Luria, A. R. (1967) *Les Fonctions Corticales Supérieures de l'Homme* (traduction française 1978) PUF.
Schmalghausen, L. L. (1969) *Problemyia Darvinisma*, Nauka, Leningrad.

MARSHALL REPLIES TO DANCHIN

It would be difficult to disagree with the central importance that Professor Danchin assigns to understanding the 'actual roots' of language universals. Neither could one doubt that those roots are grounded in neurobiology. There remains, nonetheless, the central problem of linking linguistic descriptions with their neuronal (and, ultimately, genetic) substrate. As I have previously put the issue: 'Some way surely has to be found in which results phrased in the languages of linguistics, psychology, and physiology can be brought to bear upon each other' (Marshall, 1980). Formal inquiry into the constraints on innate linguistic endowment continues to produce deeper and deeper results (Chomsky, 1985); explicit computational models of language acquisition, incorporating and extending these linguistic insights, have also shed considerable light on the 'abstract' nature of developmental growth (Berwick, 1985.)

On the more 'concretely' biological side, the anatomy, physiology, and pharmacology of cerebral dominance and of the 'language areas' is beginning to be better understood in structural terms (Geschwind and Galaburda, 1984; Benson and Zaidel, 1985). The link with functional asymmetry, however, is still primarily correlational. We still have few ideas concerning exactly what it is about the fine structure of different neuronal regions that makes them an appropriate habitat for the functions that are impaired after damage to those areas (Marshall, 1985). Even with respect to the visual system where 'we have found some likely candidates for the tissues wherein the processes corresponding to visual experience occur, we are not able, at this time, to determine just what it is about these parts of the cortex that gives them this unique property' (Anderson and Leong, 1983).

Even the link between (human) handedness and cerebral language asymmetries may yet prove of limited (or zero) significance in terms of underlying biological mechanisms (Annett, 1985; Kimura, 1983). MacNeilage, Studdert-Kennedy and Lindblom (1984) have recently demonstrated 'handedness' for complex tasks in monkeys, and hypothesized that the hierarchical nature of this collaborative hand use may be an evolutionary precursor of syntactic organization. But the speculation appears premature at a time when it seems that the relationship between language and right handedness in humans is merely coincidental. On the whole, I agree with Danchin that the hope of studying 'primitive language' (or any obvious precursor thereof) in another species (e.g. the chimpanzee) has largely evaporated (Seidenberg and Petitto, 1979). The most interesting idea currently in play about linguistic 'evolution' may be Geschwind's striking proposal that one could breed (in species other than ourselves) for specific brain regions related to language (in humans) in order to 'attempt to discover what particular behavioral features are enhanced' (Geschwind, 1984).

On the clinical front, aphasiological studies continue to reveal performance breakdowns after brain damage that cut along the lines of abstract syntactic, lexical, and semantic units, despite the fact that such findings raise more problems than they solve. In 1770, Gesner wrote that 'the vessels of the brain are surely not arranged in accordance with categories of ideas and therefore it is incomprehensible that these categories should correspond to areas of destruction.' Yet in 1985, Hart, Berndt and Caramazza could report a case of residual anomia (consequent upon cerebro-vascular accident) that was especially severe for the categories of fruit and vegetables. The patient could name to visual confrontation such comparatively rare items as an abacus or a sphinx, yet he was unable to name correctly such common fruits as peach and orange. In 1925, Vendryes wrote that 'it is wrong to think of the brain as if it were built on the plan of a grammar, cut into sections for the different parts of speech.' Yet in 1985, McCarthy and Warrington could report a case of severe agrammatism, consequent upon cerebral atrophy, in which a disorder of verb phrase constructions was the most outstanding symptom. The patient was impaired in both the production and comprehension of action names and verbs, despite excellent performance with other classes of nouns. I would greatly like to see Professor Danchin's further attempts to show how such specificity of linguistic and conceptual categories could be encoded into a well-defined neuronal substrate.

Professor Chomsky's notion of generative grammar has set the problem of language growth firmly within a biological framework; it has inspired others to the realization that formal theories of generation are appropriate to a wide range of neurobiological problems. In this context, I can do no better than close with a quotation from the immunologist Niels Jerne's Nobel Prize address of 1984:

> It seems a miracle that young children easily learn the language of any environment into which they are born. The generative approach to grammar, pioneered by Chomsky, argues that this is only explicable if certain deep, universal features of this competence are innate characteristics of the human brain. Biologically speaking, this hypothesis of an inheritable capability to learn any language means that it must somehow be encoded in the DNA of our chromosomes. Should this hypothesis one day be verified, then linguistics would become a branch of biology (Jerne, 1985).

I agree: but the route from neurons to noun phrases is tortuous enough; how much more so, the route from genes to generative syntax!

REFERENCES

Anderson, R. M. and Leong, D. C. Q. (1983) 'The placement of experience in the brain.' in Segalowitz S.J. (ed.), *Language Functions and Brain Organization*. New York, Academic Press.

Annett, M. (1985) *Left, Right, Hand and Brain: The Right Shift Theory*. London, Lawrence Erlbaum Associates.

Benson, D. F. and Zaidel, E., eds. (1985) *The Dual Brain*. New York, The Guilford Press.

Berwick, R. C. (1985) *The Acquisition of Syntactic Knowledge*. Cambridge, Mass., MIT Press.

Chomsky, N. (1985) *Knowledge of Language: Its Nature, Origin, and Use*. New York, Praeger.

Geschwind, N. (1984) 'The biology of cerebral dominance: Implications for cognition.' *Cognition*, **17**, pp.193–208.

Geschwind, N. and Galaburda, A. M., eds. (1984) *Cerebral Dominance: The Biological Foundations*. Cambridge, Mass., Harvard University Press.

Gesner, J. A. P. (1770) *Die Sprachamnesie*. Nördlingen, Beck.

Hart, J., Berndt, R. S. and Caramazza, A. (1985) 'Category-specific naming deficit following cerebral infarction.' *Nature*, **316**, pp. 439–40.

Jerne, N. K. (1985) 'The generative grammar of the immune system.' *Science*, **229**, pp. 1057–9.

Kimura, D. (1983) 'Speech representation in an unbiased sample of left-handers.' *Human Neurobiology*, **2**, pp. 147–54.

Marshall, J. C. (1980) 'The new organology.' *The Behavioral and Brain Sciences*, **3**, pp. 23–5.

Marshall, J. C. (1985) 'The duplex brain.' *Nature*, **314**, pp. 475–6.

MacNeilage, P. F., Studdert-Kennedy, M. G. and Lindblom, B. (1984) 'Functional precursors to language and its lateralization.' *American Journal of Physiology*, **246**, R912–R914.

McCarthy, R. and Warrington, E. K. (1985) 'Category specificity in an agrammatic patient: The relative impairment of verb retrieval and comprehension.' *Neuropsychologia*, **23**, pp. 709–27.

Seidenberg, M. S. and Petitto, L. A. (1979) 'Signing behavior in apes: a critical review.' *Cognition*, **7**, pp. 177–215.

Vendryes, J. (1925) *Language: A Linguistic Introduction to History*. London, Routledge and Kegan Paul.

IV: Universals and Typology

5. Universals and Typology*

NEIL SMITH

> The theory of Universal Grammar must meet two obvious conditions. On the one hand it must be compatible with the diversity of existing (indeed, possible) grammars. At the same time, UG must be sufficiently constrained and restrictive in the options it permits so as to account for the fact that each of these grammars develops in the mind on the basis of quite limited evidence. (Chomsky, 1981, p. 3)

Over the last thirty years Chomsky has consistently shaped and reshaped our thinking on the nature of language and linguistics. He has done this by constructing theories which, while achieving a level of descriptive sophistication hitherto undreamed of, have systematically subordinated description to explanation. The goal of 'complete coverage', of describing the totality of facts, is considered chimerical and is replaced by a goal more characteristic of the natural sciences, that of explaining some subset of the facts by the construction of theories with a progressively richer and more complex deductive structure.

It is not only this methodological change which distinguishes Chomsky from his predecessors, but also the redefinition of the domain that constitutes the explanatory goal of the 'generative enterprise'. The central issue is taken to be to account for the nature and form of human linguistic knowledge and how this knowledge can be acquired. Such an aim is not exclusive of other goals such as accounting for language perception and production, linguistic variation under particular social conditions, bilingualism, the phylogenetic development of language in the species, and so on. All these domains, however, presuppose some prior account of the linguistic knowledge of the individuals involved and it is this on which Chomsky has focused his attention.

---

*I would like to dedicate this article to the memory of David Kilby whose premature death has deprived linguistics of a leading researcher in the field of language universals and linguistic typology.

57

The resulting reorientation of the field is most clearly seen in Chomsky's perennial emphasis on linguistic universals, their psychological implications and their role in providing a window onto the nature of mind.

In the last decade Chomsky's ideas have begun to have a comparable effect on our understanding of language typology, raising it from a discipline with much the same status as philately to an intellectually respectable adjunct of the general theory which has now progressed sufficiently to make interesting cross-linguistic claims even in the absence of any desire for exhaustiveness. In the study both of universals and of typology, Chomsky's work has been controversial as a result of his ability to force us to rethink our assumptions about the nature of linguistics in general, largely on the basis of the development of novel kinds of argumentation and, more particularly in the present context, his resolution of the tension between description and explanation in terms of a theory of 'parametric variation'. In this chapter I want to provide a skeleton outline of the change in orientation linguistic theory has taken under Chomsky's influence, and then put a little flesh on the bones to show how work in typology can be made to depend on current theoretical proposals and thereby avoid the sterility of its previous taxonomic boundedness.

In linguistic theory we have seen a three-stage progression from a preoccupation with data via a concentration on analyses to an attempt to deal with general principles. The formal analogue of this gradation has been a transition from the study of languages to that of grammars to that of universal principles determining the form of possible grammars. As a specific illustration of this development consider the treatment of 'passive' sentences. Although it is a truism that even a description of raw data presupposes some theory—of categories, segmentation, and so on—the description of the passive in traditional and structuralist grammar left the theory inchoate and was limited largely to the listing of examples and exceptions from one or more languages, with the cross-linguistic identification of the construction simply assumed or left implicit. Thus the *Oxford English Dictionary* characterizes the passive as a construction 'in which the logical object of the action is made the grammatical subject of the assertion', an approximation to a valid generalization which it was beyond the power of structuralist linguistics to capture formally. One of the reasons for the early rise of transformational grammar was Chomsky's success in accommodating the passive within a coherent framework of rules which covered simultaneously a wide variety of other structures. It soon became clear, however, that the rules involved, in particular the so-called 'passive transformation' itself, were in many respects arbitrary and ad hoc. A plethora of 'theories' of the passive sprang up, each attempting to capture elegantly the perceived regularities in passive constructions, but none seemed convincing. Chomsky's solution was to cut the Gordian Knot by reducing the status of the passive to that of an epiphenomenon. There is no single rule of passive; rather, when the theory of grammar is correctly understood, the interaction of a number of different simple generalizations (about case, thematic structure and movement) functions to produce passive sentences as one of several side-effects. Thus, a passive such as (1):

1   Lear was deceived by Goneril

has its characteristic word order with the logical object moved into initial position as a result first of the underlying subject position receiving no thematic role, and second of the object position failing to receive objective case.[1] Each of these properties is also characteristic of constructions other than the passive. For instance, no thematic role is assigned to the subject position of raising predicates such as *seem*, as exemplified in (2):

    2   Lear seems to have suffered unduly

and objective case is not assigned to the object of the nominalized verb *depict* in (3):

    3   Shakespeare's depiction of Lear is overly pessimistic

Hence the grammar need contain no rule of passivization as such at all. The data fall out correctly as a by-product of more general principles each of which is operative elsewhere.

There are two important corollaries of such an analysis. First, there is no one-to-one correlation between constructions and rules. Whereas in early transformational generative grammar there was generally taken to be a separate rule or rules for each sentence type: passives, questions, negatives, clefts, and so on; in more recent work any one construction is a function of a number of intersecting principles, and the rules that do remain are extremely general, culminating in the maximally simple reduction of all rules involving movement to the schematic 'Move-α', where α is a cover symbol for any syntactic category or categories, the precise range being specified for each language. Second, Chomsky uses these abstract generalizations to construct an argument for the innateness of certain aspects of human linguistic ability. Having demonstrated that analyses such as that sketched above are superior in terms of their generality and deducibility from independent abstract principles, Chomsky argues that the evidence available to the child learning its first language is too impoverished to allow of any learning-theoretic mastery of the rules and principles of the grammar and hence that these must be antecedently specified, that is, part of the genotype.

This historical progression from data to analyses to universal principles is currently being repeated in the field of language typology. Typological studies have tended to lag behind the development of theory, and most work is still at the stage of collecting and categorizing data. Pre-eminent examples of such work are the 'universals' of Greenberg (1963) and the studies of Comrie (1981).

In such work languages are scrutinized for examples of particular constructions—typically, patterns of word order such as 'language X is SVO', 'language Y is SOV', 'all languages are SO'—and where possible, implicational statements are made about sets of such data: for instance, 'if a language is VSO it will have prepositions rather than postpositions.' The existence of such implicational universals means that the number of language types is not equivalent to the nth power of the relevant variables: a position which would render the classification trivial because totally unconstrained.

Once one goes beyond the recapitulation of such facts, there are severe problems with this typological paradigm, of which the least is that all the non-trivial predictions turn out to be false. For instance, the significance of the correlation of VSO word order with prepositions and of SOV word order with postpositions is undermined by the existence of languages like Papago which have VSO word order but both prepositions and postpositions. It is still possible to claim that if a language is VSO it will have prepositions,[2] but the interest of such a claim resided in large part on the implicit suggestion that such languages would not also have postpositions. But (lack of) correspondence to reality is not the worst disadvantage of this typological method. It is perhaps easiest to see the nature of the problem if we assume (counterfactually) the success of the enterprise, and think what the implications of the achievement would be. We should have a set of statements about languages of the kind given above, with perhaps a long-term possibility of predicting a wide range of further facts about language in general. What could be an explanation for such facts? The obvious response that the data are as they are because they are a function of the rules of the grammars concerned is, unfortunately, only a half-truth, as the performance data typified by the statements above are not a simple reflection of the rules of a competence grammar but are also partially determined by social, stylistic and psychological factors.

It has already been observed that the (utterances of the) sentences of a language are not in a one-to-one relationship with the rules of the grammar which generates those sentences. As a further instance, consider word order in English. English is an SVO language, but it also has a possible word order in which the (auxiliary) verb precedes the subject. This pattern can have any of a number of different functions, as in (4):

4a	Had the children come?	(Question)
b	Had the children come I should have seen them	(Counterfactual)
c	Scarcely had the children come than I left	(Negative)

yet the simplest hypothesis is that they are all produced by the same rule, move-α, which is responsible for the passive example discussed above and the cases of movement analyzed later. Furthermore, stylistic and other pragmatic effects may give rise to data (spoken or written utterances) which diverge from full acceptability, as exemplified in (5):

5a	The oats have eaten the horses	(Shakespeare)
b	His girl-friend's mother he's marrying?	(Woody Allen)
c	The bar is open for light refreshments are now being served	(Cormack, 1984)

None of these examples is a random 'mistake', but the regularities they reflect belong to different domains, as is implicit in our characterization of them as grammatical, stylistic or pathological deviations. Given such judgments, there is little reason to believe that chunks of data, often culled from disparate sources over long periods of time,[3] can throw any light on the mental mechanisms which underlie such data, and every reason to think that rules and rule systems do cast such light. That is, the most likely explanation for the multifaceted nature of the data will come from the interaction of a range of different subtheories, each with its own generalizations.

Let us assume, however, that these difficulties can be overcome: that we can discriminate among the various subtheories that jointly determine the data observed, and perhaps even idealize to a situation where rules and construction types are in a one-to-one relation. At this stage a more interesting problem emerges: namely, the status of those typological generalizations which, by hypothesis, presuppose reference to more than one language. Various types of such generalization can be distinguished, but the clearest are those exemplified by what has become known as the Keenan-Comrie 'accessibility hierarchy'. According to the accessibility hierarchy, given as 'Subject → Direct Object → Nondirect Object → Possessor' (Comrie, 1981, p. 149), the possibility in a language of forming (for example) relative clauses on a direct object entails that it will be possible to form relative clauses on a subject, but not conversely; if it is possible to form relative clauses on a nondirect object then it will also be possible to form relative clauses on direct objects and subjects, but not conversely, and so on. The accessibility hierarchy, with various modifications, has now become the subject of an extensive literature, some of which calls in doubt the exceptionless status of the claims made. However, assuming the validity of such generalizations, the same question as to what could be a possible explanation arises again. There are several possibilities which are customarily presented as alternatives: innatist, perceptual, functional and pragmatic. In fact, all four can coexist (in any combination) though the only one which is particularly well-motivated empirically is the innatist variety.[4] Indeed, even if non-innatist explanations were successful in particular instances, it would not follow that the property concerned was not also innate. For instance, it is plausible that a functional explanation for the accessibility hierarchy is, phylogenetically even if not ontogenetically, correct (cf. Comrie, 1981, pp. 25, 156), but we still have to determine the way in which this functional constraint is represented in the grammars of the individuals speaking the languages concerned. Assuming that the constraint really is a grammatical one and not simply the result of a stylistic or statistical quirk, we have two relevant possibilities: either it is learned or it is innate. The possibility that communicative conditions surrounding each child learning a particular language are such that the constraint is learnable seems implausible given that the manifestations of the accessibility hierarchy are distinct in different languages. Moreover, learning seems ex hypothesi unlikely as the constraint can only be stated accurately by reference to a number of languages, where the speaker of any of them is presumably ignorant of the others. The second alternative then seems inevitable: namely, the constraint is innate. It should be noted that for a property to be innate does not entail that it be manifest at birth, but only that the conditions for its development under appropriate triggering data be genetically determined.

It is ironic that a phenomenon associated most closely with those who eschew innatist explanations should lend most support to such explanations; it is more ironic that the common reaction of such people to an innatist explanation—that such a claim 'terminates the discussion,'[5] derives from their general avoidance of any formal theory, where what should be prompted by the hypothesis that 'phenomenon *X* is innate' is precisely the elaboration of a theory of linguistic form from which this can be deduced.

An alternative account of cross-linguistic differences has led to one of the more significant developments within generative grammar over the last few years: the incorporation of typological variation into the theoretical mainstream. In accordance with the generative emphasis on grammars and principles rather than languages and data, the treatment of typology, under the general heading of 'parametric variation', is concerned with specifying the possible choices languages may make along universal parameters. As this notion of relativized universality is often misunderstood or even considered incoherent, it may be useful to begin with an analogy. Essentially all cultures have an incest taboo. The manifestation of this taboo, however, is not everywhere the same: the specification of the kin with whom sexual relations are prohibited constituting the variation along the incest parameter. That some societies do and others do not prohibit sexual relations between uncles and nieces does not alter the fact that such a ban is an instance of the universal incest taboo.[6] Similarly with language and grammar. Until the rediscovery of object-initial languages in the late seventies (cf. Derbyshire, 1961, 1979), it was thought that languages could choose among the four word order possibilities SVO, SOV, VSO and VOS with, perhaps, a fifth 'free' word order being available too. That is, despite the obvious differences of word order to be found among the world's languages, the apparent absence of one natural class of possibilities made it seem worthwhile couching a universal statement which provided a framework into which languages had to fit. Taking the chosen parameter to be word order, the theory then specified what range of variation was possible within that parameter.[7] Because of the under-determination of grammatical rules by linguistic data discussed briefly above, one would not have expected such a claim about structures rather than rule-systems to be very fruitful, even if it had not been disconfirmed by Hixkaryana. If, however, the domain of discussion is grammar rather than language, the prospects are somewhat brighter.

Let us take an example involving the rule 'move-α' as alluded to above. All grammars appear to contain some *locality* conditions which limit the possible distance apart of the expressions referred to in the rules they contain. The most obvious such principle is 'subjacency'. This principle[8] accounts for a range of differences in the relative acceptability of sets of sentences, including those in (6) and (7):

> 6a A rise in the price of oil was announced
>   b A rise was announced in the price of oil
>   c *A rise in the price was announced of oil
> 7a The suit which I bought is big for me
>   b *The suit which you know where I bought is big for me

The example (6a) is generated phrase-structurally by a grammar including a recursive rule of the form 'NP → NP PP', giving the simplified structure in (8):

> 8 $_{NP}[_{NP}[A$ $rise]_{NP}]_{PP}[in$ $_{NP}[_{NP}[the$ $price]_{NP}]_{PP}[of$ $_{NP}[oil]_{NP}]_{PP}]_{NP}]_{PP}]$ $_{NP}]$ was announced

(6b) is then derived from (8) by a rule which moves the underlined PP from its position adjacent to an NP rightwards to the end of the sentence. The simplest formulation of such a rule, namely 'move-α', makes the prediction that (6c) is also grammatical and hence expected to be as acceptable as (6b). This prediction is clearly wrong. Similarly, on standard transformational assumptions, the example in (7a) is derived from a structure of the form given in (9):

> 9 $_{NP}[_{NP}[$The suit$]_{NP}$ $_{\bar{S}}[$which $_{S}[$I bought ___$]_S]_{\bar{S}}]_{NP}$ is big for me

where a rule moves the direct object of *bought* leftwards, as indicated by the arrow.[9] Again, the simplest formulation of such a rule (again 'move-α') predicts that (7b) is similarly grammatical. Again the prediction is false.

The ungrammaticality of examples (6c) and (7b) is in each case due to a violation of subjacency. To generate (6c) the PP *of oil* needs to be moved across two (circled) NP nodes, as indicated in (10):

> 10 $_{NP}[_{NP}[A$ rise$]_{NP}$ $_{PP}[in$ $_{NP}[_{NP}[the$ price$]_{NP}$ $_{PP}[of$ $_{NP}[oil]_{NP}]_{PP}]_{NP}]_{PP}]_{NP}$ was announced

The generation of (6b), however, involves movement across only the single NP node circled in (8). To generate (7b) the direct object of *bought* needs to be moved across two (circled) S nodes as indicated in (11):

> 11 $_{NP}[_{NP}[$The suit$]_{NP}$ $_{\bar{S}}[$which $_{S}[$you know $_{\bar{S}}[$where $_{S}[$I bought___$]_S]_{\bar{S}}]_S]_{\bar{S}}]_{NP}$ is big for me

By contrast, the generation of (7a) involves movement across only the single S node circled in (9).

Not all nodes count as 'bounding' for the purposes of subjacency. NP is generally bounding and any or all of S, $\bar{\text{S}}$, PP and perhaps others may also function as such. This latitude immediately gives rise to potential parametric variation. All languages are subject to subjacency, but two languages may differ in what they define the relevant bounding nodes to be. Thus for English the nodes are NP and S; for the Philippine language Hiligaynon[10] the bounding nodes are NP and $\bar{\text{S}}$. This difference accounts both for the parallelism between Hiligaynon and English as seen in (6a, b) and (12), and for the asymmetry between the languages as seen in (7) and (13).

12a $_{NP}[_{NP}$ [ang kamatuoran] $_{NP}$ $_{\bar{S}}$ [nga $_S[_{NP}[_{NP}[$ang bana] $_{NP}$
      the   fact   that   the husband

   $_{PP}[$sang $_{NP}[$anak niya] $_{NP}]_{PP}]$ ⓝⓟ nagpalagyo] $_S]_{\bar{S}}]_{NP}$ makahuluya guid
     of daughter her   left home   is-shameful indeed

     'The fact that the husband of her daughter left home is indeed shameful'
  b Ang kamatuoran nga ang bana nagpalagyo sang anak niya makahuluya guid
     'The fact that the husband left home of her daughter is indeed shameful'

(12b) is derived appropriately from (12a) by moving the underlined PP *sang anak niya* across the single circled NP node. If, however, more than one bounding node is crossed, as in (12c) derived by moving the same PP in (12a) further to the right, the result is ungrammatical:

12c   *Ang kamatuoran nga ang bana nagpalagyo makahuluya

     the   fact   that the husband left home is-shameful

     guid sang anak niya
     indeed of daughter her
     'The fact that the husband left home is shameful indeed of her daughter'

In (12c) so many nodes have been crossed that it is not obvious that there is any variation in subjacency between English and Hiligaynon. That Hiligaynon differs from English precisely in selecting $\bar{\text{S}}$ rather than S as a bounding node becomes apparent from an inspection of the sentences in (13):

13a   Ang bayo ko $_{\bar{S}}[$ nga $_S[$ ko gimbakal ___]] daku sa akon

     the dress my which   I bought   big for me
     'The dress which I bought is big for me'
  b Ang bayo ko $_{\bar{S}}[$ nga $_S[$bal-an mo $_{\bar{S}}[$kon diin $_S[$ ko gimbakal___]]]]

     the dress my which   know you whether where   I bought
     daku sa akon
     big for me
'The dress which you know where I bought is big for me'
  c *Ang bayo ko $_{\bar{S}}[$nga $_S[$ginapamangkot ko $_{\bar{S}}[$kon $_S[$bal-an mo

     the dress my which   wonder   I whether know you

   $_{\bar{S}}[$nga kon   diin $_S[$ko gimbakal ___]]]]]] daku sa akon

     that whether where   I   bought   big for me

(13a), parallel to (7a), is fully acceptable; (13b), parallel to the ungrammatical English (7b), is grammatical in Hiligaynon because, although the object of *gimbakal* has moved over two S nodes, it has moved over only one $\bar{\text{S}}$ node. (13c), where two $\bar{\text{S}}$ nodes have been crossed is predictably ungrammatical.[11]

Parametric variation escapes the charge of triviality that can be levelled against typological statements couched in terms of data on two counts: first, as in the case of subjacency illustrated above, a single structural principle has implication for a wide range of apparently unconnected phenomena within and across languages; second, in a more fully elaborated theory, tight constraints are placed on what can constitute a variable. The first of these points is reminiscent of the situation in biology where 'small genetic changes may have major, discontinuous effects upon morphology' (Gould, 1984; p. 181) as most clearly evidenced in homeotic mutation. The second point can be illustrated from recent work by Borer (1984) who proposes a theory of parametric variation which 'reduces all interlanguage variation to the properties of the inflectional system' (p. 29),[12] thereby locating differences essentially within the lexicon: that part of the grammar which is predominantly learned. As it stands, Borer's theory would exclude the variation in subjacency illustrated above, and it is clear that her position is currently over-restrictive. This is not a reason, however, for rejecting her programme as 'disproved'. Although falsifiability is a necessary property for any particular hypothesis, a theory with any explanatory power is never jettisoned on the basis simply of data for which it fails to account. Rather, the theory will be complicated by the addition of auxiliary hypotheses until a later synthesis provides a better account of the recalcitrant data. In general, even if some 'beautiful hypotheses' are slain by 'ugly facts', as Huxley has it, the theories from which the hypotheses derive can still survive.

One of Chomsky's achievements has been to bring to linguistics the same forms of argument as obtain in the study of the natural sciences. I began by contrasting the typical taxonomist's desire to cover all the data with the theoretician's aim to explain the data by constructing (deductive) theories. Linguistics is not yet in the position of physics where 'it is more important to have beauty in one's equations than to have them fit experiment',[13] but it is very far from being in the position where simple observations of primary data can be taken to refute edifices of the complexity now achieved. Hence comes the validity of the often repeated but often misunderstood remark that only analyses or superior theories, and not observations, are relevant to disconfirmability. As Chomsky (1980, p. 2) put it: 'linguistic principles of any real significance generally deal with properties of rule systems, not observed phenomena, and can thus be confirmed or refuted only indirectly through the construction of grammars, a task that goes well beyond even substantial accumulation and organization of observations.'

It does not follow from this that linguistics is a metaphysical or non-empirical discipline, or that Chomsky and his followers are insulating themselves against refutation by making untestable claims. It does follow that 'naive falsificationism' in the sense of Lakatos (1970) is an unfruitful stance to adopt, and that one can only contribute usefully to the debate on universals and typology if one builds on a theoretical base as complex in principle as the physicists'. For even if 'experience alone can decide on truth'[14] it can only do so in virtue of providing evidence to test alternative theories, not simply by accumulating facts.

Despite the differences and animosities that characterize the literature on universals and typology—indeed, the whole of linguistics—the divide between the

Chomskyans and their opponents can be bridged. Reconciliation of the sort sketched in the last chapter of Smith and Wilson (1979) demands not only that generativists construct grammars of increasing complexity for a growing number of 'exotic' languages: French and Italian as well as Hixkaryana and Hiligaynon; but also that descriptivists appreciate the distinction between data and evidence, and use their knowledge to construct better theories. Linguistics, like physics, has passed beyond the stage of stamp collecting.

NOTES

1 For details, cf. Chomsky (1981).
2 Cf. Comrie (1981) p. 28.
3 A salutary example of the unrevealing nature of such studies can be seen in the acrimonious and unfruitful debate over the word order (VSO, SVO or SOV) of Proto-Indo-European; cf. Smith (1981) for comment and references.
4 Cf. Smith (1982) for a discussion of specific cases.
5 Foley and van Valin (1984) p. 13; cf. also Comrie (1981) p. 24. Foley and Van Valin's extreme position is further illustrated by their remark (*ibid.*, p. 7) that 'language is thus viewed as a system of human communication *rather than* as an infinite set of structural descriptions of sentences' (emphasis added).
6 Cf. Van den Berghe (1983) for interesting recent discussion.
7 Cf. Pullum (1977) and Vennemann (1974) for typical examples.
8 Technically, subjacency says that no rule may refer to α and β in the configuration:
$$\ldots \alpha \ldots {}_x[\ldots {}_y[\ldots \beta \ldots] \ldots] \ldots \alpha \ldots$$
where x and y are 'bounding' or 'cyclic' nodes.
9 In fact the use of movement in the derivation of such examples is not crucial to the argument. Some locality condition is still necessary whether such sentences are accounted for by movement, rules of construal, or whatever.
10 Cf. Sebastian (1983). The same applies for Italian, cf. Rizzi (1982), which served as the impetus for much recent work in parametric variation, including Sebastian's work.
11 For further details cf. Sebastian (1983) from which these examples are derived.
12 It should be pointed out that Borer's definition of 'inflection' is wider than standard, extending to all relations involving the transfer of features, and hence including thematic marking of the sort cited in the earlier discussion of the passive.
13 Dirac, cited in Cohen (1980) p. 325.
14 Einstein, cited in Pais (1982) p. 350.

REFERENCES

Borer, H. (1984) *Parametric Syntax*, Dordrecht, Foris.
Chomsky, N. (1980) 'On binding', *Linguistic Inquiry*, **11**, pp. 1–46
Chomsky, N. (1981) *Lectures on Government and Binding*, Dordrecht, Foris.
Cohen, I. B. (1980) *The Newtonian Revolution*, Cambridge, Cambridge University Press.
Comrie, B. (1981) *Language Universals and Linguistic Typology*, London, Blackwell.
Cormack, A. (1984) 'Crossed brackets', paper delivered at the autumn meeting of the Linguistics Association of Great Britain.
Derbyshire, D. (1961) 'Hixkaryana', (Carib) syntax structure: I Word', *IJAL*, **27**, pp. 125–42; II, *IJAL*, **27**, pp. 226–36.
Derbyshire, D. (1979) 'Hixkaryana', *Lingua Descriptive Studies*, **1**.
Foley, W. and van Valin, R. (1984) *Functional Syntax and Universal Grammar*, Cambridge, Cambridge University Press.
Gould, S. J. (1984) *Hen's Teeth and Horse's Toes*, Harmondsworth, Penguin.

Greenberg, J. (1963) 'Some universals of grammar with particular reference to the order of meaningful elements', in Greenberg, J. (Ed.), *Universals of Language*, Cambridge, Mass., MIT Press.

Lakatos, I. (1970) 'Falsification and the methodology of scientific research programmes', in Lakatos, I. and Musgrove, A. (Eds), *Criticism and the Growth of Knowledge*, Cambridge, Cambridge University Press.

Pais, A. (1982) *'Subtle is the Lord. . .': The Science and the Life of Albert Einstein*, Oxford, Oxford University Press.

Pullum, G. K. (1977) 'Word order universals and grammatical relations' in Cole, P. and Sadock, J. (Eds), *Syntax and Semantics 8*, New York, Academic Press.

Rizzi, L. (1982) *Issues in Italian Syntax*, Dordrecht, Foris.

Sebastian, E. (1983) 'Constraints in Hiligaynon syntax', unpublished MA dissertation, University College London.

Smith, N. V. (1981) 'Consistency, markedness and language change: On the notion "consistent language"', *JL*, **17**, pp. 39–54.

Smith, N. V. (1982) Review of Comrie, (1981), in *Australian Journal of Linguistics*, **2**, pp. 255–61.

Smith, N. V. and D. Wilson (1979) *Modern Linguistics: The Results of Chomsky's Revolution*, Harmondsworth, Penguin.

Van den Berghe, P. L. (1983) 'Human inbreeding avoidance: Culture in nature', *BBS* **6**, pp. 91–123.

Vennemann, T. (1974) 'Topics, subjects and word-order: From SXV to SVX via TVX', in Anderson, J. and Jones, C. (Eds), *Historical Linguistics*, Amsterdam, North Holland.

6. Typology and Universals in Chomsky's Theory of Grammar

DAVID KILBY

CHOMSKY'S NOTION OF 'UNIVERSAL GRAMMAR'

At least since Chomsky's major methodological discussion in *Aspects of the Theory of Syntax* it has been an article of faith among transformational grammarians that linguistic theory is to be thought of as a set of principles which serve to determine the nature of possible grammars. The most interesting of these principles are 'formal universals'—concerned with the general structural properties of grammars: 'for example, consider the proposal that the syntactic component of a grammar must contain transformational rules' (Chomsky, 1965, p. 29). Chomsky continues: 'the existence of deep-seated formal universals . . . implies that all languages are cut to the same pattern' (*ibid.*, p. 30).

This position is a fairly traditional one—general principles of language structure lie at the basis of most systematic attempts at linguistic theorizing. The most readily intelligible view of language universals is that they can be cast as statements of the general form

All languages have the property P

or perhaps, bearing in mind Chomsky's views on the relationship of grammars and languages,

All grammars have the property P.

Such 'strong' universals have been proposed numerous times by linguists of many different persuasions—cf. Hockett's, 'Every human language has proper names' (1963, p. 21).

Where Chomsky differs from many linguists (including some other transformationalists) is in interpreting linguistic theory in terms of learning theory, and making conclusions from there about the nature of mind. Chomsky's conception relies on the argument that the data of language (such as might be presented to a child learning

67

that language as a first language) underdetermine the grammar of that language. If we assume that the child rapidly achieves a mastery of at least the central grammar of a language, then it is necessary, if Chomsky's position is correct, to assume that the child brings to the task of learning a first language a set of principles which will allow a grammar to be constructed even though the data are compatible with many different possible grammars. Put more generally, the child's expectations as to what a grammar can look like complement the primary linguistic data that the child is presented with, so as to enable a grammar to be constructed. General linguistic theory, or universal grammar (UG), is the linguist's attempt to construct sets of principles which will have the same effect as those which can be attributed to the child. Chomsky is on record with some rather dismissive comments about those who do not share this orientation:

> I think a linguist can do perfectly good work in generative grammar without ever caring about questions of physical realism or what his work has to do with the structure of the mind. I do not think there is any question that that is possible. It just seems to me to indicate a certain lack of curiosity as to why things are as they are. (Chomsky, 1982a, p. 31)

The evaluation in the last sentence suggests a certain lack of awareness that the objection to Chomsky's conclusions as to the structure of the mind does not follow from lack of curiosity, but rather from the feeling that the step from abstract linguistic analysis to the structure of the mind is not well-founded. But the most noteworthy thing about this passage is that, from the point of view of linguistic theory, conclusions as to mind are an optional add-on, even though for Chomsky personally they are a central motivation for studying linguistics.

In the light of this view of what linguistic theory should look like, it becomes clear why 'strong' universals such as those cited above are not likely to form the basis for general linguistic theory. Those that have been found are not particularly interesting, in the sense that they are usually fairly obvious, and also in the sense that, put together, they do not amount to a picture of what languages are like—they are merely isolated facts. UG must constitute a set of principles which suggest organized subsystems of linguistic units, rather than just individual facts. This is not to deny that there might possibly be universals of the form, 'Every language has a word for "thumb"'—but what is clear is that such universals cannot provide explanations for the acquisition of linguistic structure.

A more interesting type of universal is the implicational universal, which links the presence of one linguistic feature in a language with that of another. This type of universal is highly developed in the phonological work of Jakobson, and Greenberg (1963) is responsible for introducing it into the syntactic sphere. Note that such universals entail a typology: a universal in which the feature P implies the feature Q only makes sense if there are languages with neither P nor Q. For if Q were universal in the strong sense, the implicational universal would be otiose; and a language without Q cannot have P either (by the implicational universal). Such a universal therefore entails at least two language types. The work of Greenberg on word order (and its later refinements, e.g., by Hawkins) demonstrates that implicational universals do provide us with a coherent picture of what languages are like, and this demonstration has been repeated for other areas—most notably those which involve hierarchies of grammatical relations.

A typology is simply a way of classifying languages into types according to some feature(s) they contain. Implicational universals induce typologies; but not all typologies relate to implicational universals. There are languages with case systems and languages without; but that is a truism rather than a universal. Non-implicational universals can also define typologies: e.g., Greenberg's first universal (abstracting from its exceptions) states that subjects precede objects in basic sentence types. This suggests the by-now-well-known distinction of VSO, SVO and SOV languages. It is clear that some typologies are insignificant: if we were to divide languages into those where the word for 'man' began with a voiced segment and those where it began with a voiceless segment, the world would not leap about in admiration. But if we could correlate this division with the presence or absence of case morphology in a language, then things would be different (even though the interpretation of this particular example would be rather hard).

It appears, therefore, that we need criteria for the significance of a typology; the following is clearly the major criterion:

> The typology must not be a list of the logically-possible types of value for a feature (although of course such lists can be part of a significant typology—for instance, if the individual values correlate with the individual values of logically unrelated features).

This criterion can be relativized: a typology is more significant the greater the proportion of logically possible types that it excludes. A single implication, for instance, is less significant than an implicational hierarchy, and the more places there are in an implicational hierarchy, the stronger the claim that it makes. Thus Greenberg's implicational (near-)universal, 'In languages with prepositions, the genitive almost always follows the governing noun' (Greenberg, 1963) (almost) excludes one type of language (Prep and -NG) out of four logically possible types (assuming that both features are binary), whereas Hawkins' (1983, p. 75) implicational hierarchy (designed for prepositional languages only)

$$\left\{\begin{array}{l} \text{N-DEM} \\ \text{N-Num} \end{array}\right\} \rightarrow \text{N-ADJ} \rightarrow \text{N-GEN} \rightarrow \text{N-RELCL}$$

excludes eleven possibilities out of a possible sixteen. We can conclude that Hawkins' refinement of Greenberg is an advance, in that it makes stronger claims about possible language types.

By no means all work in the Greenberg tradition meets the criteria for significance of a typology (cf. Smith, 1981, for some relevant remarks). But even an ideally significant typology is just a beginning—it is an invitation to explain. Greenberg's work is so important because it provides us with things to explain that prior to his work we did not know were things at all. Explanation is also rare, if interpreted seriously. One might think that a generative approach ought to be able to do better.

In view of the clear advantages to be gained from adopting a typological approach in the Greenberg tradition, it is not surprising that Chomsky turned to typology, under the name of parameter-setting. Chomsky puts it well:

> What we hope is that it will ultimately be possible to derive complex properties of particular natural languages, and even to determine the full core grammar of a language with all its empirical consequences, by setting the parameters of general linguistic theory (universal grammar, UG) in one of the permissible ways. While the goal should always have been an obvious one, it is only quite recently that the task could actually be considered in a serious way, a sign of significant progress in linguistic theory, in my opinion' (Chomsky, 1982b, p. 1)

The final rhetorical flourish should not be allowed to obscure the fact that essentially this goal has always been that of linguistic typologists.

Couched in terms of learning theory, children have a universal grammar which consists of a set of basic principles, plus a set of 'parameters', each of which needs to be fixed along some dimension at a fairly early stage of language learning. For instance, if a simplified version of Greenberg's universals were assumed, a child might spot a postposition, and then immediately set the word order parameter to verb-final, modifier-modified, etc. Having made a relatively small number of such choices, the child has mastered the complete core grammar of the language. Various peripheral aspects of the grammar will presumably take more time to master.

This is, of course, a productive and necessary development in transformational grammar. It is difficult to see how it could be avoided. But how does this relate to typology in the Greenberg tradition? Is it more motivated, more explanatory, more rigorous, as we should perhaps expect of work in a generative theoretical framework? I suggest not; quite the reverse, possibly. Two reasons stand out, to do with the diffuseness of the system and the notion of markedness.

The major requirement of a typology is that it should not merely be a list of the logical possibilities. If the entire typology is that languages either do or do not have a feature, it therefore fails this requirement. But if the typological system is of great complexity, such that we cannot even establish clearly what the logical possibilities are, then the question of the significance of the typology is difficult even to approach. If the system being considered is also highly unstable (in that its basic properties may be changed) and rather fuzzy at the edges, then the logical possibilities simply cannot be enumerated. Current Chomskyan theory is all of these things; nobody could deny its overall complexity. Chomsky's method of presentation is to try varying the basic definitions (let's try a subtly different definition of the notion of 'government' and see what follows), so the system as a whole is decidedly unstable. The unclarity as to what constitutes the domain of core grammar and discourse/style/etc. is what gives it fuzziness. It is therefore hard to see that Chomsky's version of typology fulfils the fundamental requirement of a typology.

The notion of 'markedness' (a rather distant relation of the similarly named Prague School notion) further removes the typology from significance. 'Marked' is often used in linguistics as another way of saying 'unusual' or 'untypical'. In Chomskyan usage it is even further bleached, as marked phenomena may be perfectly normal. Assume (purely for the sake of the argument) the word order example mentioned above. The child meets a postposition and immediately arrives at the following system:

Postposition, verb final, modifier-modified.

If the child is learning Japanese, all is as it should be. But if the child is learning Finnish, for example, the verb is typically not sentence-final but medial. How can that be? Well, explains the typologist, Finnish has a marked verb order; as Huang (1982) so disarmingly says (p. 40) 'All head-medial languages are "untypical" in some sense.' Other languages have marked head-relative clause order instead (e.g., Hungarian or Latin) or marked adjective and relative clause order relative to the head (e.g., Diegueño or Selepet). So a parameter is set, but only for the unmarked case. The literature is a little hazy about specifying how we tell what are the unmarked cases; by frequency (as Hawkins—in a more Greenbergian tradition—has it[1])? By behavioural problems in language learning? Neither of these seems very satisfactory somehow (cf. Smith, 1981, for an excellent criticism of comparable neo-Greenbergian claims). If there is no observable correlate of markedness, no sanction against markedness, then 'marked' languages are merely those which are exceptions. In other words, languages are as UG has it, unless they are not like that. With UG being constrained in this way, it is not difficult to present an elegant theory.

On a more intuitive level it is not difficult to see that there *are* some claims which are made (or at least highly valued) by GB theorists, concerning what is or is not a possible language. I shall argue that insofar as GB does make typological claims, the results obtained are actually less satisfactory than those obtained from work in the 'traditional' typological paradigm. In doing so, I shall present one of the parameters which has received the greatest amount of cross-linguistic investigation—the 'Pro-drop' parameter—and I shall show how the initial insight seems to be diluted by the account of it which requires some ad hoc manipulation to survive.

SUBJECTLESS SENTENCES AND PRO-DROP

It has been pointed out not infrequently that some languages (e.g., English and French) differ from others (e.g., Spanish and Italian) in not allowing the subject position of normal finite sentences to remain unfilled. Even where there is apparently no semantic subject, these languages require the subject position to be filled with a dummy element (e.g., *il* or *it*) whereas in the other type of language dummy subjects seem less characteristic. David Perlmutter (in 1971) claimed this as a major typological division in the syntax of languages. Languages, he said, differed as to whether they had the following surface filter: 'Any sentence other than an imperative in which there is an S that does not contain a subject in surface structure is ungrammatical' (Perlmutter, 1971, p. 100). He contrasted comparable sentences in French and Spanish, which respectively do and do not observe this filter:

> F *avons travaillé toute la journée
> S hemos traba jado toda el día
>   (we) have worked all the day
> F *les évènements qu'il a dit que se sont déroulés
> S las cosas que di jiste que pasaron
>   the events/things that he/you said that happened
> F il pleut
> S llueve
>   it is raining

However, only comparatively recently have these issues been studied intensively, with the GB doctrine of Pro-drop. Perlmutter stipulated the typology; but any self-respecting government/binder would wish to be able to derive this property from more general properties of such languages: 'A good theory of typology should not be autonomous, but should, in the words of Ken Hale, fall out as a by-product of a proper theory of UG' (Huang, 1982, p. 35).

In French or English subjectless finite declarative sentences do not occur:

> *sommes venus   *have come

But non-finites (in subordinate clause position) do:

> je veux *venir*   I want *to come*

One GB account of this difference (Chomsky, 1981a) goes something like this: it has long been held in English transformational grammar that tense and agreement make up an auxiliary element in finite sentences, while in non-finite sentences absence of tense and agreement is characteristic. Thus the finite and infinitive clauses above have something like the following structures (where INFL = inflection):

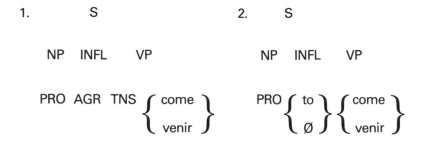

In a finite clause the subject NP and AGR in INFL are held to be coindexed (this being a relatively uncontroversial way of reflecting agreement). In non-finite clauses, on the other hand, there is no nominal element in INFL, no coindexation, no agreement. A generalization which can be made in English and French is that no structure where subject PRO is coindexed with AGR is possible. By a (relatively technical) generalization, we can further say that PRO in English and French is never governed—where the notion of government includes, for instance, the relationship between a verb and its object. We thus predict the ungrammaticality of:

J'ai lu PRO   I read PRO

where PRO is to be interpreted anaphorically—I read *it* and not just anything at all. We can use a learning theory argument to go further: empty elements are not readily observable (!) to a language learner, and therefore children cannot derive the behaviour of empty elements directly from the (degenerate) data they are presented with. From this we can conclude that empty elements must behave in similar ways in different languages if language learners are to have a hope of arriving at the correct generalization about them. PRO should therefore be ungoverned universally.

It seems bad news, therefore, when we discover that there are languages which have empty subjects of finite clauses interpreted as referring to specific things. Thus Italian (cf. Napoli, 1981):

Michele l'ha scritto   'Michael wrote it'
L'ha scritto   'He wrote it'

The mechanism that Chomsky uses (in fact only one of a variety of suggestions with similar effects) is this: recall that—given that INFL does not correspond to a word in English—the morphological expression of it appears as an ending on the verb, traditionally performed by a process such as Affix Hopping in English. This rule (Chomsky more recently calls it R) in early transformational grammar is a late rule—it applies after most other rules—and this corresponds in GB to the phonological (PF) component. So in English we find that a sentence such as:

John came

has at S-structure (following the major transformations) a structure something like (1), where INFL is immediately dominated by S, and it is at this level—the starting point for the 'semantic' (LF) component of the grammar—that principles operate such as the one which says that PRO must be ungoverned. Chomsky's proposal for Italian is relatively simple: rule R may (optionally) apply in the syntax proper rather than in the PF component.[2] By S-structure, therefore, subjects do *not* need to be governed by AGR in INFL. So subjectless sentences are possible in Pro-drop languages.

Nor is Pro-drop without associated consequences: Chomsky specifies the following:

(i)   missing subject (i.e., the basic observation)
(ii) free inversion in simple sentences
(iii) 'long wh-movement' of subject
(iv) empty resumptive pronouns in embedded clauses
(v)   apparent violations of the *[that-t] filter

The Italian examples given illustrate (i). The others are exemplified as follows:

L'ha scritto Michele 'Michael wrote it' (free inversion)
l'uomo [che mi domando [chi abbia visto]]
the man who (I) wonder who (he) saw
ecco la ragazza [che mi domando [chi crede [che
this-is the girl who I wonder who thinks that
    possa voler bene a Giorgio]]]
    (she) may love Giorgio
chi crede [che partirà]
who (you) think that will-leave

Parallel examples from French would be ungrammatical. One observation about this list: it is not clear that properties (i), (iii), (iv) and (v) are in fact different properties, as opposed to subcases of the same property. It is perhaps not worth arguing the point here, but it would suggest that the apparent correlation of multiple properties is an artifact of dividing up a single case into subcases. There are many other questions which arise, but all that I hope to have done at this stage is to provide a general outline of the nature of the Pro-drop phenomenon.

Irrespective of the specific mechanics of Pro-drop, the learning theoretic orientation of GB theorists forces us to adopt the following story. There is a set of linked phenomena which receive a unitary explanation according to UG; i.e., there is a parameter to be set. Once this parameter is set, on the evidence presumably of one of the phenomena in this linked set, then the others come 'free'. But it would appear that this does not altogether correspond to the situation as reflected in different languages. Let us assume that the 'trigger' for the parameter is the missing subject: this will apply to all of the following languages, for instance, all of which allow missing subjects: Arabic, Basque, Chinese (Mandarin), Hausa, Italian, Japanese, Mauritian Creole, Russian, Spanish, Walbiri, etc. Inversion of subjects is found in several of these languages: the interpretation of this criterion for Arabic (at least some dialects of which are typically verb initial) is obscure; and Japanese does not allow inversion in normal sentences. Thus, for example, in Japanese (Kuno, 1978):[3]

Tanaka go sono hon o yonda 'Tanaka read that book'
*Sono hon o yonda Tanaka ga

On the other hand, Japanese does allow relative word order freedom before the verb:

Sono hon o Tanaka ga yonda

Note, incidentally, that Japanese (like Mauritian Creole) has no agreement morphology on the verb to 'compensate' for missing subjects. Russian does not have long wh-movement (or in fact any who-movement out of finite clauses), although it does have omission of subject and free inversion of subject:

Borja pridet   'B. will come'
Pridet Borja

Pridet   'He will come'
*Kto vy dumaete, čto pridet?   'Who do you think that will come?'

To the mechanical GB-grammar-writer such data pose no problem: markedness considerations apply even when we have set parameters, so that virtually anything goes. The fact that Romance languages alone appear to have formed the basis for this parameter ought, however, to give cause for concern to anyone who is looking for a theory which really copes with cross-language variability. I think that the learning-theory orientation can also serve as a basis for an argument against this approach.

Faced with exceptions such as that of Russian, it is, of course, open to the linguist to say that Russian is only an apparent exception, that in fact Russian is not a Pro-drop language, and does not have free subject-verb inversion. I have already pointed out that Government and Binding Theory is a theory of core grammar; it is generally accepted that there is a whole range of phenomena (often involving movement or deletion) which are outside the range of core grammar. We might then assume that Russian does indeed have inversion and deletion of subjects, but that these occupy the periphery of Russian grammar, and that Russian core grammar shows remarkable similarity to the grammar of English or French, say. It is not difficult to formulate such an argument in apparently convincing terms—indeed Pesetsky already has (according to Franks, 1982, p. 151). But if you look at it from the point of view of the poor child who has to learn the language, things look rather different. Russian grammarians are agreed that the subject more often than not appears before the verb in Russian, but that with intransitive verbs, and especially verbs involving notions of existence or appearance on the scene, verb-subject order is extremely frequent. It is also very common, especially in spoken Russian, for subjects to be omitted. On the other hand, by virtue of the fact that 'long wh-movement' does not occur in Russian, not to mention the fact that it only could conceivably occur in fairly complex sentences, children will not be in a position to judge the acceptability of long wh-movement cases. The same will surely have to be true for Italian, where the more obscure grammatical properties differ from those of Russian, but the more common properties are identical. So the Italian and the Russian child will both be presented with data of a similar sort, and yet they will be expected to set their parameters in different ways, the Russian child recognizing that inversion and omission are peripheral, and therefore not part of core grammar, the Italian child deciding just the opposite. Such a scenario lacks any credibility. It is possible that there are other features of Russian and Italian which correlate with this difference, but that would remain to be demonstrated.

CONCLUSIONS

Chomsky has several times formulated an argument to the effect that language universals of the more interesting types can best be discovered within the framework of the investigation of single languages, and that the comparison of numerous languages is less effective in this respect. The argument derives from the greater depth that, for instance, transformational investigations have tended to achieve in comparison with more purely descriptive approaches. It also has recourse to the learning theory argument; if there are highly abstract properties of a grammar which can derive only by detailed study of rather obscure sentence types in a language, then it is not likely that a child could construct, on the basis of relatively simple language data, a grammar which would have these abstract properties. We may then infer that these properties follow from innate principles, and if they do indeed follow from such principles, they must be universal, as children are not innately predisposed to learn any particular language.

Leaving aside quibbles about the depth and reliability of many analyses within transformational grammar, there are two objections to this sort of argument. The first relies on the 'track record' of such an approach. Let us assume that Chomsky's general argument about innateness goes through—I personally feel no great commitment to it, but find it quite plausible nonetheless. It does not then follow that any particular mechanisms derived from transformational grammars can plausibly be understood as innately specified, or indeed that they can be derived from innately specified principles. Where are the widely accepted universals based on single-language work? Where is the transformational equivalent of Greenberg? The fact is that the proposals that exist are of two sorts:

(i)   the proposal that all grammars of human languages contain a transformational component is of one type—the vacuous type, because nothing follows about the nature of a language from the fact that its grammar contains a transformational component;

(ii) the proposal that, for instance, subjacency or the Case filter are univeral is of the second type; as soon as such mechanisms are proposed for one language they will be claimed to be universals, and when they are replaced, or rejected, this claim will simply lapse.

In other words, the first type of 'universal' makes no claim about what languages can be like, while the second type of 'universal' is purely declarative—evidence is not required. It is perfectly legitimate to do this—what is being claimed is that these principles are not interesting unless they are universal in some sense. But more substantial evidence is required if their universality is to be taken seriously.

The second type of objection to Chomsky's argument relates to the accessibility of UG to the linguist. In discussing parameters, Chomsky says:

> If these parameters are embedded in a theory of UG that is sufficiently rich in deductive structure, then the languages that are determined by fixing the parameters one way or another will appear to be quite diverse, since the consequences of one set of choices will be very different from the consequences of another set: yet at the same time fairly restricted evidence, just enough to fix the parameters of UG, will determine a grammar that may be very intricate and will in general lack any grounding in experience in the sense of an inductive basis (Chomsky, 1981b, p. 124).

So we assume that the child has UG and can construct grammars which do not have a purely inductive basis; but how does the *linguist* do it? If there is no inductive basis for the 'correct' grammar, then the linguist should be unable to construct the grammar. One popular answer to this has always been that the linguist has to make up this deficit by looking at the data of numerous languages. *One* language may underdetermine its grammar, and hence UG, but if different languages complement each other, there is some possibility that universal principles could be arrived at.

NOTES

1   Why any purely linguistic principles should correlate with frequency is, however, a complete mystery,

especially given that quite exotic grammatical phenomena are still being discovered in hitherto undescribed languages, and that these languages could well be representative of many others which either remain undescribed or have lost their speakers with the advent of 'civilization'. The fact that some of the major European languages have had well-attested influence on other languages should also make us pause to consider the significance of frequency distributions. See Smith (1981) for a discussion of these issues.

2   This is only one of several possible solutions to the Pro-drop phenomenon; for instance, Chomsky has more recently proposed (1982b) that the empty subject pronoun in Italian is not PRO as described here, but 'pro'—an empty element with rather different properties. Numerous other interpretations exist.

3   Non-verb-final sentences exist quite freely in colloquial Japanese: but Kuno (1978, pp. 60–4) points to a considerable amount of evidence that the postverbal elements are *afterthoughts* rather than syntactically integrated elements.

REFERENCES

Chomsky, N. (1965) *Aspects of the Theory of Syntax*, Cambridge, Mass., MIT Press.
Chomsky, N. (1981a) *Lectures on Government and Binding*, Dordrecht, Foris.
Chomsky, N. (1981b) 'Markedness and core grammar', in Belletti, A. *et al.* (Eds), *Theory of Markedness in Generative Grammar*, Pisa, Scuola Normale Superiore, pp. 123–46.
Chomsky, N. (1982a) *The Generative Enterprise*, Dordrecht, Foris.
Chomsky, N. (1982b) *Some Concepts and Consequences of the Theory of Government and Binding*, Cambridge, Mass., MIT Press.
Franks, S. (1982) 'Is there a Pro-drop parameter for Slavic?' *Papers from the 18th Regional Meeting of the Chicago Linguistics Society*, pp. 140–54.
Greenberg, J. H. (1963) 'Some universals of grammar with particular reference to the order of meaningful elements', in Greenberg, J. H. (Ed.), *Universals of Language*, Cambridge, Mass., MIT Press.
Hawkins, J. (1983) *Word Order Universals*, New York, Academic Press.
Hockett, C. F. (1963) 'The problem of universals in language', in Greenberg (1963).
Huang, C. (1982) 'Logical relations in Chinese and the theory of grammar', unpublished PhD thesis, Massachusetts Institute of Technology.
Kuno, S. (1978) 'Japanese: A characteristic OV language', in Lehmann, W. P. (Ed.), *Syntactic Typology*, Brighton, Harvester Press, pp. 249–76.
Napoli, D. J. (1981) 'Subject pronouns: The pronominal system of Italian vs. French', *Papers from the Seventeenth Regional Meeting of the Chicago Linguistic Society*, pp. 249–76.
Perlmutter, D. M. (1971) *Deep and Surface Structure Constraints in Syntax*, New York, Holt, Rinehart and Winston.
Smith, N. V. (1981) 'Consistency, markedness and language change: On the notion "consistent language"', *Journal of Linguistics*, **17**, pp. 39–54.

Interchange

SMITH REPLIES TO KILBY

Despite making a number of positive points, Kilby fails in my opinion to characterize Chomsky's programme accurately, and draws negative conclusions which do not follow from his arguments. Kilby correctly observes (p. 67) that for Chomsky the relevant domain of study is grammar rather than language, but then ignores this insight in his subsequent discussion of implicational universals, thereby overlooking the radical effect of Chomsky's work on the study of universals and typology. Thus I find it implausible that linguistic typologists had essentially always had the goal of 'determin(ing) the full core grammar of a language ... by setting the parameters of ... universal grammar', as Kilby suggests (p. 69).

This oversight reflects Kilby's deeper misapprehension about the nature of explanatory theories in general and of typological ones in particular. He says that the major requirement of a typology is that it 'not merely be a list of the logical possibilities' (p. 70), criticizing current government-binding theory for being both too complex and too unstable to be able to meet this criterion. As the list of logical possibilities is presumably infinite, I take Kilby to mean that a typology should be both explicit and also have enough deductive structure for the effects of changing one variable to be traceable throughout the system. That certain logical possibilities should remain unspecified and that the theory should be in a state of developmental flux, such that the predictions made differ as the claims become more refined, seems not only inevitable but desirable. Kilby tendentiously describes GB work on the null-subject parameter (PRO-drop) as a 'doctrine' (p. 71). In fact, as his other criticisms make clear, nothing could be further from the truth than to call the bundle of competing theories which have arisen in an attempt to explain these phenomena a 'doctrine'.

Kilby accepts that PRO-drop phenomena need an explanation and even appears to grant the force of 'poverty of the stimulus' arguments, where the fact of language acquisition can only be adequately accounted for if a complex innate structure is ascribed to the infant. He then claims that exceptions to the generalizations captured by one standard treatment of the phenomena (in terms of the ungoverned status of PRO) undermine the whole treatment of empty subjects and even invalidate the transformational paradigm more generally. Kilby's arguments are flawed. His position is initially vitiated by his relegation of the difference between Pro and PRO to a footnote; the basis for the PRO-drop parameter is not just Romance (p. 74), but draws on such languages as Hungarian, Hebrew and Japanese as well; the attempt to minimize the importance of the clustering of properties associated with PRO-drop, as

formal constraints, towards a functionalist view, which arguably does not presuppose any innate bioprogram or universal grammar. However, Muysken (1981), while suggesting that the 'TMA' markers in creoles fulfil a wider range of semantic functions than is allowed for by Bickerton, argues that they represent the universal category of Aux, and that the elements of tense, mood and aspect are interpreted by a semantic component constrained by the principles of core grammar. One of these principles would determine that aspect is interpreted before mood, and mood before tense. Another principle would determine that elements closer to the verbal stem would be interpreted before elements further away from it, which as Muysken points out, leads to two possible orderings of the elements: TMA before the verb, or AMT after it. Compared with Bickerton's approach Muysken reflects a more formal, Chomskyan view of universal grammar, and as we shall see, this formal view enables us to see more clearly how the same aspect of universal grammar is reflected in sign languages, despite their difference of medium.

Because sign languages have a three-dimensional signing space available, they cannot be analyzed purely in terms of linear order. However, we can order elements in relation to their proximity to the main verb, on the assumption that simultaneity with the verb involves the closest proximity, followed by temporal (or linear) adjacency, followed by some temporal separation from the verb. It is interesting to discover that T, M and A elements are certainly found in sign languages, and that while the A element is close to the verb, M and T are progressively further away. It is true of all sign languages I have investigated so far that aspect marking is done by inflection on the verb itself, modality is marked by an auxiliary placed either before or after the verb, and time is marked by an adverbial placed often at some distance from the verb. In sign languages verb inflections are achieved by the modification of one of the formational components of the verb sign, generally its movement, which may be repeated for aspect marking. Table 1 shows how various categories of aspect are marked in four different sign languages, at least as far as can be shown by research to date.

Table 1. *Aspect Marking by Verb Inflection in Four Sign Languages*[1]

Sign language	*Slow repetition*		*Fast repetition*		*Slow movement*
	+ punctual verb	*− punctual verb*	*+ punctual verb*	*− punctual verb*	
BSL[2]	iterative		habitual	durative	
ASL[3]	iterative	durative	habitual		
FSL[4]	iterative				durative
RSL[5]	iterative				

Notes: 1 Data based on Deuchar (1984a), Klima and Bellugi (1979), Moody (1983) and Zaitseva (1983).
  2 British Sign Language.
  3 American Sign Language.
  4 French Sign Language.
  5 Russian Sign Language.

To give an example from British Sign Language (BSL), slow repetition of the movement of a verb can indicate iterative aspect. Thus the sign QUARREL, which in its citation form consists of little fingers, extended from fists, touching twice in neutral space, can mean 'to quarrel repeatedly' if the touching movement is repeated slowly. Another sign, COME, which is a sign with inherently punctual meaning made by moving the index finger towards the signer, can be inflected for aspect by repeating the movement quickly. Finally, the sign TALK, an inherently non-punctual verb which is made by the index fingers, extended from the fists, touching twice, can be inflected for durative aspect by fast repetition of the movement. A similar process, with slightly varying functions, is also found in the other three sign languages listed in Table 1. Aspect marking occurs simultaneously with the verb rather than sequentially to it, and hence is as close to the verb as is possible.

While aspect is marked by inflection of the verb itself in these sign languages, modality is marked by a separate lexical item, which is placed as close to the verb as it could be without actually being an inflection: that is, it is adjacent to the verb, occurring either before or after it. In BSL, markers of modality include items glossed as WILL, MUST, CAN and CANNOT for example, which can be placed either before or after the main verb. Thus we find in a data corpus (see Deuchar, 1984b) the sequence WILL ASK for 'I will ask', and AGREE WILL YOUNG for 'The young will agree.' Work on ASL reports modality markers such as CAN, CANNOT and MUST (cf. Wilbur, 1979, p. 122), and on FSL, CAN and WILL (VA-VA) for example (cf. Moody, 1983, pp. 99, 100). These markers, like those in BSL, can occur either before or after the main verb. Thus in sign languages, like creoles, aspect is marked closest to the verb, followed by modality.

In creoles, tense marking is farthest from the verb, and this is true of sign languages. In the case of sign languages we would probably want to call it time marking rather than tense marking, however, since time is marked by what appear to be sentence adverbials whose position is fairly free, and often at some distance from the verb. Examples from BSL include BEFORE, TOMORROW, NOW, NEXT-WEEK and LAST-WEEK, and an illustrative item from the data corpus (see Deuchar, 1984b) is the following: WASHINGTON BEFORE NAME WASHINGTON SEE ('I saw the place called Washington'). Sentence adverbials which function in a similar way in ASL are YESTERDAY, TOMORROW, LAST-WEEK and FUTURE, and in FSL YESTERDAY and LAST-SATURDAY. I shall later argue that sign languages are examples of creoles, and yet time instead of tense marking is more characteristic of pidgins than creoles (cf. Muysken, 1981, p. 188). However, as time marking often becomes tense marking in the process of pidgins becoming creoles (e.g., Sankoff and Laberge, 1973), sign languages might be considered early creoles where the development of the tense marker is not yet complete. In any case, it is interesting to note that in sign languages, like creoles, the time marker is further from the verb than both the modality and aspect markers.

The next grammatical characteristic which is common to both creoles and sign languages is that existential and possessive sharing the same lexical item. Bickerton (1981) observes that this is true of a wide range of creoles, and Fischer (1978) shows that it is true of both Hawaiian Creole English and ASL. In ASL the sign for both 'have' and 'there is' is made by two hands touching the chest, palms facing towards the signer. In BSL the same two meanings are again conveyed by one lexical item: an open hand closing into a fist shape in neutral space. In FSL the item which fulfils the same two functions is a thumb touching the chest with the fingers of the hand spread out. Clearly this similarity in both sign languages and creoles, despite formational differences, needs to be explained.

Not all languages have copulas, and it is interesting to note that creoles as a group seem to lack copulas. This is also true of sign languages, as the following examples show: HE NO-GOOD (BSL: 'He is no good'; see Deuchar, 1984b); LYNN SINGLE (ASL: 'Lynn was single'; see Edge and Herrmann, 1977); LOUP LUI (FSL: 'He is a wolf'; Moody, 1983). A characteristic related to the absence of copulas is that there is no clear distinction between verbs and predicative adjectives, so that the latter may show the characteristics of verbs. This has been pointed out by several creolists, as Bickerton (1981) says, and in his analysis of Ile-de-France creole, Corne (1981) proposes replacing the distinction between verbs and adjectives with a semantic category of 'verbals', which can be subdivided further into categories of state, process and action. This proposal would appear to be helpful for sign languages also, since some signs which might be translated as adjectives function grammatically more like verbs. For example, in BSL the sign GOOD takes negative inflection, in ASL SICK marks durative aspect marking, and in FSL a stative adjective such as GRAVE ('serious') can be negated by being juxtaposed with a negation sign, as in GRAVE PAS ('It's not serious').

Finally, creoles and sign languages have in common the absence of a passive construction. The absence of the construction in creoles is referred to by Craig (1971) and Bickerton (1981), and in sign language its absence is clear from the literature at least on the following sign languages: British, American, Danish, French, Russian and Swedish. This phenomenon might be accounted for in terms of two specific factors: an apparent preference for topic-comment semantic order in informal communication and in emerging languages (cf. Givon, 1979; Ochs, 1979), and the lack of a grammatical subject in emerging languages as well as some others (cf. Givon, 1979; Li and Thompson, 1976). The grammatical category of subject is usually associated with agency as well as topic-hood (cf. Comrie, 1981), and a passive construction serves the purpose of separating these two categories in languages with subjects. In languages without subjects, however, agent and topic are not expected to go together necessarily: hence where the topic is not the agent there is no special need for a passive construction.

We have now seen that a set of grammatical characteristics appears to be shared by both creoles and sign languages, despite the different media in which they are realized. Bickerton (1981) argues that the characteristics which creoles share reflect the nature of the language bioprogram, which according to him has a particular effect on new or emerging languages. So are sign languages new emerging languages of the same kind as creoles? I shall argue that they are, since in addition to the structural similarities, there are similarities in the way creoles and sign languages develop.

Just as a creole first develops as a child's first language, on the basis of rather limited input from a pidgin, sign languages are generally learned by children on the basis of rather limited sign language input. This is because the majority of deaf children's parents are hearing and do not sign to them, or sign in a very limited way. Most deaf children first learn sign language by communicating with other deaf children at a residential school for the deaf. In such schools, especially in Britain, it is common for the teachers to be unable to sign and for the official mode of communication in the classroom to be spoken language. Nevertheless, children sign among themselves, but since only a minority (10 per cent or less) of them will have deaf parents and already be able to sign, it seems that they in fact 'invent' a sign language system which is only influenced by very limited input from the adult sign language. Little research has been done on the process by which sign languages are created in schools (but see James, forthcoming), but Fischer (1978, p. 329) argues that 'most deaf children are forced to *re*creolize ASL in every generation.' Because few deaf children have deaf signing parents *and* they are not usually exposed to the signing of other adults, the chain of transmission from deaf adult to deaf child is very weak, and hence children have to invent their own sign language. Because of this weakness of transmission, sign languages do indeed seem to be creoles, and one might expect them to remain so until direct transmission of sign languages occurs from deaf adult to deaf child. This would require a change of educational policy in most countries, including the recognition (so far not widespread) of sign languages as natural languages. Meanwhile, however, sign languages will continue to be new, emerging languages with each generation.

We saw earlier how the 'monogenesis' or genealogical explanation of the similarities between pidgins and creoles was influenced by the work of the neo-grammarians of the nineteenth century. Their same influence can also be discerned in work from the early days of sign language research, when it was assumed that FSL and ASL were historically related, and that this accounted for similarities between them. It is true that there was some contact in the early nineteenth century between American and French educators to the deaf, but this fact led to the myth that one French person (Laurent Clerc) had 'brought' FSL to the United States, and that ASL was directly descended from FSL as a result. Against this position Woodward (1978) argues that the differences between ASL and FSL are too great to make direct descent feasible, and suggests instead that varieties of ASL underwent radical restructuring through contact with FSL. He does not, however, consider accounting for the similarities in terms of language universals. This may be because of the abstract nature of Chomskyan universals and because work in formal syntax has not dealt to any great extent with sign language. (The latter was more data oriented, partly because few linguists were native signers.) However, I would suggest that the recognition that sign languages might be creoles (cf. Fischer, 1978; Ladd and Edwards, 1982; Deuchar, 1984a), combined with a language universals approach to pidgins and creoles (cf. Kay and Sankoff, 1974; Todd, 1974; Bickerton, 1981), has led to new possibilities of explanation in the field of sign language research. In particular, it makes similarities between historically unrelated sign languages, such as BSL and ASL, less difficult to account for.

Thus research on creoles, including sign languages, has benefitted from the inspiration provided by Chomsky's theoretical perspective on language universals. We shall now see how sign language research in particular provides empirical evidence relevant to another aspect of Chomsky's work on universal grammar: his ideas about the relation between universal grammar and language learning.

Chomsky's views on the relation between universal grammar and the mind, discussed earlier, are closely linked to his views on language learning. According to him, universal grammar both constrains the form of the grammars of particular languages, and since he conceives of universal grammar as represented in the human mind, it also constrains the way in which grammars of particular languages are acquired by speakers in childhood. In support of the latter argument Chomsky and others put forward what has come to be called the 'poverty of the stimulus argument' (Chomsky, 1980, p. 34; Hornstein and Lightfoot, 1981; pp. 9–10): children's gram-matical knowledge is underdetermined by the input data they receive. In earlier writings this claim was made in general terms, on the assumption that the primary linguistic data to which children are exposed is 'restricted and degenerate' (Chomsky, 1968, p. 27), or, in other words, finite in quantity and containing examples of ungrammatical utterances as a result of performance errors. This claim gave rise to some empirical work on the nature of the linguistic input to children (e.g., Snow and Ferguson, 1977), and though the claim of finiteness could not be questioned, the amount of ungrammaticality in speech to children was found to be very low.

More recently, the poverty of the stimulus argument has been formulated more specifically as involving the claim that some aspects of the grammatical knowledge demonstrated by children could not possibly have been acquired by induction from the data alone, but require the postulation of abstract principles which are determined by universal grammar. In favour of this position at least two kinds of arguments are put forward. The first is that although children produce many utterances which are ungrammatical from an adult point of view during the process of language acquisition, they conform to certain principles which may be universal. The second is that some grammatical constructions allow alternative analyses, the correct one only being obvious from negative evidence about ungrammatical sentences, and yet this is not available to the child.

The first type of argument can be illustrated by taking Chomsky's claim that the principle of structure dependence is part of universal grammar. In support of this he argues (Chomsky, 1975, p. 173) that on the basis of input data like (1), children might be expected to form questions as in (2) rather than (3):

(1)   The man who is tall is in the room.
(2)   *Is the man who tall is in the room?
(3)   Is the man who is tall in the room?

In (2) they would simply be fronting the first verb in the sentence independently of its structural position, whereas in (3) they would be conforming with a principle of structure dependence. It is argued that the lack of utterances like (2) in children's output supports the idea of a principle of structure dependence being given in universal grammar, rather than being worked out on the basis of the data available. This argument seems generally reasonable, except that it does assume that children learn to form questions as constructions related to declaratives in the input, rather than to the form of questions in the input.

The second type of argument is illustrated by Chomsky's discussion of the interpretation of the English expression *each other* (e.g., Chomsky, 1981b). He argues that without being given negative evidence, language learners know that certain sentences containing *each other* are grammatical, while others would be ungrammatical. This can be exemplified by the following;

(4)   The men like each other
(5)   They believe the men to like each other
(6)   *The men believe me to like each other

A child presented with data of the kind represented in (4) and (5) would have no way of knowing that (6) is ungrammatical, especially as it is in fact interpretable. However, Chomsky suggests that its ungrammaticality can be accounted for by postulating a principle of universal grammar: that a reciprocal expression like *each other* must be bound by an antecedent in the embedded clause. In (5) *each other* has an antecedent, *the men*, within the embedded clause, whereas in (6) *the men* is outside the embedded clause and hence (6) is ungrammatical. If the ungrammaticality of sentences like (6) is determined by a principle of universal grammar as Chomsky claims, children will know the principle without having to learn it. White (1981) points out that the empirical evidence suggests at first sight that children do not necessarily know this principle automatically. However, as she shows, it is difficult to design an empirical test of their knowledge of this principle alone, without also testing whether they understand embedded sentences.

We have now discussed two kinds of argument relating to the poverty of the stimulus. While they are interesting and worthy of consideration, the first suffers from assumptions made about those aspects of the linguistic input which are relevant to language learning, and the second from difficulties in empirical testing of children's knowledge about language. Both arguments are made with reference to normal language learning situations, where the child is receiving a certain amount of linguistic input from the target language, although it is argued that this input is not enough. What is needed is a situation where linguistic input is absent or severely reduced, so that assumptions need not be made about it, and so that linguistic output from the child can be assumed to reflect his or her linguistic knowledge unadulterated by the input. Such a situation would be unethical if designed as such, but as we have seen, it exists naturally in situations where sign languages are acquired and, to a lesser extent, where creoles are developed on the basis of pidgins. The problem with the latter is that we do not know enough about the type and quality of the input.

In the case of sign language development, however, we have seen that it is common for no adult input to be available at any stage. Feldman *et al.* (1978) did a detailed study of the development of sign language among several deaf children whose parents did not sign to them. They found that the children developed gesture systems with language-like properties including rule-governed combinations and recursion (see Goldin-Meadow, 1982). James (1985), in a pilot study of sign language development among children in a school for the deaf, almost none of whom had had any adult signing input, found that children appeared to be developing grammatical characteristics very similar to those found in creoles and in the adult sign language. Research results are so far sparse, and produce a different kind of evidence from that adduced by Chomsky, in that they show what child grammars include when deprived of input data rather than what they exclude when exposed to limited data. While Chomsky's work so far might be said to be oriented towards determining the limits or boundaries of universal grammar, the sign language evidence could be said to give support to the idea that there *is* a universal grammar, as well as some concrete indications of what it minimally might contain.

CONCLUSION

I hope to have shown in this chapter how Chomsky's work on universal grammar has provided a new theoretical perspective for work on pidgins and creoles, as well as for work on a particular category of creoles, sign languages of the deaf. In turn, the way in which sign languages develop under very reduced conditions of input gives empirical support to Chomsky's claim that principles of universal grammar constrain the structure of languages in general.

ACKNOWLEDGEMENT

I am grateful to Trevor Pateman for comments on an earlier draft of this chapter.

REFERENCES

Bickerton, D. (1981) *Roots of Language*, Ann Arbor, Mich., Karoma Publishers.
Bickerton, D. (1984) 'The language bioprogram hypothesis', *The Behavioral and Brain Sciences*, **7**, pp. 173–221.
Chomsky, N. (1968) *Language and Mind*, New York, Harcourt Brace Jovanovich (enlarged edition, 1972).
Chomsky, N. (1975) *Reflections on Language*, London, Fontana.
Chomsky, N. (1980) *Rules and Representations*, Oxford, Basil Blackwell.
Chomsky, N. (1981a) *Lectures on Government and Binding*, Dordrecht, Foris Publications.
Chomsky, N. (1981b) 'Principles and parameters of syntactic theory', in Hornstein and Lightfoot (Eds), pp. 32–75.
Comrie, B. (1981) *Language Universals and Linguistic Typology*, Oxford, Basil Blackwell.
Corne, C. (1981) 'A re-evaluation of the predicate in Ile-de-France Creole', in Muysken (Ed.), pp. 103–24.
Craig, D. (1971) 'Education and Creole English in the West Indies: Some sociolinguistic factors', in Hymes (Ed.), pp. 371–91.
Decamp, D. (1971) 'The study of pidgin and creole languages', in Hymes (1971), pp. 13–39.
Decamp, D. and Hancock, I. (Eds) (1974) *Pidgins and Creoles: Current Trends and Prospects*, Washington, D. C., Georgetown University Press.
Deuchar, M. (1984a) *British Sign Language*, London, Routledge and Kegan Paul.
Deuchar, M. (1984b) *Diglossia in British Sign Language*, Bloomington, Ind, Indiana Linguistics Club.
Edge, V. and Herrmann, L. (1977) 'Verbs and the determination of subject in ASL', in Friedman, L. (Ed.), *On the Other Hand: New Perspectives on American Sign Language*, New York, Academic Press, pp. 137–79.
Feldman, H., Goldin-Meadow, S. and Gleitman, L. (1978) 'Beyond Herodotus: The creation of language by linguistically deprived deaf children', in Lock, A. (Ed.), *Action, Gesture and Symbol: The Emergence of Language*, London, Academic Press, pp. 351–414.
Fischer, S. (1978) 'Sign language and creoles', in Siple (Ed.), pp. 309–31.
Givon, T. (Ed.) (1979) *Syntax and Semantics, Volume 12, Discourse and Syntax*, New York, Academic Press.
Givon, T. (1979) 'From discourse to syntax: Grammar as a processing stategy', in Givon (Ed.), pp. 81–112.
Goldin-Meadow, S. (1982) 'The resilience of recursion: A study of a communication system developed without a conventional language model', in Wanner, E. and Gleitman, L. (Eds), *Language Acquisition: The State of the Art*, Cambridge, Cambridge University Press, pp. 51–77.
Hornstein, N. and Lightfoot, D. (Eds) (1981) *Explanation in Linguistics: The Logical Problem of Language Acquisition*, London, Longman.
Hornstein, N. and Lightfoot, D. (1981) 'Introduction', in Hornstein and Lightfoot (Eds), pp. 9–31.
Hymes, D. (Ed.) (1971) *Pidginization and Creolization of Languages*, Cambridge, Cambridge University Press.
James, H. (1985) 'Pidgin Sign English in the classroom?', in Stokoe, W. and Volterra, V. (Eds) *Proceedings of the Third International Symposium on Sign Language Research*, Silver Spring, Md., Linstok Press, pp. 351–5.
Kay, P. and Sankoff, G. (1974) 'A language-universals approach to pidgins and creoles', in Decamp and Hancock (Eds.), pp. 61–72.
Klima, E. and Bellugi, U. (1979) *The Signs of Language*, Cambridge, Mass, Harvard University Press.
Ladd, P. and Edwards, V. (1982) 'British Sign Language and West Indian Creole', *Sign Language Studies*, **35**, pp. 101–26.
Li, C. and Thompson, S. (1976) 'Subject and topic; a new typology of language', in Li, C. (Ed.), *Subject and Topic*, New York, Academic Press, pp. 457–89.
Moody, B. (1983) *La Langue des Signes*, Vincennes, International Visual Theatre.
Muysken, P. (Ed.) (1981) *Generative Studies on Creole Languages*, Dordrecht, Foris.
Muysken, P. (1981) 'Creole tense/mood/aspect systems: The unmarked case?', in Muysken (Ed.), pp. 181–99.

Ochs, E. (1979) 'Planned and unplanned discourse', in Givon (Ed.), pp. 51–80.

Sankoff, G. and Laberge, S. (1973) 'The acquisition of native speakers by a language', in Decamp and Hancock (Eds), pp. 73–84.

Snow, C. and Ferguson, C. (Eds) (1977) *Talking to Children: Language Input and Acquisition*, Cambridge, Cambridge University Press.

Siple, P. (Ed.) (1978) *Understanding Language through Sign Language Research*, New York, Academic Press.

Todd, L. (1974) *Pidgins and Creoles*, London, Routledge and Kegan Paul.

White, L. (1981) 'The responsibility of grammatical theory to acquisitional data', in Hornstein and Lightfoot (Eds), pp. 241–71.

Wilbur, R. (1979) *American Sign Language and Sign Systems*, Baltimore, Md., University Park Press.

Woodward, J. (1978) 'Historical bases of American Sign Language', in Siple (Ed.), pp. 333–48.

Zaitseva, G. (1983) 'The sign language of the deaf as a colloquial system', in Kyle, J. and Woll, B. (Eds) *Language in Sign*, London, Croom Helm.

8. Other Keyholes: Language Universals from a Pidgin-Creole Viewpoint

JEAN AITCHISON

Scientists are 'peeping toms at the keyhole of eternity', according to the British philosopher Arthur Koestler (1972, p. 140). This picturesque metaphor applies equally well to linguists, many of whom might well agree with Chomsky that 'the most challenging theoretical problem in linguistics is that of discovering the principles of universal grammar that interweave with the rules of particular grammars to provide explanations for phenomena that appear arbitrary and chaotic' (1972, p. 48).

Linguists are indebted to Chomsky for focusing their attention on language universals. It was largely due to his inspiration in the 1960s that many of us moved from an obsession with descriptive trivia to a search for broad-based principles underlying language. However, the fact that many of us were inspired by Chomsky does not mean that we uncritically accept his views and outlook. To return to the keyhole imagery, some of us find the view offered through Chomsky's peephole somewhat limited. Not only do keyhole peepers sometimes glimpse unsuspected vistas, they also see only a part of the landscape. They are restricted to the particular portion captured through the tunnel vision of the keyhole. This chapter will suggest that, while Chomsky's approach to language universals is valid and interesting, it ignores the equally valuable glimpses which can be gained through other keyholes, so leading to a perhaps distorted and fragmentary view of human language.

The chapter is divided into two main sections. In the first, possible reasons for language universals will be discussed. In particular, a distinction will be drawn between 'internal' or 'innatist' explanations, and 'external' or 'functional' ones. It will be argued that functional explanations are likely to be at least as important as innatist ones. Their importance lies in the fact that they sometimes allow us to give a coherent account of why certain structures and constraints have come into existence. This is in

93

many ways more satisfying than an innatist approach which encourages one to believe that language is full of unmotivated peculiarities (cf. Fodor, 1984).

In the second section, it will be argued that pidgins and creoles, which are languages in infancy, can help to shed light on why languages behave in the way they do. When pidgins start to develop into 'full' languages, their simple initial state allows only a finite number of options, which in turn lead to further options. Some of these early options produce stable structures which proliferate, while others give rise to less satisfactory structures which remain marginal, or fade out. In particular, this section will argue that, as a language develops, a simple SVO system will tend to favour the leftward movement of constituents rather than rightward movement. This in turn may help us to understand why in languages in general leftward movement tends to be unbounded, whereas rightward movement is restricted. Such a viewpoint can usefully supplement Chomsky's view that movement rules are governed by arbitrary innate constraints, such as 'subjacency'.

EXPLANATIONS FOR LANGUAGE UNIVERSALS

Language universals can, in theory, be divided into two broad categories, based on their probable origin: on the one hand, we have those that are innate, in the sense that they are preprogrammed to emerge in any normal human because they are written into the genetic code. For example, humans, like cows or chickens, may be programmed to use the vocal-auditory tract as a medium of communication. The use of structure-dependent operations is another plausible example of a genetically encoded linguistic ability. On the other hand, we have universals that are non-innate, in the sense that while occurring universally, they need not be attributed to a genetic blueprint. For example, the observation that all languages seem to have nouns may be simply due to the fact that the world in which humans live is composed to a large extent of separable objects. Obviously we have to assume that there is some genetic determinism involved for humans to be able to recognize objects, but there is no need to claim that there is a language blueprint containing the component 'noun'.

In practice, there is often a good deal of overlap between the two types of reason, which are sometimes labelled 'internal' versus 'external' explanations, or perhaps more opaquely 'formal' versus 'functional' ones. It is possibly naive to think that we can ever draw up two separate lists assigning any universal to one or the other, just as it is oversimplistic to try and divide human behaviour into that which is 'natural' and that which is 'nurtured'. However, in spite of the difficulty of separating the two, linguists often veer towards one or the other type of explanation.

Chomsky, as is well known, favours the first type. He has suggested that various 'mental organs' might develop in specific ways, each in accordance with the genetic programme, much as bodily organs develop. He therefore argues that 'in certain fundamental respects we do not really learn language; rather, grammar grows in the mind' (1980, p. 134). As he notes, 'No one finds it outlandish to ask the question: what genetic information accounts for the growth of arms instead of wings? Why should it be shocking to raise similar questions with regard to the brain and mental faculties?' (1979, p. 84).

However, there is an increasing realization that to label something 'innate' may simply be a way of evading an issue, since it allows one to avoid seeking a rational explanation for something insufficiently understood. A growing number of linguists are therefore exploring the role of 'external' or 'functional' explanations (e.g., Butterworth, Comrie and Dahl, 1984).

As always in linguistics, there is a certain amount of terminological confusion, in that the word 'functional' is vague and at times ambiguous (Hyman, 1984). However, the general trend of this work is clear. Linguists are unwilling to accept a magic wand labelled 'innatism' or 'genetic programming' which relieves them of the responsibility of further research. Instead, they have begun to assemble a number of possible factors relating to communicative needs—ease of parsing, expressive considerations, and so on—which might help to explain why languages are the shape they are. 'Innatist' explanations are not dismissed, but they are regarded as a last resort, to be proposed only when no suitable alternative explanations can be found. In brief, the 'core' of Chomsky's 'core grammar' may well be pared down to a kernel somewhat smaller than he currently envisages.

One useful way of dealing with language universals from a functional viewpoint is to see whether they belong to a set of logically possible solutions to a particular problem. Let us explain this notion further. One fairly obvious observation about human life is that, for most problems, there are usually a finite number of possible solutions. Quite often the same solution will be rediscovered by generation after generation. For example, why down through the ages have human beings tended to run away when unexpectedly confronted by a lion? Are they preprogrammed with an innate fear of lions? Or, viewing the size of the lion's claws and its teeth, do they calculate that a wrestling match might be too great risk? Of course, if one adopts the second solution, one has to assume that humans have a certain computational ability, but this is a fairly general skill compared with an inbuilt fear of lions. As Bates (1984, p. 188) notes:

> Many universal or at least high-probability outcomes are so inevitable given a certain 'problem space' that extensive genetic underwriting is unnecessary. To be sure, some kind of genetic determinism is necessary to place the organism in the right ballpark for the problem to be encountered and solved. But the genetic contribution often proves to be far smaller and far less direct than one might expect given the reliability of the phenomenon in a given species.

As an example, Bates points to the formation of honeycombs. A casual observer might be tempted to assume that the perfect hexagonal structure of honeycombs was due to some innate hexagonal principle genetically encoded in the bees. However, it is now realized that the hexagons are the inevitable outcome of the 'packing principle', a mathematical law which says that hexagons result when spheres are placed together with even or random pressure from all sides. Therefore 'the bees' 'innate knowledge of hexagons' need consist of nothing more than a tendency to pack wax with their hemispheric heads from a wide variety of directions' (Bates, 1984, p. 189).

In the realm of language universals, then, it would be interesting to discover if certain structures are the inevitable result of linguistic 'packing principles'. Recent writings have suggested that this is a viable and useful avenue of enquiry. For example, Lindblom, MacNeilage and Studdert-Kennedy (1984) have shown that one might usefully approach sound structure in this way. In the realm of syntax, Sampson (1980) has argued that hierarchical structures must emerge in the course of language evolution, Hopper and Thompson (1984) have proposed a discourse basis for lexical categories, and Hurford (1984) has shown how certain standardized numeral expressions are likely to emerge. From the psycholinguistic point of view, Fodor

(1984) has suggested that parsing needs might influence the structure of language.

Where should we go from here? Since 'full' languages are immensely complex structures, it makes sense to try to identify some of the working principles involved in a simplified situation. Since pidgins and creoles are languages in infancy, it is here that we might usefully begin our search. It is becoming increasingly obvious that the processes of change found in pidgins and creoles are also those found in 'ordinary' languages (Aitchison, 1983; Woolford, 1979), so they can usefully be regarded as a microcosm in which we can observe the natural development of language.

THE PIDGIN AND CREOLE LIFEGAME

Let us begin by defining what we mean by the terms 'pidgin' and 'creole'. Perhaps the least controversial definitions are functional ones: a pidgin can be defined as a subsidiary or auxiliary language used for communication by people who have no common language, whereas a creole can be defined as a pidgin which has become someone's first language (Todd, 1984).

The problem with these definitions is that they say nothing about structure, which is likely to vary widely, depending on the stage of development reached (Mühlhäusler, 1980). A pidgin starts out as a jargon, an unstable and erratic mixture of borrowed words and phrases, with little consistent syntax. In the course of time, this is likely to develop into a stable pidgin with its own rules. These are likely to be fairly consistent, though the phonology, syntax and lexicon will be simpler (more regular) and somewhat impoverished (utilizing fewer resources) in comparison with a normal language. If used over a lengthy period, a stable pidgin may well develop into an extended pidgin, with the growth of morphology, movement rules, and complex sentences. Creolization—adoption of the pidgin as a native language—can take place at any of the stages outlined above.

Inevitably a pidgin in its early unstable stages is likely to be very different from a stable pidgin which might have existed for decades, or even generations. Similarly a creole formed from an unstable pidgin is likely to differ considerably from that arising from a stable pidgin.

However, in spite of the wide range of variation found, pidgins and creoles everywhere show considerable similarities, provided we leave out the earliest jargon phase, which may perhaps be classified as an incipient pidgin stage. Todd (1984, p. 28) suggests that 'a wide-ranging study of pidgins, creoles and child language makes it possible to suggest that universal grammar may involve some or all of the following characteristics:

1   fixed word order, possibly with SV as the basic pattern;
2   two types of words, one type being multifunctional and semantically full; the second type consisting of a very limited number (possibly only one) of prepositions or postpositions which are capable of indicating location and possession;
3   a set of pronouns containing at least two items, equivalents for 'me' and 'you';
4   no inflections;
5   no bound forms;
6   few or no transformations;

7 temporal and aspectual distinctions are carried by context or, like interrog ation and negation, by one or more word forms placed outside the statement;
8 systematic use of reduplication;
9 verb serialization as a means of differentiating nominals without using case or prepositions.

There is some argument as to whether all these characteristics are inevitably present. However, they are certainly found in a number of pidgins at an early stage of development. At the very least we can say that pidgins tend to have a fixed word order, sparse or non-existent morphology, and are composed mainly of 'content' words.

Why do unrelated pidgins and creoles exhibit so many similarities? One interpretation is that we are witnessing the surface reflexes of an innate 'bioprogram' (Bickerton, 1981, 1984). There are, however, a number of problems with the bioprogram view (Aitchison, 1983; Open Peer Commentary on Bickerton, 1984). An alternative interpretation is that the similarities represent the best solutions to certain problems which recur in simplified language situations. As Bates notes: 'Universal and high-probability structures shared by creoles need not necessarily reflect innate tendencies of any direct sort. They may reflect the consistent rediscovery of a set of logically possible solutions to a problem space whose structure is still not well understood' (1984, p. 189).

Indeed, pidgins provide linguists with an unparalleled opportunity to study the 'lifegame' of a language. 'Lifegame' is a computer game with biological implications (Gardner, 1970). A mathematician noted that if one started with a particular configuration of 'cells', these could be added onto in various ways. The new cell configurations, after the additions, then provided a range of further possibilities. Some of the methods of cell proliferation turned out to be stable ones, causing the 'organism' to expand progressively. Others stopped the cells progressing, and led to an impasse.

This is what we see happening in pidgins and creoles. Given a very simple initial state, there are only a few logically possible ways of extending it. If a language system is composed almost entirely of content words, then the predominant syntactic device available to it is word order. This in turn will restrict the options that are available to it as it develops (see below). It is not always clear whether non-existent patterns are precluded by the human brain, or whether the existing ones have simply been found more fruitful. In many cases, however, non-existent patterns are simply harder to process, and so are passed over in favour of ones which make communication easier.

This is the situation which will now be illustrated. It will be shown that, if one starts with a pidgin with subject-verb-object word order, as the language develops, leftward movement of constituents is considerably more likely to occur than rightward movement. This in turn may shed light on the well-known fact that in many 'full' languages unbounded leftward movement is possible, whereas rightward movement is restricted.

It so happens that the arguments below rely mainly on ease of parsing, though this is not necessarily a claim that the needs of comprehension outweigh all other considerations. The true situation is likely to be considerably more complex, as pointed out by Fodor (1984). However, space precludes a full discussion.

The following examples are from Tok Pisin, also known as Neo-Melanesian or New Guinea Pidgin. This is an English-based pidgin which has been in existence for over a hundred years, and is the lingua franca which makes communication possible between the speakers of Papua New Guinea's several hundred mutually unintelligible languages. Mostly, Tok Pisin is a stable, extended pidgin, having been regularized and codified over the decades, particularly by missionaries. Recently, however, it has increasingly become creolized, as transport becomes modernized and intermarriage between people whose only common language is pidgin becomes more usual. In such circumstances the children grow up speaking a pidgin as a first language. At this stage the pidgin has by definition become a creole. The phenomena discussed, however, occurred while it was still a pidgin. Note that although the examples are drawn only from one pidgin/creole, the structures described are not unique to Tok Pisin, and can be readily identified in many of the other pidgins and creoles of the world.

Tok Pisin has SVO word order, a fact which is well-documented. For example:

(1)   'Ei, yupela, mi siutim em pinis, tispela supia bilong mi i bruk, em i go antap pinis' (Laycock, 1970, p. 53).
      hey—you—I(S)—shoot (V)—it (O)—PAST—this—spear—of me (S)—broke (V)—it (S)—go (V)—up—PAST.
      'Hey, you, I shot it [a crocodile], my spear broke, it swam upstream.'

Now suppose a human language system with mainly content words and SVO word order needs to draw attention to some part of a sentence, what procedures could it adopt? There are several logical possibilities:
(a)   word order change, i.e., movement of constituents;
(b)   repetition;
(c)   coining a deictic word;
(d)   use of prosodic features
It seems likely that all of these may be used. From the point of view of understanding how languages develop, however, the first two, word order change and repetition, are particularly interesting since they potentially destroy, or at least alter, the existing SVO structure. Let us examine how one might use these to emphasize an NP in sentence (2):

(2)   Blackpela dok i lukim bikpela snek
      black—dog—see—big—snake
      'The black dog sees/saw a big snake.'

(*i* is an obligatory preverbal particle, which may originally have been a pronoun referring to the initial NP: 'The big dog, he sees the big snake.' It may, however, have been reinforced by a preverbal particle found in some indigenous languages.)
(a) *Word order change (movement).* If we wanted to emphasize the NP *blakpela dok* (subject), we cannot move it to the beginning of the sentence as it is already there. We could move it to the end, as in (3).

(3)   *i lukim bikpela snek blakpela dok
      see—big—snake—black—dog
      'The thing that saw the big snake was the black dog.'

However, as the asterisk indicates, this structure is unlikely to occur in the stable pidgin. The reason for the lack of this logically obvious pattern is presumably the ambiguity which would result. With no morphological devices to help speakers and hearers to keep track of the sentence, the word order alteration would simply destroy clarity of meaning without adding the emphasis required. Indeed, the most likely interpretation would be to assume that someone (unspecified) saw the big snake and the black dog.

This does not mean that movement has to be abandoned as a device for focusing attention on the subject. Movement can occur, provided it is combined with pronominalization. If a pronominal copy of the moved NP is left in situ, the structure of the original sentence remains transparent. Moving the subject leftward, and leaving a pronominal copy (*em* 'he, she, it'), we get:

(4) blakpela dok, em i lukim bikpela snek
     black—dog—it—see—big—snake
     'It is the black dog which saw the big snake.'

This is a very common construction (and, as we noted earlier, may have given rise to the preverbal particle *i*: a pronoun following a fronted NP is likely to be reanalyzed first as a topic marker, then as part of the verb, cf. Givon, 1979). For example:

(5) bipo muruk em i no wokabaut long graun (Laycock, 1970, p. 57).
     previously—cassowary—it—not—walk—on—ground
     'Long ago the cassowary did not walk on the ground.'

Leftward movement of the subject, then, is perfectly acceptable, providing a pronominal copy is left. However, if we try to move the subject rightward, leaving a pronominal copy, we get:

(6) ?? em i lukim bikpela snek, blakpela dok
     it—see—big—snake—black—dog
     'The thing that saw the big snake was the black dog.'
     ('He saw the big snake and the black dog.')

The problem with (6) is that it involves backward pronominalization, something which has been known for a long time to be less natural in language than forward pronominalization (Postal, 1970). This is because languages have a superficially linear structure based on real time, so that it is natural to refer to the full NP before its anaphor. Utterances which go against this are harder to process, since they involve potential ambiguity: the pronoun may or may not be coreferential with the NP that follows it. Sentence (6), therefore, could equally well be interpreted as 'He saw the big snake and the black dog.'

Thus leftward movement of the subject works well, provided a pronominal copy is left, whereas rightward movement is less satisfactory. Let us now turn to the object. If we move it leftward, we get (7):

(7) bikpela snek, blakpela dok i lukim
     big—snake—black—dog—see
     'It was the big snake that the black dog saw.'

This is a perfectly acceptable sentence, and the construction occurs reasonably often, for example:

(8) 'Oi, wanpela mi kikim pinis' (Laycock, 1970, p. 53).
     oy—one—I—touch with foot—past
     'Oy, I felt one [crocodile] with my foot.'

Although in theory it might be possible to interpret the two initial NPs as conjoined, in practice the context usually precludes this as a possibility. In addition, Tok Pisin reliably distinguishes transitive from intransitive verbs by means of the bound suffix *-im*, which means that the hearer seeks an object for the verb. The suffix *-im* was possibly originally an object pronoun derived from English *him*. It is probable that at an earlier stage leftward movement of the object was often combined with leaving a pronominal copy, as in:

> (9)   bikpela snek, blakpela dok i lukim em
> big—snake—black—dog—see—it
> 'It was the big snake that the black dog saw.'

This construction is still found, though is not particularly common, for example:

> (10)   na bikpela snek i stap long wara, em i ken kisim em (Laycock, 1970, p. 52).
> and—big—snake—stay—in—water—they—may—catch—it
> 'And the big watersnake, they may catch it.'

Leftward movement of the object then gives acceptable results, whether or not a pronominal copy is left behind. Rightward movement of the object alone is impossible, as it is already located at the end of the sentence under discussion. Leaving a pronominal copy gives (11):

> (11)   ?blakpela dok i lukim em, bikpela snek
> black—dog—see—it—big—snake
> 'The black dog saw it, that is, the big snake.'

This again involves backward pronominalization: although, intuitively, the close proximity of the pronoun and the NP would seem to favour a co-referential interpretation, in spite of the backward pronominalization, in practice this is a rare or even non-existent pattern. At any rate, no Tok Pisin example was locatable.

In brief, leftward movement gives acceptable sentences for both the subject (with a pronominal copy) and the object (with or without a pronominal copy), whereas rightward movement presents problems in both cases.

(b) *Repetition.* Repetition, or reduplication, is widely used in pidgins (Todd, 1984). It is used to avoid homophony: *was* 'watch', *waswas* 'wash'; for repeated or protracted actions: *em i krai i krai* 'he kept on shouting'; to mean 'each': *em i lukim wan wan* 'he saw each one individually'; for intensification: *bikpela bikpela snek* 'a really big snake'. It seems to be used most commonly to repeat syllables or single words. Repetition of whole NPs is not impossible, as shown by (12):

> (12)   wanpela barata bilong mi, wanpela barata bilong mi, i dai pinis...
> (Laycock, 1970, p. 53).
> a—brother—of—me—a—brother—of—me—died.
> 'One of my brothers died...'

More usually, however, such repetition involves some slight change or additional information, for example:

> (13)   tispela ol diwai, bikpela diwai mi kolim nem bilong ol pinis, long dispela
> diwai ... (Laycock, 1970, p. 48).
> these—trees—big trees—I—call—name—of—them—past—in—
> these—trees
> 'These trees, the big trees I told you the name of, in these trees ....'
> (14)   mipela go painim tispela haus bilongen nau, haus bilong tispela pukpuk
> ... (Laycock, 1970, p. 53).

we—go—find—this—house—of it—now—house—of—this—crocodile
'We went to find its nest, the nest of this crocodile.'

One reason for the relative rarity of the exact repetition of whole NPs might be that such repetitions take too long to produce. Another possibility is that the repetition of whole NPs might seem like a self-correction strategy: when people correct themselves they frequently return to the beginning of the phrase involved, according to some early work on this topic (Maclay and Osgood, 1959; though later researchers have not confirmed this claim, e.g., Schegloff, 1979)—and this might have been the explanation for the repeated NP in (12), since it was preceded by a self-correction:

(15) wanpela ... wanpela man ... wanpela barata bilong mi, wanpela barata
       bilong mi ....
       'One ... one man ... one of my brothers ... one of my brothers ....'

Whatever the reason for the rarity of the repetition of whole NPs, there is no need to abandon the strategy of repetition. As with movement, the answer is to use pronominalization. By leaving a pronominalized copy of the NP, it is possible to avoid sequences of two whole NPs, while still retaining the device of repeating items. So let us consider what happens when repetition is combined with pronominal copying.

With repetition and forward pronominalization of the subject, we get:

(16) blakpela dok, em i lukim bikpela snek
       black—dog—it—see—big—snake
       'It was the black dog that saw the big snake.'

Note that this produces the same surface pattern as (4)–(5). In other words, repetition and pronominalization of the subject NP produce the same result as leftward movement and pronominalization. This outcome would be likely to reinforce the surface pattern of NP + pronoun followed by a VP.

With repetition and forward pronominalization of the object, we get:

(17) ??blakpela dok i lukim bikpela snek em
       black—dog—see—big—snake—it
       'What the black dog saw was the big snake.'

This pattern is not impossible in pidgins, and is found in Cameroon Pidgin (Todd, 1984). It sounds somewhat strange in Tok Pisin, however, so may not be an obvious pidgin pattern, perhaps because a pronoun at the end of a sentence would tend to become phonetically reduced and would then merge with the preceding word, failing to provide the required emphasis. Also, in Tok Pisin a pronoun following an NP would be most naturally interpreted as the first word in the following clause, for example:

(18) em i lukim wanpela bikpela pik, wanpela wail pik em dispela snek i kilim
       (Wurm, 1969, p. 163).
       he—saw—a—big—pig—a—wild—pig—it—this—snake—kill.
       'He saw a big pig, a wild pig which this snake had killed.'

In summary, if an SVO language system which contains mainly content words needs to place emphasis or focus on an NP, it can, among other devices, utilize word order change and repetition. There are problems associated with the use of these devices by themselves, but with pronominalization they become feasible. However, the logical probabilities are not all equally satisfactory in that some of them lead to parsing problems. The most satisfactory is leftward movement which works equally well with both subject and object. Rightward movement is problematic for both. Repetition works best with the subject. This situation is shown below:

	Rep.	L-ward	R-ward
Subject	+	+	−
Object	?	+	−

Note that with the subject leftward movement (examples (4) and (5)) and repetition (example (16)) give exactly the same result:

(16)   blackpela dok, em i lukim bikpela snek.

Together, therefore, these processes may be regarded as forming a 'conspiracy', a situation in which different processes combine to create the same surface structure (Kisseberth, 1970). The outcome of a conspiracy inevitably becomes a surface structure target for future structures (Haiman, 1974).

In brief, if one assumes that language minimizes pointless variety, and avoids unnecessary opacity, then one would assume that it would maximize structures that happen to be the end result of a number of different processes, especially if this end result is easy to parse. In relation to the structures discussed here, it seems likely that SVO language systems in their early stages would have a strong preference for a surface structure target of a fronted full NP followed by a canonical SVO sentence with a pronominal copy of the fronted NP, which would be analyzed as leftward movement.

Of course, the developmental stages which occurred between this early stage and the complexities of a 'full' language need to be examined. Moreover, there are undoubtedly phenomena in mature languages which pose interesting questions unthinkable in a pidgin. But this does not invalidate the point being made here: one should at least query whether the unboundedness of leftward movement rules and the constraints on rightward movement might not fall out naturally from a desire to avoid unnecessary opacity, and the maximization of a surface structure which happened to be the result of different processes, before we start proposing apparently unmotivated innate constraints.

This is not to suggest that Chomsky is wholly wrong. Indeed, he is almost certainly right in arguing that some part of language is genetically programmed. The point at issue is simply one of emphasis. This chapter has argued that a genetic programming explanation should be a last resort, to be adopted only when other solutions fail. If this approach were adopted, we might find that Chomsky's 'core grammar' turned out to be the metaphorical equivalent of a small apple pip. In particular, I have suggested that it is worthwhile contemplating the possibility that a number of apparently puzzling conditions on rules in human language could fall out naturally from a very few, rather obvious facts which are observable in simplified linguistic situations. At the very least, then, pidgins and creoles may provide other keyholes through which we may catch additional glimpses of the elusive principles which underlie human language.

ACKNOWLEDGEMENT

I am grateful to Brian Butterworth, Margaret Deuchar, Jim Hurford, and Peter Mühlhäusler for their helpful comments on an earlier draft of this chapter.

REFERENCES

Aitchison, J. (1983) 'On roots of language', *Language and Communication*, **3**, pp. 83–97.
Bates, E. (1984) 'Bioprograms and the innateness hypothesis', *The Behavioral and Brain Sciences*, **7**, pp. 188–90.
Bickerton, D. (1981) *The Roots of Language*, Ann Arbor, Mich., Karoma.
Bickerton, D. (1984) 'The language bioprogram hypothesis', *The Behavioral and Brain Sciences*, **7**, pp. 173–88.
Butterworth, B., Comrie, B. and Dahl, O. (1984) *Explanations for Language Universals*, The Hague, Mouton (Linguistics, 21, 1 (1984)).
Chomsky, N. (1972) *Language and Mind*, enlarged edition, New York, Harcourt, Brace, Jovanovich.
Chomsky, N. (1979) *Language and Responsibility*, Brighton, Harvester Press.
Chomsky, N. (1980) *Rules and Representations*, Oxford, Basil Blackwell.
Fodor, J. D. (1984) 'Constraints on gaps: Is the parser a significant influence?', in Butterworth, Comrie and Dahl (1984).
Gardner, M. (1970) 'Mathematical games', *Scientific American*, October, pp. 120–3.
Givon, T. (1979) *On Understanding Grammar*, New York, Academic Press.
Haiman, J. (1974) *Targets and Syntactic Change*, The Hague, Mouton.
Hopper, P. J. and Thompson, S. A. (1984) 'The discourse basis for lexical categories in universal grammar', *Language*, **60**, pp. 703–52.
Hurford, J. (1984) 'A socio-diachronic explanation of a linguistic universal', *Work in Progress, 1984,* Edinburgh, Department of Linguistics, University of Edinburgh, pp. 135–47.
Hyman, L. (1984) 'Form and substance in language universals', in Butterworth, Comrie and Dahl (1984).
Kisseberth, C. W. (1970), 'On the functional unity of phonological rules', *Linguistic Inquiry*, **1**, pp. 291–306.
Koestler, A. (1972) *The Roots of Coincidence*, London, Hutchinson.
Laycock, D. (1970) *Materials in New Guinea Pidgin (Coastal and Lowlands)*, Canberra, Australian National University, Pacific Linguistics, D-5.
Lindblom, B., MacNeilage, P. and Studdert-Kennedy, M. (1984) 'Self-organizing processes and the explanation of phonological universals', in Butterworth, Comrie and Dahl (1984).
Maclay, H. and Osgood, C. E. (1959) 'Hesitation phenomena in spontaneous English speech', *Word*, **15**, pp. 19–44.
Mühlhäusler, P. (1980) 'Structural expansion and the process of creolization', in Valdman, A. and Highfield, A. (Eds), *Theoretical Orientations in Creole Studies*, New York, Academic Press.
Postal, P. (1970) *Cross-Over Phenomena*, New York, Holt, Rinehart and Winston.
Sampson, G. (1980) *Making Sense*, Oxford, Oxford University Press.
Schegloff, E. A. (1979) 'The relevance of repair to syntax for conversation', in Givon, T. (Ed.), *Syntax and Semantics 12: Discourse and Syntax*, New York, Academic Press.
Todd, L. (1984) *Modern Englishes: Pidgins and Creoles*, Oxford, Basil Blackwell.
Woolford, E. (1979) *Aspects of Tok Pisin Grammar*, Canberra, Australian National University, Pacific Linguistics, B-66.
Wurm, S. A. (1969) *New Guinea Highlands Pidgin: Course Materials*, Canberra, Australian National University, Pacific Linuistics, D-3.

Interchange

DEUCHAR REPLIES TO AITCHISON

Aitchison and I appear to agree that language universals may be accounted for in both psycho-biological and functional terms, though there is plenty of room for discussion about the load to be borne by each kind of explanation. In my chapter I concentrated on phenomena which seem particularly amenable to explanation in psycho-biological terms, though I recognized the possibility of functional explanations as an alternative. In this reply I wish to concentrate, with Aitchison, on functional explanations. However, my own analysis of her data will lead to a different conclusion as to what phenomena should be accounted for, and to a different kind of functional explanation from that proposed by her.

Aitchison argues that focusing of constituents in Tok Pisin is achieved by leftward rather than rightward movement rules, and that this can be accounted for in terms of the functional consideration of parsability. I shall show that what appears to be focusing may in fact be topic marking, and that the prevalence of topic marking constructions in pidgin/creole data can be accounted for in terms of the functional consideration of ease of processing in a situation of communicative stress.

Aitchison assests that Tok Pisin has a canonical SVO order, as represented in her sentence (2):

Blakpela dok i lukim bikpela snek
'The black dog sees/saw a big snake.'

This would indeed seem to represent SVO order, especially if we assume, with her, that *i* is an obligatory preverbal particle. However, it is interesting to note that, as Sankoff (1980) shows, it is likely to have been a topic marker at an earlier stage of the language. Givón (1976) argues that subject agreement of the kind exemplified in (2) may arise diachronically from the frequent use of topic marking constructions under conditions of communicative stress. Such conditions are clearly common where pidgins and creoles are used.

However, Aitchison is interested not in devices which mark topic, but in those which mark focus. (I am assuming that the term 'topic' refers to known or given information, while 'focus' refers to asserted or emphasized material.) She selects for our consideration those devices which are available for focusing a particular constituent, and which involve a departure in word order from SVO. I shall deal only with constituent movement.

For focusing on the subject, Aitchison says that the preferred device is 'moving the subject leftward, and leaving a pronominal copy.' She illustrates this with her sentence (4):

blakpela dok, em i lukim bikpela snek
'It is the black dog which saw the big snake.'

The English translation of this sentence shows that Aitchison interprets 'blackpela dok' as focus, and yet it is not clear why it should be focus rather than topic (and translated something like 'As for the black dog, it saw the big snake'). In fact, this kind of construction is analyzed by Sankoff (1980) as involving topic marking. Indeed, Aitchison says that it is a very common construction and that 'a pronoun following a fronted NP is likely to be reanalyzed first as a topic marker ....' To illustrate this she then gives her example (5), where leftward movement and pronominalization seem clearly to mark topic rather than focus.

A possible confusion between topic and focus also arises when we look at the data showing object movement. Aitchison's example (7), showing leftward movement of the object, is as follows:

bikpela snek, blakpela dok i lukim
'It was the big snake that the black dog saw.'

It is not clear why 'bikpela snek' should be interpreted as focus, particularly since another example she gives of this construction, (8), is as follows:

Oi, wanpela mi kikim pinis
'Oy, I felt one [crocodile] with my foot.'

The translation given is neutral as between assigning 'wanpela' to topic or focus, but the anaphoric function of 'wanpela' suggests strongly that it is a (known) topic rather than an (asserted) focus.

One might argue that whether one considers the constructions in Aitchison's data as topic marking or focus marking does not really matter, since the constructions she selects in any case show leftward movement (assuming a theoretical framework that allows for movement rules at all). However, if this is a topic marking device it could be accounted for in different terms from those of parsability: i.e., in terms of a tendency for known information to come first and to be marked as such under conditions of communicative stress. Furthermore, a clear distinction between topic and focus might have allowed further exploration of when constituent movement is a possibility and when it is not. Following Creider's (1979) argument that SVO languages treat initial position as topical and final position as focusing, we might predict that topic marking of subject and focus marking of object in Tok Pisin could not be done by constituent movement alone. The first of these two predictions might be supported by a reanalysis of Aitchison's data, while we should need further data to test the second.

REFERENCES

Creider, C. (1979) 'On the explanation of transformations', in Givón, T. (Ed.) *Syntax and Semantics Volume 12. Discourse and Syntax*, New York, Academic Press.

Givón, T. (1976) 'Topic, pronoun and grammatical agreement', in Li, C. and Thompson, S. (Eds.) *Subject and Topic*, New York, Academic Press.

Sankoff, G. (1980) 'Variability and explanation in language and culture: Cliticization in New Guinea Tok Pisin', in Sankoff, G. (Ed.) *The Social Life of Language*, Philadelphia, University of Pennsylvania Press.

AITCHISON REPLIES TO DEUCHAR

In my chapter I argued that Chomsky's innatist view of language universals was valid and interesting, but that he overemphasized this approach. I suggested that a genetic programming explanation for language universals should be a last resort, to be proposed only when we cannot find any suitable alternative explanation. Instead of being innate, I argued that a number of seemingly arbitrary universals or near universals might be the most probable response to certain communicative needs, and might therefore fall out naturally in a particular set of circumstances. That is, given certain basic propensities for coping with language (such as an ability to sequence and to use structure-dependent operations), speakers of different languages might rediscover the same solutions repeatedly and independently of one another.

Deuchar in her chapter claims that she is supporting Chomsky. Her basic argument is that there are characteristics shared by pidgins, creoles and sign language, which appear to arise independently. She suggests that these characteristics are likely to be genetically programmed. Yet the particular features which she selects for comment are those which fit well into the scenario I have proposed: they are the inevitable or most likely solution to a particular set of communicational problems.

For reasons of space it is possible to consider the first of these only: the claim that in pidgins, creoles and sign language, aspectual markers are closest to the verb, then modal markets, then tense or time markers. Before examining this claim, we need to note that the apparent ubiquity of this neat pattern is to some extent an artefact of the various analyses, since in practice it is often extremely difficult to assign verbal markers reliably to temporal, modal or aspectual categories, since they all overlap. For example, past time tends to overlap with perfectivity, futurity cannot be easily disentangled from intentionality, and so on. In addition, the labels tense, mood and aspect are each used to cover a wide and sometimes heterogeneous collection of verbal markers (Aitchison, in press).

Perhaps the most that one can do is to agree on prototypical examples of tense, mood and aspect, and to compare their order. Even here one runs into a problem, in that in pidgins and in the early stages of a creole preverbal markers are scarce, and are rarely combined. This makes the question of which is closest to the verb somewhat academic. However, if we regard prototypical aspect as being the expression of iterativity or durativity, and prototypical temporal marking as being [− present], it does seem to be true that aspectual markers are typically closer to the verb than temporal ones, though the modal situation is less clear.

Yet the nearness of prototypical aspect markers to the verb is no deep mystery, and certainly requires no genetic programming. Not surprisingly, the most obvious way of expressing iterativity or durativity is by means of repetition, e.g., Tok Pisin *mi ron ron ron i ron* 'I kept running'. A common alternative is to substitute an all-purpose marker for the second verb. This marker itself may be repeated, e.g., *mi ron yet i go i go i go i go* 'I was still running', or may occur once, e.g., *mi ron i go yet* 'I was still running'. (These examples are all taken from Wurm, 1969, p. 168). In other words, an iconic marker, repetition of a verb for repetitive action, eventually develops into a conventional non-iconic marker, based on the surface pattern of the repeated verb. Its closeness to the verb is therefore almost inevitable. This hardly requires genetic programming.

To turn to time, this need be marked only when the time is not obvious from the context. Hence, the present time will be largely unmarked, but an additional phrase is likely to be needed to express remoteness from the present, e.g., *mi sik* would imply 'I am ill now', whereas *asde mi sik* 'yesterday I was sick', would specify that the sickness was remote in time from the present. It makes sense that something expressing remoteness from the present should be outside the critical sentence nucleus. In addition, in a narrative there is a tendency to topicalize the time reference, which again moves it away from the verb, e.g., *long moningtaim man bilongen i go* . . . 'In the morning, her husband went . . .' (Laycock, 1970, p. 59). Some of these adverbial phrases are likely in the long run to become tense markers, as in the case of Tok Pisin futurity marker *bai*, which is usually considered to be derived from *baimbai* 'by and by'. Such tense markers will therefore tend to be further away from the verb than prototypical aspectual ones.

The scenario envisaged above can account quite naturally for the typical, though not inevitable, relative positions of temporal and aspectual markers in pidgins, creoles and sign language. In brief, in this case as in a number of others, apparently arbitrary innate features can be explained as the most obvious response to a particular set of communicative needs.

REFERENCES

Aitchison, J. (in press) 'Tense and aspect in child language, pidgins and creoles', *Osmania Papers in Linguistics*.

Laycock, D. (1970) *Materials in New Guinea Pidgin (Coastal and Lowlands)*, Canberra, Australian National University, Pacific Linguistics, D-5.

Wurm, S. A. (1969) *New Guinea Highlands Pidgin: Course Materials*, Canberra, Australian National University, Pacific Linguistics, D-3.

IV: Chomskyan Distinction Between Core Grammar And Periphery

9. Core Grammar and Periphery

RAPHAEL SALKIE

> I will be concerned now with a kind of 'core grammar' for English consisting of a few general rules and some general conditions governing the operation of these rules. (Chomsky, 1977, p. 72)

The distinction between core grammar and periphery was not an explicit part of Chomsky's work until the mid-1970s. It was then that statements like the one cited above began to appear. The idea of core grammar was developed considerably in later work, and has now become a central assumption in work by Chomsky and his co-workers.

In this chapter I try to explain the importance of the core-periphery distinction in Chomsky's recent work. Section 1 argues that the distinction is a natural consequence of Chomsky's central aim in studying language. Section 2 looks at how the distinction affects the way that Chomsky goes about constructing a generative grammar. In section 3 I try to evaluate the core-periphery distinction, firstly within Chomsky's general framework of assumptions, and secondly from a broader viewpoint.

1 CHOMSKY'S CENTRAL AIM

Chomsky's declared aim is to apply the approach of the natural sciences, as he understands it, to the study of human language. For Chomsky the key feature of natural sciences is that they are concerned with explaining the world rather than just describing it. An explanation is a response to a puzzle—a problem which does not have an immediately obvious solution. Each science formulates a puzzle of some sort and attempts to solve it.

Adopting this approach in linguistics, Chomsky formulates his puzzle like this:

how is language acquisition possible? His solution is the theory of universal grammar, assumed to be innate. This is very different from the aim of writing a comprehensive descriptive grammar of a language or a range of languages. If this had been Chomsky's aim, the criteria for success and failure would have been very different. In descriptive work it is comprehensiveness that counts—how many phenomena can be subsumed under a particular descriptive framework. In the natural sciences it is the quality of the explanation—the 'explanatory depth' to use Chomsky's term—that is crucial.

We can use two main criteria to assess the 'depth' of a scientific explanation. The first is the chain of reasoning which starts with the principles of the theory and ends with the actual phenomena to be explained. The longer this chain is—and hence the more abstract the theory is—the greater the depth of explanation achieved by the theory. The second criterion is whether the theory can relate phenomena which at first sight seem unrelated.

Chomsky often uses Galileo as an example of a scientist who consistently aimed for explanatory depth rather than a comprehensive descriptive scheme. He refers to Galileo when he sets out the basic question he is concerned with in linguistics:

> . . . To what extent and in what ways can inquiry in something like the 'Galilean Style' yield insight and understanding of the roots of human nature in the cognitive domain? Can we hope to move beyond superficiality by a readiness to undertake perhaps far-reaching idealisation and to construct abstract models that are accorded more significance than the ordinary world of sensation, and correspondingly, by readiness to tolerate unexplained phenomena or even as yet unexplained counterevidence to theoretical constructions that have achieved a certain degree of explanatory depth in some limited domain, much as Galileo did not abandon his enterprise because he was unable to give a coherent explanation for the facts that objects do not fly off the earth's surface?
>
> . . . I am interested, then, in pursuing some aspects of the study of mind, in particular, such aspects as lend themselves to inquiry through the construction of abstract explanatory theories that may involve substantial idealisation and will be justified, if at all, by success in providing insight and explanations. From this point of view, substantial coverage of data is not a particularly significant result; it can be attained in many ways, and the result is not very informative as to the correctness of the principles employed. It will be more significant if certain fairly far-reaching principles interact to provide an explanation for crucial facts—the crucial nature of these facts deriving from their relation to proposed explanatory theories. It is a mistake to argue, as many do, that by adopting this point of view one is disregarding data. Data that remain unexplained by some coherent theory will continue to be described in whatever descriptive scheme one chooses, but will simply not be considered very important for the moment. (Chomsky, 1980, pp. 9–12)

Notice here the insistence that scientists who adopt the 'Galilean Style' will inevitably have to limit the range of phenomena they consider, and idealize those phenomena, if they want to explain the world rather than simply to describe it. We can also see in embryo the distinction between core grammar and periphery when Chomsky refers to 'crucial facts' on the one hand and 'data that remain unexplained by some coherent theory' on the other.

Anyone familiar with Chomsky's work will be aware of the limitations and idealizations which Chomsky claims are necessary if explanation is to be achieved in linguistics. These include:

1 ignoring sociolinguistic variation—the notion of a 'homogeneous speech-community' (Chomsky, 1980, pp. 24–6);

2 paying no attention to the functions of language (Chomsky, 1980, pp. 229–30);

3 restricting attention to competence rather than performance (Chomsky, 1965, pp. 3ff);

4 treating competence as perfect—the notion of an ideal speaker-hearer who knows the language perfectly (Chomsky, 1965, p. 3);

5 the distinction between 'grammaticality' and 'acceptability' (Chomsky, 1965, pp. 10ff);

6 treating syntax in isolation from semantics—the autonomy thesis (Chomsky, 1957, p. 17);

7 treating the language faculty in isolation from other mental faculties—modularity (Chomsky, 1980, pp. 40ff);

8 treating language acquisition as instantaneous (Chomsky, 1975, pp. 119ff).

What Chomsky does in his discussion of these issues is to set out, clearly and consistently, the price that must be paid *if* linguistics is to become an explanatory science. Whether or not that price is worth paying is a debatable issue, of course; we return to it in section 3.

Chomsky's puzzle, then, is to explain language acquisition. The proposed explanation looks like this:

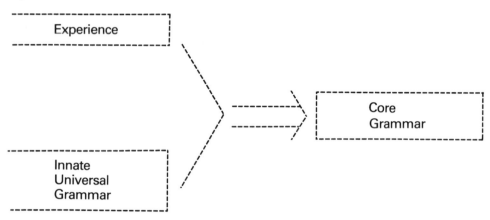

The language learner experiences a mass of linguistic data. Using the resources of universal grammar (UG), which are innate in the brain, she/he arrives at a core grammar for her/his native language. The puzzle for Chomsky is to elaborate the rules and principles of UG which make it possible for the language learner to go from experience to core grammar. In earlier discussions of the acquisition puzzle, Chomsky used to write 'grammatical competence' in the output box now called 'core grammar'. Now only certain grammatical rules and principles are located in this box. Why the change?

The answer is that the list of idealizations given above is not quite complete. So far, we have seen how Chomsky clears away the areas that he is not concerned with in order to concentrate on grammar. As work based on this approach proceeded, it was virtually inevitable that in the grammar itself it would be necessary to single out those areas where the 'Galilean Style' looked appropriate. Put rather crudely, core grammar is the name for those areas of grammar where Chomsky's approach has achieved or seems likely to achieve some measure of success. Anaphora, for example, has been an area where explanation has looked possible, while the topic of gapping has not (Chomsky, 1982, pp. 81ff).

Those aspects of competence which in Chomsky's view are not amenable to explanation in this way are called the 'periphery'. It is in the periphery that considerations of markedness apply. Constructions that are in the periphery of the grammar may violate the rules and principles of UG at a cost. Such constructions will be marked and should exhibit the following properties: rarity, variation from speaker to speaker, difficulties for the language learner, and diachronic instability.

Hence Chomsky is not just saying that certain grammatical phenomena are amenable to explanation while others are not. Clearly, historical relics, foreign borrowings and the like will have to be analyzed in other terms. The claim is that the areas which are amenable to explanation are the central ones—the ones that are less likely to change and easier to acquire. In principle this is an empirical claim, though not an easy one to test (for a discussion of some of the problems, cf. White, 1982, pp. 95–6).

The distinction between core grammar and periphery can thus be seen as the logical last step in Chomsky's list of idealizations and simplifying assumptions which are needed if linguistics is to become an explanatory science. The other assumptions are the large-scale ones which limit attention to grammar. The idea of core grammar is that within the grammar itself one can and should focus primarily on those areas like anaphora which seem to shed light on UG. Other areas are consigned to the periphery.

2 CORE GRAMMAR IN ACTION

Let us now look at an example of work in core grammar, bearing in mind that it is UG which is Chomsky's prime concern, and to which core grammar is intended to open the door. Here are four sentences:

(1)   Rachel controlled the dog
(2)   The women helped Rebecca
(3)   Rachel controlled herself
(4)   The women helped each other

The first two sentences can be put into the passive. Sentences (3) and (4) cannot:

(5)   The dog was controlled by Rachel
(6)   Rebecca was helped by the women
(7)   *Herself controlled Rachel
(8)   *Each other were helped by the women

Descriptive grammars like Quirk *et al*, (1972, p. 806), and some generative grammarians (Brame, 1979, pp. 189ff; Gazdar, 1982, p. 467) have tried to account for this by saying that reflexive pronouns like *herself* and the reciprocal expression *each other* are object pronouns like *me, us , them*, etc., and hence cannot appear as the subject of a sentence.

Chomsky's account of these sentences is very different. He calls reflexives like *herself* and the reciprocal phrase *each other* ANAPHORS. (This is a traditional term used by grammarians; Chomsky uses it in a slightly restricted way.) Chomsky proposes that there is a general principle which applies to anaphors (what follows is highly simplified so that it is easier to understand):

Binding principle: An anaphor must be bound in its governing sentence.

To understand this principle, you will need to know what some of the words in it mean. Every anaphor normally has an *antecedent*—a word or phrase that comes before it and indicates to what the anaphor refers. In examples (3) and (4), *Rachel* is the antecedent of *herself* and *the women* is the antecedent of *each other*: We say that the antecedent *binds* the anaphor. So to say that an anaphor is bound is simply to say that it has an appropriate antecedent.

Government is a highly technical term, and much current research is concerned with the correct way to define it. The definition offered here gives the basic idea:

Let *A* and *B* be two items in a sentence. We will say that *A* governs *B* if:

(i)   *A* is a noun, verb, adjective or preposition; and

(ii)   *B* is to the right of *A* and part of the same phrase.

The instances of government which concern us here are where *A* is a verb or a preposition, and *B* is its object. So we say that in (3), the verb *controlled* governs *herself*, its object; in (4), *helped* governs *each other*; and in examples like this, the preposition *with* governs *herself*:

(9)   Rachel was delighted with herself

The *governing sentence* of an anaphor is the smallest sentence containing the anaphor and the nearest word which governs it. In simple sentences like the ones looked at so far, the 'governing sentence' will simply be 'the same sentence'. In such cases the binding principle says, in effect: 'An anaphor must be governed, and it must be bound.' In complex sentences like (10) and (11), which consist of more than one clause, the word 'smallest' is crucial:

(10)   Paul expected that Rachel would control herself

(11)   I noticed that the women helped each other

These two sentences consist of a *main clause* '*Paul expected [something]*' or '*I noticed [something]*' and a *subordinate* or *dependent clause*, introduced by *that*. To find the governing sentence for the anaphors in (10) and (11), we first find the word or phrase that governs it. It is the verb of the subordinate clause in each case: *control* in (10) and *helped* in (11). The governing sentence is the smallest sentence containing both the anaphor and the word that governs it. In both cases it is the subordinate clause which is the governing sentence.

We are now in a position to see how the binding principle works. In sentence (3), the anaphor is *herself*. It is bound by the antecedent *Rachel*, and the antecedent is in the same sentence as the anaphor. So sentence (3) conforms to the binding principle and is grammatical. Consider now the passive (7), repeated here:

(7)   *Herself was controlled by Rachel

The anaphor here has no antecedent at all. An antecedent must *precede* the anaphor it binds (otherwise it would not be an antecedent). So (7) violates the binding principle—the anaphor is not bound at all, hence it certainly is not bound in its governing sentence.

Not all uses of English reflexive pronouns can be accounted for by the binding principle. Reflexive pronouns can be used for emphasis; in such cases they can occur much more freely:

(12)   I wouldn't go there myself

(13)   I myself wouldn't go there

(14)   Myself, I wouldn't go there

In this last example the reflexive precedes its antecedent, violating the binding principle. Other uses of reflexives which violate the principle are cited in Scheurweghs (1959, p. 124):

(15)   The only reality was themselves
(16)   Nathaniel Ellis. That was myself
(17)   Myself and my own misery drum in my ears
(18)   ... as long as no one but myself is hurt

Chomsky would have to say that such uses of reflexives do not come under core grammar and are therefore not subject to the binding principle. They are in the periphery of the grammar where the principles of UG can be relaxed. The claim is that they are rare and vary from speaker to speaker; this appears to be correct.

Returning to core grammar, the binding principle will also handle complex sentences like (10). The anaphor is *herself* again, and the antecedent is *Rachel*. The anaphor is governed by the verb *control*, so the governing sentence is the subordinate clause. By the binding principle, the antecedent must be in the subordinate clause as well. This is the case, so the sentence is grammatical. Similar reasoning shows that (11) also conforms to the binding principle.

Suppose we construct sentences like (10) and (11), except that the antecedent is not in the subordinate clause but in the main clause. The binding principle predicts that such sentences will be ungrammatical, and this turns out to be correct:

(19)   *Rachel expected that Paul would control herself
(20)   *The women noticed that I helped each other

In (19), *herself* requires an antecedent in the subordinate clause. The only word available is *Paul*. But that does not work: the antecedent of *herself* must be female. The obvious candidate for antecedent, *Rachel*, is not available because it is in the main clause. Similarly in (20), the only permitted antecedent is the word *I*. But *each other* requires a *plural* antecedent, and *I* is singular. So the binding principle predicts, correctly, that native speakers of English reject these sentences as ungrammatical. Examples like (19) and (20) are important in Chomsky's view. He points out that they simply cannot express the meaning one would expect. So we cannot use (19) to mean (19') or (20) to mean (20'):

(19')   Rachel expected that Paul would control her
(20')   The women each noticed that I helped the other

The fact that there is nothing wrong with the meaning of (19) and (20) is strong evidence in support of the binding principle. The other account of reflexive and reciprocal constructions that we mentioned briefly above does not help us at all with more complex cases like (19) and (20): *herself* and *each other* are the object of their sentence in these examples. It is worth mentioning also that the binding principle has a much wider application than just to sentences of the type discussed here. Chomsky treats movement transformations as leaving behind 'traces' of the moved items which can also be considered as anaphors and hence are subject to the principle. The link between movement and anaphora is one of the key achievements of Chomsky's recent work.

Let us now look at the key question for Chomsky: how do speakers of English acquire the binding principle? At first sight there may seem to be no problems of principle in answering this question. Presumably a young person acquires the binding principle in the same way as she acquires other grammatical rules: by listening to the sentences spoken around her, trying out sentences of her own, and so on. One might need to investigate in more detail the stage of development at which this principle is acquired, or whether some young people have special difficulties with it. But there seems to be no reason why we should be unable to give a general account of how it is acquired.

Now in certain cases, what I have said in the preceding paragraph is probably correct. It is a rule of English, for example, that adjectives generally precede the noun they modify: we say *a good cry*, not **a cry good*. A young person learning English will hear innumerable examples where the adjective comes first, and almost none where the noun comes first. It will clearly be possible for her to arrive at the rule that adjectives come first. Of course, this whole process is unconscious, just as most language acquisition is. But there is no difficulty in reconstructing this unconscious process of acquisition.

While this account may be true of adjectives, it cannot be true of the binding principle. To see why, we must bear in mind a simple but important fact about language acquisition: the only information available to a young person acquiring a language is that certain sentences are acceptable. In general, young people are rarely informed that certain sentences are *not* acceptable, and more rarely still are they informed *why* certain sentences are not acceptable. Linguists say that children have access to 'positive evidence' (grammatical sentences), but not to 'negative evidence' (ungrammatical sentences).

This simple fact puts the acquisition process in a new light. A young person only hears a small sample of sentences. There are an enormous number of possible sentences that she has never heard. Of these, some are grammatical and some are not. If adult speakers uniformly agree that a sentence which they have not encountered before is ungrammatical, then whatever rule they are applying must be based solely on the evidence from grammatical sentences which they *have* encountered.

In our discussion of reflexives and reciprocals we argued that the binding principle worked better than the simpler account we considered. The evidence was examples (19) and (20): the simpler account could not explain why these two sentences, which would be judged unacceptable by any speaker of English, were ungrammatical. It was these two *un*grammatical sentences which were crucial evidence in favour of Chomsky's analysis.

Linguists analyzing English can easily obtain judgments about examples like (19) and (20). Unlike linguists, a young person acquiring English does not have access to the information that these two sentences are not grammatical. But such sentences are the *only* evidence for choosing the binding principle rather than the other alternative. If young people do not have access to this evidence, how is it that they invariably choose the binding principle? One would expect instead variation from speaker to speaker, and hesitation in judging sentences like (19) and (20) to be unacceptable. But we do not find this: any speaker of English would not hesitate to rule them out. Why is this? Chomsky's by now familiar answer is that the binding principle is part of UG and is innate. All a learner needs, according to Chomsky, is evidence that words like *herself* and *each other* are anaphors: UG does the rest. The binding principle is thus part of the core grammar of English because it is part of universal grammar.

Chomsky has proposed that UG consists of a number of parameters along which languages can vary. A core grammar for a particular language is the result of choosing, from the evidence available to the language learner, the values of the parameters for that language. To take a simple example, some languages have relatively fixed constituent order, while in others the order is fairly free. This is presumably the kind of thing that a young person acquiring a language can determine without much difficulty. Chomsky (1981, pp. 127ff) proposes that the learner can then choose from the two options that UG makes available: a 'configurational' syntactic structure and movement transformations for languages like English with fixed order, and a 'flat' structure and random assignment of grammatical functions for languages like Japanese with free order. (For criticism, see Gazdar *et al.*, 1983, and Horrocks, 1983.)

3 EVALUATION

The theory of core grammar can be evaluated in two ways. Firstly, one can assume that Chomsky's basic aim in the study of language is a valid one and assess notions like core and periphery in terms of whether they contribute to that basic aim. Secondly and more fundamentally, one can look at the kind of work that core grammar advocates have produced and ask whether this is what linguists should be spending their time on.

Taking the first approach, there is little doubt that the core-periphery distinction has enabled Chomsky and his co-workers to propose interesting hypotheses about language which have a considerable amount of depth (in the sense discussed above). Binding theory and the other principles and systems of core grammar discussed in Chomsky (1981) interact to account for a considerable range of data. The notion of parameters of core grammar has led to many interesting attempts to reduce apparently unrelated differences among languages to one underlying difference: see, for example, Kayne (1981) and Borer (1984). Chomsky and others are now able to assume a set of rules and conditions on rules which are tightly integrated, so that a small change in one area of the grammar can have large consequences. This is an ideal starting point for theoretical research and debate.

If we now take a broader perspective, the picture is less clear. The core-periphery distinction is one of the idealizations which Chomsky says is necessary if linguistics is to adopt the 'Galilean style' of the natural sciences. Even if Chomsky is now beginning to succeed in his aim, the question must be whether the notion of core grammar is just one more way of removing Chomsky's work from reality—in particular, from the reality of language acquisition. We are still waiting for the theory of UG and empirical work on language acquisition to interact in fruitful ways. It is true that learning a language involves other forms of development than just UG—motor skills, memory, attention span, and so on—and this means that links between UG and empirical research will not be straightforward. But substantial results have been slow to appear. To be fair, the theory of core grammar is only a few years old. (For some initial attempts to link theory and acquisition data, see Tavakolian, 1981.)

Generative grammar continues to be a puzzling mixture: more intellectually exciting than ever, but always with the worry that it is of little practical use to anyone. Nevertheless, even if an explanatory theory of language turns out to be an illusion, it is a tribute to Chomsky that so many people have thought the attempt to build one worthwhile.

REFERENCES

Borer, H. (1984) *Parametric Syntax* Cambridge, Mass., MIT Press.
Brame, M. (1979) *Essays toward Realistic Syntax*, Seattle, Wash., Noit Amrofer.

Chomsky, N. (1957) *Syntactic Structures*, The Hague, Mouton.

Chomsky, N. (1965) *Aspects of the Theory of Syntax*, Cambridge, Mass., MIT Press.

Chomsky, N. (1975) *Reflections on Language*, London, Temple Smith.

Chomsky, N. (1977) 'On *wh*-movement', in Akmajian, A., Culicover, P. and Wasow, T. (Eds), *Formal Syntax*, London, Academic Press, pp. 71–132.

Chomsky, N. (1980) *Rules and Representations*, Oxford, Basil Blackwell.

Chomsky, N. (1981) *Lectures on Government and Binding*, Dordrecht, Foris.

Chomsky, N. (1982) *Some Concepts and Consequences of the Theory of Government and Binding*, Cambridge, Mass., MIT Press.

Gazdar, G. (1982) Review of M. Brame, *Base Generated Syntax* (Seattle, Wash., Noit Amrofer, 1978) and *Essays toward Realistic Syntax* (Seattle, Wash., Noit Amrofer, 1979) in *Journal of Linguistics*, **18**, pp. 464–73.

Gazdar, G., Klein, E. and Pullum, G. K. (1983) 'Introduction', in Gazdar, G., Klein, E. and Pullum, G. K. (Eds), *Order, Concord and Constituency*, Dordrecht, Foris, pp. 1–8.

Horrocks, G. (1983) 'The order of constituents in modern Greek', in Gazdar, G., Klein, E. and Pullum, G. K. (Eds), *Order, Concord and Constituency*, Dordrecht, Foris, pp. 95–111.

Kayne, R. (1981) 'On certain differences between French and English', *Linguistic Inquiry*, **12**, pp. 349–71.

Quirk, R. *et al.* (1972) *A Grammar of Contemporary English*, London, Longman.

Scheurweghs, G. (1959) *Present Day English Syntax*, London, Longman.

Tavakolian, S. (Ed). (1981) *Language Acquisition and Linguistic Theory*, Cambridge, Mass., MIT Press.

White, L. (1982) *Grammatical Theory and Language Acquisition*, Cambridge, Mass., MIT Press.

10. On the Scope of Grammatical Theory

DAVID GIL

1 CHOMSKY'S QUERY: WHAT DOES GRAMMAR INCLUDE?

Noam Chomsky views linguistics as a branch of cognitive psychology, concerned with the study of one particular mental faculty, namely grammar. Central to Chomsky's approach is the autonomy thesis, whereby grammar is endowed with unique structural characteristics distinguishing it from other mental faculties such as music and vision.[1] Thus, for example, Chomsky asserts that:

> There are a number of cognitive systems which seem to have quite distinct and specific properties .... The language faculty is one of these cognitive systems. There are others. For example, our capacity to organize visual space, or to deal with abstract properties of the number system, or to comprehend and appreciate certain kinds of musical creation, or our ability to make sense of the social structures in which we play a role, which undoubtedly reflects conceptual structures that have developed in the mind, and any number of other mental capacities. As far as I can see, to the extent that we understand anything about these capacities they appear to have quite specific and unique properties. That is, I don't see any obvious relationship between, for example, the basic properties of the structure of language as represented in the mind on the one hand, and the properties of our capacity, say, to recognize faces or understand some situation in which we play a role, or appreciate music and so on. These seem to be quite different and unique in their characteristics.[2]

Similarly, Chomsky views the internal organization of the language faculty as being modular in nature, consisting of a number of autonomous systems, such as—in one recent formulation[3]—bounding theory, government theory, θ-theory, binding theory, Case theory, and control theory.

A second characteristic feature of Chomsky's approach is the distinction between *grammar*—a 'real' object, worthy of scientific inquiry—and *language*—which is 'epiphenomenal', and of little, perhaps even no significance whatsoever to linguistic research. Thus, Chomsky states that 'grammars have to have a real existence, that is, there is something in your brain that corresponds to the grammar. . . . But there is nothing in the real world corresponding to language. In fact, it could very well turn out that there is no intelligible notion of language.'[4] Resulting from this distinction is a state of affairs whereby grammar grossly underdetermines language. Thus, in recent formulations, Chomsky has abandoned earlier assumptions to the effect that a generative grammar must specify the set of well-formed sentences in a language.[5] Instead, grammar is viewed as accounting for a limited set of linguistic phenomena, leaving additional phenomena to be accounted for outside grammatical theory.

In fact, these remaining phenomena may be accounted for by invoking other mental faculties existing alongside grammar. Thus, for example, Chomsky writes:

> what we loosely call 'knowledge of language' involves in the first place knowledge of grammar . . . and beyond that other cognitive systems that interact with grammar . . . [6]
> an actual language may result only from the interaction of several mental faculties, one being the faculty of language. There may be no concrete specimens of which we can say These are solely the product of the language faculty; and no specific acts that result solely from the exercise of linguistic functions.[7]

Language is thus a joint product of grammar and a number of other mental faculties. For any linguistic phenomenon, the question accordingly arises whether it may be more adequately explained within grammatical theory or, perhaps, a theory of some other mental faculty. For example, while the unacceptability of *The candidates wanted me to vote for each other* may be grammatically explicated, e.g., in terms of principles of government and binding, the unacceptability of *The cantaloupes wanted me to vote for them* might be explained in terms of what Chomsky refers to as our 'commonsense' faculty—specifically, our shared belief that cantaloupes cannot want. However, the question which mental faculty or faculties are to be invoked in the explanation of a given linguistic phenomenon is, in general, far from being trivial. Linguistic phenomena do not present themselves to the researcher labelled grammatical or otherwise; researchers have no a priori basis for determining whether a given linguistic phenomenon is a product of grammatical competence or of any number of other mental faculties affecting language.[8] The scope of grammatical theory is thus an open question—one that is to be addressed through empirical inquiry, not dogmatic pronouncement.

This query—what does grammar include?—has been recently formulated by Chomsky. Assuming a modular approach to mind consistent with the autonomy thesis, and invoking an analogy between mental and bodily organs, Chomsky asks:

> what is to be included under aspects of form and meaning properly assigned to the language faculty? . . . if one believes the modular approach to have some merit . . . the question is a reasonable one. It is on a par with the question: what is the human visual system, or the heart, or the circulatory system? Such systems are not physically isolable. As in the case of a 'mental organ', which I am taking to be an integrated system of rules and principles generating representations of various sorts, the question is one of appropriate idealization at a certain level of theoretical discussion, a question with empirical content, no doubt, but *one that can be fully resolved only in the context of a broader study of a system that incorporates the given idealized 'organ' as a part.*[9] (my emphasis)

Chomsky's conclusion merits closer attention. What is this 'broader study of a system that incorporates the given idealized "organ" as a part', and why is it a sine qua non for the resolution of the question posed above? To the best of my knowledge, Chomsky provides no elaboration on this in any of his other writings.

In what follows I wish to formulate and defend a proposal concerning the ways in which the scope of grammatical theory may be determined—a proposal which, I believe, is implicit in the above passage by Chomsky. Specifically, I shall propose that in order to determine the limits of grammatical theory, it is necessary to conduct detailed investigations into a variety of domains of non-verbal mental activity, for example, music, vision, mathematics. Such investigations reveal numerous non-trivial structural properties shared by language and various domains of non-verbal mental activity: these shared properties, it is subsequently argued, must be accounted for outside grammatical theory, in terms of mental faculties governing both verbal and non-verbal activities. Thus, in section 2 it is argued that a certain structural principle manifested in natural language, artificial language, and music—and currently accounted for, in the context of natural language, within grammatical theory—ought rather to be accounted for within the framework of a theory of prosody characterizing a mental faculty that is essentially autonomous of grammatical competence. Similarly, in section 3 it is suggested that an array of abstract structural features shared, inter alia, by language, vision, and mathematics—some of which are currently represented within grammatical theory—should be factored out of theories of grammar, vision, and mathematical competence, and relocated within a single mental faculty of an algebraic nature.

Investigation of music, vision, mathematics, and other domains of non-verbal mental activity may thus have surprising ramifications *vis-à-vis* linguistic theory, leading to a theory of grammar that is considerably more impoverished than is assumed in most current models of generative grammar. Phenomena as diverse as syllable structure, agreement and case marking morphology, word order, logical inference, and others will be argued in the continuation to possess structural analogues in domains of non-verbal mental activity, thereby suggesting that at least some aspects of these phenomena fall outside the scope of grammatical theory. Our argumentation will consequently engender a paradox of sorts, in that it is shown how adopting Chomsky's methodological assumptions—the autonomy thesis, the grammar-language distinction, and the view that language is a joint product of a number of mental faculties—leads inevitably to a theory of grammar substantially different from that espoused by Chomsky and his followers: a theory of considerably narrower scope.

2 ABSTRACTING AWAY FROM GRAMMAR: THE SMALL-PRECEDES-LARGE PRINCIPLE

Aristotle, in *The Poetics*, states that 'we speak many iambs when talking to each other.'[10] In this section it is argued that a principle of iambicity underlies numerous aspects of our verbal and non-verbal mental activity. Specifically, it is shown how a variety of phenomena—some linguistic: phonological, morphological, and syntactic, others in the realm of artificial language and music—instantiate a general tendency to order elements in such a way that smaller items precede larger ones.[11] After adducing several phenomena exemplifying this tendency, it is suggested that the small-precedes-large principle may be most appropriately accounted for within the framework of a theory of prosodic competence.

Consider the following set of data:

(1) (a) Pins and needles   (*needles and pins)
    (b) Kit and kaboodle   (*kaboodle and kit)

(2)   John ――― eats durians ――
    (a)   √   * seldom
    (b)   ?   √ every Monday and Thursday

(3)   I wish to put―― forward ――― in this paper ―――
    (a)   √   *   * it
    (b)   √   √   √ a certain claim
    (c)   *   *   √ the claim that S

(4) (a) Un garçon intelligent   (French)
         a-m boy   intelligent-sgm
         'An intelligent boy'
    (b) Un beau   garçon
         a-m handsome-sgm boy
         'A handsome boy'
    (c) Un joli   garçon
         a-m nice-sgm boy
         'A nice boy'
    (d) Un garçon beau   et   joli
         a-m boy   handsome-sgm and nice-sgm
         'A nice and handsome boy'

Each of the above examples instantiates a principle whereby smaller expressions occur before larger ones. Example (1) illustrates the effect of Pāṇini's compound rule, according to which in frozen expressions words with fewer syllables precede words with more. Sentence (2) exemplifies a constraint on the location of adverbial expressions in English, whereby the shorter expression must occur before the VP, while the longer one occurs preferably after the VP. Example (3) illustrates the combined effect of two rules of English—particle shift and heavy-NP shift: the larger the direct object NP is, the further to the right it occurs in the sentence. Example (4) presents some facts pertaining to adjective order in French: while most adjectives, e.g., *intelligent*, follow their head nouns, a small class of generally short adjectives, e.g., *beau* and *joli*, precede them; however, if two such adjectives are conjoined, e.g., *beau et joli*, the resulting longer adjectival phrase must follow its head.

  Each of the above examples thus illustrates an ordering of smaller expressions before larger ones; nevertheless, most linguists would probably argue that such examples are in some sense peripheral, failing to penetrate the 'hard core' of syntax. Let us now generalize the ordering principle to make reference to the size not of individual expressions, but rather of syntactic categories. For example, we shall say that the category of VP is larger than the category of subject NP since, in an overwhelming majority of actually occurring sentences, the VP expression is larger than its subject NP expression. The generalized ordering principle will now stipulate that smaller syntactic categories occur before larger ones. For example, it predicts that subject NPs will precede their VPs—and this prediction is borne out in the basic word orders of about 90 per cent of the world's languages.[12] In (5)–(8) below a number of constituent order universals are stated and exemplified, each of which instantiates the general principle whereby smaller syntactic categories precede larger ones:

(5) *Subject NP precedes VP*
[$_{NP}$ John] [$_{VP}$ eats durians every Monday and Thursday]
(6) *Topic NP precedes S*
[$_{NP}$ As for durians,] [$_S$ John eats them every Monday and Thursday]
(7) *WH-NP precedes S*
[$_{NP}$What] [$_S$ does John eat every Monday and Thursday]
(8) *VP precedes Sentential NP*
It [$_{VP}$ seems] [$_{NP}$ that John eats durians every Monday and Thursday]

The principle whereby smaller syntactic categories precede larger ones may also be invoked to account for a variety of constituent order phenomena generally subsumed under the title of 'mixed' word orders. For example, in many languages basic word order is different for pronouns than for corresponding full NPs; in all such cases the pronouns, which are smaller as a syntactic category, occur before the corresponding full NPs, which are larger. Consider the following:

(9) (a) Jean mange un durian   (French)
John eat-3sg a-m durian
'John is eating a durian'
(b) Jean le mange
John acc-3sgm eat-3sg
'John is eating it'
(10) (a) Natati oto leyehohanan   (Hebrew)
gave-1sg acc-3sgm to-John
'I gave it to John'
(b) Natati lo et hadurian
gave-1sg to-3sgm acc the-durian
'I gave him the durian'

In French, as in many other languages,[13] direct objects follow the verb if they are full NPs, as in (9a), but precede if they are pronouns, as in (9b). Similarly, in Hebrew the order of direct and indirect objects is determined, at least in part, by whether they are pronouns or full NPs: if one is a pronoun and the other a full NP, the pronoun will precede the full NP, as in (10a, b), regardless of which is the direct and which the indirect object.

This same principle may also account for the numerous violations of various 'serialization' principles that have been proposed in the literature[14] in order to account for constituent order universals. For example, it has been suggested that all nominal modifiers—quantifiers, adjectives, relative clauses—must line up on the same side of their nominal heads, either before, as in Japanese and Tamil, or after, as in Swahili and Fulani. Nevertheless, most languages just do not work that way; most languages have some modifiers preceding their nominal heads and others following. A closer look, however, reveals that when serialization is violated, it is almost invariably the case that smaller modifier categories precede their nominal heads, while larger modifier categories follow. As syntactic categories, quantifiers are smaller than adjectives, which in turn are smaller than relative clauses. Consider the state of affairs represented in (11) below:

(11)

	Quantifiers	*Adjectives*	*Relative Clauses*	*Examples*
(a)	precede	precede	precede	Japanese, Tamil

(b)	precede	precede	mixed	Finnish, Turkish
(c)	precede	precede	follow	English, Quechua
(d)	precede	mixed	follow	French, Italian
(e)	precede	follow	follow	Persian, Maori
(f)	mixed	follow	follow	Hebrew, Malay
(g)	follow	follow	follow	Swahili, Fulani

Whereas cases (a) and (g) exemplify perfect serialization, cases (b) to (f) violate serialization; however, they do so in a manner conforming with the principle whereby small syntactic categories precede large ones. For example, in English and Quechua—case (c)—the largest modifiers, relative clauses, follow their head nouns, whereas the smaller modifiers, adjectives and quantifiers, precede. This principle predicts that while languages may violate serialization, as in cases (b)–(f) above, they may not do so in a large number of other logically possible ways—for example, by having quantifiers and adjectives follow their heads but relative clauses precede, as in a hypothetical mirror-image English. This prediction is borne out cross-linguistically by an overwhelming majority of the world's languages.

As indicated by (1)–(11) above, a wide variety of linguistic phenomena instantiate a general linear-ordering principle whereby smaller items are made to precede larger ones. While in examples (1)–(4) the principle pertains directly to the phonological size of expressions, in examples (5)–(11) it makes reference to a more abstract notion of size attributed to syntactic categories. In both cases, however, the net effect is an ordering of linguistic material in which small precedes large.

In all the examples considered so far, a small-precedes-large order was obtained by taking as given the size of expressions or syntactic categories, and assigning them linear order in accordance. However, a variety of further linguistic phenomena conspires to effect a small-precedes-large order in an opposite manner, namely, by taking as given the linear order of expressions—either surface or basic—and increasing the size of expressions occurring further to the right. Consider, for example, the following two varieties of an existential construction in Hebrew:

(12) (a) Hasefer yešno
the-book is-3sgm
(b) Yěs et hasefer
is acc the-book
'The book is there'

Example (12) illustrates the role of agreement and case marking morphology in increasing the size of expressions occurring toward the ends of sentences. To begin, the above example instantiates the universal tendency[15] for agreement to proceed in a left-to-right direction: while in (12a) the existential particle *yeš* bears a subject-agreement suffix *-no*, in (12b) agreement with the now sentence-final subject NP is suspended. Secondly, this example illustrates a universal tendency[16] for case marking to increase the size of expressions occurring further to the right: whereas in (12a) the subject NP receives a phonologically zero nominative case marking, in (12b) the same NP is marked with the non-zero accusative preposition *et*. Thus both agreement suffix *-no* and case marking preposition *et* occur only when the expression they apply to is located to the *right* of its clause-mate; agreement and case marking thus functioning in unison to increase the size of the second expression, whichever it may be.

Other rules in language have a similar effect. Consider the following phenomena pertaining to conjunction:

(13)   Joel, Rommel, Dado, and David   (*Joel and Rommel, Dado, David)
(14)   He and them   (*Him and they)

Many languages, e.g., English, Hebrew, Turkish, Tagalog, have a rule whereby a conjoining element may occur, as in (13), between the last two conjuncts in a list but not elsewhere; however, no languages have a mirror-image rule according to which a conjunction may occur between the first two conjuncts but not elsewhere. Similarly, some languages, e.g., Nandi, certain dialects of Classical Hebrew, and also English, marginally, in the nominal system, cf. (14), have a rule whereby the second of two conjoined nouns is marked in the accusative case.[17] Observe that both the conjoining element and the accusative marker serve to increase the phonological size of the last of two or more conjuncts in a phrase.

Another rule functioning to increase the size of expressions occurring further to the right is the nuclear stress rule,[18] according to which the strongest lexical stress falls on the last of a sequence of words in a phrase or clause. For example, in (12a) the strongest stress is on *yešno*, in (12b) on *hasefer*, in (13) on *David*, and in (14) on *them*. Viewing stress as one particular instance of size,[19] the effect of the nuclear stress rule in examples such as these is thus identical to all the other rules considered above, namely to increase the size of the last of a given sequence of expressions.

As before, an even larger number of linguistic phenomena may be accounted for by generalizing the above principle, this time so that it makes reference not to the surface order of expressions but rather to basic constituent order; specifically, rules tend to increase the size of expressions occurring further to the right in basic order. Observe that in almost all the world's languages subject NPs precede direct object NPs in basic word order. The above principle may be invoked to explain the following universal hierarchies governing agreement and case marking morphology:

(15)   *NPs Triggering Verbal Agreement*[20]   *Examples*
    (a)   none   Chinese, Japanese
    (b)   subject NPs   English, Hebrew
    (c)   subject NPs and direct object NPs   Hungarian, Georgian
(16)   *NPs with Zero Case Marking*[21]   *Examples*
    (a)   none   Japanese, Georgian
    (b)   subject NPs   Bengali, Quechua
    (c)   subject NPs and direct object NPs   English, Malay

Since subject NPs generally precede direct object NPs in basic word order, they are more likely to precede the verb, and hence, subject-verb agreement—if obtaining—is more likely to be left-to-right than direct-object-verb agreement. In fact, as indicated in (15), languages may have subject-verb agreement without direct-object-verb agreement, e.g., English, Hebrew, but not direct-object-verb agreement without subject-verb agreement. Similarly, since subject NPs generally precede direct object NPs in basic word order, a non-zero accusative case marker will increase the size of an expression occurring further to the right than will a non-zero nominative case marker. Hence, as indicated in (16), languages may have zero nominative case marking and non-zero accusative case marking, e.g., Bengali and Quechua, but not non-zero nominative case marking and zero accusative case marking. Note the close parallel between agreement and case marking in the Hebrew existential constructions in (12) on the one hand, and the universal hierarchies in (15) and (16) on the other. While in (12) agreement and case marking are determined by the surface order of expressions, in (15) and (16) they are determined by basic constituent order. However, in both cases agreement and case marking function together to increase the size of expressions occurring further to the right, thereby contributing to the general principle whereby smaller items precede larger ones.

Examples (1)–(16) all illustrate the small-precedes-large principle in a domain that may be broadly characterized as sentence-level. However, reflexes of the same principle may also be observed at levels below and above that of the sentence. At a lower level consider, for example, the fact that—according to current theories of phonology[22]—syllables consist of an *onset*, containing the initial consonants, if any, plus a *rhyme*, containing the vocalic nucleus plus the final consonants, if any, for example:

(17)   [$_{onset}$ P] [$_{rhyme}$ it]

As phonological categories, onsets are clearly smaller than rhymes. In linear order, onsets always precede rhymes. Observe the striking parallel between the [consonant] [vowel consonant] parsing of syllables, as in (17), and the [noun] [verb noun] parsing of sentences, as in (5).[23] In both phonology and syntax, the most basic parsing yields a linear ordering in which a smaller category—onset or NP—precedes a larger category—rhyme or VP.

The same tendency for small units to precede large ones may be discerned, albeit in a considerably less systematic fashion, at a level above that of the sentence— namely, the text. Consider the following examples:[24]

(18)   (a)   [1]Space.
              [2]The final frontier.
              [3]These are the voyages of the starship Enterprise.
              [4]Its five year mission:
                  [a]to explore strange new worlds,
                  [b]to seek out new life, new civilizations,
                  [c]to boldly go where no man has gone before.

        (b)   [1]In bath he is Hylas and imprint of naked young foot on bathmat
              while I drink dry his cool water-stippled flesh;
              [2]Ganymede in dining-room, feeling the felony fascination of that
              fraîche face which tacitly disapproves over glass of milk that has
              white-mustached him;
              [3]Endymion in bedroom which steals illumination from his body's
              golden shimmer as if he were the source of all light, blinding animate
              and inanimate alike in a kind of perpetual myopia;
              [4]And triumphant Eros everywhere though not without protest:
                  [a]soft carpet savages his bare feet,
                  [b]sun in dim room hurts his eyes,
                  [c]he feels drafts on still, hushed days,
                  [d]and wasps/hornets/mosquitoes in screened house pierce his
                  pretty hide.

Both of the above texts exemplify a 'crescendo' effect very widespread in a variety of discourse types. Each text consists of four constituents of generally increasing size; moreover, in each text the fourth constituent contains, in turn, a sequence of three or four subconstituents, again of mostly increasing size. Like the sentence-level pheno- mena in (1)–(16) and the syllable-level phenomenon in (17), the above texts thus exemplify the general tendency for smaller items to precede larger ones.

The phenomena illustrated in (1)–(18) accordingly attest to the productivity and pervasiveness of the small-precedes-large principle in a variety of domains of ordinary natural language. Quite clearly, however, current models of generative grammar offer no means for this principle to be represented.[25] This is due, primarily, to the fact that the above phenomena straddle a large number of independent systems of rules and principles, thereby rendering highly implausible any unified formulation of the requisite generalization. Thus, for example, examining the above phenomena with respect to systems of rules, we find that the generalizations pertaining to violations of serialization in (11) belong to the base component, WH-fronting in (7) to the transformational component, the agreement and case marking phenomena in (15) and (16) to the morphology, heavy NP-shift in (3) to the interpretive PF component, and Paṇini's compound rule in (1) to the lexicon. Similarly, examining the same phenomena with respect to systems of principles, we find that most, perhaps all, of these systems are represented in the data in question: government theory, binding theory, X-bar theory, Case theory, and so on. Moreover, these systems do not suffice to cover the diversity of the phenomena considered above, specifically the facts in (17) and (18), lying solidly outside the scope of syntactic theory.[26]

Current models of grammatical theory thus do not provide the tools for representing the small-precedes-large principle. As things stand now, the facts have to be stated over and over again: in the base, transformational, and interpretive components; in the theories of government, X-bar, and Case. But how much of a loss is this? Adopting Chomsky's own criterion of explanatory adequacy: a substantial loss indeed. In accordance with explanatory adequacy, redundancy is to be avoided at all costs; if a structural parallel crops up in supposedly unrelated systems of grammar, this is 'probably an indication that something is wrong'[27] with whatever framework permits such redundancy. In the light of the diverse phenomena discussed above, the logical step is thus to 'factor out' the small-precedes-large principle from the several grammatical systems over which it is presently spread, and to locate it—perhaps with some related principles—within a separate autonomous system, interacting with other systems of grammar in order to yield the facts illustrated in (1)–(18).

The question arises where to locate this separate autonomous system within a 'map of the mind'; specifically, whether to include it as another 'module' within grammar alongside government, X-bar, Case, and other theories, or, alternatively, to extricate it entirely from grammatical theory and attribute it to another mental faculty. Example (18), pertaining to the organization of texts at a supra-sentential level, provides prima facie support for the latter alternative. In what follows, further evidence is adduced supporting the claim that the small-precedes-large principle falls outside the scope of grammatical theory.

We shall argue that this principle is an important component of man's prosodic faculty, providing data showing that the organization of linguistic material according to quantity is a characteristic feature of a variety of types of metered verse. Consider the following specimens of metered verse:

(19) Hó Hó Hó Chi Mính   (*Hó Ho Hó Chí Mính)

(20) Músic to héar, why héar'st thou músic sádly?[28]

(21) ¹Ońe twó thrée four fíve   (*Zéro óne two thrée four fíve
      ²Ónce I caúght a físh alíve   Í caúght físh alíve)

(22) ¹Sílence augménteth gríef, wríting increáseth ráge,
      ²Stáled are my thoúghts which lóved and lóst the wónder óf our áge.[29]

(23) ¹Šɔmɔ́h lišmɔmɔ́   'They have made it desolate,
      ²ʔɔbəlɔ́ ʕɔláy šəmemɔ́   and being desolate it mourneth unto me;
      ³Nəšámmɔ kɔl-hɔʔɔ́rɛṣ   the whole land is made desolate,
      ⁴Kí ʔén ʔíš šɔ́m ʕal-léb   because no man layeth it to heart.'[30]

Each of the above specimens of verse illustrates a metrical system upholding the small-precedes-large principle: a prosodic unit containing fewer syllables or words precedes a prosodic unit containing more syllables or words. Example (19) exemplifies a cross-linguistically widespread pattern of cheer in which a four-beat structure is made to accommodate five syllables: typically, the extra unstressed syllable—in the above example *Chi*—occurs between the third and fourth beats, and not, say, between the first and second beats—as, for example, in the unacceptable variant also indicated above. Thus cheers following the pattern of (19) consist of two halves, or hemistiches, the first containing two syllables and the second three.[31] A similar phenomenon is evident also in lines of iambic pentameter, of which (20) is a typical example. Lines of iambic pentameter generally consist of ten syllables, of which the even-numbered ones are stressed and the odd-numbered ones unstressed; example (20) displays two common variations from this pattern, exhibiting stress on the first rather than the second syllable, and an eleventh final unstressed syllable. Of interest to us is the position of the caesura—the line-internal 'break' indicated by a comma; in this example it occurs between the fourth and fifth syllables, thereby dividing the line into a first hemistich with four syllables and a second hemistich with seven. While in general the position of the caesura in lines of iambic pentameter is free, there exists a statistically significant tendency for the caesura to occur towards the beginning of the line, thereby parsing the line in such a way that the first hemistich contains fewer syllables than the second.[32].

Examples (21) and (22) illustrate metrical schemes in which the first line contains fewer syllables than the second. Example (21) presents a common four-beat couplet pattern typical of cheers and nursery rhymes in a variety of languages. While the first line contains five syllables, in a pattern identical to that of example (19), the second line contains seven. A mirror-image pattern with seven syllables in the first line but only five in the second is ill-formed.[33] Example (22) is an instance of Poulters Measure, in which a line of iambic hexameter, containing twelve syllables, is followed by a line of iambic heptameter, containing fourteen syllables. Thus both (21) and (22) exemplify metrical schemes upholding the small-precedes-large principle, with a line containing fewer syllables preceding a line containing more.

Finally, example (23) in Biblical Hebrew illustrates a common quatrain pattern in which the fourth and last line contains more words—or, equivalently, stressed syllables—than each of the preceding three lines. In the Biblical verse the first three lines contain two, three, and two words respectively, while the fourth line contains five words. Note the similar crescendo effect in (23), a specimen of metered verse, and the two examples of prose in (18)—in all three cases the last of a sequence of four constituents is the largest.[34] Each of the above five examples of metered verse exemplifies a state of affairs in which prosodic units containing fewer syllables or words precede prosodic units containing more. Examples (19)–(23) thus exemplify five distinct metrical schemes, each of which upholds the small-precedes-large principle.

The small-precedes-large principle thus underlies a variety of metrical systems governing the form of metered verse. Quite clearly, however, the regular patterns formed by this principle are, like other metrical regularities, in no sense of the word grammatical. Prosodists have traditionally assumed that a unit of metered verse exhibits, simultaneously, independent prosodic and grammatical structures.[35] Within a generative framework, autonomous prosodic and grammatical structures are generated independently of each other, subsequently associated by means of mapping or correspondence rules to yield units of metered verse.[36] Underlying most generative theories of prosody—as well as some pre-generative ones—is the assumption that man is endowed with two autonomous mental faculties—grammar and prosody— joining forces to produce metered verse.[37] Most importantly, metric schemes upholding the small-precedes-large principle, such as those illustrated in (19)–(23), are attributed to the faculty of prosody; their rightful place is thus within prosodic theory, and not a theory of grammar.[38]

Consider, now, the fact—previously demonstrated—that the small-precedes-large principle underlies not only a variety of metrical schemes but also a wide range of phenomena within the realm of ordinary, non-stylized language, e.g., those illustrated in examples (1)–(18). Given that the small-precedes-large principle is part of man's prosodic competence, considerations of explanatory adequacy and the avoidance of redundancy dictate that the ordinary language phenomena upholding this principle also be attributed to the prosodic faculty. The phenomena illustrated in (1)–(18) thus fall within the scope of prosodic theory, and outside the scope of a theory of grammar.

To this point, instances of the small-precedes-large principle have been adduced solely from the domain of natural language, either ordinary or stylized. Strong further support for the claim that phenomena exemplifying this principle lie beyond the scope of grammatical theory may be obtained by examination of additional instances of the principle occurring solidly outside the realm of natural language. Consider, first, artificial languages of the type commonly used to express mathematical or scientific statements, or for a variety of other purposes. Examples (24)–(26) are of simple expressions in basic mathematical notation:

(24) $a(b+c)$

(25) $\sin x = x - \dfrac{x^3}{3!} + \dfrac{x^5}{5!} - \dfrac{x^7}{7!} + \dots$

(26) $e = mc^2$

Example (24) represents the product of two terms, a and $(b+c)$. Since multiplication is commutative, it is equivalent to the expression $(b+c)a$. However, most users of mathematical notation evince a stylistic preference for the expression represented in (24), where a constituent containing one syllable precedes a constituent containing four, over the reverse-order expression, in which a four-symbol constituent precedes a constituent with only one. Similarly, in (25) the relation of equality is symmetric; hence the expression is equivalent to one in which the terms on both sides of the 'equals' sign are interchanged. However, most mathematics textbooks will cite the series expansion as in (25), where a constituent with two symbols, $\sin x$, precedes a constituent with several, and not in the logically equivalent reverse order. Finally, the well-known relativistic formula (26) encapsulates the phenomena represented in (24) and (25). Why not $e = c^2 m$, or $mc^2 = e$, or $c^2 m = e$? Because in (26), e—one symbol—precedes mc^2—three symbols; moreover, within mc^2, m—one symbol— precedes c^2—two symbols. Examples (24)–(26) thus provide clear instantiations of the small-precedes-large principle in artificial languages.

In many further cases the small-precedes-large principle effects not just a

language may be accounted for in terms of communicative function, for example, the distinctions between topic and comment, foreground and background; typically, such properties will be shared by language and by other systems of a semiotic nature.[50]

The faculty of algebra may be posited to underlie various abstract structures, e.g., groups, rings, fields, Boolean algebras, shared by diverse domains of mental activity such as mathematical reasoning, vision and language. Regarding the first of these, Chomsky notes that 'In mathematics certain areas seem to correspond to exceptional human aptitudes: number theory, spatial intuition.'[51] These very same areas of mathematics are heavily exploited in the domain of vision. Consider, for example, what is involved in recognizing a certain object, say John's face, as seen from a variety of angles and distances. Clearly, we must have knowledge of the metric properties of two- and three-dimensional Euclidean spaces, in order to be able to take a two-dimensional image and reconstruct a three-dimensional object. Moreover, we must have knowledge of the group-theoretic properties of the set of rotations of a given object in space, in order to be able to recognize a number of different images as being of the same object.[52] Finally, the same abstract structures occur throughout language, for example, in model-theoretic semantics, which relies heavily on the notion of Boolean algebra.[53] Rather than positing knowledge of these algebraic structures redundantly, within mathematics, vision and language, the abstract structures shared by these and other domains of mental activity may be abstracted out of the respective mental faculties and assigned uniquely to algebraic competence—an autonomous mental faculty which, like grammar and vision (but not mathematical reasoning), is tacit, and acquired automatically in early childhood.[54]

We may thus view any given sentence as representing a joint product of these and probably other mental faculties. Consider, for example, sentence (5), reproduced below as (35):

(35)   John eats durians every Monday and Thursday.

This sentence embodies a variety of phenomena accountable for within different theoretical frameworks. For example, grammatical theory provides for its syntactic parsing into NP *John* and VP *eats durians every Monday and Thursday*; prosodic theory accounts for the main sentence stress occurring on *Thursday*; pragmatic theory may characterize *John* as topic and the remainder of the sentence as comment; and algebraic theory accounts for the fact that sentence (35) entails that John eats durians every Monday. However, other phenomena may be less straightforwardly attributable to one theory or another. For example, the fact that in (35) the NP precedes the VP is attributed by Chomsky to grammatical theory, by many other linguists to pragmatic theory, but by us, in section 2, to a theory of prosody.

(However, another possibility must also be acknowledged, namely that everybody is right. Recall the candle burning in the corner of the room: why is it burning? Because chemical combustion is taking place, or because somebody lit it, or because it is Sabbath eve? In some sense all three explanations are equally valid. Why should not the same be true also for the constituent order exhibited by sentence (35)? Perhaps the NP precedes the VP because of a grammatical phrase-structure rule *and* because topics generally precede comments, *and* because small items generally precede large ones. If, however, grammar, pragmatics and prosody are autonomous mental faculties, this would mean that the mind is horrendously redundant. Perhaps this is the case. After all, the human digestive system has its appendix, a useless relic of an earlier evolutionary stage: why should not the mind, surely of greater complexity than the digestive system, have its useless evolutionary relics too? Possibly, at an earlier stage of the language, NP–VP constituent order was prosodically (or pragmatically) motivated, but, as time elapsed, it became grammaticalized. Scenarios such as these are quite plausible. Nevertheless, lacking evidence in support of specific proposals, the optimal course would still seem to be striving to avoid redundancy wherever possible. As a result, if phenomena such as the NP–VP constituent order of sentence (35) can be related—via prosodic theory—to phenomena in artificial language and music, we shall conclude that they ought to be excluded from the scope of grammatical theory.)

It should be emphasized that this view—whereby language is a joint product of several interacting mental faculties—is entirely consistent with the autonomy thesis, according to which each such faculty is endowed with unique structural properties distinguishing it from all other faculties. The relationship between these two assumptions is made clear in the following passage by Lightfoot. Commenting on John Searle's contention that grammatical theory should make mention of the communicative function of certain phenomena such as the distribution of *please* in English, Lightfoot notes:

> if the distribution of *please* can be accounted for by a pragmatic rule, that would support the autonomy thesis, since one would not want the syntax to explain the distribution redundantly. In general, the autonomy thesis (or 'modularity') is supported when one has an independent (e.g. pragmatic) account of some phenomenon, permitting the syntax to avoid any consideration of it.[55]

Lightfoot's observations are, of course, equally germane to the prosodic and other non-grammatical accounts of linguistic phenomena suggested herein.

We are thus faced with the alternative of accepting Chomsky's methodological assumptions—the autonomy thesis, the grammar-language distinction, and the view that language is a joint product of a number of mental faculties—but at the same time rejecting current models of grammatical theory in favour of a theory of considerably narrower scope, one that excludes phenomena that are amenable to non-grammatical—e.g., prosodic, aesthetic, pragmatic, algebraic—explanations. In addition, we are faced with a further methodological moral of far-reaching consequence. Within the generative framework it has been argued that in order to construct a grammar of English, it is necessary to investigate other languages, thereby constructing a universal grammar from which the grammar of English may be obtained by setting the values of certain parameters.[56] The arguments presented herein lead to the even stronger conclusion that in order to construct a universal grammar—in particular, in order to determine what belongs within grammatical theory and what does not—it is necessary to investigate not only language but also a variety of other domains of human mental activity, for example, mathematical reasoning, vision, music. Specifically, in order to determine whether a given phenomenon is grammatical, it is necessary to search a variety of domains of non-verbal mental activity for possible structural analogues; only after the search has been conducted and no analogues found is it possible to conclude that the phenomenon is indeed grammatical. What this means is that a theory of grammar cannot be developed in isolation, but only in conjunction with theories of other mental faculties, such as prosody, aesthetics, pragmatics and algebra.[57]

This, I believe, is the message implicit in Chomsky's remark, cited in section 1, that the scope of grammatical theory may be determined 'only in the context of a broader study of a system that incorporates the given idealized organ as a part.' If this proposal is heeded—and the arguments presented herein suggest that it should be—

then conscientious linguists are going to have to spend a lot of time and effort familiarizing themselves with new and diverse disciplines of study.

ACKNOWLEDGEMENTS

I am very grateful to Noam Chomsky for extensive comments on an earlier version of this paper. In several footnotes, I have cited some of these comments and added further observations of my own, attempting to establish a rudimentary dialogue in the spirit of the format adopted by this volume. The present version of this paper has also benefited from helpful comments by Edith Moravcsik and Betsy Ritter.

NOTES

1   Chomsky has taken issue with the above sentence, maintaining that the autonomy thesis 'is not, as stated later several times [in this article], an "assumption" that I make; rather, it is a conclusion that I draw, tentatively.' Indeed, as evidenced by the above-cited passage, Chomsky does hold the autonomy thesis to be an empirical hypothesis. However, to the best of my knowledge there have been no explicit attempts to put this hypothesis to the test: nobody has looked seriously at music, vision, etc., and then asked if these mental faculties possess analogues of those structural characteristics supposedly unique to grammar. In the absence of such attempts, the autonomy thesis assumes the de facto status of a working assumption, even if its empirical basis is continually (and correctly) proclaimed. I shall, accordingly, continue to refer to the autonomy thesis as an 'assumption'; nothing crucial in this chapter will hinge on this terminological choice.

2   Cited in Reiber (1983, pp. 33–4). For more detailed discussion of the autonomy thesis see Chomsky (1975a, 1975b, 1980).

3   Chomsky (1981, p. 5); cf. also Chomsky (1982a, p. 6).

4   Chomsky (1982b, p. 117). For other formulations of this position see also Chomsky (1980, pp. 82–3, 127, 217) and Chomsky (1982a, p. 14).

5   Chomsky has objected to my contention that his views have undergone evolution, claiming that 'I have never made any such assumption . . . about a grammar specifying WF sentences.' In support of this objection he cites the 'elaborate theory of degrees of grammaticalness' developed in *Logical Structure of Linguistic Theory* (Chomsky, 1955). However, what is at issue here is not the possibility that grammaticality might be a matter of degree, but rather that grammaticality might fail to be recursively enumerable—and on this score Chomsky's views have indeed changed. Thus in *Syntactic Structures* Chomsky asserts that 'The grammar of L [is] a device that generates all of the grammatical sequences of L and none of the ungrammatical ones' (Chomsky, 1957, p. 13). However, in *Rules and Representations* he is willing to entertain the possibility that ' . . . a grammar does not in itself define a language . . . ' and that ' . . . languages may not be recursively definable' (Chomsky, 1980, p. 126; this view is foreshadowed also in Chomsky, 1976, p. 342). Surely this constitutes a change in view. In Gil (1984) I provide what appears to be conclusive evidence that Chomsky's latter view is the correct one. Our quibble, then, is on a point of history, and bears no substantive consequences.

6   Chomsky (1980, p. 90).

7   Chomsky (1975b, p. 43).

8   This point is made by, among others, Lightfoot (1980, pp. 142–3).

9   Chomsky (1980, p. 60).

10   Aristotle's *Poetics*, Chapter 4, as translated by Leon Golden.

11   In language the tendency for smaller items to precede larger ones has been commented upon by, among others, Malkiel (1959), Bolinger (1962), Hetzron (1972), Cooper and Ross (1975) and Dik (1978). The full extent of the phenomenon has not, however, received due attention.

12   According to Keenan (1978), about 90 per cent of the world's languages have one of the subject-initial basic word orders, SOV or SVO.

13   For example, Italian, Greek, Swahili, Guarani—cf. Greenberg (1963) Universal 25.

14   For example, Hawkins (1979), Jackendoff (1977b), Keenan (1978), Lehmann (1973), Vennemann (1973) and many others.

15 See, for example, Greenberg (1963) Universal 33, and Moravcsik (1978, p. 365).

16 For discussion of this tendency see Gil (1982a).

17 For more detailed discussion of these facts see Gil (1982a).

18 See Chomsky and Halle (1968).

19 Experimental studies—cf. Lehiste (1970)—have revealed three phonetic correlates of stress: intensity, duration, fundamental frequency. Of these three parameters, the first two relate clearly to the notion of size or quantity.

20 See Moravcsik (1978, p. 364) for further discussion.

21 These facts are captured, in part, in Greenberg (1963) Universal 38.

22 For example, Selkirk (1980), Cairns and Feinstein (1982).

23 This point is discussed further in Gil and Radzinski (to appear).

24 The first text is the well-known introduction to the American television serial *Star Trek*. The second text is from a novel by Casimir Dukahz: *The Asbestos Diary* (New York, Oliver Layton Press, 1966, p. 143). In both examples the parsing of the text into constituents is my own, based in the first example on the long pauses occurring between adjacent constituents, and in both examples on the obvious syntactic and semantic parallelisms.

25 Chomsky comments that this statement 'is correct'; however, the conclusions he draws from it are different from my own (cf. note 45 below).

26 Data such as those cited in (1)–(18) may thus appear to run counter to the modularity of grammatical theory; specifically, the principle of *phonology-free syntax* as advocated by Zwicky (1969) and Zwicky and Pullum (1983). Hetzron (1972) cites similar data to make precisely this point. However, since, as I suggest here, the small-precedes-large principle is extra-grammatical, a product of man's prosodic competence, the facts in (1)–(18) do not constitute an 'impermissible interaction' between phonological and syntactic components: they are entirely consistent with the principle of phonology-free syntax and the modularity of grammatical theory.

27 Chomsky (1982b, p. 76).

28 Shakespeare, *The Sonnets*, Number 8.

29 Fulke Greville, Lord Brooke, *Epitaph on Sir Philip Sydney*.

30 The Old Testament of the Bible, Jeremiah 12:11; translation according to the *King James Authorized Version*.

31 For examples and analyses of cheers such as (19) in English, Hebrew and other languages, see Gil (1978) and Stein and Gil (1980, pp. 194–5).

32 See Tsur (1977, Ch. 2) for a statistical analysis supporting this tendency in lines of iambic pentameter in English and Hebrew.

33 For additional examples and discussion of this metrical scheme, see Gil (1978) and Stein and Gil (1980, p. 209).

34 For a detailed prosodic analysis of (23) and other specimens of Biblical Hebrew verse exhibiting the same pattern, see Gil and Shoshany (to appear) and Shoshany (to appear b). Other examples of this quatrain structure are discussed in Burling (1966), Stein and Gil (1980, pp. 205–6), Gil and Shoshany (1984), Gil (to appear c) and Shoshany (to appear a).

35 This assumption dates back at least as far as the traditional Arab grammarians, who distinguished between abstract metrical patterns, called *wuṣul*, and particular lines of verse instantiating them.

36 See, for example, Halle and Keyser (1971), Kiparsky (1975, 1977), Stein (1975) and Stein and Gil (1980). But for a minority viewpoint, according to which prosodic structures are not independently generated but rather parasitic upon grammatical ones, cf. Bierwisch (1970).

37 See, for example, Halle and Keyser (1971, p. 140), Kiparsky (1975, p. 577), Chomsky, as cited in Reiber (1983, p. 42), and for a more explicit formulation of this assumption Gil and Shoshany.

38 However, many theories of prosody have chosen to ignore facts such as those illustrated in (19)–(23), restricting their attention to patterns of suprasegmental phenomena such as stress. For an explicit account of the small-precedes-large principle within a generative prosodic framework, see Stein and Gil (1980) and Gil and Shoshany (1984, to appear).

39 From Schubert's Symphony No. 5 in B flat. For an analysis of the rhythmic structure of this piece see Cooper and Meyer (1960, p. 103).

40 Cooper and Meyer (1960, p. 61). As observed, however, in Stein and Gil (1980), music—as opposed to recited verse—is often characterized by trochaic, i.e., beginning-accented structures, at lower hierarchic levels.

41 Lightfoot (1980, p. 142).

42 For some proposals in this direction see Stein and Gil (1980), Gil and Shoshany (1984, to appear) and

Gil (to appear a) from a linguistic perspective, and from a musicological viewpoint Jackendoff (1977a), Jackendoff and Lerdahl (1980) and Lerdahl and Jackendoff (1977, 1983).

43 These mapping rules are formalized within the theoretical framework developed in Stein and Gil (1980) and Gil and Shoshany (1984, to appear) in terms of *prosodic markers*, in particular, the prosodic marker NUMBER OF SYLLABLES.

44 A number of variants of the standard generative framework—for example, Sanders (1975a, 1975b) and Keenan and Faltz (1978, 1980)—have questioned the central role played by linear order within generative theory, choosing instead to abstract linear order away from other grammatical phenomena. More recently, and within the orthodox generative framework, Stowell (1982) and Chomsky (1982a, 1982b) have raised the possibility that linear order may be assigned not in the base component but rather in terms of other factors.

45 In his comments on this section of the chapter Chomsky agrees that the small-precedes-large principle 'should not be part of grammar'; however, he rejects the conclusions that I draw *vis-à-vis* grammatical theory, suggesting instead that the examples in (1)–(18) should be accounted for within the framework of a theory of markedness:

> . . . your short-precedes-long principle is quite plausible, but it isn't at all clear how invoking it in some other (or super-) system would change the writing of grammars or the formulation of UG at all. What the examples suggest is that your principle is extra-linguistic, and may enter somehow into the theory of markedness, though exactly how is far from clear.

And in another passage:

> I would change nothing, say, in *Lectures on Government and Binding* or *Sound Pattern of English* except to say that some of the markedness principles might be related to the small-precedes-large principle that seems to hold of other cognitive faculties. As far as I can see, everything else remains the same.

To deal adequately with Chomsky's counterproposal would require much more space than is presently available. I shall, therefore, restrict myself to two preliminary comments on Chomsky's suggestion. First, a 'markedness' account of the data does nothing to overcome the problem of redundancy, since markedness is part of grammar. (However, it is quite conceivable that this is the correct account of at least some of the facts. Consider a plausible diachronic scenario whereby some of the effects of the prosodic small-precedes-large principle, e.g., subject-NP-precedes-VP constituent order, become grammaticalized. In such a case, grammar takes over from prosody, but continues to uphold the small-precedes-large principle: the resulting grammatical rule is accordingly characterized as 'unmarked' with respect to the small-precedes-large principle. Quite clearly, much detailed work is required to adjudicate between such scenarios.)

My second comment on Chomsky's counterproposal is not substantive, but a state-of-the-art qualm regarding the theory of markedness. As is well known, there is no worked out theory of markedness, only some general proposals as to what such a theory might involve. On the other hand, there does exist an explicit theory of prosody—cf. Stein and Gil (1980), Gil and Shoshany (1984, to appear)—in which the small-precedes-large principle may be couched in a natural way. Hence, if one wishes to propose a markedness account of the principle, one must assume the burden of fleshing out the details, in order to show explicitly how this may be done. Until this is acheived, the existing prosodic explanation will remain more attractive.

46 Lightfoot (1980, p. 143).

47 Lightfoot (1980, p. 142).

48 See Gil (to appear a) for discussion of another such structural property, yielding a prosodic typology of languages involving correlations between basic word orders and syllable structure, phonological segment inventory, and the existence of phonemic tonal distinctions.

49 For further discussion see Gil and Shoshany (to appear), where it is suggested that the aesthetic faculty may subsume the faculty of poetics as posited, for example, by Bierwisch (1970) and Tsur (1983a, 1983b).

50 Much recent work in linguistics—cf. Givón (1979), Kuno (1980), Hopper and Thompson (1980) and others—has been devoted to showing how various putative rules of grammar may be more insightfully accounted for in terms of communicative function. Such arguments are often couched in strong anti-Chomskyan terms; however, they need not be: as suggested above, there is no reason not to suppose that some linguistic phenomena may be grammatical while others are explicable in terms of communicative function. Chomsky, himself, has on numerous occasions—e.g. Chomsky (1977a, p. 78), Chomsky (1980, pp. 59, 90, 206, 224–5)—made reference to the existence of a pragmatic competence underlying language use.

51 Chomsky (1977b, p. 67). For further discussion of the relationship between the faculties of mathematical reasoning and grammar, see Gil (1983).

52 Although Chomsky makes numerous references to the faculty of vision, e.g., Chomsky (1977b, pp. 46, 49, 51–3), Chomsky (1982b, pp. 8–11), I have found only one instance—Chomsky (1975b)—where he draws attention in passing to possible structural analogues between vision and language. Elsewhere, e.g., Chomsky (1975b, p. 229, footnote 7), he argues against the existence of interesting structural parallels.

53 See, for example, Keenan and Faltz (1978, 1980) and Keenan (1981, 1983). Although Chomsky has disassociated himself from model-theoretic approaches to semantics, the phenomena shown by Keenan and Faltz to be Boolean fall clearly within the domain of Logical Form, as defined in Chomsky (1976), and ipso facto within the domain of grammatical theory, as perceived by Chomsky.

54 Chomsky comments that 'the fact that one finds Boolean phenomena hardly seems surprising. How could it be otherwise?' But I am not familiar with any explicit arguments to the effect that Boolean structures—in language and elsewhere—are a logical, rather than a biological cognitive necessity. In at least one limited domain, namely, the morphosyntactic expression of the so-called 'logical connectives', it is not even clear whether Boolean properties are a logical *or* a biological necessity: as shown in Gil (1982b, Ch. 9), an American Indian language, Maricopa, has no expressions corresponding to the Boolean connectives represented by English *and* and *or*.

    Chomsky goes on to state that '. . . it has always been assumed in generative grammar . . . that the theory of grammar and its mental representation involves some elements of mathematics. That's central to the whole approach to the language faculty as a system of rules and representations, a computational system of some sort.' This is obviously true. What I am suggesting, however, is that grammar 'involves' mathematics in a particular way, namely, by making use of an algebraic faculty which itself lies outside grammar.

    For a further proposal regarding a structural principle belonging to the algebraic faculty, namely, X-bar Structure, see Gil (to appear d).

55 Lightfoot (1979, pp. 43–4).

56 Of course, generative grammar has also gained a justified reputation of doing just the opposite: investigating English in order to establish properties of universal grammar. These two approaches are consistent with each other, and are both sound. However, in Gil (1982b), I argue that greater emphasis than is currently fashionable should be placed on the empirical investigation of a wider range of typologically diverse languages.

57 See Gil (to appear b) for further support for this conclusion, based on an analysis of NP configurationality and the count-mass distinction.

REFERENCES

Bierwisch, Manfred (1970) 'Poetics and linguistics', in Freeman, D. C. (Ed.), *Linguistics and Literary Style*, New York, Holt, Rinehart and Winston, pp. 96–115.

Bolinger, Dwight L. (1962) 'Binomials and pitch accent', *Lingua*, **11**, pp. 34–44.

Burling, Robin (1966) 'The metrics of children's verse: A cross-linguistic study', *American Anthropologist*, **68**, pp. 1418–41.

Cairns, Charles E. and Feinstein, Mark H. (1982) 'Markedness and the theory of syllable structure', *Linguistic Inquiry*, **13**, pp. 193–225.

Chomsky, Noam A. (1955) *The Logical Structure of Linguistic Theory*, Cambridge. Mass., MIT Press.

Chomsky, Noam A. (1957) *Syntactic Structures*, The Hague, Mouton.

Chomsky, Noam A. (1975a) 'Questions of form and interpretation', *Linguistic Analysis*, **1**, pp. 75–109.

Chomsky, Noam A. (1975b) *Reflections on Language*, New York, Pantheon Books.

Chomsky, Noam A. (1976) 'Conditions on rules of grammar', *Linguistic Analysis*, **2**, pp. 301–51.

Chomsky, Noam A. (1977a) *Essays on Form and Interpretation*, New York, North Holland.

Chomsky, Noam A. (1977b) *Language and Responsibility*, New York, Pantheon Books.

Chomsky, Noam A. (1980) *Rules and Representations*, New York, Columbia University Press.

Chomsky, Noam A. (1981) *Lectures on Government and Binding*, Dordrecht, Foris.

Chomsky, Noam, A. (1982a) *Some Concepts and Consequences of the Theory of Government and Binding*, Cambridge, Mass., MIT Press.

Chomsky, Noam, A. (1982b) *The Generative Enterprise: A Discussion With Riny Huybregts and Henk van Riemsdijk*, Dordrecht, Foris.

Chomsky, Noam, A. and Halle, Morris (1968) *The Sound Pattern of English*, New York, Harper and Row.

Cooper, Grosvenor and Meyer, Leonard B. (1960) *The Rhythmic Structure of Music*, Chicago, Ill., University of Chicago Press.

Cooper, William E. and Ross, John R. (1975) 'World order', in Grossman, R. E., San, L. J. and Vance, T. J. (Eds), *Papers from the Parasession on Functionalism*, Chicago, Ill., Chicago Linguistic Society, pp. 63–111.

Dik, Simon C. (1978) *Functional Grammar*, North Holland Linguistic Series, Amsterdam, North Holland.

Gil, David (1978) 'Hašofet Ben Zona: Hebrew soccer cheers and jeers', *Maledicta*, **2**, pp. 129–45.

Gil, David (1982a) 'Case marking, phonological size, and linear order', in Hopper, P. J. and Thompson, S. A. (Eds), *Studies in Transitivity, Syntax and Semantics 15*, New York, Academic Press, pp. 117–41.

Gil, David (1982b) *Distributive Numerals*, PhD dissertation, University of California, Los Angeles.

Gil, David (1983) 'Intuitionism, transformational generative grammar, and mental acts', *Studies in History and Philosophy of Science*, **14**, pp. 231–54.

Gil, David (1984) 'Remarks on nonrecursivity in syntax', *Linguistic Inquiry*, **15**, pp. 344–8.

Gil, David (to appear a) 'A prosodic typology of language', *Folia Linguistica*, **20**.

Gil, David (to appear b) 'Definiteness, noun-phrase-configurationality, and the count-mass distinction', in Reuland, E. and Meulen, A. G. B. ter (Eds), *The Representation of (In)definiteness*, Cambridge, Mass., MIT Press.

Gil, David (to appear c) 'The *Muwaššaḥ*: Artistic convention or cognitive universal', in Somekh, S. (Ed.), *Studies in Classical Arabic Poetics and Poetry* (tentative title), Leiden, Brill.

Gil, David (to appear d) 'What does grammar include?', *Theoretical Linguistics*.

Gil, David and Radzinski, Daniel (to appear) 'Georgian syllable onsets: Some arguments for unordered hierarchic phonological structures', in *Phonologica 1984, Proceedings of the Fifth International Phonology Meeting*, Cambridge, Cambridge University Press and Poznan, Adam Mickiewicz University.

Gil, David and Shoshany, Ronit (1984) 'On the scope of prosodic theory', in Dressler, W. U., Pfeiffer, O. E. and Rennison, J. R. (Eds), *Discussion Papers, Fifth International Phonology Meeting, June 25–28 1984, Eisenstadt, Austria*, Wiener Linguistische Gazette, Supplement Beiheft **3**, pp. 78–82.

Gil, David and Shoshany, Ronit (to appear) *Aspects of Prosodic Theory, Studies in Biblical Hebrew Poetry*, Albany, State University of New York Press.

Givón, Talmy (1979) *On Understanding Grammar*, New York, Academic Press.

Greenberg, Joseph H. (1963) 'Some universals of grammar with particular reference to the order of meaningful elements', in Greenberg, J. H. (Ed.), *Universals of Language*, Cambridge, Mass., MIT Press, pp. 73–113.

Halle, Morris and Keyser, Samuel J. (1971) *English Stress: Its Form, Its Growth, and Its Role in Verse*, New York, Harper and Row.

Hawkins, John A. (1979) 'Implicational universals as predicators of word order change', *Language*, **55**, pp. 618–48.

Hetzron, Robert (1972) 'Phonology in syntax', *Journal of Linguistics*, **8**, pp. 251–65.

Hopper, Paul J. and Thompson, Sandra A. (1980) 'Transitivity in grammar and discourse', *Language*, **56**, pp. 251–99.

Jackendoff, Ray (1977a) 'Review of *The Unanswered Question* by Leonard Bernstein', *Language*, **53**, pp. 883–94.

Jackendoff, Ray (1977b) $\bar{X}$ *Syntax: A Study of Phrase Structure*, Cambridge, Mass., MIT Press.

Jackendoff, Ray and Lerdahl, Fred (1980) *A Deep Parallel between Music and Language*, Bloomington, Ind., Indiana University Linguistic Club.

Keenan, Edward L. (1978) 'On surface form and logical form', in Kachru, B. B. (Ed.), *Linguistics in the Seventies: Directions and Prospects*, Studies in the Linguistics Sciences 8.2, University of Illinois, pp. 163–203.

Keenan, Edward L. (1981) 'A Boolean approach to semantics', in Groenendijk, J. A. G., Janssen, T. M. V. and Stokhof, M. B. J. (Eds), *Formal Methods in the Study of Language*, Dordrecht, Reidel, pp. 343–79.

Keenan, Edward L. (1983) 'Boolean algebra for linguists', in Mordechay, S. (Ed.), *UCLA Working Papers in Semantics*, University of California, Los Angeles, pp. 1–75.

Keenan, Edward L. and Faltz, Leonard M. (1978) *Logical Types for Natural Language*, UCLA Occasional Papers in Linguistics **3**, University of California, Los Angeles.

Keenan, Edward L. and Faltz, Leonard M. (1980) 'A new approach to quantification in natural language', in Rohrer, C. (Ed.), *Time, Tense and Quantifiers*, Linguistische Arbeiten **83**, Tubingen, Max Niemeyer Verlag, pp. 223–68.

Kiparsky, Paul (1975) 'Stress, syntax, and meter', *Language*, **51**, pp. 576–616.

Kiparsky, Paul (1977) 'The rhythmic structure of English verse', *Linguistic Inquiry*, **8**, pp. 189–247.

Kuno, Susumu (1980) 'Functional syntax', in Moravcsik, E. A. and Wirth, J. R. (Eds), *Current Approaches to Syntax, Syntax and Semantics 13*, New York, Academic Press, pp. 117–35.

Lehiste, Ilse (1970) *Suprasegmentals*, Cambridge, Mass., MIT Press.

Lehmann, Winfred P. (1973) 'A structural principle of language and its implications', *Language*, **49**, pp. 47–66.

Lerdahl, Fred and Jackendoff, Ray (1977) 'Toward a formal theory of tonal music', *Journal of Music Theory*, **21**, pp. 111–71.

Lerdahl, Fred and Jackendoff, Ray (1983) *A Generative Theory of Tonal Music*, Cambridge, Mass., MIT Press.

Lightfoot, David W. (1979) *Principles of Diachronic Syntax*, Cambridge, Cambridge University Press.

Lightfoot, David W. (1980) 'Trace theory and explanation', in Moravcsik, E. A. and Wirth, J. R. (Eds), *Current Approaches to Syntax*, New York, Academic Press, pp. 137–66.

Malkiel, Yakov (1959) 'Studies in irreversible binomials', *Lingua*, **8**, pp. 113–60.

Moravcsik, Edith A. (1978) 'Agreement', in Greenberg, J. H. (Eds), *Universals of Human Language, Volume 4*, Stanford, Calif., Stanford University Press, pp. 331–74.

Reiber, Robert W. (1983) *Dialogues on the Psychology of Language and Thought*, New York, Plenum Press.

Sanders, Gerald A. (1975a) *Invariant Ordering*, The Hague, Mouton.

Sanders, Gerald A. (1975b) 'On the explanation of constituent order universals', in Li, C. N. (Ed.), *Word Order and Word Order Change*, Austin, Tex., University of Texas Press, pp. 389–436.

Selkirk, Elisabeth O. (1980) 'The role of prosodic categories in English word stress', *Linguistic Inquiry*, **11**, pp. 563–605.

Shoshany, Ronit (to appear a) 'A prosodic explanation for a textual alteration in Bialik and Ravnitzky's "Sepher Haagada"', in Shamir, Z. (Ed.), *Research Papers on the Works of C. N. Bialik* (tentative title), Tel Aviv, Dvir (in Hebrew).

Shoshany, Ronit (to appear b) 'Prosodic structures in Jeremiah's poetry', *Folia Linguistica Historica*.

Stein, David N. (1975) *On the Basis of English Iambic Pentameter*, PhD dissertation, Urbana, Ill., University of Illinois.

Stein, David and Gil, David (1980) 'Prosodic structures and prosodic markers', *Theoretical Linguistics*, **7**, pp. 173–240.

Stowell, Tim (1982) 'A formal theory of configurational phenomena', in Pustejovsky, J. and Sells, P. (Eds), *Proceedings of the Twelfth Annual Meeting of the North Eastern Linguistic Society*, Amherst, pp. 235–257.

Tsur, Reuven (1977) *A Perception-Oriented Theory of Metre*, Tel Aviv, Tel Aviv University, Porter Institute for Poetics and Semiotics.

Tsur, Reuven (1983a) *Meaning and Emotion in Poetry: On the Roots of Poetic Intuition*, Tel Aviv, Tel Aviv University, Katz Research Institute for Hebrew Literature.

Tsur, Reuven (1983b) 'What is cognitive poetics?', *Papers in Cognitive Poetics* **1**, Tel Aviv, Tel Aviv University, Katz Research Institute for Hebrew Literature (in Hebrew).

Vennemann, Theo (1973) 'Explanation in syntax', in Kimball, J. P. (Ed.), *Syntax and Semantics* **2**, New York, Academic Press, pp. 1–50.

Zwicky, Arnold M. (1969) 'Phonological constraints in syntactic description', *Papers in Linguistics*, **1**, pp. 411–63.

Zwicky, Arnold M. and Pullum, Geoffrey K. (1983) 'Phonology in syntax: The Somali optional agreement rule', *Natural Language and Linguistic Theory*, **1**, pp. 385–402.

VII: Part Three: Linguistics and Psychology

11. Grammar and Psychology

P.N. JOHNSON-LAIRD

Modern psycholinguistics began with the impact of Chomsky's work on psychologists studying language. George Miller, who had collaborated with Chomsky on the development of formal models of language and its users, was the first to exploit ideas derived from transformational grammar in a theory of linguistic processing (Miller, 1962). But from the start it was clear that the relations between Chomsky's generative linguistics and psychological phenomena are subtle and complex. There can be no straightforward importation of the theory into psychology for the very good reason that the rules of grammar are not necessarily intended to characterize mental processes. Nevertheless, Chomsky has always maintained that linguistics, as he conceives it, is a part of cognitive psychology. The claim is no whimsical aside but a fundamental tenet of a carefully articulated theory.

If Chomsky is right, then it is a matter of some surprise that there has been considerable resistance to his ideas: one is bound to wonder why so many psycholinguists have failed to accept his conception of psychology in its entirety. Of course there are some spurious reasons for this relative lack of acceptance even on the part of those who concede the profundity of his linguistic theories. Despite the developments in transformational grammar over the last thirty years, and three major stages in its evolution—the initial theory (Chomsky, 1957), the standard theory (Chomsky, 1965), and the theory of government and binding (Chomsky, 1981, 1982)—there is no complete account of the syntax (and *a fortiori* the semantics) of any natural language, and no generally accepted and definitive linguistic theory—no theory sufficiently explicit to be translated into an effective procedure for acquiring a grammar for a language, given a corpus of sentences from that language. Judged by the strictest criteria of scientific achievement, the Chomskyan programme has yet to succeed; compare its course with, for instance, that of Crick and Watson's theory of the structure of DNA. Psychologists ought not to be put off by this comparison since they have few, if any, achievements of their own comparable to transformational grammar. Yet inevitably the appeal of Chomsky's theory is diminished by the apparently slow degree of progress, which to a disinterested outsider is often hard to discern amongst the wranglings of one group of grammarians with another, or within the seemingly perpetual 'treason of the clerks' as successive generations of generative linguists part company with the founding father.

Are there perhaps deeper reasons for psychologists' distrust of Chomsky's view of their subject? I believe that there are, and that these reasons arise primarily as a result of failures on the part of psychologists to grasp some principal home truths that Chomsky has been telling us for a long time. Error is not perhaps all on one side, however. What I shall try to do in this chapter is to sort out Chomsky's conception of psychology and of how grammar relates to the mind. There are, I suspect, some important morals to be drawn from trying to establish a proper notion of the psychology of language.

A SCIENCE OF THE MIND

Chomsky works within a particular conception of how science, and particularly a science of the mind, should be developed. From his earliest works he has always made three fundamental assumptions: first, the aim of science is to discover explanatory principles; second, in order to establish such principles it is necessary to make idealizations; and, third, facts have no intrinsic interest—other than as curiosities to students of natural history—but interest only in relation to explanations. This conception is at marked variance with the methodology advocated by many psychologists, even some latterday cognitive psychologists. Indeed, he accuses many of them of having adopted a suicidal definition of their subject, namely, that it is the study of performance (Chomsky, 1979, p. 49).

A further methodological principle that distinguishes Chomsky from his predecessors in linguistics, and from many psychologists, is his insistence that theories, and grammars in particular, should be precise, explicit and interpretable without recourse to intuition. He is well aware of the expository difficulty of too much formalism, with the result that some critics, such as the late Richard Montague, have accused him of expressing his theories in an insufficiently formal manner. However, there is no reason to suppose that he has abandoned this goal. As he wrote in *Syntactic Structures*, obscure and intuition-bound theories can seldom be shown to lead to absurd consequences—a productive way of advancing the field; nor are they likely to yield solutions to problems other than those which they were designed to solve (Chomsky, 1957, p. 5). There are cognitive psychologists (e.g., Bruner, 1984, p. 99) who still argue that formalism, whether in the form of a mathematical notation or a computer model, inhibits imagination. A persuasive case against this view could be based on Chomsky's use of formal notation and Marr's (1982) deployment of computer models in his study of vision.

In short, Chomsky is right to defend the aim of explaining the mind rather than predicting behaviour or accounting for the results of experiments. The results of psychological experiments, like any other facts, are of interest only if they bear on explanatory principles. The same moral has been defended from other quarters (e.g., Newell, 1973), but psychologists often continue to gamble that the fastest route to understanding is the accretion of experimental data. Likewise, Chomsky is right to defend the goal of explicit theorizing. The history of psychology is littered with theories that take far too much for granted, and that as a result are poorly understood (often by their progenitors) and difficult to refute. What is remarkable, as I have pointed out elsewhere (Johnson-Laird, 1983, pp. 5–6), is that it often seems to be impossible to determine whether empirical predictions *follow* from the statement of a psychological theory. Psychologists have no right to be alienated by Chomsky's demands for rigorous explanations in place of intuition-bound predictions.

COMPETENCE AND PERFORMANCE

As his work developed in the late 1950s, it became increasingly clear to Chomsky that linguistics is part of cognitive psychology (see the introduction to Chomsky, 1975, the book based on his PhD thesis of 1955). The psychology of language, he came to believe, comprises the study of the cognitive system of grammar, the way in which it is acquired, how it is used and its underlying neurophysiological substrate. In principle, any one of these subdomains may illuminate any other. In practice, however, Chomsky (personal communication) holds that psycholinguistic studies of the perception of sentences have yet to inform the theory of grammar. This failure is curious: psycholinguists have been carrying out such studies for twenty years or more, but they tend to regard them as addressing the problems of how language is understood rather than the issue of its essential structure. Nevertheless, Chomsky (e.g., 1980, p. 51) continues to insist that experimental studies may one day illuminate grammatical rules. It remains unclear what sort of experiment would in principle do the trick, and how it could establish a structural point that would not yield to the methods that Chomsky himself employs. His commitment here, I suspect, derives from his views about the proper way to study the mind.

The first step in Chomsky's paradigm of psychological research is to identify a reasonably self-contained cognitive domain, such as vision or language. The second step is to attempt to formulate theories about the structure of that domain. In a famous passage at the beginning of *Aspects of the Theory of Syntax*, he (1965) wrote:

> Linguistic theory is concerned primarily with an ideal speaker-listener, in a completely homogeneous speech-community, who knows its language perfectly and is unaffected by such grammatically irrelevant conditions as memory limitations, distractions, shifts of attention and interest, and errors (random or characteristic) in applying his knowledge of the language in actual performance. This seems to me to have been the position of the founders of modern general linguistics, and no cogent reason for modifying it has been offered. To study actual linguistic performance, we must consider the interaction of a variety of factors, of which the underlying competence of the speaker-hearer is only one.

This passage states Chomsky's well-known distinction between competence and performance, a distinction that is to be found in his earlier writings and that he continues to maintain (e.g., Chomsky, 1962, 1981). Although the general distinction between knowledge, especially tacit knowledge, and its application occasionally savours of paradox—as, for example, when one considers knowledge about performance errors and how to cope with them—the general line of demarcation is clear enough and certainly all that one can reasonably ask of a pre-theoretical distinction. A comparable distinction, as Chomsky (1963, p. 326) pointed out, was drawn by Lashley, Tolman and other psychologists.

GRAMMAR AS TACIT KNOWLEDGE

The theories to be constructed during Chomsky's second stage of a psychological investigation are precisely theories of competence, that is, of the intuitive and unconscious knowledge that makes performance possible. Such a theory in the case of language consists of a grammar, and a grammar is accordingly a scientific hypothesis about tacit knowledge. The term 'grammar' does double-duty: it denotes both a theory constructed by a linguist and the entity that the theory is about, namely, linguistic competence (Chomsky and Halle, 1968). Granted that grammar is mentally instantiated (a point to which I shall return later), then Chomsky is obviously right in claiming that psychologists should not attempt to study performance without first determining the competence upon which it is based. Thus, on the one hand Chomsky argues that studies of performance can in principle illuminate the nature of competence, but on the other hand he claims that the theory of competence should come first: if psycholinguists are to make progress, they must base their work on a better model of competence (Chomsky, 1979, p. 50). In other words, all components of the psychology of language are equal, but some are more equal than others. That is why psycholinguistic results, though in principle relevant to the theory of competence, have so far failed to contribute to it.

Chomsky (1965, p. 27) dubs a grammar as *descriptively adequate* if it describes the linguistic competence of the idealized native speaker of the language. He assumes that the major, though not incorrigible, sources of evidence about competence are intuitions—usually the linguist's intuitions—about the language. He believes that these are clear-cut in a sufficient number of cases to allow descriptively adequate grammars to be formulated. However, it is clear that a grammar based on intuitions about grammaticality has an uncertain status, and there are no overwhelming reasons for assuming that it is to be found in the minds of competent speakers. This claim is supported by at least two independent reasons.

The first reason is the uncertain status of the grammatical intuitions themselves. Obviously, as Chomsky recognizes, there is no way of directly tapping competence, because even the exercise of linguistic intuition is an aspect of performance (see also Levelt, 1974, Ch. 2). But there is a potentially more serious problem that can be illustrated by considering a different domain, where the argument may be clearer.

Musical improvization is essentially a syntactic skill unencumbered by semantics since musical phrases do not have truth conditions. Competent improvizers can devise a melody to a chord sequence that they know by heart at very high speed, e.g., producing notes at the rate of twelve or more per second. Because working memory has a limited processing capacity, it is likely that the unconscious mechanisms on which they rely are able to generate notes with only a minimum of musical structure. I have put this conjecture to the test by devising an algorithm equivalent to a finite state transducer that takes as input a chord sequence and that outputs melodic phrases (of a creditable verisimilitude). The algorithm employs a regular grammar that allows notes to be produced with the minimum of structuring.

The invention of chord sequences for use in improvizing is not subject to the same real-time constraints because musicians can work on harmonic progressions in a piece-meal way, and use only the finished product as a framework for their subsequent improvizations. They can write down their efforts rather than have to rely on working memory. Hence, it is not surprising that chord sequences have rather more structure and that their generation goes through several stages. An algorithm that I have implemented, which produces acceptable chord sequences, depends on three stages: an initial use of a context-free grammar to generate a basic sequence, the use of a context-sensitive transducer to substitute chords according to the cycle of fifths, and a final context-sensitive transducer to make further substitutions. (The final two stages are very similar to an unpublished theory proposed by Mark Steedman.)

In music there thus appear to be major differences in the competence underlying improvization and composition, since the former is subject to severe working memory constraints whereas the latter is not constrained in this way. There may be similar differences in competence between speech and writing, especially if the comparison is made between the speech of non-literate cultures and languages with a long tradition of literacy. Existing theories of competence have been largely developed on the basis of linguists' intuitions, and therefore inevitably reflect a grammatical knowledge of the written language. Perhaps in the case of language, unlike music, there are no major distinctions in the competence underlying improvized performance and written composition, but until the point is established one way or the other, the status of existing theories remains uncertain.

The second reason for doubt about the psychological status of Chomsky's theory of competence is the peculiar role of its grammatical rules. The knowledge embodied in the theory is supposed to be implanted in the mind, but the rules used in the formal specification of sentences are not necessarily supposed to play any direct part in the process of understanding or producing sentences. As Chomsky (1965, p. 9) wrote: 'When we say that a sentence has a certain derivation with respect to a particular generative grammar, we say nothing about how the speaker or hearer might proceed, in some practical or efficient way, to construct such a derivation.' The irrelevance of the rules of grammar to performance is borne out by the history of psycholinguistic theories.

The first important psycholinguistic theory assumed that phrase-structure rules had nothing to do with mental processes, but that the process of perception did call for the undoing of grammatical transformations in order to recover the simpler underlying structures (Miller, 1962). When it became clear that psychological complexity failed to correspond to transformational complexity, it was obvious that some component of the theory was false. Logically speaking, theorists might have argued that the theory of competence was at fault, and that sentences should not be derived in the formal theory by way of transformations. What happened, however, was that theorists maintained the theory of competence but abandoned the idea that transformations had any direct part to play in performance—at least adult performance. They assumed instead that underlying structure is recovered by a series of heuristic processes (Fodor, Bever and Garrett, 1974). One heuristic interprets sequences of the form: noun … verb … noun, as putative underlying clauses; another heuristic treats the first noun as the underlying subject of the clause, the verb as the main verb of the clause, and the second noun as the underlying object. Hence, in this theory, and in algorithmic alternatives to it (e.g., Kaplan, 1972), neither phrase-structure rules nor transformational rules play any role in performance. What is strange, of course, is that both sets of rules, as components of the theory of competence, are supposed to be embodied in the mind. They play a part in representing grammatical knowledge, but they play no part in the use of that knowledge: sentences are understood, or spoken, using entirely different procedures.

This duplication of effort is plainly unparsimonious, and a theory of performance would be altogether more satisfactory if it could employ all the knowledge posited in the theory of competence. The mind should make use of the rules of the grammar if the grammar is seriously intended as an account of the unconscious knowledge that enables it to speak and to understand a language. Of course, the rules will have to be supplemented by procedures that make use of them in parsing or constructing sentences, but there is nothing problematical about the design of automata that employ grammars in this way.

GRAMMAR AS AN ACCOUNT OF WHAT IS COMPUTED

There is an alternative view about the relation between grammar and the mind that may make better sense of the status of Chomskyan theory. This view also derives from a paradigm of how psychological theory should be developed (see, e.g., Adrian, 1954; Marr, 1982; Broadbent, 1983; Johnson-Laird, 1983). The first step is to characterize what the mind is doing in a particular cognitive domain; the second step is to formulate a theory of how the mind carries out the task and how the relevant procedures are acquired; and the third step is to establish the neurophysiology underlying performance. In other words, first characterize the function that the mind computes, and then formulate the algorithm, or effective procedure, that it uses to compute that function. This approach leads to the following 'ecumenical' principle about the proper relations between linguistics and psychology (Stanley Peters, personal communication): linguistics aims to specify the functions to be computed (from speech to the representation of meaning, and vice versa) and psychology aims to specify the procedures by which these functions are computed (the interpretation and production of sentences).

This principle resolves the uncertain status of linguistic theory. There is no need to suppose that a grammar is explicitly represented in the mind of a speaker even if the speaker's intuitions entirely conform to that grammar. One might thus accept a transformational grammar of English in its entirety as an account of the grammatical structure and logical form of English sentences without necessarily having to assume that it is implanted in the minds of English speakers. It is possible in principle that the procedures underlying a speaker's intuitions and linguistic performance employ an entirely different system. There are indeed always many ways, infinite in number, of computing the same function (see, e.g., Rogers, 1967).

In certain cognitive domains the existence of radically different ways of carrying out a task has been clearly demonstrated. For example, when people draw deductions of their own, they tend to formulate conclusions that do not throw away information in the premises, but rather re-express that information more parsimoniously. In the case of propositional inferences, their performance can be accounted for by assuming that they possess the formal rules of inference of the propositional calculus together with some extra-logical principles that constrain them to non-trivial conclusions. However, there is a natural alternative to this purely formal, syntactic procedure. Their performance may be based on a knowledge of meaning. It can be accounted for by a procedure that substitutes truth values for those constituents of complex propositions that correspond to simple premises, and that then attempts to simplify the resulting expressions from its knowledge of the meaning of propositional connectives. Where no initial substitution is possible, a complex proposition can be divided recursively in order to pursue the substitutional consequences of its separate constituents (see Johnson-Laird, 1983, Ch. 3).

A more radical thesis is defended by 'connectionist' theorists, who assume that there are no tacit rules represented in the mind, but only relational patterns embodied in neuronal systems from which such rules are emergent properties. If connectionism is correct, the mind behaves as if it were rule governed, though in fact it contains no rules whatsoever (Anderson and Hinton, 1981).

The moral of these considerations is simple: even if a grammar describes the intuitions of the idealized native speaker perfectly, it may have no psychological reality. It is an account of a function that is computed, but not necessarily an account of the speaker's unconscious knowledge of the language, which may be represented in quite a different form.

THE ACQUISITION OF GRAMMAR

How does one determine the nature of the mental representation of grammar if descriptive adequacy is not enough? One clue is that the grammar has to have a form that can be acquired by children. A descriptively adequate grammar, as Chomsky has always recognized, is not the final goal of linguistic theory. Given such a grammar, then he advocates that one should seek for an explanatorily adequate theory, that is, an account of how the mind constructs the grammar from a corpus of utterances of the language (Chomsky, 1965, p. 25). There have been various studies of the theoretical learnability of classes of grammars in the Chomsky hierarchy (regular, context-free, context-sensitive, and transformational grammars of various sorts), and, given certain technical assumptions about the nature of learning, it has been shown that there are severe limits on identifying a particular grammar from a corpus of sentences (Gold, 1967; Wexler and Culicover, 1980; Osherson and Weinstein, 1984). However, a factor that overrides the generative power of the grammar—its position in the hierarchy—is the ease of selecting it from the set of grammars accessible to human beings (Chomsky, 1965, pp. 61–2). If relatively few grammars have to be tried out and the choice amongst them is easy, then even a grammar with the power of a universal Turing machine could still be acquired.

For Chomsky, a grammar develops in a way akin to the growth of a bodily organ. He assumes that there are innate constraints on the grammars for natural languages. The constraints constitute a 'universal grammar', and a grammar for a particular language—strictly speaking, the set of its grammatical subsystems—is acquired by using a corpus of utterances to set the values of each parameter in the universal grammar (see, e.g., Chomsky, 1982, p. 3). Since there is only a finite number of parameters and each parameter has only a finite number of permissible values, there is only a finite number of grammars accessible to human beings. Whether this account is correct remains an open question. Piaget (1980) and others have argued that the innate component is not specific to language, but underlies the general development of sensory-motor intelligence; Putnam (1980) and others have argued that the acquisition of syntax is dependent on the acquisition of semantics. Although Chomsky's proposals remain a long way from an effective procedure, they do provide a more comprehensive account than these rival theories, and one that would be refuted by the occurrence of a natural language outside the scope of the theoretical parameters.

PERFORMANCE PHENOMENA AS CONSTRAINTS ON GRAMMAR

A different clue to the nature of the grammatical information in the mind is provided by studies of performance. Although I have suggested that experimental investigations of perception and production are unlikely to lead to modifications in the rules of a grammar (*pace* Chomsky), the results of such studies can be informative about certain general design features of the grammatical knowledge embodied in the mind. The logic of the argument is simple. As Chomsky would allow, the phenomena of performance depend on two major components: mental processes and a tacit representation of a grammar. Let us suppose that a grammar posited as an account of what the mind computes is assumed to be represented in the mind, and that its rules and structures are also assumed to be directly used by the processes underlying perception and production. If the resulting psychology of language is not corroborated by experimental results, then one or other of the two components is in error. Moreover, if no evidence is forthcoming to suggest that the structures of the grammatical theory are mentally represented or its rules directly employed in comprehension or speech, then it is reasonable to assume that the grammar, though it is an accurate account of the function that is computed, is not represented in the mind.

This hypothetical case history appears to correspond closely to the fate of the standard theory of transformational grammar. After the abandonment of transformational rules as psychologically real, it became apparent that there was no unequivocal evidence that deep structure is ever mentally represented (see Johnson-Laird, 1983, p. 278). Hence, the psychology of language seems to require a grammar that makes no use of transformations and *a fortiori* no use of deep structure. Just such grammars have been independently advocated by a number of theorists (e.g., Brame, 1978; Gazdar, 1981; Ades and Steedman, 1982; and unpublished work of Stanley Peters described in Johnson-Laird, 1983, Ch. 12). These grammars have the further advantage that a semantics can be framed to run in parallel with them—with a semantic rule for each of their syntactic rules. Since some of them are context-free, it is provable that they can be parsed efficiently (Hopcroft and Ullman, 1979), and, more importantly, a variety of parsing algorithms have been fully implemented for context-free languages (see Johnson-Laird, 1983, Ch. 13 for a review).

The proofs of parsing efficiency apply to classes of grammar, but there is no doubt that efficient parsers for individual transformational grammars could also be developed (Berwick and Weinberg, 1982). It is not yet clear whether such parsers can meet some further performance constraints, such as an equal efficiency with both left-branching and right-branching structures. Likewise, comprehension proceeds so swiftly in comparison with the response time of a neuron—a few milliseconds—that performance must be rooted in parallel algorithms (Marslen-Wilson, 1975; Tyler and Marslen-Wilson, 1977; Posner, 1978). The essence of parallel processing, however, is that one computation is carried out in ignorance of the results of another. An interpretation of the meaning of an expression cannot begin until the meanings of some of its constituents have been assembled, and this latter process cannot begin until some words have been identified. The feasibility of parallel processing therefore depends on the nature of the algorithm, and it is a major analytical problem to determine which of its components can in principle be executed in parallel. There are algorithms for parsing context-free grammars that can operate in parallel and perform in a time proportional to the length of the input sentence (see Johnson-Laird,

1983, Ch. 13). There do not yet appear to be any such algorithms for transformational grammars.

These considerations are obviously not decisive for the psychology of grammar. On the one hand, the existence of efficient parsers is at most suggestive evidence for a particular conception of tacit grammatical knowledge. On the other hand, psycholinguists have made few explorations of the consequences for theories of performance of the theory of government and binding. In particular, the claim that people do not represent deep structure in the process of understanding sentences, but rather recover meaning directly from surface structure appears to be compatible with Chomsky's latest views.

REFERENCES

Ades, A. E. and Steedman, M. J. (1982) 'On the order of words', *Linguistics and Philosophy*, **4,** pp. 517–58.

Adrian, E. D. (1954) 'Science and human nature', *Advances in Science*, **11,** pp. 121–8.

Anderson, J. A. and Hinton, G. E. (1981) 'Models of information processing in the brain', in Hinton, G. E. and Anderson, J. A. (Eds), *Parallel Models of Associative Memory*, Hillsdale, N. J., Erlbaum.

Berwick, R. and Weinberg, A. (1982) 'Parsing efficiency, computational complexity, and the evaluation of grammatical theories', *Linguistic Inquiry*, **9,** pp. 641–71.

Brame, M. K. (1978) *Base Generated Syntax*, Seattle, Wash., Noit Amrofer.

Broadbent, D. E. (1983) 'The functional approach to memory', *Philosophical Transactions of the Royal Society, Series B*, **302,** pp. 239–49.

Bruner, J. S. (1984) *In Search of Mind: Essays in Autobiography*, New York, Harper and Row.

Chomsky, N. (1957) *Syntactic Structures*, The Hague, Mouton.

Chomsky, N. (1962) 'Explanatory models in linguistics', in Nagel, E., Suppes, P. and Tarski, A. (Eds), *Logic, Methodology, and the Philosophy of Science*, Stanford, Calif., Stanford University Press.

Chomsky, N. (1963) 'Formal properties of grammars', in Luce, R. D., Bush, R. R. and Galanter, E. (Eds), *Handbook of Mathematical Psychology, Vol. II*, New York, Wiley.

Chomsky, N. (1965) *Aspects of the Theory of Syntax*, Cambridge, Mass., MIT Press.

Chomsky, N. (1975) *The Logical Structure of Linguistic Theory*, New York, Plenum.

Chomsky, N. (1979) *Language and Responsibility*, Trans J. Viertel, Brighton, Harvester Press.

Chomsky, N. (1980) 'On cognitive structures and their development: A reply to Piaget', in Piattelli-Palmarini, M. (Ed.), *Language and Learning: The Debate between Jean Piaget and Noam Chomsky*, Cambridge, Mass., Harvard University Press.

Chomsky, N. (1981) *Lectures on Government and Binding*, Dordrecht, Foris.

Chomsky, N. (1982) *Some Concepts and Consequences of the Theory of Government and Binding*, Cambridge, Mass., MIT Press.

Chomsky, N. and Halle, M. (1968) *The Sound Pattern of English*, New York, Harper and Row.

Fodor, J. A., Bever, T. G. and Garrett, M. F. (1974) *The Psychology of Language*, New York, McGraw-Hill.

Gazdar, G. (1981) 'Unbounded dependencies and coordinate structure', *Linguistic Inquiry*, **12,** pp. 155–84.

Gold, E. M. (1967) 'Language identification in the limit', *Information and Control*, **10,** pp. 447–74.

Hopcroft, J. E. and Ullman, J. D. (1979) *Formal Languages and Their Relation to Automata*, Reading, Mass., Addison-Wesley.

Johnson-Laird, P. N. (1983) *Mental Models: Towards a Cognitive Science of Language, Inference, and Consciousness*, Cambridge, Cambridge University Press; Cambridge, Mass., Harvard University Press.

Kaplan, R. M. (1972) 'Augmented transition networks as psychological models of sentence comprehension', *Artificial Intelligence*, **3,** pp. 77–100.

Levelt, W. J. M. (1974) *Formal Grammars in Linguistics and Psycholinguistics, Vol. III: Psycholinguistic Applications*, The Hague, Mouton.

Marr, D. (1982) *Vision: A Computational Investigation in the Human Representation of Visual Information*, San Francisco, Calif., Freeman.

Marslen-Wilson, W. D. (1975) 'Sentence perception as an interactive parallel process', *Science*, **189,** pp. 226–8.

Miller, G. A. (1962) 'Some psychological studies of grammar', *American Psychologist*, **17,** pp. 748–62.
Newell, A. (1973) 'You can't play 20 questions with nature and win', in Chase, W. G. (Ed.), *Visual Information Processing*, New York, Academic Press.
Osherson, D. N. and Weinstein, S. (1984) 'Formal learning theory', in Gazzaniga, M. S. (Ed.), *Handbook of Cognitive Neuroscience*, New York, Plenum.
Piaget, J. (1980) 'The psychogenesis of knowledge and its epistemological significance', in Piattelli-Palmarini, M. (Ed.), *Language and Learning: The Debate between Jean Piaget and Noam Chomsky*, Cambridge, Mass., Harvard University Press.
Posner, M. (1978) *Chronometric Explorations of Mind*, Hillsdale, N. J., Erlbaum.
Putnam, H. (1980) 'What is innate and why: Comments on the debate', in Piattelli-Palmarini, M. (Ed.), *Language and Learning: The Debate between Jean Piaget and Noam Chomsky*, Cambridge, Mass., Harvard University Press.
Rogers, H. (1967) *Theory of Recursive Functions and Effective Computability*, New York, McGraw-Hill.
Tyler, L. K. and Marslen-Wilson, W. D. (1977) 'The on-line effects of semantic context on syntactic processing', *Journal of Verbal Learning and Verbal Behavior*, **16,** pp. 683–92.
Wexler, K. and Culicover, P. (1980) *Formal Principles of Language Acquisition*, Cambridge, Mass., MIT Press.

12. The Modularity of Meaning in Language Acquisition

THOMAS ROEPER

INTRODUCTION

What do the old debates on language acquisition look like in a modern light? What is the innateness claim? Chomsky's earliest notions of an innate transformation were barely more constrained than the notion of 'rule' itself. There was very little that a transformation could not do (i.e., copy, delete, move, permute) and its domain of application was not even limited to sentences (i.e., generalized transformations).[1]

In retrospect Chomsky's position might seem nearly as abstract and unconstrained as Skinner's notions of stimulus and response or Piaget's use of 'general cognition'. However, there was and is a fundamental conceptual difference: the notion that language capability was genetically *constrained* in ways that 'general' cognition was not. The early conceptions were heavily constrained by an 'evaluation metric' which selected among possible grammars. The constraints themselves, Chomsky argues, have a character at once so abstract and so subtle that there is no conceivable avenue to learning them. In this chapter we will explicate and buttress this argument.

Parameters and Constraints

Modern linguistics reflects a shift from formal principles of language variation (based on transformational complexity) to more substantive forms of what is called 'parametric variation' (based on specific patterns found in language families).[2] In effect, current work (which we review below) has shown that language ability is far more narrowly constrained than the earliest work suggested. Therefore, the gulf has

157

widened between Chomsky and Skinner or Piaget. Chomsky is claiming that natural language is an even narrower subset of the possible 'cognitive' languages.

The 'doctrine of constraints' presents one primary empirical challenge to the Piagetians. It is *not* to provide an explanation for how a child could cognitively represent language. The set of cognitively possible languages is far larger than the set of actually occurring ones. Computer languages, for instance, are instances of cognitively possible languages but not naturally occurring ones. Therefore, it is necessarily the case that linguistic knowledge can be represented as the output of cognitive ability. The theory of linguistics itself is not the result of linguistic ability, but of cognitive problem-solving ability.

The empirical challenge therefore is quite different. It is to show how a child knows that certain sentences are *disallowed* or ungrammatical: how can a child avoid use of structures and forms which are *not* found in human language? In a word, what prevents a child from uttering ungrammatical sentences?

Excluding Agents

To be specific: How does a child know that it is possible to say

> (1)   the boat was sunk by Bill

but not

> (2)   *the boat sank by Bill?

Most of the sentences that a child uses are original. Therefore the fact that the child has not heard (2) does not inform him that he cannot utter (2). Now we will follow the system of replies a Piagetian might make. He might retort: the child has not heard 'structures' like (2). This is correct, but before the child can use that knowledge he must be able to identify what structure is involved. If the child hears:

> (3)   the boat sank by the river's edge.

then the sentence is acceptable. Now, one might say: the *by-phrase* cannot refer to AGENT. When is the reference to AGENT eliminated? Answer: if the structure is not a passive. This is also incorrect: we can say *the sinking of the boat by Bill*. Now we can elaborate the claim:

> (4)   if the object is in subject position and the sentence is not a passive, then no *by-phrase* agent can occur.[3]

This formulation may prove to be adequate. However, the formulation is not 'heard', nor is it 'taught', nor does it have any definable context. We have simply reconstructed a corner of linguistic theory. Our reconstruction is just an ad hoc statement, therefore totally unlearnable in the absence of instruction. Linguistic theory, providing a common definition for many structures, embeds the generalization (4) in a system of simple principles from which (4) can be deduced. The deduction is automatic if the principles are innate.[4] The question is the focus of much current research.

This, then, is the challenge to Piagetian approaches: the exclusion of non-allowable sentences. It is never addressed in the Piagetian literature.[5] We will provide several illustrations of how innate principles can do what induction cannot do.

Interactions

A similar evolution (from rather abstract to more concrete claims) can be seen in the controversy over whether language ability is *interactive* or *autonomous*. Piaget is associated with the 'interactive' view and Chomsky with the 'autonomous' view. In retrospect the entire debate has a premature quality. Originally Chomsky advanced the claim that syntax might be acquired entirely in formal terms, and the effect of extra-linguistic knowledge was limited to defining the content of words. Current work in linguistic theory, abandoning a single transformational notation, exhibits very intricate 'interactions'. However, in Chomsky's view the interactions themselves are innately stipulated connections between and among linguistic and non-linguistic domains, known as 'modules'. In Piaget's view the connections are the result of experience and a child's powers of induction (see Piatelli-Palmarini, 1980). The existence of interactions, in Chomsky's account, does not lessen the need for a task-specific, genetically controlled acquisition of language. The gulf over innateness remains.

In what follows we shall show that a child's 'experience', the evidence available to him, is *contradictory*. Therefore experience, using Piaget's perspective, leads nowhere. From Chomsky's perspective the contradictory evidence is immediately rendered non-contradictory by the application of a crucial distinction from universal grammar: *core* versus *peripheral* rules.

AFFECTEDNESS AND MOVEMENT

Let us move to an illustration. The microscopic subtlety of current linguistic analysis involves the 'interaction' of concepts quite alien to initial work in linguistic theory. Consider the notion 'affectedness' which is linked to a distinction between two classes of movement rules.[6] We can say both:

(5) the destruction of the city
(6) the city's destruction

But we cannot say both (7) and (8):

(7) the appreciation of the play
(8) *the play's appreciation

The generalization is: only 'affected' objects can be preposed in all structures (nominalizations, middles, compounds, −able), except passive. For instance, we cannot have a middle form *plays appreciate easily*, while the form *cities destroy easily* is fine. We find that the same constraint applies in compounds. While we can have both *the man illustrated the book* and *a book-illustrating man* we cannot have *the man illustrates the problem* (= he is the problem) and have *the problem-illustrating man*. In the former case the book is affected by illustration, but 'equative' usages do not involve any affect on the object (the problem). For −ables we can have: *the answer is discoverable by the layman* but not *four is equallable by two and two*.

There is a major exception, which might seem curious: the passive. Clearly *the play was appreciated* is fine. However the exceptionality of passive is not a local accident. It is exceptional throughout. It allows extraction from prepositions (*Bill was relied on*), where nominalizations (and the others) do not (**Bill's reliance on*), and it allows extractions from sentences (*Bill was believed to be smart*), where nominalizations do not (**Bill's belief to be smart*).[7] How does the child know that the passive does not generalize to the other object movement structures?

The answer is that he has a pre-existing definition of exceptionality: non-affected objects, extraction from prepositions, or from complement sentences are all exceptional. Moreover universal grammar (UG) stipulates: (A) operations which are 'exceptional' belong to the periphery of grammar, and (B) peripheral operations do not generalize. The core/periphery distinction is then a prerequisite for the avoidance of ungrammatical overgeneralizations (such as **John's belief to be smart*). In effect, despite existing examples, the child is born knowing that *Bill was relied on* is exceptional and therefore may not generalize.

It is interesting that the notion of 'affectedness' itself is very difficult to formulate. We can have:

(9)   the discovery of America
(10) America's discovery

but not:

(11) the discovery of our common interests
(12) *our common interests' discovery

One might think that the act of discovery does not affect a country, but that 'common interests' might be affected by the act of discovery. These examples reveal that we must regard the label 'affectedness' as a cover term for a complex cognitive and perceptual object (or module) that we do not fully understand. The presence of this mystery does not blockade our linguistic efforts, though. It is clear that a semantic factor is interacting with a syntactic factor in a specific way. There is no deductive logic that leads to this association, although a biological logic, far beyond our current research capacities, might lead to this conclusion. For instance, there could be a neurological factor, or perhaps an accident of evolution which explains this modular interaction.

The acquisition process itself might lead to this pattern. Lebeaux (1985, and references therein) observes that children's passives initially obey the affectedness constraint. They seem to have forms like *John was hit* but not *John was liked*. He argues that affectedness is a clear indicator of the verb-object relationship (while other -ed forms might be analyzed as adjectives). It follows that the affected object of a passive or a nominalization, now in subject position, must have been put there by movement from the verb phrase. Therefore, the notion of 'affectedness' could be a crucial trigger in the recognition of a transformation. Once passive is recognized, it operates wherever the appropriate morphology is present. Consequently, affectedness is no longer crucial to the grammar but remains nonetheless in less frequently used structures. What appears rather arbitrary in the adult language is rendered quite sensible when the problem of acquisition is included, and we see that affectedness triggers a child's knowledge and then is longer needed in passives.

Cognitive and Linguistic Agents

The claim that language is modular can be dramatically illustrated by a demonstration that language has a *separate* version of certain cognitive distinctions. Consider the following contrasts:

(13) the robber of the bank
(14) *the thief of the bank
(15) the cooking of stew
(16) *the cook of stew

Both *robber* and *thief* have the notion of *agency* associated with them. Only one allows an *of-phrase*. The existence of *bankthief* and *stewcook* show that without *of* the words are connectable and the same meaning is attainable.

Dan Finer and I have argued that the linguistic notion of AGENT is distinct from the cognitive notion of agent.[8] Moreover, the linguistic notion of THEME (= direct object) must be linked to a linguistic notion of AGENT. The preposition *of* marks the linguistic THEME. This formal uniformity in the treatment of AGENT and THEME is required by UG.[9] It resembles the fact that grammatical gender (like *le, la* in French) is distinct from semantic gender.

The compound noun forms (*bankthief*), in contrast, have two words freely associated. The free association naturally results in regarding *thief* as an agent and *bank* as a theme, although some other reading is possible. For instance, if I invent *holidaythief* then one is more likely to project the meaning 'steals on holidays' than 'steals holidays' (although both are possible). The linguistic notion is connected to both a verb (like *rob*) and to a formal marker (like *-er* or *-ing*). The ungrammaticality of (16) indicates that an underlying verb is not sufficient. Three features must be present to satisfy the linguistic notion of AGENT:

(17) a cognitive agent, a verb, and an affix.

The connection between these three elements is what we attribute to UG.[10] A virtue of this approach is that it is very concrete. If we assume the presence of an innate universal grammar, then the child must simply search for a simple clue: the presence of an affix indicates that linguistic thematic roles are present.

What is the consequence of this claim? First, it shows that the simple recognition of agency in the world does not provide the child with enough information to fix the role of AGENT in a theory of grammar. This means that any theory which claims that children's grammars are 'semantic' in nature has simply not examined the crucial acquisition puzzles. The 'semantic' claim has come from many quarters (including the Piagetian school and others). Where the cognitive agent and the linguistic agent coincide, acquisition is easy, as in canonical subject-verb-object sentences.[11] The problem is to explain that part of acquisition where they do not correspond. Once again, what prevents a child from saying *the thief of the bank*? I have never seen any evidence that children make errors of this kind. No teacher explains it to them.

Evidence as Contradictory Input

What is the role of evidence? First, we should observe that it is *contradictory*. Let us illustrate. The relationship between *-er* and *of* is productive. We can say anything: *the licenser of dungeons* is perfectly acceptable. However, there are substantial numbers of exceptional examples, which seems to contradict any claim that the non *-er* nominalizations are ungrammatical:

(18) the author of the book
      the push of a button

The exceptionality is revealed by the fact that they do not generalize; in a word, they are not productive:

(19)   *the poet of a book
       *the force of a button

A great deal of discussion has been directed toward the claim that a child has only *positive evidence* as a basis for determining his grammar. Here we have two kinds of positive evidence: *-er and of* which is productive, and *denominal verb and of* which is unproductive. The latter are produced only in moments of literary creativity. How does the child know that he cannot generalize (18) to produce (19) but he may generalize *the robber of the bank* to produce whatever he wants? In effect the evidence, by itself, is contradictory.

Universal grammar, however, if assumed, makes this array of data perfectly predictable. The distinction between *core* and *periphery* tells the child that one form cannot be generalized. The evidentiary criterion is the same: where no affix is present, a formal thematic role is excluded (or peripherally acceptable). Under such a definition the child knows *automatically* that *the push of a button* is exceptional. And he knows that **the push of a child* is ungrammatical while *the pushing of a child* is grammatical. In effect, an expression like *the push of the button* is a complex lexical item (or an idiom) and not a productive syntactic structure.[12] In sum, the *-er and of* combination is recognized by the child as the formally satisfactory case that UG was looking for. Formally deficient forms are automatically assigned to the periphery of the grammar, as either ungrammatical or exceptional.

The difference between ungrammatical and exceptional, from this perspective, is less important than the distinction between core and periphery. The data, in effect, reveal both the grammatical and the exceptional/ungrammatical. It is only the principles of UG which reveal the difference. The child must have the power to know not only why some forms never appear, but also why some forms which do appear do not allow overgeneralization.[13]

The differences here cannot be recognized by a notion of 'frequency'. The exceptions are quite frequent themselves, just as the number of words in our vocabulary is large. The productive cases are almost 100 per cent productive (although other modules may interact), while the unproductive cases merely have hundreds of examples. The reader can prove this to himself by seeing that all verbs allow -ing nominalizations (the buying of clothes), while bare nominalizations are frequent but not general (*an image, *a create*) and those with *of* are fewer (*a good buy* but **the good buy of clothes*).

The Fixation of Primary Data

It should be noted that we are discussing acquisition at a middle point. As we noted above, there are earlier steps which are necessary and which, in principle, could mislead the child if not executed properly. For instance, the child must be able to subdivide a word in order to recognize its deverbal character. Children who go through a stage where they mispronounce *phoTOGrapher* as *PHOtoGRAPHer* are presumably learning to see the verb within the noun.[14] This process, which we could call the fixation of primary data, constitutes a separate and interesting phenomenon.

If we dig into the primary data, an important question arises: what role does UG play? If the child has the notion of *derivation* from UG, then he might always attempt to relate similar words. He would then form a hypothesis about a connection between *and* and *band*. Or it might be oriented toward words, like verbs, that automatically trigger subdivision. Or some other feature might prove to be a critical trigger. We have little to say about this question. Our hunch is that the way to approach the question is from the adult grammar working backwards to the child grammar. This reflects the research we shall summarize below.

Agency and Acquisition Evidence

I have perused acquisition data for many years. Nowhere have I seen examples of children producing forms like *the thief of the bank*. There exist instances of the overgeneralization of *of*: *watch out of that* or *I'm bored of that* but, as these examples illustrate, only in contexts where a linguistic theme is appropriate.

Janet Randall (1982) has made an intricate and important study of how children interpret complements in morphologically derived structures. Her experiments explore the connection between complements of verbally derived nouns and non-verbal nouns. It is a classic argument of morphology that nominalizations *inherit* the complement structure of verbs (Chomsky, 1970). A child should know automatically that the verbal structure for *the enemy destroyed the city* is paralleled by the nominalization *the enemy's destruction of the city*.

The *-er* nominalization is only partially obedient to the inheritance principle. We find that *a player of games* is grammatical but **a player with him* is not (under the reading 'I play with him'). Only the direct-object may be inherited with *-er*, unlike with *-ing* (*the playing of games with him*). She predicts that children will overgeneralize the *-er* to allow full inheritance. Anecdotal evidence supports the claim. Children say, *I'm not so much a player with him* and *He's a bikerider without hands*, where *without hands* modifies the activity of riding a bike and does not describe a limbless person.[15]

In a carefully constructed set of experiments with picture-choices Randall shows that children take the verbal reading with *-er* for ambiguous *with-phrases*. The *with-phrases* refer to either *instrument* or *accompaniment*. We will focus on the most pertinent of her experiments. It involves four each of the phrases:

(20) a writer with a candybar
(21) a chef with a fork

The *chef* is a cognitive agent while *writer* has a thematic agent. Since *chef* is a non-verbal noun, however, it should be open to the accompaniment reading. For adults the same is true for *writer* in (20). However, Randall shows, as does our anecdotal evidence, that children will overgeneralize *-er* to allow the instrumental reading, connected to the underlying verb.

Pictures were used with a person holding (a) a candybar and (b) writing with a candybar, and having (a) a fork or (b) cooking with a fork (with other control pictures where no fork was present). She had eighteen 5-6-year-old children and twelve adults in this experiment. The children were encouraged to choose as many of the four pictures as they wanted. For *chef* 100 per cent of both children and adults chose the accompaniment reading: a picture where the *fork* was present but not involved in cooking. For *writer* 27.7 per cent of the responses excluded the accompaniment reading where the activity was ongoing, while 31.9 per cent excluded the accompaniment reading where no activity occurred but a candybar was present: only the instrumental (verbal) reading was allowed.[16]

In effect, two-thirds of the children interpreted *writer with a candybar* as if it were *he was writing with a candybar* where the instrumental reading is virtually obligatory. This occurred although pragmatically candybars are not a very likely instrument for writing. For *chef* they chose the accompaniment reading which is appropriate for ordinary nouns (like *a shelf with a candybar*). In sum, these children exhibited knowledge of the distinction between a cognitive agent and a linguistic agent in a very subtle contextual environment, which goes against pragmatics (chefs naturally use forks).

TWO CONCEPTS OF VARIABLE BINDING

We turn now to another instance where there is both a cognitive and linguistic representation for the same concept: *distributed reading* and its linguistic analogue, *variable binding*. A distributed reading can be illustrated with sentences like *people have noses*. The sentence does not usually mean that individuals have a set of noses (as in *people have eyes*), but rather that a set of individuals collectively has noses. In addition we are able to infer an isomorphic relation based on our knowledge of the world: each person has one nose. This interpretation is reached by adding an inference to the meaning of the utterance *people have noses*.

If the correct interpretation is attainable for these sentences via inference, then inference should be enough to interpret (22):

(22)   every person has a nose

Why should a person ever learn the more restricted linguistic code: the fact that (22) allows *only* the 'distributed' reading? In linguistic terms sentences with quantifiers achieve a distributed reading via 'bound variables'. *Every* and *a nose* each have variable reference, but they are bound to each other. How does the child learn that the collective reading is excluded and only the bound variable reading is available for (22)? Why not infer that (22) means either people have multiple noses or they have one each. Context is then used to make a choice.

Inferences

This contextual scenario is what is implicitly or explicitly proposed in much of the acquisition literature.[17] We confront again the crucial question: if the child has a powerful inference capacity, which he can (and must) apply to language, then what would cause him to exclude certain sentences, or certain interpretations as ungrammatical?

Virtually every sentence requires that we use some capacity for inference based on context or knowledge of the world. If I say, *John's eyes are red*, I do not mean that his eyeballs are red, since red is excluded genetically as a possible eye colour, but that there is red in the whites of his eyes. How does a child know that he must go beyond these everyday inferences in his analysis of sentences with *every*? He might, somehow, learn the meaning of *every*, but what reveals that it will covary with the article?[18]

Wh-Movement and Binding

We can examine the same issue in far more subtle environments:

    (23)   who thinks he has a hat
    (24)   who does he think has a hat

In (23) there is a bound variable reading: a set of people all thinking, separately, about themselves. In (24) there is only one *he*, a person thinking about other people. How does a child learn the difference between these sentences? How, given inference, can he exclude the bound variable reading for (24)?

We can exclude the bound variable inference if, once again, we assume a theory of stipulated modular interactions. Consider now another example: it is possible to have 'backwards anaphora' in certain contexts (John = he):

    (25)   Near him$_i$, John$_i$ put his shoes

while forward coreference is blocked (John $\neq$ he):

    (26)   Near John$_x$, he$_y$ put his shoes.

Now suppose the child had a simple commonsense inductive generalization, found in most traditional grammars;

    (27)   pronouns must have an antecedent.

Therefore, the antecedent must precede the pronoun. This generalization is immediately falsified by the examples (25, 26). How can we explain the phenomenon? It can easily be explained if we assume the concept of a transformation:

    (28)   Near him, John put his shoe *trace*

The trace represents *near him* and allows the child to fix the coreference relations in terms of the original generalization (pronouns have antecedents). The reconstructed sentence (i.e., deep structure) is: *John put his shoes near him.* One important argument on behalf of innate principles is that they allow a child to learn language when he is faced with such contradictory evidence. It is only the principle of the transformation which rescues the child from the false notion that there is no generalization at all (pronouns can go backwards or forwards).

He cannot assume that a module for anaphora has order sensitivity unless he assumes that a transformational module interacts with the anaphora module to preserve its simplicity.[19] Therefore, the innate knowledge has to function as a *presupposition* to analysis. It is in this profound sense that the concept of transformation radically simplifies a child's knowledge while it seems to add power. Without the use of two modules in conjunction, the child can only conclude that there is no principle at all and inference must be used everywhere. This may be true of the limited speech forms of retarded children.

Now we have a solution to the problem of bound variables as well. If we assume that *who* is a name in its relation to a pronoun *he*, and if we use transformations, then we can see that the origin of (30) is in fact (29):

    (29)   he thinks who has a hat
    (30)   who does he think *trace* has a hat

The *he* precedes *trace* and is non-coreferent with it just as with a proper name *he thinks John has a hat*. In effect, coreference must be determined at deep structure. If it is non-coreferent, then it cannot be bound and therefore cannot be a bound variable. In addition, we can see that the inference system is subordinate to the grammar. The child cannot impose an inferred bound variable reading if the linguistic modules exclude that reading.[20]

Acquisition Evidence

These structures are ripe for acquisition research and the first steps have been taken. Lust (forthcoming) has carried out a series of experiments that show a greater capacity to block forwards coreference for (26) with children as young as 3. Her results also show a greater inclination to allow coreference than in the comparable unmoved structure (*he put his shoes near John*). The non-equivalence of the moved and unmoved sentences shows that children have some capacity to use 'order' by itself as a criterion for coreference.[21] Nevertheless, if the fact is sustainable that very young children will block forward coreference, then it shows that there is no principled delay in the interaction of the anaphoric and the transformational module. Those who fail to block forward coreference are, presumably, unable to provide a full syntactic analysis and therefore use the simplest principle available.

Ingram and Shaw (1981) report no significant block on forward coreference at this age. Their work invites the view that some children may systematically analyze these structures in a different way. We must, therefore, provide an explanation both for those children who correctly analyze the sentences and for those who do not.

One reason why forwards anaphora may occur is simply, as we said above, that the child disregards some of the syntactic structure. Another reason is that it may be plausible to argue that children generate an initial prepositional phrase without a transformation. In a sentence like, *At the private home of the president, he keeps his personal papers*, no movement has occurred, and therefore forward coreference is possible. The child must be aware that the verb requires a PP within its scope before a transformation is required. Ingram and Shaw used ambiguous verbs, and not ones like *put* sentences which must have a prepositional phrase with them.

What is our method here? We interweave naturalistic data, data and principles from linguistic theory and experimental results. Factors of frequency, context and experimental bias could (and sometimes do) influence children. They are irrelevant at this level of subtlety unless their role can be demonstrated clearly.

Binding

How does binding emerge? Matthei (1983) and Otsu (1981) have both shown that children at the age of 3 know that reciprocals (like *each other*) function as bound variables. Binding in complex wh-extraction sentences has been examined in a set of experiments that I have carried out with Mats Rooth, Lupy Mallis and Satoshi Akiyama.[22] We have done six experiments on a wide variety of structures involving more than 100 children from 3 to 10. The bulk of the experiments involved children marking one or more pictures from an array of four. For instance, in one picture two people would be lifting their own hats, while Big Bird lifts another person's hat. Then we would say:

Here's Big Bird and his friends. They like hats:

    (31)   whose hat is he lifting
or   (32)   who is lifting his hat

At no age did the children make incorrect choices on these sentences ((31) ⇒ Big Bird, (32) ⇒ other two). This suggests that the children could perceive the relation between the anaphoric module and the trace since the deep structure of (31) is: *whose hat is he lifting trace*. The *he*. once again, precedes the *trace*.

The more complex sentences produced systematic errors. The pictures contained thought-bubbles which the children were easily able to interpret.

Here is Big Bird and his friends. They like clothes:

    (33)   who thinks he is wearing a hat
    (34)   who does he think is wearing a hat

The children, until the age of 8, allow a bound variable reading for both of these sentences in equal amounts (roughly 25 per cent). They were exactly as likely to have two 'friends' thinking about themselves for (34) as they were likely to select Big Bird thinking about one of them. The putative origin structure for (34) is (35):

    (35)   who does he think [$_S$ *trace* is wearing a hat$_S$]

Why should it be difficult for children to carry out the same interpretive operation on these sentences? We have noted above that extraction from sentences is generally exceptional. Hence we do not find nominalizations that permit extraction: *the persuading of John to go/*John's persuasion to go*. It is therefore not surprising that children should choose a different path at this point? But what is that path?

We would argue that there is an empty category which is equivalent to a pronoun which can appear in such contexts. It is like a residual pronoun found in semi-grammatical structures like *?who does he think Bill and him are wearing hats*. In fact, such sentences are grammatical in other languages. In effect, the child, in an attempt to avoid exceptionality, chooses a different language family for a time. Other information in the language, linked to quite different phenomena (like expletives), eventually reveals to the child that English is not a residual pronoun language.[23]

TRIGGER THEORY

We have argued that the linguistic and cognitive systems for certain semantic notions are not identical. We have not exlcuded the possibility that some relation exists between the two systems. What is the relation between extra-linguistic cognitive knowledge and linguistic modules? We assume that cognitive concepts are a prerequisite for related linguistic concepts (see Chomsky, 1981). As such they can bear a *trigger* relation to linguistic concepts. A trigger, a notion which comes from biology, does not bear a deductive relation to the thing triggered. It is like any other feature of biological growth: the structure triggered is far more complex than the triggering information.

It is important to note that a theory of triggers is quite compatible with a theory of maturation. It could be that the organism must mature in two ways. It must have *cognitive maturity* before it is possible to trigger certain linguistic concepts. Secondly, the trigger itself might be sensitive to maturational processes.[24] For instance, in the example just discussed, one could imagine that a child might fail to have the notion of bound variables at either the cognitive or linguistic level. If maturation is involved, then a child's grammar could be defined in a different notation at earlier stages. This has often been suggested, though not persuasively demonstrated, when the argument is made that a child's earliest grammars are semantic.

Current Models

How does our discussion relate to current models of acquisition? In general terms we can abstract three models from the literature: the continuity hypothesis (the grammatical abilities of the child are the same at every stage, but new rules are added);[25] the parametric hypothesis (grammars are in adult notation, but undergo radical redefinition with new input),[26] and the maturation hypothesis (early grammars are in a different notation, certain triggers cause a reformulation).[27] These are crude characterizations of a complex process which we do not yet understand.

In fact, there is no reason to choose among these hypotheses. It is quite possible that all three could be applicable to different parts of the acquisition process. One must examine each structure and each stage in acquisition to see how the evolution occurs. In effect, an explanatory theory of grammar, coupled with an *account* of the acquisition process should be the appropriate input to a biological theory. In that sense, there may be no independent theory of language acquisition. However, the account of acquisition may be as important as linguistic theory itself in a biological model.

CONCLUSION

We have argued that meaning itself has modular origins. The definition of agent or variable can be linked to quite different parts of the mind: an inference system or a syntactic system. The modules are connected by a trigger relation but, we have argued, they require a separate definition in each domain. In certain respects this solution resembles Piagetian notions of 'interaction'. Perhaps he would agree with the current trends in linguistics.

Our discussion, inevitably, has wandered into technical details of analysis. Technical details, of course, do not lend themselves to cross-theoretical comparison. In general most theories, in their internal structure, cannot readily be compared. This is true of theories within generative grammar or, for that matter, within government-binding. Can no theory, then, attain superiority? Or are acquisition stages described in terms of core and periphery/productive and unproductive features of universal grammar simply the equivalent ('notational variants') of Piaget's notion of *decalage*? The problem is obscure, but not troublesome. The comparison of theories is not the goal of science. If a comparison must occur, it should occur at another level, typical for biology. Are the theories equally *robust* and do they both offer a subtle *fit* between theory and fact? Impressionistically, the Piagetian theory seems programmatic and unable to address subtle features of human language. Most of the central problems are left untouched.

Psychology and Methodology

One reason that there exists a persistent disjunction between work in psychology departments and work in linguistic departments has to do with the assumption that we know what the domain of inquiry is, what language is. But linguistic research constantly discovers new data which shift the centre of research and in effect shift our view of what a theory must explain, what language is. Much of the crucial data of language, though spoken every day, has been as hidden from view as if it has been at the bottom of the sea. For instance, one recent discovery is a difference in coreference when focus is present, as in the contrast between: *John's₁ FATHER likes him₁* and **JOHN'S₁ father likes him₁* where in the latter *him* cannot be *John*. In fact, the whole theory of anaphora interacts with how focus works. At what point do children know that a focused possessive rules out forward anaphora?

It is often asserted that children of 5 have mastered English grammar. Yet most of the structures currently under scrutiny in linguistic theory have never undergone acquisition research. We know little of how or when children comprehend quantifiers, wh-movement is complex structures raising and nominalizations. There is a vast descriptive deficit in acquisition work and a huge bias toward simple syntactic forms. For instance, a great deal of work has been devoted to the passive, but I am unaware of any work that addresses the interaction between passive and raising: *John seems to have been left*?

Does raising appear when other movement rules appear, like 'tough-movement': *John is easy to please*? The answer seems to be, judging from a small sample of naturalistic data, that tough-movement appears at the age of 3 while raising does not arise until the age of 6. This is a mammoth chronological difference and calls for an explanation. Yet the question itself remains unknown to most workers in the field.

Part of the problem lies in allegiance to the methods of the psychologist and not to the methods of the field linguist. We need, first, a rough sense, obtainable by informal conversation, of what lies in children's grammars, and then a refined sense of how each step is taken. The distinctions are subtle and sharp enough (like those between (23) and (24) above) that any consistent difference in interpretation (in virtually any experimental context) will be significant. This approach calls for constant interaction between linguistics and developmental work.

Here Chomsky and Piaget may meet (in methodology). Piaget's interview techniques resemble the methods of the field linguist and they become more and more relevant as the sophistication of linguistic theory grows. It seems that Piaget knew, intuitively, that essential features of human nature appear in subtle and evanescent ways, like occasional traces of subatomic particles on photographic paper. In this important sense Chomsky and Piaget share a common grasp, not of language, but perhaps of human beings.

NOTES

1   I would like to thank N. Chomsky for comments on the first draft of this chapter. See Chomsky (1957). Chomsky (1984) provides the best current account of Chomsky's views on language acquisition. See also Chomsky (1965, 1975).

2   The parametric theory is described in Chomsky (1981). For a particularly interesting discussion in the light of language acquisition, see Hyams (1983, forthcoming) and Otsu (1981, forthcoming), also

papers in Roeper and Williams (in preparation) and references. Background is also available in Tavakolian (1981) and Baker and McCarthy (1981).

The parametric approach is carefully enunciated within the theory of government and binding, which will serve as the basis for this discussion. Most of what we argue is transferable to other current versions of generative theory, e.g., lexical-functional grammar. See Pinker (1984) for a discussion in that framework along with numerous other interesting arguments about the role of theory in acquisition research.

3 This formulation is highly simplified and neglects pertinent data, such as preposing in nominalizations. The formulation is intended for expository purposes only.

4 See Keyser and Roeper (1984), Finer and Roeper (forthcoming) and Burzio (forthcoming).

5 My knowledge of Piagetian literature is not extensive. It includes the work in Piatelli-Palmarini (1980) and Sinclair-de-Zwart, Chipman, and others who have addressed problems in complex syntax. My construal of Piaget therefore may be artificially narrow in order to make the contrast with Chomsky sharper.

6 See Anderson (1979), Roeper (1986) and Jaeggli (1984).

7 See Keyser and Roeper (1984) for extensive discussion and modification.

8 Finer and Roeper (forthcoming).

9 This argument is highly simplified. Numerous complications arise which, via principled explanation, strengthen the basic hypothesis.

10 Note that if an −ing affix is present in a compound, then the relations are once again fixed: in *government-selecting* the *government* must be the object, while in *government selection* the *government* can be either agent or object.

11 See Pinker (1984), and Grimshaw (1981) for a discussion of this point using the notion 'semantic bootstrapping'. The term seems unfortunate to me because it does not make clear whether the stages are guided by general induction or, as I argue here, by universal grammar. Thus the central question is left obscure.

12 There are subregularities in this system (see Roeper, 1986). For instance, it is generally the subject and not the object which appears when no affix is present, as in *the bite of the dog*, as opposed to *the biting of the dog* which favours the object reading.

13 The term *periphery* has several important uses in linguistic theory, of which this is one. The connection between productivity and acquisition is not usually discussed.

14 Note that we have, quite predictably, *the phoTOGrapher of weddings* which contrasts with *the PHOtoGRAPHer of weddings*. The latter is at least marginally better.

15 These examples are drawn from a corpus I have collected.

16 Randall (1982, p. 173).

17 Bates (1976) and a large literature in developmental journals.

18 Maratsos (1976) shows that children know the meaning of articles from virtually the one-word stage. See Macnamara (1982).

19 See Chomsky (1981) and Solan (1983) for extensive discussion of how the anaphoric principle should be stated. It has been argued that the principle is entirely hierarchical and makes no reference to order. We assume, with Solan, that order sensitivity is the unmarked condition.

20 Note that a single coreferential reading is possible under inference. I can say *he saw who the murderer was in the mirror.*In this case a preceding *he* does refer to a subsequent *who*. However, unlike (23), only a single person, not a set of people can be referred to by this inferential mechanism. In other words, no bound variables are present.

21 See Lust (forthcoming) also work in Tavakolian (1981), Solan (1983), Jacubowicz (1984), Phinney (1981), Goodluck (1978) and many others.

22 Roeper, Rooth, Mallis and Akiyama (1984)

23 This is a highly simplified version of a complex theory. See Hyams (1983, forthcoming) for an extensive and illuminating discussion, also Roeper and Williams (forthcoming).

24 See Roeper (1982) and Borer and Wexler (1984).

25 Klein (1982) and Pinker (1984).

26 Hyams (1983).

27 Borer and Wexler (1984) and Roeper (1980).

REFERENCES

Anderson. M. (1979) *Noun Phrase Structure*, dissertation, University of Connectcut.

Barker, C. L. and McCarthy, J. (1981) *The Logical Problem of Language Acquisition*, Cambridge, Mass., MIT Press.

Bates, E. (1976) *Language and Context*, New York, Academic Press.

Borer, H. and Wexler, K. (1984) 'The maturation of syntax', (to appear) in Roeper, T. and Williams, E. (Eds) *Proceedings of the Conference on Parameter-Setting*, Reidel.

Chomsky, N. (1957) *Syntactic Structures*, The Hague, Mouton.

Chomsky, N. (1965) *Aspects of The Theory of Syntax*, Cambridge, Mass., MIT Press.

Chomsky, N. (1970) 'Remarks on nominalizations', in Jacobs, R. and Rosenbaum, P. (Eds) *Readings in Transformational Grammar* Ginn.

Chomsky, N. (1975) *Reflections on Language*, Pantheon.

Chomsky, N. (1981) *Lectures on Government and Binding*, Dordrecht, Foris Publications.

Chomsky, N. (1984) *Knowledge of Language: Its Nature, Origins, and Use*, ms, MIT.

Finer, D. and Roeper, T. (1983, to appear) 'From cognition to thematic roles: The projection principle and language acquisition', in May, R. and Matthews, R. *Proceedings of the Ontario Conference on Learnability*.

Goodluck, H. (1978) *Linguistic Principles in Children's Grammar of Complement Subject Deletion*, dissertation, University of Massachusetts.

Grimshaw, J. (1979) 'Complement selection and the lexicon,' *Linguistic Inquiry*, **10, 2.**

Grimshaw, J. (1981) 'Form, function, and the language acquisition device', in Baker, C. L. and McCarthy, J., *The Logical Problem of Language Acquisition*, Cambridge, Mass., MIT Press.

Hyams, N. (1983) *The Acquisition of Parameterized Grammars*, dissertation, City University of New York, (to appear) Holland, Reidel.

Ingram, D. and Shaw P. (1981) 'Acquisition of pronouns', ms, University of British Columbia.

Jacubowicz, C. (1984) 'On markedness and binding principles', *NELS*, **15.**

Jaeggli, O. (1984) 'Passive', ms, University of South Carolina.

Keyser, S. J. and Rocper, T. (1984) 'On the middle and ergative constructions in English', *Linguistic Inquiry*, **15, 3.**

Klein, S. (1982) *Syntactic Theory and the Developing Grammar*, dissertation, University of California at Los Angeles.

Lebeaux, D. (1985) 'The acquisition of passive and affectedness', ms, University of Massachusetts.

Lust, B. (forthcoming) (Ed.) *Studies in the Acquisition of Anaphora: Defining the Constraints*, Holland, Reidel.

Macnamara, J. (1983) *Names for Things*, ..., Bradford.

Maratsos, M. (1971) *The Acquisition of the Definite and Indefinite Articles*, Cambridge, Cambridge University Press.

Otsu, Y. (1981, forthcoming) *Universal Grammar and Syntactic Development in Children*, dissertation, MIT (forthcoming) Reidel.

Phinney, M. (1981) *Syntactic Constraints and the Acquisition of Embedded Sentential Complements*, dissertation, University of Massachusetts.

Piatelli-Palmarini, M. (1980) *Language and Language Learning*, Cambridge, Mass., Harvard University Press.

Pinker, S. (1984) *Language Learning and Language Development*, Cambridge, Mass., Harvard University Press.

Randall, J. (1982) *Morphological Structure and Language Acquisition*, dissertation, University of Massachusetts.

Roeper, T. (1980) 'Introduction', in Burke, V. and Pusteovsky, J. (Eds), *Markedness and Learnability*.

Roeper, T. (1982) 'Linguistic universals and the acquisition of gerunds', in Wanner and Gleitman.

Roeper, T. (1984) 'Implicit arguments', ms, University of Massachusetts.

Roeper, T. and Williams E. S. (Eds) (to appear) *Parameter-Setting*, Holland, Reidel.

Roeper, T., Rooth, M., Mallis, L. and Akiyama, S. (1984) 'On the problem of empty categories in language acquisition', for *Cognition*.

Solan, L. (1983) *pronominal Reference: Anaphora and Child Language*, Reidel. Conference on Parameter-Setting, University of Massachusetts.

Tavakolian, S. (Ed.) (1981) *Language Acquisition and Linguistic Theory*, Cambridge, Mass., MIT Press.

13. Language: A Gift of Nature or a Home-Made Tool?

HERMINA SINCLAIR*

During much of its history, the study of language has had links with philosophy, logic, psychology and other human sciences. However, in general, the links were either fairly loose (other human sciences taking up terms from linguistics and using them to describe or classify phenomena observed elsewhere) or they were so close as to produce almost a fusion and not a link between at least partly autonomous disciplines. Chomsky is one of the rare linguists (and maybe the only one) whose work not only proclaims the autonomy of grammar, but also follows this principle in its analysis, and who has, at the same time, exercised great influence on the world of intellectual enterprise as a whole, and on philosophy and psychology in particular.

I am certainly not capable of sketching the impact of Chomsky's work, either on his followers or on his opponents, even in the case of Piagetian constructivist psychologists (amongst whom I count myself, after having, a long time ago, been a student of historical linguistics). I consequently decided to concentrate on the only view I am sure of, my own, and to describe in a personal and rather unsystematic way the impact Chomsky's work has had on myself.

My first acquaintance with Chomsky's work brought me at least two great moments of insight. I must, of course, have 'known' that human beings were capable of understanding and producing an indefinitely large number of sentences of indefinite length, but I had not been aware of it and I had certainly not realized its implications. The result of my becoming aware of this property of everybody's language competence was that I had a different view on (or different feeling about) every single sentence or utterance I read or heard, even such simple ones as 'John left' or 'Who?' Seeing a sentence as 'a simple affirmative active sentence' is very different from seeing it as merely one realization from an indefinitely large number of possibilities. A similar shift in perspective must occur when one realizes that there is no limit to the set of natural numbers, i.e., that 'you can count on and on for ever, and

*The experimental work on which this chapter is based was made possible by grants from the 'Fonds national suisse de la recherche scientifique', FN 1.133.69, FN 1.190.75 and FN 1.769.0.83.

173

if you stop somebody else can go on', as a child once explained. After this discovery, numbers and their combination into additions, etc. appear in an entirely new guise.

Another moment of insight came when I understood something about transformations. Underlying strings, let me call them sentence patterns, can be twisted and they can be combined with other sentence-patterns, much like a mobile can take on different configurations of its elements and combine with another mobile. But only certain constellations can appear under certain conditions; there are rules, and these rules are internal to the structural system itself. Even now, with considerable scope for hindsight, I am not altogether sure what makes me think of this insight as something quite fundamental. I suppose I interpreted the extensive discussions on transformations in Chomsky's writings as meaning that a language system is both defined by and defines the transformations that can be effected within it. Moreover, I suppose that this insight fitted in with a Piagetian principle: a child's (or adult's, for that matter) knowledge in the large sense, i.e., the way he organizes the world he lives in and his own thoughts about it, stems from the transformations he carries out and becomes aware of (even just turning one's head and looking at a toy from another angle is a transformation). Action, not passive recording of exterior reality (out of reach in any case), is what builds knowledge.

Other passages in Chomsky's writings had a different kind of impact on me: they did not provide new moments of insight, but reinforced the anti-empiricist, anti-positivist, and anti-associationist positions I had derived from Piaget. Many of Chomsky's arguments when he deals with his opponents in this area seem particularly incisive. For example, Chomsky's discussion on the 'psychological reality' of linguists' constructions and the kinds of evidence that allow the linguist or psychologist to 'impute existence to certain mental representations and to the mental computations that apply in a specific way to these mental representations' (1978, p. 206) deals with objections to his theories that are very similar to those often raised against Piagetian psychology.

Some of Chomsky's statements in this context are parallel to statements we have often felt obliged to make about our approach to the study of child language. Compare, for example, Chomsky (1978, p. 203) and Sinclair *et al.* (1976, p. 172). Chomsky argues as follows:

> Our investigation of the apparatus of the language faculty, whether in its initial or final steady state, bears some similarity to the investigation of thermonuclear reactions in the solar interior that is limited to evidence provided by light emitted at the periphery. We observe what people say and do, how they react and respond, often in situations contrived so that this behavior will provide some evidence (we hope) concerning the operative mechanisms. We then try, as best as we can, to devise a theory of some depth and significance in regard to these mechanisms, testing our theory by its success in providing explanation for selected phenomena. Challenged to show that the constructions postulated in the theory have 'psychological reality' we can do no more than repeat the evidence and the proposed explanations that. involve these constructions.

In the very similar passage indicated above we explained that we try to reach the competence of the child through many 'peripheral' approaches (experimental, often contrived, situations where either the child's comprehension of certain sentences is investigated or his production is elicited, studies of the way he judges certain sentences and other meta-linguistic studies, comparative studies in different languages, etc.) since there is no direct way of studying this competence. Exactly like Chomsky, when challenged we can do no more than 'repeat the evidence and the proposed explanations.' Also like Chomsky, we explain that we try to devise a theory in regard to what we have observed and to test this theory by its success in providing explanations. In other words, both Chomsky and the Genevan psycholinguists defend their approaches to the problem of language competence as scientific, and as the only possible ones (in our own views) given the nature of the object of our enquiries.

So far, I am, first, indebted to Chomsky, and, secondly, in perfect agreement with his approach. Let me now try to explain where I disagree. As was pointed out in the above-mentioned article (pp. 172–3), from a psychological point of view we consider the object of our studies, the language competence and the way it develops in the child, as an integral part of a general cognitive competence. In the first place, utterances heard and produced by children express meanings (interests, desires, ideas, observations, etc.), and the construction of meanings begins extremely early in life to reach an elaborate state before language (in the sense of understanding conventional words and, maybe a little later, producing them) starts. Secondly, it seems to us implausible that the numerous mechanisms the child applies to his task of understanding his physical and social environment would not also be applied to his efforts to come to grips with those curious strings of sounds he hears from other people (and which are very important to the baby, extremely early and possibly from birth, in comparison with other sounds). From Piaget's epistemological perspective, language is neither the source of cognitive structures, nor a particular type of knowledge distinct from other types. This does not mean that we consider language, or maybe better grammar, as not having any particular features that set it apart from other products of the human mind. One such property is no doubt that of transposing a hierarchical thought-structure into a sequential string of words. Nor does our hypothesis deny that human genetic endowment determines both constraints on and possibilities for human knowledge, and that some of the genetic determining factors may be specific to language. Our theory-building efforts are thus directed towards finding out what is particular to language (but linguistically universal) in comparison with other human capacities (especially other means of representation and communication) and what is specific to one (or some) language(s) compared to others. In other words, we do not contest that something is innate in all cognitive competence and even in language competence, but we feel that the scope of this 'something' is a neuro-biological question. Until further neuro-biological evidence becomes available, the plausibility of a theory in this matter depends only on the linguistic and psychological data and arguments its author may adduce.

The basic difference between Chomsky's theories and our own needs to be clearly stated. Howard Gardner (1980, p. xxiii) succinctly gives Chomsky's position as it appeared in his debate with Piaget (1979, 1980): Chomsky sees 'the human mind as a set of essentially pre-programmed units, each equipped from the first to realize its full complement of rules and needing only the most modest environmental trigger to exhibit its intellectual wares.' In fact, Chomsky goes even further than this statement indicates: he also thinks that one of the hypothetical components of the human mind, namely universal grammar, is in principle not different from other components that will exhibit what may be called 'anatomical wares', such as the genetic properties that determine that an embryo will have arms rather than wings (1981, 1984).

I differ from Chomsky's position on two counts. First, I do not believe that no real ontological development of important cognitive structures takes place, and secondly, I cannot see language competence, in the form of universal grammar with the particular properties Chomsky bestows on it, as a separate unit (not even if one accepted a modular view of the human mind).

On the first point, I accept Piaget's theory that genetic endowment (and especially human genetic endowment) does not determine development in any direct way: 'between the level of hereditary characteristics and that of the acquisitions due to environmental factors, there is a level of self-regulation or equilibration which plays a vital role in development. This does not oblige or even authorize us to think of everything which is not due to exogenous learning as innate' (Piaget and Inhelder, 1971, p. 122). In human beings these epigenetic self-regulations become self-constructive mechanisms. The knowing subject is highly active in a rich social and physical environment; his constructions and the difficulties that have to be overcome can often be followed, especially in short longitudinal experiments such as described by Inhelder *et al.* (1974).

On the second point, I see language as a tool constructed by the human mind (on the basis of its innate capacities) in the service of representation and communication, when humans became capable of and felt the need for the construction of such a tool. Therefore, even in a modular conception of human cognition, I cannot see universal grammar as a primary, independent unit, but believe basic language competence to be constructed by the child subsequent to and on the model of the child's fundamental achievements during the pre-verbal practical intelligence period—achievements that bear on his knowledge of the physical as much as of the social world he lives in.

On both points, I admit freely that my convictions are not based on hard evidence. On the first, there are the innumerable studies by Piaget that render a constructivist view plausible, and in my view inescapable. On the second, chronology is in our favour: many authors have noted the approximate synchrony of the beginnings of language and such other cognitive conquests as the permanence of objects (in its elaborate stage), pretend play, a certain level of communicative behaviour (Bates, 1979; Nicolich, 1981; Smolak, 1982; Veneziano, 1981, 1984). Once again, none of this means that I contest that innate capacities were used by human beings in their construction of language and speech, nor that I think that children do not use such capacities to build up their language (they do and there is clear evidence for it). We also agree that children have to develop specific linguistic rules. Very early in their careers as native speakers, children come to grips with problems that are specifically linguistic, for example, the sequential nature of speech. More and more such specifically linguistic problems will have to be solved as the child's knowledge of his language grows. But even then, as I will try to show below, the general-purpose cognitive mechanisms brought to light by Piaget and his collaborators appear to play an important part.

This leads me to my next point which has to do with the way we think we find evidence for our respective theories. Chomsky starts from facts (mainly drawn from judgments adults are capable of giving about certain sentences) pertaining to the adult state of language knowledge. For example, he shows how adults' knowledge allows them to give precise and correct interpretations of sentences such as the following:

John is too stubborn to talk to Bill.
John is too stubborn to talk to.
John is too clever to expect us to catch Bill.
John is too clever to expect us to catch him.

These facts can be accounted for by the theory of government and binding. Chomsky then goes on to argue that it is implausible to suppose that speakers of English have had sufficiently numerous data at their disposal to master this knowledge by processes such as induction and confirmation, and that in many instances it would be difficult to imagine what such data might be. Therefore, concludes Chomsky, it is reasonable to suppose that such properties of the grammar reflect intrinsic properties of the human mind-brain, just as it is highly probable that innate properties determine that a human embryo develops a mammalian eye rather than the eye of an insect (1981, 1984). Chomsky's procedure and his way of arguing (which are both perfectly clearly described) appear to me as exactly parallel to our own procedures and arguments.

In general, we start with the hypothesis that a certain sentence pattern will probably not be understood in the adult way by children below the age of, say, 4 or 5. Having verified this, we then construct multiple ways of sounding out how children of different ages interpret, produce, repeat, judge and answer questions about such sentences (e.g., Sinclair and Ferreiro, 1970; Ferreiro, 1971; Ferreiro *et al.*, 1976; Berthoud and Sinclair, 1978). So far, the results of such experiments fit into a Piagetian constructivist framework, whereas they seem to be incompatible with the hypothesis of the (however gradual) unfolding of a genetically preprogrammed grammar.

Let me take an example I have already discussed in a paper in English (1978, pp. 187–98). Ferreiro (1971) studied children's growing mastery of the means that speakers of French use to express the correct succession of two events, *P* and *Q*, when starting their description with event *Q*. For example:

The boy went upstairs when the girl had washed him.

Before the boy went upstairs, the girl washed him.

The boy went upstairs after the girl had washed him.

To study their comprehension of such sentences, she asked her subjects to show what the sentences meant, using dolls, other toys and a doll's house. To study children's production of such sentences, she showed the combined event described by sentences such as those given above, and asked her subjects, first, to relate what had happened (free description), and then to do so again but this time to begin with the boy going upstairs (inverse-order description). Other questions were also asked, and the event was performed (and imitated by the child) as often as necessary to make sure that no memory difficulties remained. Ferreiro observed many interesting (i.e., unexpected, but systematically occurring) behaviours; let me give a few examples of such behaviours as noted in the inverse-order description task. The youngest, least advanced children (around 4 years of age) usually, but not always, give their free description in the order *P*, *Q*, with the two propositions loosely connected by *and* or *and then*. For the inverse-order description they simply say *Q* and *P*, with both verbs in the same tense, 'The boy went upstairs and the girl washed him.' At the next level of development, the children always give their free description in the form *P*, then *Q*, with both verbs in the same tense (present or past). But for them the demand for the inverse-order description creates a conflict: these children declare, 'It cannot be done; it would come out wrong, it would be the wrong way around.' When they are encouraged to try anyway, curious compromise solutions are proposed, such as the following :

    (a)   Event *Q* is described in an inverted way: in the example given, 'The boy goes upstairs' becomes 'The boy goes downstairs.' The total event is then (incorrectly) described as follows: 'He goes downstairs and the girl washes his hands.'

    (b)   The agents of events *P* and *Q* are inverted: 'The boy washed the girl and then she goes upstairs.'

The children who propose these solutions know full well that their descriptions do not fit the events they were shown. They seem to know that the inversion demanded by the instruction to start with event Q has to be compensated for by some other modification of their initial description, but they cannot yet find the way to do this, although all the verbal means (before, after; later, but first; already; tenses) are at their disposal as was verified through other questions. The most advanced subjects (age 8 or 9) have no difficulty in using these different means to describe correctly the events in the order Q, P.

This type of development, i.e., the 'falling apart' of an initial organization that works well and creates no conflict, followed by conflict and efforts to resolve it, leading to a higher organization, is frequently observed in other domains of knowledge (cf. Inhelder *et al.*, 1974). In language acquisition such patterns escape psycholinguists when the children's comprehension of certain sentence-forms is studied experimentally, and also when a corpus of spontaneous utterances is analyzed: only ingenious elicitation of production will bring them to light. Several of our experiments have yielded this type of data (cf. Sinclair and Ferreiro, 1970; Berthoud and Sinclair, 1978).

My argument is, then, as follows: I see no way to render these data compatible with a theory that posits the triggering of an innate endowment with as one of its components a universal grammar as specific as the one proposed by Chomsky. By contrast, the data fit well with Piaget's constructivism, which gives a reasonable explanation for such progress.

Thus, Chomsky starts from facts about adults' knowledge, performs a highly technical analysis on certain sentences, brings the system of rules he has uncovered back to a universal principle, and concludes it is implausible that this principle, and thus the more specific rules, could have been induced by native speakers from the evidence they dispose of.

We start from facts about children's behaviour in experimental situations, analyze the facts in a psycholinguistic manner and conclude that it is implausible that the developmental line we uncovered could be the result of an unfolding innate competence.

I think that both methods are justifiable, and that neither is more 'scientific' or more 'explicit' than the other. Each chooses data considered pertinent for their problem: Chomsky starts with linguistic data pertaining to adult knowledge, the Piagetian psycholinguists start with developmental data. Both should be taken seriously; and as far as the Piagetian psycholinguists are concerned their theoretical conclusions should be taken as preliminary. As we have said many times, we do not yet possess a theory of language acquisition (or, if preferred, of the development of grammar), though we do have a theory of cognitive development in general; and until a theory about language acquisition has taken at least some more or less explicit form, the data we now see as pertinent to such a theory may turn out to be pertinent to some other theory. However, in my opinion, the same goes for the data adduced by Chomsky.

I would like to make one final remark on this point. If asked the question suggested by Gruber (1980): supposing that something important in language is innate, would the Piagetians go about their studies of child language in a different way? My answer is: no, we would not. We would still want to investigate how a preprogrammed system of structures unfolds; or, in Chomsky's words, we would want to study how syntactic structure maps onto lexical properties which he considers to be discovered by the child through experience (Chomsky, 1984, p. 16).

To conclude, I wish to raise a point also mentioned by Gruber. This is the question of how linguistic competence evolved in the species.

> How could a proto-human lift itself by its cognitive bootstraps into the world of words and sentences? . . . Even if the transition to linguistic competence were a sudden evolutionary jump, the result of the macro-mutation or a final transforming mutation, a problem would still remain. We would have to believe *either* that the first child carrying the new hereditary blessing came into a world without language and began to speak, *or* that the child and her descendants were the vehicles through which language evolved over an indefinite number of generations. The first alternative is implausible, and the second means that a series of precursors to human language can be imagined, which is indistinguishable from Piaget's constructivism. (Gruber, 1980).

This is, indeed, the point where so-called nativists (but now I no longer refer to Chomsky himself) find themselves making highly questionable statements.

All human languages have been created by humans and are therefore dependent on human biological capacities. It is trivial to take this to mean that all human beings (pathological accidents apart) can hear a certain range of sound and can produce a certain variety of sounds. It goes further than that, and means, for example, that all languages are based on phonological principles that could not function but for the innate capacity of what is called categorical perception. A number of experiments with infants in their first weeks of life have brought to light this type of auditive perceptual mechanism for speech sounds (though categorical perception is no doubt limited neither to humans nor to speech sounds). But to state that human language is constructed on the basis of this categorical perceptual capacity is rather different from saying that children are born with perceptual (and other) mechanisms specially adapted to human speech.

Eimas, to whom we owe many interesting experiments on the perception of speech in infants, asserts, for example: 'Categorization occurs because a child is born with perceptual mechanisms that are tuned to the properties of speech' (1985, p. 37). This is putting the cart before the horse. It seems to me that sometime, somewhere, some humans found that they had a problem and the means to solve it. The problem certainly included the need for the transmission of messages about the past and the future. Among the means to solve it were the manifold capacities implied in the human genetic make-up such as categorical perception (and probably also a general capacity for pattern-building and pattern-recognition, and many other specifically human talents including consciousness). I would, therefore, turn Eimas' above-mentioned sentence around and say the properties of human speech are tuned to the perceptual mechanisms the child is born with. Eimas' formulation leads him to a peculiar conclusion: 'It may be that like the specialized anatomy of the vocal tract and the speech centers in the brain these innate perceptual capacities evolved specifically for the perception and comprehension of speech. They are an evolutionary answer to the need for each infant to acquire its parents' language and culture as early in life as possible.' Does this mean that articulated speech existed first in humans who did not have these innate capacities? who made up some kind of language un-suited to the then existing human innate abilities, that was therefore difficult (or even well-nigh impossible) to learn? and that later the human genetic make-up changed so as to fit this language better? This is a most peculiar view of phylogenesis. Two other possibilities seem much more natural: the one I mentioned, that language started from the innate endowment which was its basis, or, possibly, that the specific capacities evolved hand in hand with the construction of language.

The origins of human language may forever remain shrouded in mystery, but the question of how children who are born into a culture that is permeated with language acquire what is called their mother-tongue should receive an answer. If and when it does, it will be in no small measure due to Chomsky, whose precise and explicit theoretical formulations incited both his followers and his critics to re-examine their premises and to ask themselves new questions.

REFERENCES

Bates, E. (1979) *The Emergence of Symbols*, New York, Academic Press.

Berthoud, I. and Sinclair, H. (1978) 'L' expression d'éventualités et de conditions chez l'enfant', *Archives de Psychologie*, **46, 179**, pp. 205–33.

Chomsky, N. (1978) 'On the biological basis of language capacities', in Miller, A. G. and Lenneberg, E. (Eds), *Psychology and Biology of Language and Thought*, New York, Academic Press, pp. 199–220.

Chomsky, N. (1984) 'La connaissance du langage', *Communications*, **40**, pp. 7–24, originally published in English in 1981 in the *Philosophical Transactions of the Royal Society of London*.

Eimas, P. (1985) 'The perception of speech in early infancy', *Scientific American*, January.

Ferreiro, E. (1971) *Les Relations temporelles dans le Language de l'Enfant*, Geneva, Droz.

Ferreiro, E. *et al.* (1976) 'How do children handle relative clauses?' *Archives de Psychologie*, **45, 3**, pp. 229–66.

Gardner, H. (1980) Foreword, in Piatelli-Palmarini, M. (Ed.), *Language and Learning: The Debate between Jean Piaget and Noam Chomsky*, Cambridge, Mass., Harvard University Press.

Gruber, H. E. (1980) 'Language learning', in *New York Book Review*, 19 October, pp. 250–6.

Inhelder, B., Sinclair, H. and Bovet, M. (1974) *Apprentissage et Structures cognitives*, Paris, PUF; English translation: *Learning and the Development of Cognition*, London, Routledge and Kegan Paul.

Nicolich, L. McLune, (1981) 'Toward symbolic functioning: Structure of early pretend games and potential parallels with language', *Child Development*, **52**, pp. 785–97.

Piaget, J. and Inhelder, B. (1971) 'The gaps in empiricism', in Koestler, A. and Smythies, J. R. (Eds), *Beyond Empiricism*, Boston, Beacon Press.

Sinclair, H. and Ferreiro, E. (1970) 'Etude génétique de la compréhension, production et répétition des phrases au mode passif', *Archives de Psychologie*, **40, 160**, pp. 1–42.

Sinclair, H. *et al.* (1976) 'Recherches en psycholinguistique génétique', *Archives de Psychologie*, **44, 171**, pp. 225–31.

Sinclair, H. (1978) 'Conflict and progress', in Miller, G. A. and Lenneberg, E. (Eds), *Psychology and Biology of Language and Thought*, New York, Academic Press, pp. 187–98.

Smolak, L. (1982) 'Cognitive precursors of receptive vs. expressive language', *Journal of Child Language*, **9**, pp. 13–22.

Veneziano, E. (1981) 'Early language and nonverbal representation: A reassessment', *Journal of Child Language*, **8**, pp. 541–63.

Veneziano, E. (1984) *A Search for Formal and Structural Precursors of Language*, doctoral thesis, Hebrew University, Jerusalem.

Interchange

ROEPER REPLIES TO SINCLAIR

Professor Sinclair upholds the tradition of Piaget with clarity, grace and an attempt to make a fair-minded comparison between Piaget's approach and Chomsky's. I think her approach, though not as precise as I believe to be appropriate, might be on the right track in describing the growth of *language*.

However, we can ask whether it is appropriate for the explanation of *grammar*. The terms 'grammar' and 'language' refer to vastly different phenomena in current linguistic theory.[1] The term 'language' refers to the interaction of grammar with knowledge of the world, social factors, perceptual factors, parsing factors, etc. The term 'grammar' refers only to the deductive principles which are common to all languages.

Are her conclusions about language or grammar? First, the claims are simply not deductive; they are at best enlightening metaphors. For instance, she alludes to a period of 'falling apart', followed by a sense of conflict and efforts to resolve it. In what fashion does it fall apart, what causes the reconstruction and toward what linguistic end? Perhaps one might use his language to describe the interaction between a feature of grammar and an aspect of cognition, but the grammar itself remains untouched by it. Instead, the fact of a transition stage is being elevated here to a kind of 'principle' where no deductive structure is offered.

Let us examine a non-linguistic parallel: the ability to walk. Walking is generally considered to be innate. Nonetheless, it involve stages of crawling, then intermediate stages of crawling, falling, reeling off balance, and other fairly extreme-looking behaviour. The child's occasionally reeling off balance, knowing that he is not walking, strikes me as similar to the child's radical restructuring of an input sentence in the effort to fulfil a task beyond its capacities. I think it is comparable to the radical restructuring to which Sinclair alludes (i.e., 'the boy went downstairs instead of upstairs'). She suggests the child also knows that his rendition is wrong, just as the reeling child knows he cannot yet walk.

Sinclair-de-Zwart has chosen an example (the learning of temporal conjunctions) which represents the Piagetian style of acquisition research quite well. I think that the potential for using conversational elicitation techniques is particularly important for probing older children's knowledge of complex grammar. It is unfortunate the technique is so often ignored in American acquisition research. However, her approach to the 'learning' of conjunctions is entirely semantic. The experiment essentially explores how the child learns the *meaning* of a word like 'before' and its relation to the sequence of utterances. Meaning, of course, may involve any aspect of

181

real-world knowledge and therefore no particular syntactic knowledge is involved. In fact, 'before' has syntactic consequences which one might usefully explore. It allows prior reflexive structures:

(1)   Before washing himself, John ate dinner

How and when does the child learn to reconstruct the missing subject of the 'before' clause, which in turn justifies the use of the reflexive? How does the child know that the subordinating conjunction originates after the main clause, allowing a grammatical coreference reading:

(2)   John ate dinner before—washing himself

These are the questions which a deep explanation of acquisition must address. It would be extremely interesting to know if the child's capacity to comprehend 'before' led *immediately* to the capacity properly to construe these reflexives. Then we would know that the syntactic consequences of subordination had been triggered. It is just at this subtle point that we do *not* expect to see overt transitory behaviour of the sort that Sinclair has described.[2] In sum, one can see Sinclair's approach as compatible with Chomsky's as long as one recognizes that her approach simply addresses issues of language and not grammar.

Let me conclude with a few remarks about Piaget's contribution. In the intellectual history of the twentieth century Piaget may well be seen as the first to open the door to the systematic study of cognition. To those who pass through, not surprisingly, the interior may not match what he imagined. Piaget set as the goal the creation of a direct connection between biology and cognitive activity. In a way, this leaves out psychology as a domain of independent coherence. If true, then local cognitive coherence, mapped directly onto neurological descriptions may eventually reveal that 'general cognition' or 'general psychological mechanisms' are a collection of epi-phenomena. This is not Piaget's personal conclusion, but the thrust of his work is open to this interpretation I believe.

Instead of 'psychology' we have *modular* systems which have individual neurological roots. Sometimes modules reproduce the same knowledge in different domains (like stereoscopic eyes and ears), sometimes they interact mechanically (like the heart and lung), and sometimes they interact in unsystematic ways producing the bewildering array of behaviour that typically occurs on any day in the life of a human being. The challenge, now as then, is to see where interesting principles lie and to avoid the bottomless effort to explain our myriad, but momentary, behavioural moods.

NOTES

1   Chomsky (1985) makes this distinction and it is fundamental to the modular perspective on language.
2   It is noteworthy that prior reflexives are generally unacceptable:

   (3)   Bill undertook the education of himself
   (4)   *the education of himself cost Bill a lot

   Therefore a specifically structural phenomenon is involved. Our analysis of these phenomena entails an innate feature: subordination allows a prior reflexive to occur. This in turn follows from deeper principles of hierarchical structure. The technical features involved is *c-command*. There is now a large acquisition literature on the topic showing that children are sensitive to the distinction. See Solan (1983) and Lust (forthcoming) and references therein; see also Lasnik and Crain (to appear) for some evidence that Solan's claims hold at even younger ages.

REFERENCES

Chomsky, N. (1984) *Knowledge of Language: Its Nature, Origins, and Use*, ms, MIT.
Lust, B. (forthcoming) *Studies in the Acquisition of Anaphora: Defining the Constraints*, Dord recht. Reidel.
Lasnik, H. and Crain, S. (forthcoming) Review of *Pronominal Reference* Lingua.
Solan, L. (1983) *Pronominal Reference: Child Language and the Theory of Grammar.*

SINCLAIR REPLIES TO ROEPER

On the whole, I see more convergence than conflict between Roeper's position and my own. I agree that as yet there is no proper theory of language acquisition: it is, in Roeper's words, 'a complex process which we do not yet understand' (p. 168). He gives a number of examples that raise interesting questions, outlines the main orientation of his approach to the study of language acquisition, and presents a 'challenge' to Piagetians. I will briefly respond to these three points.

Discussing the principle of 'affectedness' (which, as Roeper shows, accounts very neatly for many intriguing facts of English grammar), Roeper states, 'it is clear that a semantic factor is interacting with a syntactic factor in a specific way. There is no deductive logic that leads to this association, although a biological logic, far beyond our current research capacities, might lead to this conclusion. For instance, there could be a neurological factor, or, perhaps, an accident of evolution which explains this modular interaction' (p. 160). I feel rather sceptical about neurological or evolutionary factors intervening in something as particular as the exceptionality of passive sentences. However, in his next paragraph Roeper proposes that 'the acquisition process itself might lead to this pattern.' This, in my opinion, is a purely constructivist Piagetian proposal, and I am happy to agree. Moreover, Roeper goes on to say that Lebeaux's observations show that 'children's passives initially obey the affectedness constraint.' Indeed they do, as was concluded from a lengthy series of experiments on the comprehension, production and repetition of passive sentences in French, English and Swiss-German with children between $3\frac{1}{2}$ and 8 years old (Sinclair and Ferreiro, 1970; Sinclair, Sinclair and de Marcellus, 1971; Caprez, Sinclair and Studer, 1971). We noticed a gap of several years between the mastery of sentences such as 'the boy is knocked down by the girl' and that of sentences such as 'the boy is followed by the girl', and concluded that this difference could only be accounted for by the fact that in the second sentence the verb expresses an action without any contact which results only in a displacement of both 'agent' and 'patient'. Semantic factors, we concluded, interact with syntactic factors in a complex way. In other words, so far Roeper and I seem to be in perfect agreement.

On the second point, the methodological approach to the study of the acquisition of language, there is indeed a difference. Roeper's hunch is that 'the way to approach important questions about UG is from the adult grammar working backwards to the child grammar' (p. 163). We prefer to start with the study of child grammar in order to avoid an adulto-centric bias, which at worst makes for experimental methods that lead the child towards responses that fit a hypothesized development, and at best does not allow the observation of intermediate stages (which may be 'evanescent', as Roeper himself remarks). However, there is no obvious reason why there might not be a meeting-point in the middle of our itineraries; a combination of both approaches certainly seems most promising—if difficult.

The third point, the 'challenge to the Piagetians' of the 'exclusion of nonallowable sentences' (p. 158), is the most difficult to comment upon and is a challenge for constructivist theory in general: why do only certain 'wrong ideas' appear in development? Why does the child's construction of knowledge in many domains tend towards 'better', 'more powerful' ideas? Much of Piaget's later work dealt with precisely this question. Piaget's solution may be briefly described as follows.

Within a system constructed by the child, however primitive, and at whatever level of development, the internal coherence of its rules renders certain actions or thought-operations necessary and others possible. What appears necessary to the child may not appear so to the adult, but it determines what is possible at a certain stage, just as what is regarded as possible determines what is necessary. A complex interaction takes place between success in solving a problem and trying to understand why a particular strategy is successful, as well as between feeling confident with a certain thought-pattern and feeling free to try others so that new experience can be 'admitted' into the system. The internal consistency of the system both sets norms at a certain stage and modifies them at another.

We are only beginning to see how this constructivist principle could be applied to language acquisition, but Roeper's hypothesis about 'affectedness' fits perfectly into this theoretical framework. Moreover, it leads (necessarily? possibly? at our present level of understanding . . .) to Roeper's hypothesis (p. 160) that 'what appears rather arbitrary in the adult language is rendered quite sensible when the problem of acquisition is included'—an idea which delights my constructivist heart!

REFERENCES

Caprez, G., Sinclair, H. and Studer, B. (1971) 'Entwicklung der Passivform im Schweizerdeutschen', *Archives de Psychologie*, **41, 161,** pp. 23–52.

Piaget, J. (1981) *Le Possible et le Nécessaire*, Paris, PUF.

Sinclair, A., Sinclair, H. and Marcellus, O. de (1971) 'Young children's comprehension and production of passive sentences', *Archives de Psychologie*, **41, 161,** pp. 1–22.

Sinclair, H. and Ferreiro, E. (1970) 'Etude génétique de la compréhension, production et répétition de phrases au mode passif', *Archives de Psychologie*, **40, 160,** pp. 1–42.

VIII: Part Four: Artificial Intelligence

14. Chomsky and Artificial Intelligence

I think the network of connections loosely around the cognitive sciences . . . form a pretty natural nexus. My own guess, frankly, is that if the kind of linguistics I am interested in survives in the United States, it may very likely be in that context, rather than in linguistics departments. (Chomsky, 1982, p. 8)

Although it would be wrong to underestimate the immense effect which Chomsky's work has had in many branches of intellectual activity, the enthusiasm with which some have traced his influence has scarcely known any bounds. So much so that not many years ago, for example, discussions on the intellectual antecedents of universal grammar had reached a stage where, per impossibile, there was a paper to be written on Chomsky's influence on the *Modistae*, the medieval modistic grammarians.

Artificial Intelligence (AI) has a head start over the *Modistae*: it is at least logically possible that Chomsky's work has influenced AI, and equally that AI has influenced Chomsky's own work in linguistic theory. Alan Turing's seminal paper, 'Computing machinery and intelligence', often taken to mark the advent of AI, was published in 1950, just five years before Chomsky wrote (but did not publish) his *Logical Structure of Linguistic Theory*, on which *Syntactic Structures* (1957) was based.

In his paper Turing considered under what conditions we would be prepared to ascribe intelligence to an artificial device, to a machine. He argued (to simplify somewhat) that if a person communicating at a distance (via a keyboard, for example) is unable to detect whether he or she is interacting with an unseen human or an unseen machine when in communication link with both, then we can reasonably assign intelligence to the non-human machine, as well as to the human. This, in essence, is the basis for the famous Turing test for (artificial) intelligence.

In arguing thus Turing was concerning himself in particular (though not exclusively) with that part of intelligence commonly thought to be more directly associated with language. AI, as it has developed over the years, has been concerned far more widely with the modelling of human cognitive abilities: there has been important work on vision (notably that of David Marr), for example, and on human reasoning. These wider concerns are reflected in the other labels under which (more or less) the same field is covered by different practitioners: *congitive science, cognitive studies* and (more recently) *knowledge engineering*.

What connections, then, can we establish, should we establish, between the work of Chomsky and studies in this polyonymous field? What relevance, if any, does his work have? What influence has it had? And are there others in the same field as Chomsky whose work also merits consideration with respect to AI? These are the issues we shall be considering in this chapter. It is difficult to summarize the conclusions in advance, for not all of the questions have very straightforward answers (as we shall see), but broadly speaking we shall argue that:

(1)   Chomsky's influence on AI has been considerably less than his influence on other areas identified in this volume (although considerably more than his influence on the *Modistae*);

(2)   notwithstanding the different nature of the two fields, as we shall detail it, there is a clear sense in which AI would benefit if it were to draw far more on the work of linguists, and (in particular) to incorporate some of the *methodological* insights of current grammatical theories.

Readers of the journal *Cognition* of some ten years ago may be forgiven for thinking that at least part of the remainder of this chapter is likely to be an action-replay of the Dresher and Hornstein (1976) paper in which they questioned the value of the contributions of AI, compared to linguistics, to 'the scientific study of language'. It is certainly true that that paper, perhaps more than any other, stimulated a lively (and sometimes heated) debate on the questions of the relative contributions of the two fields to our study of language, with replies by Winograd (1977) and Schank and Wilensky (1977) and rejoinders by Dresher and Hornstein (1977a, 1977b). Whilst the conclusions of Dresher and Hornstein are to some extent redrawn in this chapter, the forum for discussion has changed most decisively in the last ten years: this means that we can now re-evaluate some of the earlier discussion, and that in addition we can address a range of issues not resolved in the earlier discussion, with a view to seeking a *rapprochement* of sorts.

We begin by sketching some of the central tenets of Chomsky's position on the 'scientific study of language'. Most of the details will already be very familiar to most readers (and some at least are covered elsewhere in this volume) but it may nevertheless be useful to rehearse them here, especially since we shall find them systematically (and non-systematically) challenged in the AI literature.

Central to any presentation of Chomsky's contribution to the 'scientific study of language' must be an exposition of the (much-discussed) *competence/performance* distinction. In *Aspects of the Theory of Syntax* (Chomsky, 1965) a fundamental distinction is drawn between *what a speaker* (actually the 'ideal speaker-hearer') *knows* by virtue of which he or she has mastery of the language, and *what a speaker* (or hearer) *does*. A study of the former yields a theory of *competence*; of the latter, a theory of *performance*. A *grammar* of a language is an *explicit statement* of *competence*: 'We thus make a fundamental distinction between *competence* (the speaker-hearer's knowledge of his language) and *performance* (the actual use of language in concrete situations)' (Chomsky, 1965, p. 4). This distinction has, it would not be an exaggeration to say, received great attention—not least from philosophers. In particular they have frequently questioned the use of the term 'knowledge' for something of which we are not consciously aware: knowing a language, in this sense, is not like knowing the names of the capital cities of Europe. Nor, to refer back to a distinction originally made by Ryle, does knowing a language resemble *knowing how* rather than *knowing that*: knowledge of grammar does not amount to possession of a skill.

Chomsky's consistent response to these charges has been essentially to suggest that, as Higginbotham (1984, p. 116) puts it, 'these philosophical considerations merely show the impoverishment of the conceptions of knowledge that analytic philosophers have typically allowed in recent years', for there is an obviously cognitive state of *knowing English*, or French, or Arabic. If the term 'knowledge' continues to give offence, Chomsky suggests, then we may replace it by a technical term like 'cognition' and speak of a person's 'cognizing' his or her grammar.

There is, however, a further point about the notion of competence, and one that is highly relevant to the present discussion. In developing an account of competence the Chomskyan linguist is laying claim to be engaged in establishing a set of rules, which we have internalized, which (as a matter of fact) give us mastery of our language. A (transformational) grammar is an explicit statement of these rules, which collectively generate (in the mathematical sense attributable to Post) all and only the sentences of the language. The evidence for a theory of competence comes at a variety of levels of abstraction. The finer details, which have inevitably changed in Chomsky's exposition over the years, need not concern us here. Suffice it to note that at the simplest level a theory of competence must yield a grammar which not only generates all and only the sentences of the language under consideration but also assigns them the correct structural description (on the basis, largely but not entirely, of native-speaker intuitions), and that given that many distinct grammars are compatible with this evidence, Chomsky establishes for a linguistic theory the further goal of explanatory adequacy (to be achieved modulo an effective evaluation metric). This goal is to be met by abstracting away from particular descriptively adequate grammars to a level at which it is possible to establish linguistic universals which will be 'sufficiently rich and detailed to account for the facts of language learning' (Chomsky, 1965, p. 46), and perhaps ultimately to a level at which it will be possible to establish biological universals which will 'lay the foundations for a significant theory of human learning in various domains' (Chomsky, 1980, p. 254).

This is a rich and engaging intellectual programme: one that is characterized above all by the search, at increasing levels of intellectual abstraction, for linguistically significant generalizations, which will yield in turn increasing levels of explanation for the phenomena of language and language learning. Yet, as we shall see in the next section, there are many, in AI and elsewhere, who would question the very basis for such a programme; and who would certainly question its relevance to the hard-nosed business of getting a very different sort of program running on a computer. First, however, it will be helpful to draw out a further corollary to Chomsky's position.

The rules of a transformational grammar are, mathematically, production rules of an axiomatic system of the form:

$$x_1, x_2, \ldots, x_{n-1} \rightarrow x_n$$

For any string y, y can be proved to be a theorem of the system if and only if there is a linearly ordered sequence of strings $y_1, y_2, \ldots y_m$ such that every string in the sequence is either an axiom (e.g., the initial symbol *S* of Chomskyan grammars) or follows by one of the production rules from one or more of the strings preceding it. Such an ordered sequence is a derivation or proof. In linguistic terms, then, a given string constitutes a well-formed sentence of the language in question just in case the body of rules yields a derivation (proof) of that string. The (transformational) linguist is thereby committed to effectively sorting strings/sentences into the well-formed and the ill-formed—a perfectly reasonable and obvious position to be committed to, one might think, and one which is symbolic of Chomsky's fundamental break with earlier work in linguistics; the era of the linguist's '*'. Yet the *derivational paradigm*, as it has come to be known, has been fiercely resisted in many AI circles.

We considered in the last section the nature and extent of the evidence for establishing the competence of the ideal speaker-hearer, that which gives mastery of the language. There are two types of objection to this endeavour; the first relatively subtle, the second rather more brusque. Both are found in the AI literature (and elsewhere). The first takes the line that whatever evidence we can currently come up with for competence will seriously underdetermine the theory based on that evidence, so that we will have no right to argue that this is the body of knowledge which *does* give mastery; only that this is the body of knowledge which *would* give mastery (of the language in question) were it to be what we actually have in our heads. Whether or not we do have such a body of knowledge in our heads is precisely what is not determined by the data. (A variety of this line of objection is to be found in, for example, Foster, 1976.) The objection here is that we lack evidence for the 'psychological reality' (to use a much-abused phrase) of the linguist's constructs.

Chomsky's response to this is essentially Quinean in character (although Chomsky himself acknowledges a different intellectual debt). He argues in *Rules and Representations* that linguistics is in the position of any empirical science in that the data will always underdetermine the theory, so that 'at best, we can settle on one of the indefinitely many possible theories that account for crucial evidence' (Chomsky, 1980, p. 191).

This is a point to be taken. But Chomsky takes the issue one step further in a very revealing passage:

> The literature takes a rather different view. Certain types of evidence are held to relate to psychological reality, specifically, evidence deriving from studies of reaction time, recognition, recall, etc. Other kinds of evidence are held to be of an entirely different nature, specifically, evidence deriving from informant judgments as to what sentences mean, whether they are well formed, and so on. Theoretical explanations advanced to explain evidence of the latter sort, it is commonly argued, have no claim to psychological reality. (Chomsky, 1980, p. 192)

Clearly some have argued in this way. Chomsky's point is that the evidence from reaction times, etc. is not evidence of a higher status, more relevant to psychological reality, but simply . . . more evidence. He is clearly right on this point. Yet all other things being equal we would prefer a theory supported by *both* kinds of evidence, meshing together to yield a higher degree of explanatory insight.

This is a most central issue for any comparison between linguistics and AI, for the latter has always been concerned inevitably with *processing*. Take some typical AI language tasks: suppose that we want to build an automatic syntactic parser which will model in a machine (a computer) how we parse (some subset of the) sentences of English, or how we assign them a semantic interpretation, or how we effect morphological analysis. In each case we are concerned with establishing automatic processing mechanisms. In each case we may investigate to what extent the mechanism we devise does or does not offer a plausible and 'psychologically real' model of what the human processing mechanism does.

It has seemed to some people working in AI (and indeed to other commentators on Chomskyan linguistics) that the competence/performance distinction which Chomsky draws sits uneasily with any discussion of processing. There have been responses within AI to this lack of fit and it would be useful to distinguish them. There are at least four, with some slight degree of overlap.

1   The first response is that most commonly attributed to those in AI, certainly in conversation, although the one for which it is least easy to find a clear reference in the literature: it is that the competence/performance distinction is only half relevant to AI, since AI is concerned with the way language is *used*, and that is a matter of performance.

2   This response (common in the 1980s) represents the second, more brusque, objection mentioned earlier to Chomsky's characterization of competence. It amounts to an acceptance (often implicit) of the competence/performance distinction as such, but a rejection of the particular model of competence Chomsky offers, as made explicit in the grammar, as being, frankly, fundamentally irrelevant to the needs of a discipline concerned, centrally, with processing.

3   The third is a more subtle response: it involves essentially a rejection of the first response in favour of a competence/performance distinction which applies *across* the domain of processing. On this view a theory of competence should hook up with processing phenomena (in some way not typically very clearly articulated), although it is accepted that some aspects of processing will need to be covered by a theory of performance.

4   The final response is almost certainly one which many AI people who have persevered with the chapter thus far will have had. In its most basic form it runs something like this: 'I don't have time for all this self-indulgent philosophizing. That's not what the people who pay me want. They want a system which is up and running—yesterday.' (There are more, and less, polite versions of this response, as those of you who are smiling will recollect.)

It is clear that if there is to be (or has been) any fruitful contact between Chomskyan linguistics and AI then the third response, or some minor variant on it, has to be the accepted one. Of the other responses, the second favours a link-up between linguistics and AI but rejects Chomskyan linguistics as a suitable partner. Steady relationships have been noted recently between AI and generalized phrase structure grammars, daughter dependency grammars, and lexical-functional grammars, to name but some. The other two responses (the first and the last) suggest that there can be no thought of any productive union between Chomskyan linguistics and AI. These are the issues, then, at the very heart of the matter. That they have given concern to linguists for some time cannot be doubted. They have certainly given concern to students studying linguistics and worrying about 'where it fits in'. But they are equally issues which have troubled those in AI, if not always consciously. As Henry Thompson recently remarked in reflecting on the Cognition debate of the 1970s:

> Considerable heat and perhaps some light were generated, but one suspects that in the end both sides retired from the field secure in the knowledge they had won (the naively optimistic ones) or at least supposing they had demonstrated the internal consistency of their own and their friends'

position (the realists). Overt interest in the issue has since died down almost as quickly as it blew up, but I fear that on the AI side of the fence this is a classic case of repression, and we are suffering the predictable consequences: schizoid neurosis. (Thompson, 1983, p. 22)

The 'schizoid neurosis' has arisen in AI, Thompson thinks, precisely because those working in the field are divided over whether or not they think their own work has any significance for linguistic (or psychological) theory. Yorick Wilks and Karen Sparck Jones make not the same but a complementary point when they candidly remark (in the same volume) that:

It would be convenient, and intellectually tidy, if *automatic* natural language parsing could be discussed without any extended reference to the history of theoretical linguistics, as if computational analysis had its own autonomous life; and it is true that at times artificial intelligence workers have disregarded the concerns of contemporary theoretical linguistics. For others, however, autonomous parsing must be intellectually disreputable, mere amateur posturing: for them computational parsing ought to be the application of (well-founded) linguistic theory. (Wilks and Sparck Jones, 1983, p. 11)

With these words ringing in our ears, we turn to consider more fully the numbered responses distinguished above, ignoring the first. Subsequently we shall consider how other aspects of the 'Chomskyan paradigm' (as AI-ers have dubbed it) have fared within computational analysis.

We begin with those responses which support the null hypothesis: that there is no correlation between advances in AI and developments in Chomskyan linguistics, starting (contrariwise) with the fourth response. As the quotes from Thompson and from Wilks and Sparck Jones reveal those in AI are, as it were, only half serious when they dismiss Chomskyan linguistics in favour of 'getting on with the job'; or, if you prefer, they are only half serious when they deny that they dismiss . . . . What reasons might the (Chomskyan) linguist give in favour of altering the fraction in favour of linguistic theory?

One of the striking facts about much of the work done in AI on language is what Moore and Biggs (1977) called its parochialism. In the SHRDLU system, for example, Terry Winograd gives a procedural definition for the instruction to the computer to PICK UP *X*, where PICK UP is defined in terms of more primitive subactions such as RAISE HAND and GRASP (Winograd, 1972). As Yorick Wilks pointed out (in Wilks, 1976) the account which Winograd gave is wholly system-dependent. It is an expression of a set of procedures for picking up blocks in the blocks-world of the SHRDLU system—no less and no more. We cannot generalize from this to other linguistically straightforward uses of 'pick up'. One might argue, though here we are in danger of reactivating the rather fruitless and inconclusive proceduralist-declarativist debate of the 1970s, that Winograd does not characterize *any* linguistic use of the English verb 'pick up', but rather gives a procedural definition of the system-command PICK UP.

This point is intended not so much as a criticism of Winograd's work as by way of an observation. The current state of word semantics in linguistic theory does not offer a way of improving on Winograd's work in quantum leaps. Indeed, it is probably true to say—and worth saying—that linguists have often been open to the charge that they have criticized the AI treatment of some particular linguistic point without being in a position to offer a preferable alternative. Where linguistics has been noticeably more successful than AI, however, has been in producing analyses which are at least in principle extendable to other cases not currently under consideration.

The solutions offered are (in the successful cases) non-ad-hoc; rather, they capture linguistically significant generalizations. As we saw earlier the intention is that the generalizations should hold at increasing levels of explanatory adequacy as we move to more abstract levels of theorizing about language, perhaps (ultimately) to a level at which we establish biological universals from which the linguistic universals will fall out.

The picture in AI language work has in general been very different. A good example was the early work on speech recognition, which was based essentially on pattern-matching. As a piece of applied acoustics the work has been very impressive; linguistically it is largely uninformed (as its developers readily admit) by any syntactic, semantic, prosodic or pragmatic analysis.

At this point in such discussions those in AI are wont to become faintly irritated. 'Give us a chance,' is the common response, 'we can't do everything at once.' (This is just one of the many reasons why those criticized by Dresher and Hornstein felt aggrieved.) But this is to miss the real point of the matter. To the extent that AI language work involves bolting on extra levels as and when the funds/manpower/ time-scale allow, then it is constantly in danger of recapitulating some of the difficulties of the structuralist approach in linguistics. Not that AI-ers are insisting as a matter of principle, as Hockett did, that there shall be no mixing of levels. Quite the contrary, a good deal of work in the 1970s was concerned to argue that it was linguistics which had been too rigid in its separation of syntax and semantics. But in practice much of the work done in AI has been piecemeal, parochial and partisan: there has been no unifying theme, no overall framework within which work on different levels of analysis can be integrated. Some might argue that this lack of a single vision of the field has been AI's blessing, that it has enabled it to develop rapidly, to throw up a vast range of interesting ideas and analyses, and (above all) to get programs running which people can actually use, be it for a natural language front-end to a data base, a semi-automatic translation facility, an expert system or any one of a host of other applications. The time has now come, however, in the development of AI where there is a felt need both to integrate work on different levels of linguistic analysis for both theoretical and practical reasons (as in some of the very large-scale projects now being undertaken in Europe, the United States and Japan) and, even more importantly, to provide a sustaining meta-theory for the work in AI. It is this, perhaps still largely unconscious, need which has given rise to the 'schizoid neurosis' of which Thompson writes.

This brings us back to the second numbered response. For if AI needs an overall theoretical framework and sustaining meta-theory, then the crucial question must be: where is it to get these from? It would be bizarre, perhaps even conceptually incoherent, to suppose that linguistic theory could have no part in this. But then the issues are: how large a part, and whose linguistic theory? It is, sadly, beyond the scope, and indeed the remit, of this chapter to consider in any detail the rival attractions of alternative grammars to the Chomskyan model, but any discussion of the links between AI and Chomskyan linguistics has ultimately to be seen in the wider context of comparison with these alternatives. Dick Hudson's *Daughter-Dependency Grammar* (first introduced in detail in Hudson, 1976) has been taken up computation-ally by Mike McCord (in, for example, McCord, 1982), and Kaplan and Bresnan (1982) offer the promise of a computationally plausible lexical-functional grammar. The most discussed alternative grammar, and the one which AI workers in a number of countries have become excited about, is the *generalized phrase structure grammar*

(GPSG) of Gerald Gazdar and others, developed largely over the last six years or so, and drawing on much earlier work by Gilbert Harman (1963). In a series of papers (for example, Gazdar, 1981, 1982) and in a new book (Gazdar *et al.*, 1985) an alternative model has been developed of a generative grammar without transformational rules, where all analysis is carried out at a single (surface structure) level by a context-free phrase-structure grammar. One of the reasons why there has been so much interest in GPSG in AI is because the entire class of context-free languages is known to have, in a mathematical sense, *efficient* parsing algorithms (Earley, 1970).

Interest there certainly has been, in a wide range of smaller and larger projects in Europe, the United States and Japan, including the large GPSG-based database access project at Hewlett Packard. On the parsing side, important work has been done on constructing a chart-parser for GPSG, notably by Henry Thompson at Edinburgh, although we may hesitate to accept in its entirety his claim in 1983 that he does not think it 'too far-fetched to see in the near future, for example, a chart parser of GPSG on a chip, which you could buy together with a reasonably extensive grammar to plug into your expert system product' (Thompson, 1983).

There has also, predictably, been a strong reaction from the Chomskyan side, notably in the work of Robert Berwick and Amy Weinberg, in their 1982 article and their book (Berwick and Weinberg, 1982, 1984). One of their countering moves involves accepting the mathematical validity of Earley's Algorithm but denying that this assigns a uniquely privileged *linguistic* status (as opposed to a *mathematical* status) to context-free phrase-structure languages. For this set, they argue, will contain many *non-natural* context-free languages (such as those generating palindromes, like *abbaabba*). Hence efficient parsability in the mathematical sense cannot be the sole criterion and 'a mathematically relevant class need not be coextensive with a cognitively relevant one' (Berwick and Weinberg, 1982, p. 177).

We need not, therefore, accept Gazdar's restriction to CF languages for (a) as we have just seen parsability is not the only criterion and (b) there are many non-context-free languages which are also efficiently parsable. If Berwick and Weinberg are right, then there is a choice to be made between placing further restrictions on the class of context-free grammars to rule out the palindromic and other non-natural languages, and finding a measure of 'relevant cognitive complexity' which will enable us to identify the relevant subset, of the indefinitely large set of non-context-free grammars, which are appropriate as grammars of natural languages. It is not immediately obvious that the balance lies heavily in favour of Berwick and Weinberg.

The upshot of the discussion of the two numbered responses we have considered so far has been that we have argued strongly in favour of the need for AI to seek, at this stage in its development, a sustaining meta-theory, with the suggestion that this might well come (at least in large part) from linguistic theory. At the same time we see that there are a number of possible grammars which might lay claim to being friendly to computational parsing. We might well wonder about the possibility, as it were, of a negotiated settlement.

Our first task, however, must be to consider the third numbered response to the apparent lack of fit between the competence/performance distinction which Chomsky draws and the notion of processing. The third response, it will be recalled, involves arguing that a theory of competence *should* hook up with processing phenomena, although it is accepted that some aspects of processing will need to be covered by a theory of performance.

A variant of this response first appeared, to the best of my knowledge, in Schank and Wilensky's response to Dresher and Hornstein (1977). They rightly object to the rather cavalier strictures which Dresher and Hornstein place on linguistic theory, such that the latter exclude from study 'problems of how language is processed in real-time' (Dresher and Hornstein, 1976, p. 328). Schank and Wilensky go on to suggest, albeit very sketchily, that whilst AI is concerned with processing it is also concerned with abstracting away in the manner of competence: 'almost every AI model of language use is [of] an ideal user' (Schank and Wilensky, 1977, p. 135).

A more recent, and much more clearly articulated, version of this response is the following:

> If we accept—as I do—Lenneberg's contention that the rules of grammar enter into the processing mechanisms, then evidence concerning production, recognition, recall, and language use in general can be expected (in principle) to have bearing on the investigation of rules of grammar, on what is sometimes called 'grammatical competence' or 'knowledge of language'.

Those who do not recognize the quote may, perhaps, be surprised to find that it is from the author of *Aspects of the Theory of Syntax*, in his more recent *Rules and Representations* (Chomsky, 1980, pp. 200–1). This passage seems to indicate a marked and relatively unheralded change in Chomsky's position. A suspicion that he may not be totally committed to this new position, however, is supported by his subsequent remark in the same paragraph that: 'Some evidence may bear on process models that incorporate a characterization of grammatical competence, while other evidence seems to bear on competence *more directly, in abstraction from conditions of language use.*' [my emphasis]. These remarks are made in a passage in which Chomsky now allows that processing evidence and evidence from 'language use in general' can count in discussions of 'psychological reality' but argues that evidence of this sort has no especially privileged character. This point we have already accepted in our preliminary discussion on 'psychological reality' (although others have not). But by the same token the traditional Chomskyan evidence does not have the especially privileged character implied in the above quote. As he himself notes earlier (p. 200): 'The new evidence might or might not be more persuasive than the old; that would depend on its character and reliability, the degree to which the principles dealing with this evidence are tenable, intelligent, compelling, and so on.' Quite so.

We have been considering so far ways in which we might be able to establish conceptual links between Chomskyan linguistics and AI. A natural question to ask is: what *actual* links are there? That we have only just raised the question at this point in the chapter is not because of some absurd oversight, but rather because until we understand in some detail the broader issues we have been discussing then it is not really clear what would count as a link of the relevant kind. It might be felt that there are some glaring counter-examples to this line of reasoning. Surely, it might be argued, however the broader issues are settled, the work of Marcus (1980), for example, is a clear illustration of the way in which the insights of Chomskyan grammar, in this case the extended standard theory (EST), have shaped and informed a specific implementation, namely PARSIFAL. It is not at all clear, however, when one reads Marcus' book that the implementation, impressive though it is, is *directly motivated by EST*, rather than justified post hoc, despite the fact that it is a linguistically exceptionally informed piece of work. Again we come back to the question—to borrow a phrase of Woods from a rather different context—'what's in a link?'.

We have argued that AI is, for both theoretical and practical reasons, in need of a sustaining meta-theory. Chomsky's recent discussion in *Rules and Representations* suggests that a (new style) competence-based theory might well be developed to serve that function. Which grammar will turn out in the end to be more user-friendly to the computer, government and binding, or generalized phrase structure grammar, or one of the other alternatives, is a matter for debate—but not here. Whatever the outcome, we have detailed here a fundamental Chomskyan paradigm which is competence-based, and which seeks increasingly explanatory theories at higher levels of abstraction, moving first to linguistic universals, and ultimately to a level of biological universals which will 'lay the foundations for a significant theory of human learning in various domains' (Chomsky, 1980, p. 254). This programme of escalating levels of explanatory generalizations is on offer to AI. There is every reason to think that Artificial Intelligence would benefit very considerably from adopting such a methodology.

If, as the quote from Chomsky at the beginning of this chapter suggests, theoretical linguistics of the Chomskyan kind will flourish in the future not in linguistics departments but within (post-Modistic) centres for cognitive studies, there is every reason to suppose that its effect on AI will be both positive and significant. There is also every reason to suppose that in such circumstances the effect of AI on linguistics will be similarly positive and significant. But that is another chapter.

REFERENCES

Berwick, R. and Weinberg, A. (1982) 'Parsing efficiency, computational complexity, and the evaluation of grammatical theories', *Linguistic Inquiry*, **13, 2**, pp. 165–91.

Berwick, R. and Weinberg, A. (1984) *Language Use and Language Acquisition*, Cambridge, Mass., MIT Press.

Chomsky, N. (1957) *Syntactic Structures*, The Hague, Mouton.

Chomsky, N. (1965) *Aspects of the Theory of Syntax*, Cambridge, Mass., MIT Press.

Chomsky, N. (1980) *Rules and Representations*, Oxford, Blackwell.

Chomsky, N. (1982) *The Generative Enterprise* (A discussion with Riny Huybregts and Henk van Riemsdijk), Dordrecht, Foris.

Dresher, E. and Hornstein, N. (1976) 'On some supposed contributions of Artificial Intelligence to the scientific study of language', *Cognition*, **4**, pp. 321–98.

Dresher, E. and Hornstein, N. (1977a) 'Reply to Schank and Wilensky', *Cognition*, **5**, pp. 147–50.

Dresher, E. and Hornstein, N. (1977b) 'Reply to Winograd', *Cognition*, **5**, pp. 377–92.

Earley, J. (1970) 'An efficient context-free parsing algorithm', *Communications of the ACM*, **13**, pp. 94–102.

Foster, J. (1976) 'Meaning and truth theory', in Evans, G. and McDowell, J. (Eds), *Truth and Meaning*, London, Oxford University Press.

Gazdar, G. (1981) 'Unbounded dependencies and coordinate structure', *Linguistic Inquiry*, **12**, pp. 155–84.

Gazdar, G. (1982) 'Phrase structure grammar', in Jacobson, P. and Pullum, G. (Eds), *The Nature of Syntactic Representations*, Dordrecht, Reidel, pp. 131–86.

Gazdar, G. *et al.* (1985) *Generalized Phrase Structure Grammar*, Blackwell, Oxford.

Harman, G. (1963) 'Generative grammars without transformational rules: A defense of phrase structure', *Language*, **39**, pp. 597–616.

Higginbotham, J. (1984) 'Noam Chomsky's linguistic theory', in Torrance, S. (Ed.), *The Mind and the Machine: Philosophical Aspects of Artificial Intelligence*, Chichester, Ellis Horwood.

Hudson, D. (1976) *Arguments for a Non-Transformational Grammar*, Chicago, Chicago University Press.

Kaplan, R. M. and Bresnan, J. (1982) 'Lexical-functional grammar: A formal system of grammatical representation', in Bresnan, J. (Ed.), *The Mental Representation of Grammatical Relations*, Cambridge, Mass., MIT Press.

McCord, M. (1982) 'Using slots and modifiers in logic grammars for natural language', *Artificial Intelligence*, **18,** pp. 327–67.

Marcus, M. (1980) *A Theory of Syntactic Recognition for Natural Language*, Cambridge, Mass., MIT Press.

Moore, T. and Biggs, C. (1977) 'Questions of parochialism in semantics', in Seuren, P. (Ed.), *Proceedings of a Conference on Empirical and Methodological Foundations of Semantic Theories for Natural Language*, Nijmegen, The University, Nijmegen.

Schank, R. and Wilensky, R. (1977) 'Response to Dresher and Hornstein', *Cognition*, **5,** pp. 133–45.

Thompson, H. (1983) 'Natural language processing: A critical analysis of the structure of the field, with some implications for parsing' in Sparck Jones, K. and Wilks, Y. (Eds), *Automatic Natural Language Parsing*, Chichester, Ellis Horwood, pp. 22–31.

Turing, A. (1950) 'Computing machinery and intelligence', *Mind*, **59.**

Wilks, Y. (1976) 'Parsing English I', in Charniak, E. and Wilks, Y. (Eds), *Computational Semantics*, Amsterdam, North-Holland.

Wilks, Y. and Sparck Jones, K. (1983) 'Introduction: A little light history', in Sparck Jones, K. and Wilks, Y. (Eds), *Automatic Natural Language Parsing*, Chichester, Ellis Horwood, pp. 11–21.

Winograd, T. (1972) *Understanding Natural Language*, Edinburgh, Edinburgh University Press.

Winograd, T. (1977) 'On some contested suppositions of generative linguisitics about the scientific study of language', *Cognition*, **5,** pp. 151–97.

15. Bad Metaphors: Chomsky and Artificial Intelligence

YORICK WILKS

One cannot take up this subject with much optimism that any intellectual exchange will take place. The precedents are too grim: the Chomsky and Schank exchange (Chomsky, 1980) degenerated into *ad hominem* sneers, such as Chomsky's references to the low value of studies of language use in selling hamburgers in restaurants, and his assertion that the work of Schank's group is 'virtually without issue'. Nonetheless, I will use that article of Chomsky's as the basis for this piece, for it remains, I think, the most compact and accessible statement of his general views on the nature of cognitive science and the 'language faculty', and hence the place where some relevance to the task of artificial intelligence (AI) may be sought.

What follows will consist of general remarks on AI, on transformational-generative grammar (TGG) and on the history of the relationship between the two bodies of ideas. These sections will be highly general, as both the space available and the well-known character of the material dictates. I will not resort to deep footnotes and quotations to make my points since I do not believe the positions I state require that: they are either well-known, or totally denied by those they refer to, or in some cases both. At the end I shall turn briefly to the central matter of the language faculty. The burden of this piece will be that much of the distance between Chomsky's approach and AI has been the product of his tendency to pick and stick to bad metaphors to support his theoretical paradigm.

ARTIFICIAL INTELLIGENCE

AI is a study that eludes any clear definition, beyond a listing of the computational enterprises that have come under its banner and, to be fair, a second listing of closely related activities that often prefer not to be seen as AI (e.g., expert systems and logic programming). What excludes those activities is, to some degree, the continuing preoccupation of many of those in AI with the modelling of cognitive functions, as opposed to the construction of performing inferential devices, or 'knowledge engineering'. Other excluded studies are pattern recognition and cybernetics, and here the distaste is normally on the part of the AI researchers, and it is for quantitative methods and the use of lower-order mechanisms that do not allow the use of logical reasoning and the explicit coding of propositions or theories.

This point is of some relevance to our theme here, in that it shows how close are some of the concerns of many AI workers and Chomsky himself. In his (1980) article Chomsky compares the operation of two missiles, one guided by trained pigeons, operating on Skinnerian principles and pecking so as to steer the missile to its destination, while the other is steered by a theory of planetary motion plus appropriate computations, etc. Chomsky proposes that, although examination of their behaviours would not distinguish the missiles, a 'deeper look' might cause us to attribute a property he calls *cognizing* to the second missile and to speak of it as having something like a *mental state* (*ibid.*, p. 11).

This opposition, of an 'abstract characterization' to something rather less, is familiar to all students of Chomsky's view of the language faculty, and indeed of cognitive functions in general. However, if we forget all that, and stand back and think (perhaps remembering a little elementary philosophy), we see that Chomsky's opposition of the two missiles is grossly inappropriate as a model of cognitive functioning, at least as that relates to actual and possible evidence available to researchers. Chomsky confuses, as he always has, what we know, on the one hand, as scientists/researchers/plain men of some aspect of the world and (on the other hand) what there is any reason to believe our brains code or process when confronted with the same phenomenon. The two only meet when we have real evidence (and that will mean physiological evidence in the last resort, but *at least* psychological evidence) that the brain is operating with the theory under discussion. The missile case has relevance to human cognition insofar as (and no further than) we can be *as sure* that human brains use any given theory of (language, planetary motion or whatever) *as we can be that the rocket does.* It needs no great schooling in the human sciences to know that the evidence in the two cases is utterly different. But not for Chomsky, of course: it is one of his most endearing features that he really does seem to *know* that the language faculty operates with an abstract characterization of just the type he has given of languages over the years. But again, as every first-year philosophy student knows, that kind of knowledge is beyond all test, and ultimately vacuous. Chomsky's total assault on 'psychological reality' and, more generally, the evidence yielded by psychology (1980, p. 12) might be of genuine value in a context where it did not serve those particular anti-evidential ends. But anyone reading it cannot divorce himself from the knowledge that psychological experiment has consistently failed to confirm the reality of the structures Chomsky has predicted.

The missile example, whatever its inherent value, serves a bridge function with AI precisely because it clashes so clearly with Papert's well-known catching-the-ball example of the space of possible cognitive rules. Papert pointed out some years ago that we theorize about moving projectiles with the geometry of parabolas (just as we would program missiles to take account of planetary motion, in gross form at least). Hence we might come to believe that the brain of a ball player operates with just that theory when catching one. However, as Papert pointed out, there is a far simpler equivalent rule of thumb available: if the ball is going up the sky, move back; if down, move forward; if stationary, stay where you are and it will hit you.

The moral here is not at all that therefore the brain works with the rule of thumb and not the geometry of Euclid. To so argue would be to commit the very fallacy under discussion. The consideration to influence the intellect, however, is to compare the probable length of time humans have caught objects, or had the motor skills that make up that skill, with the time scale of knowledge of 'abstract parabolic characterization' (where we can be pretty precise: 2500 years) and to consider which one evolution might have picked. Nothing about the cognitive faculty follows from this discussion, except wonderment at the mental processes of those who simply *know* about our cognitive endowments.

However, when all that is said, it is not hard to find those in AI who might take a distinctly more Chomskyan than Papertian position on these issues. McCarthy has been on record for a decade defending the claim that a governor of a steam engine is in a cognitive state. This is not equivalent to Chomsky's (1980, p. 9) cognizing exactly, since McCarthy in effect reduces the content of his claim to what is required to explain behaviour, whereas Chomsky has independent knowledge of the second missile's abstract guidance system. The difference can be seen from the fact that McCarthy would probably assign a cognitive state to both rockets, which at least avoids the problems we have just discussed about direct, evidence-free, knowing an entity's internal structure. However, the positions are very close, and it is worth noting that McCarthy has always defended a definition of AI that encompassed the characterization of intelligent behaviour in humans or machines, *independently of its implementation*. This position opens up the competence-performance distinction on which so much of Chomsky's work rests: *i.e.* on McCarthy's view there can be logical characterizations of intelligence within AI that may or may not correspond to the properties of implemented programs. However, and here the analogy between their views weakens considerably, to discuss the competence and performance of programs, whatever that may mean, is to discuss two notions with a clear formal relationship, unlike the situation of human language use.

Again, nothing follows from this demonstration that there is more than one view in AI on this issue. One can in fact discern two tendencies: the cognitivist tendency that takes psychological evidence seriously and is wary of claims about mentality and cognition, knowing as it does their tricky status and, on the other hand, the logicist tendency, concerned with the nature of representations and, perhaps, effective programs, independent of cognitive import. What is interesting is that it is the latter tendency that shares a heritage with Chomsky back through Carnap, all of which is quite consistent with Chomsky's current attitude to psychological evidence, if not with his claims over many years to be doing a form of psychology.

That there is still methodological division in AI should be seen as part of a general phenomenon of new organisms or organizations having a weak exterior: other entities can, as it were, thrust their way in, because of weak definition. Thus Marr's meditations on 'physiological bottom-up AI' found a way in and made immediate impact in AI, as Chomsky noted (1980, p. 53) when discussing Schank, though I think they are fully digested by now. Similarly, there is intelligent and interesting work at MIT AI Laboratory by Berwick and others on syntactic learning, which is effectively a computational extension of Chomsky's own views. Anything that is fundamentally computational and bears, however remotely, on the modelling of intelligent or cognitive activity can find a way into AI, and properly so. Given the MIT provenance of the AI researchers mentioned, it will be seen there is also what Chomsky might term a 'locality effect' at work. However, there are also forms of modern syntactic theory such as Gazdar's GPSG (1981) which share many of Chomsky's general assumptions, while being firmly separated from TGG by an attitude to transformational versus phrase structure rules. However, GPSG's are designed explicitly to be computationally parsable though without need of the shielding the competence/performance distinction gave from the harsh world of evidence. There is no reason why such research efforts could not be accommodated within AI, for there are no points at issue that cannot be settled by computation or other forms of evidence. This fact makes it harder yet more important to seek out what has divided the AI and TGG paradigms for so long. The burden of this chapter is that it has been Chomsky's attachment to a sequence of bad metaphors to explain and support his paradigm, and his progressive detachment from all known canons of evidence.

However, given the point about the weak boundary to AI, and the possibility of a competence-oriented AI in the sense of McCarthy, it is important to remember that the subject nevertheless has a clear methodological mission: the implementation of real computational processes making use of representations of knowledge. However simple, this provides a clear test of the adequacy of programs: they either model a phenomenon at issue or they do not, which will be a matter, in the future, for appropriate statistical tests. Further questions, such as the psychological or physiological plausibility of the representations used to achieve the machine behaviours, or the inherent logical interest of the representation itself, are not strictly matters for AI at all.

TRANSFORMATIONAL GRAMMAR

What follows is a travesty of the detailed and meticulous work that has gone into the establishment of the transformational-generative paradigm over the last thirty years, but is, in essence, true.

The metaphor behind TGG, and the one with respect to which Chomsky explained it for many years, was *automata theory*, which is to say the characterization of a device that would generate all and only the well-formed sentences of a natural language. The details underwent much discussion, e.g., 'generate', 'well-formed', etc. and changed over the years but the outline remained fairly clear. Moreover, the rule syntax chosen to express the content of the automaton was that of 'transformational rules', a term coined by Carnap, but owing its logical heritage to Post's production rules for theorem proof in general logic.

I mention all this well-known material only to make a point about *processes*: a notion fundamental to AI and computer science but one which Chomsky has always sought to keep out of the description of TGG, for he has always dismissed concrete implementations as being concerned with performance rather than with a process-free competence. Even here there have been enormous muddles, for it would be perfectly proper to have a process-explication of a competence model: in a sense, all computational logic is just that, but let us leave this aside here.

The initial bad metaphors in which Chomsky was caught were *automaton* and *transformation*. These notions, in terms of which he initially cast TGG, were inherently process-oriented and cannot be divorced from them. It is no accident that the pedagogy of TGG has always had to explain in process terms: beginning with an S symbol, applying PS rules to obtain, etc. Students are then told by the stricter masters that it was all only a metaphor, and TGG is to be seen correctly as a set of (non-process) functions that map one set of structures to another without any implications as to how that is achieved (any more than $x^2 + y^2 = z^2$ implies processes for calculating z from x and y). But that was all nonsense and self-deception, for it was automaton and transformation that were the real metaphors underlying the system, and 'function' cannot be appended arbitrarily later so as to withdraw their force.

This matter can be seen very clearly in the development in TGG of generative semantics (GS): an attempt to combine the virtual processes of TGG that generate sentences with the claim that the underlying structures generated were logical in form. It was not widely appreciated at the time (though see Wilks, 1972) that the clash of process and non-process accounts had become explicit and devastating: if the generative-transformational processes were logical-inferential (as the generative semanticists at times seemed to claim, see Lakoff, 1970), there was no possible way in which they could also be non-directional. Yet it was an important part of the 'non-process' view held by Chomsky that the functions involved in TGG (as well as a 'notational variant' like GS) were indifferent to transformational direction (i.e., as between the analysis and production of actual sentences). But logic processes are not symmetrical in that way, in that p→q certainly lends no deductive support to q→p!

An important addition to the theory came with the claim that native speakers *knew* the grammar of their language and that what such speakers said about the *structure* of their language (i.e., in saying more than what was and was not a well-formed sentence) was to count as evidence when selecting one representation in preference to another; this was the so-called level of 'descriptive adequacy'. It was here that *know*, the grandest of the bad metaphors, entered in, and philosophers have never been able to take TGG totally seriously since.

In the clear sense of 'know' established earlier, when discussing the ball-catching example of Papert, people cannot possibly know any such thing: the phlogiston-believers still had lungs that worked by oxygenation, and if there had been any connection between their explicit theoretical beliefs and their inner processes they would have choked to death.

It is at this point that Chomsky introduces 'cognize' to cover the situation humans are in where they do not know the rules of language they operate with, and where philosophers keep reminding Chomsky of the fact, but nevertheless one where Chomsky wants very much to claim that we do more-or-less know the rules and they are those of TGG: 'If a person who cognized the grammar and its rules could miraculously become conscious of them, we would not hesitate to say that he knows the grammar and its rules' (*ibid.*, 1980, p. 9). Yes, of course, but this is a counter-to-fact assumption that, if true, would make us organisms of a quite different sort, where none of our existing assumptions about cognition would hold. It is not just some accidental fact about us that we do not know such things, but one essential to the nature of language, consciousness and mental functioning generally.

The sheer naivité of Chomsky's point is only equalled by his audacity: he calls to his support at just this point such names as Wittgenstein (*ibid.*, p. 7) with his 'insights into the use of language against the background of belief, intent ... ' when Wittgenstein more than any other philosopher showed the pitfalls into which views like Chomsky's must fall. At that point Chomsky refers yet again to 'the mental state of knowing a language'. If Wittgenstein taught anything at all, it was the error in such forms of talk: there can be no such state, in the sense of a self-justifying state, whose reportage can be trusted in any serious sense, even by the holder of such a putative state. Anyone may sincerely believe they speak French, and believe themselves to be in the mental state of speaking French, while in fact speaking it very badly, speaking not a single word, or speaking Spanish, believing it to be French, to take just a few from a range of exotic but serious possibilities.

Chomsky may very well be right to insist that there is knowledge of language, and that it is different from world knowledge, while not being a skill or technique, though that is a much weaker matter than the last. Here, though he would not accept it, is a point where AI programs could perhaps be of conceptual assistance: in a program like Winograd's (1972) there is a coding of language quite separate from that of truths about the world, together with an area of semantic knowledge (e.g., that robots are not human) that could be assimilated to either or both of the other categories. The three forms of 'knowledge' were coded by Winograd in different representations, but that was an arbitrary feature and the fashion in AI would now be to code them all in the same format and use them differently or similarly according to the interpretation task to hand (a comparison with Carnap's *material* and *formal mode* for expressing the same facts might be historically instructive here). In such a system there is no need to draw a strict division between types of knowledge, indeed the boundary could shift depending on the task. Curiously, Chomsky has no interest in such matters.

Of course, such a device would not help at all with the deeper problems of mapping the representations between areas the system could be said to know explicitly or even 'consciously', as opposed to the attributions of performative senses of 'know'. But that is an area where AI researchers usually refrain from excessive claims and so do not get into Chomsky's tangles about knowing and cognizing.

Honesty compels one to admit that there is one sub-area of AI that has become committed to a methodology very close to Chomsky's acceptance of native-speaker accounts of language structure. That is known as expert systems, where 'knowledge' is elicited from an expert and coded up as a series of inferences and facts so as, ultimately, to replace the expert with a program. Here one finds exactly the same assumption that an expert can not only perform but has conscious access to how he does things and can report it, even though there is a solid body of psychological evidence to the contrary.

But again, naive though it is, expert systems research has a clear methodology in an overall sense, and will either succeed or fail: the systems will mimic experts or not, and if they do it will be of no fundamental interest whether or not it is by the methods the experts in fact use, as opposed to what they report.

The real problem with Chomsky's theories is that he has progressively cut himself off from all the areas of intellectual endeavour with the ability to test claims: programs either work or not, psychology has experiments, but Chomsky rejects such evidence, and, as is also well-known, he has cut himself off over the years from the testability criteria of linguistics, namely acceptable data, on the ground (Chomsky, 1965) that theories determine their own data.

A reader who came across Chomsky's work only recently would be unlikely to be moved by the appeals to data he does make: in (1980, p. 4) he rests his overall case on such examples as

Which class was the lesson harder than the teacher had told that it would be?

'Evidently', Chomsky writes, 'this is not a well-formed question, though its intended sense is clear enough . . . .' I suspect that out in these remote reaches of English it is equally evident that any psychological experiment would show that people judge such sentences to be well-formed precisely to the extent that they can interpret them in context. Beyond that they have only the shakiest intuitions of well-formedness, just as they do for multiple centre-embedded sentences like

The dog the cat the man bought bit died,

which, of course, Chomsky considers well-formed, contrarily and for purely theoretical reasons.

But no serious theory of language should have to rely on examples like this to make general points: it may well be that there are 'general rules of movement' that bear on the *lesson* example, but such simple processes (sic) are available within a wide range of formalisms in linguistics and AI, many of them owing no debt whatever to Chomsky's work. Indeed, what procedural language could lack such operators? As always, no thought seems to enter Chomsky's mind of the vast space of alternative claims that could cover the few data there are as well as his own. Having cut himself off in turn from all established areas and traditions of evidence in this way, it may be that Chomsky is making some very long-term bet on vindication by physiology, in which case it will be a long wait.

One remaining area to which Chomsky has paid increasing attention since the formulation of the notion of 'explanatory adequacy' has been learning: a theory would be explanatorily adequate (Chomsky, 1965) to the extent to which it showed how particular classes (and only those) of grammars could be learned. At the same time Chomsky has insisted with increasing fierceness that languages are not truly learned (*ibid.*, p. 3) because of the rich innate genetic endowment of the child, and the 'poverty of the stimulus'. No quantitative measures of these are ever given, but it is surely worth remarking the paradox of making learning central to a theory which denies that there is learning in the broadly accepted sense, as opposed to development of pre-existing faculties. I would go further and suggest that *learning* is yet another bad metaphor within Chomsky's system of ideas: as with psychology in general, he claims it is central to him, but a little examination shows his system has been set up so as to deny its relevance.

I mention learning in this chapter concerned with AI for two reasons: first, it has been a strong criticism of AI since Dreyfus (1972) that its products could not be taken seriously until they showed how learned intelligence was possible, for simply to pump knowledge into a program was not enough, since we are essentially creatures that grow up in an environment. AI has taken this message to heart, and much research has been done that may, in the end, meet Dreyfus' requirement. But the demand and the response were for real learning, not for an avoidance of the issue by repacking learning as innate endowment.

Secondly, Chomsky has taken encouragement from recent developments of Gold's (1957) work on sequence extrapolation that now goes under the name 'learnability theory'. This attempts to specify abstract requirements on transformational schemes that would allow them to come within an abstractly learnable class, given certain assumptions about the data presentation process, etc. There were initial difficulties because it seemed that only decidable classes of grammars could be learned and TGG was notoriously not one of them, but some repair work seems to have been done there. More seriously, a key constraint on presentation is that the input strings be presented to the learner/child along with their semantic interpretation. One does not need to be a Quinean to have serious doubts about how any such enterprise could fall within what we normally consider as learning a first language. It is not at all clear how the child can be presented with a semantic representation in any sense.

An instructive AI parallel would be an ingenious program of Power and Longuet-Higgins (1977) where they did cause a program to learn the number systems of a range of languages (but not Roman, interestingly enough) given the linguistic strings *and the numerals together with a knowledge of arithmetic*. This program did contain the presentation of language strings and semantics in the sense of learnability theory; it was also very good AI, but who (and certainly not its constructors) could consider it a serious model of the child learning!?

AI AND TGG: THEIR MUTUAL HISTORY

Here, alas, there is little to report, except that both emerged as representational studies from predecessors that were in a strong sense anti-representational (cybernetics and structural linguistics, respectively). Early AI work on the analysis and understanding of general natural language (Simmons, 1970; Wilks, 1967; Schank, 1968) was much preoccupied by what its practitioners saw as the wrongheadedness of Chomsky's preoccupation with syntax and by the need for semantics-based methods to understand language. In doing so they may well have overlooked much that was of value in Chomsky's system: but on balance they were right, for TGG itself has changed to give a far greater role to logic, semantics and surface considerations than was then the case.

The lasting linguistic debt of AI work in natural language (apart from Winograd and Wilks to Halliday, and Schank to Lamb and Hays) was to one of TGG's unwanted offspring: case grammar (Fillmore, 1968). It is fascinating to compare its almost total rejection within the TGG community with its universal acceptance within AI. It is too early to be clear about the reason for this, but part of it is the ubiquity in the AI paradigm of predicate logic representation, and the ease with which case grammar can be adapted to predicate-argument format.

THE KEY ISSUE: MODULARITY AND THE 'LANGUAGE FACULTY'

We have postponed the key matter at issue between Chomsky and much of AI, as it is between certain groups of AI workers: the modularity of knowledge and whether there is, in any useful sense, a language faculty. There is sometimes a confusion of terms here, in that Chomsky (along with Fodor and others) uses 'module' to distinguish gross faculties, whereas in AI the term has a more empirically-founded usage to denote any self-contained body of code that can be evaluated without reference to other such modules.

The principal question is not easy, but can be thrown into sharper relief by an extreme position, held in AI by those associated with the expert systems movement, and sometimes expressed as 'language is a side effect'. That is to say, language is merely one among many alternative ways of achieving human ends, and often no more than a side effect of other processes, as when we shout 'Ouch' on being hurt.

This view is perhaps the strongest of those that fall under the functional view of language, adopted by Searle and Schank among others (*ibid.*, 1980). In replying to Schank, Chomsky finds it necessary to write explicitly that 'language is not a task-oriented device' (*ibid.*, p. 53). This is an extraordinary remark, devoid of any general support in that paper or elsewhere in Chomsky's work, and all the more strange coming from one who has recently adopted the manner of speaking of the 'language organ' and its similarity to other organs of the human body. For to speak of organs and their development, let alone of genetic endowment, as Chomsky also does, *is* to speak of their function. However much it may be the case that many humans now talk for fun and without purpose, what person who accepts evolution in general can doubt that language is, in its origin and essence, task-oriented?

Organ may prove to be only the latest, and one of the most blatant of Chomsky's bad metaphors, for if language is in any sense an organ, then not only is it task oriented, but it has an evolutionary history and may be expected to exist at the same time in a range of forms of development. That will be a consequence of the analogy hard to explain to much of the linguistic community.

This is no place to review the associated false inferences Chomsky has made with regard to genetic endowment for language and its relation to his theories. He often seems to argue that those who question the content of his own theory of universal grammar also question the possibility of genetic coding for language and are no more than unreconstructed empiricists, or tabula rasa men.

Again, and as always, to do this simply ignores the huge gap between assertion and evidence, a gap into which a thousand different theories could be fitted. Anyone can accept that there is some genetically determined component to language, but it may be very small and may be piggy-backed, as it were, on another ability. Chomsky himself is now writing qualifications to his earlier unwiser claims: 'we should not exclude the possibility that what we now think of as language might consist of quite disparate cognitive systems that interweave . . .' (1980, p. 7). A language faculty or organ of almost any size and capacity is consistent with that. There may be no further serious dispute if that quotation really represents Chomsky's considered position.

When peering into the space of alternatives that is left open, an AI researcher would be particularly intrigued, for example, by Lieberman's (1984) speculation that the genetic foundation for language is very small and may consist (apart from a sound-producing mechanism) in the ability to piggy-back rules (such as syntactic rules) onto pre-existing planning rules of identical syntax. Again, there are Simon's (1981) well-known speculations that hierarchicality has nothing in particular to do with phrase structure but would be found as a representational formalism in any organism capable of complex planning. Both these suggestions are quite compatible with the way nature is known to do things during evolution, highly compatible with the emphasis on planning in AI, but may leave Chomsky with an uncomfortably small 'innate language' area.

In conclusion, I should declare a personal interest: I am much interested in the procedural explication of language mechanisms and the relationship of meaning and knowledge. Unlike many in AI, I most certainly believe that there must be distinctive representations and characterizations for the language phenomenon, and that these cannot be replaced by side-effect explanations or by general world-knowledge mechanisms. There is all the evidence one needs for that position, most of it known to Chomsky. However, Chomsky's arguments, repeated assertions, and ultimately self-defeating metaphors unshackled to any form of testable evidence, are of no help in that endeavour but rather an intellectual embarrassment.

REFERENCES

Chomsky, N. (1965) *Aspects of the Theory of Syntax*, Cambridge, Mass., MIT Press.

Chomsky, N. (1980) 'Rules and representations', *Behavioral and Brain Sciences*, **3**, pp. 1–15.

Dreyfus, H. (1972) *What Computers Can't Do*, . . . Harper and Row.

Fillmore, C. (1968) 'The case for case', in Bach & Harms (Eds), *Universals of Linguistic Theory*, Holt, Rinehart and Winston.

Gazdar, G. (1981) 'Unbounded dependencies and coordinate structure', *Linguistic Inquiry*.

Gold, E. M. (1957) 'Language identification in the limit', *Information and Control*.

Lakoff, G. (1970) *Linguistics and Natural Logic*, Studies in Generative Semantics, no. 1. Linguistics Deot., Ann Arbor, Mich.

Lieberman, P. (1984) *The Evolution and Biology of Language*, Harvard University Press.

Power, R. and Longuet-Higgins, C. L. H. (1977) 'Learning to count', *Proceedings of the Royal Society London*, **193**, pp. 21–42.

Schank, R. (1968) 'Semantic categories', Tracor Doc. No. 68–551–U.

Simmons, R. (1970) 'Some semantic structures for representing English meaning', Tech. Rept. NL–1, University of Texas at Austin.

Simon, H. (1981) *Sciences of the Artificial* Cambridge, Mass., MIT Press.

Wilks, Y. (1967) 'Computable Semantic Derivations', Systems Development Corporation, Memo No. SP–3018.

Wilks, Y. (1972) 'Lakoff on linguistics and natural logic', Stanford AI Laboratory Memo, no. AIM–170.

Winograd, T. (1972) *Understanding Natural Language*, Edinburgh, Edinburgh University Press.

Interchange

BIGGS REPLIES TO WILKS

When the editors of this volume invited me to contribute an article on 'Chomsky and Artificial Intelligence', paired with Yorick Wilks, I made it clear before accepting that whilst I understood that the general intention in having paired views was to stimulate a vigorous debate between *pro* and *con*, it was likely that my views would emerge as occupying a fairly central point on whatever might be regarded as the appropriate scale of measurement in these matters. This indeed turned out to be so. One of the main conclusions of my article was that Chomsky's work has not so far been perceived as especially relevant to Artificial Intelligence and that his influence in this area of intellectual endeavour has been considerably less than in many other areas considered in this volume. I suggested, however, that there were *potential* benefits to be derived from Chomskyan linguistics, notably in that it is able to offer AI something which it currently lacks: a sustaining meta-theory. I also supposed that AI had valuable contributions to make to the future development of linguistics.

Within this context it is not surprising that Yorick Wilks and I should, perhaps, find ourselves rather more in agreement that our editors might have wished. We both accept that contact and influence have so far been minimal; we agree that one of the chief obstacles to future progress in establishing stronger links between linguistics and AI has lain in Chomsky's expressed attitudes towards psychological reality, and in particular towards the accounts of language processing; we have both noted that Chomsky seems to have changed his attitude towards issues of this kind in recent years; and, equally, we have both expressed scepticism about whether this perceived change of attitude marks quite the shift in intellectual posture that we would wish to have. These, then, are matters on which there is broad agreeement between us. Interleaved with these, however, is a set of issues where we are very clearly in sharp disagreement.

One of the most central of these issues concerns our respective perceptions of the essential characteristics of Chomskyan linguistics. Within the space available I shall have to restrict my comments and focus on one or two principal issues. First, however, a comment on Wilks' use of the key term 'Artificial Intelligence'. In his initial characterization of the field he assigns expert systems and logic programming to the distinct (although 'closely related') field of knowledge engineering. 'What excludes those activities is, to some degree, the continuing preoccupation of many of those in AI with the modelling of cognitive functions, as opposed to the construction of performing inferential devices, or "knowledge engineering"'. This is a most curious opposition, especially if we consider (as we clearly must in a discussion of the work of

Chomsky) the role of AI in modelling natural language understanding. It is perhaps not surprising, therefore, that Wilks subsequently, but inconsistently, remarks that 'honesty compels one to admit that there is one sub-area of AI that has become committed to a methodology very close to Chomsky's acceptance of native-speaker accounts of language structure. That is known as expert systems.' There is indeed a parallel to be drawn here: the linguist is, in the intended sense from knowledge engineering, an *expert*. It ought therefore to be possible, in principle, to model the inferential processes which the linguist goes through in first describing and subsequently explaining any given level of language: to construct, that is, an expert system to model the linguist modelling natural language. A modest initial attempt at this, at the level of morphology, is now being carried out by a group of us at the University of Reading.

The idea of expert systems, however, Wilks finds 'naive', whatever that means. Furthermore—and here we connect again directly with Chomsky—'the systems will mimic experts or not, and if they do it will be of no fundamental interest whether it is by the methods the experts in fact use, as opposed to what they report'. The problem of psychological reality has re-emerged. It is Wilks' view that Chomsky has 'cut himself off from all established areas and traditions of evidence' that might make his work testable. This is, as should be clear from the arguments in the main article, a hasty conclusion to reach, and one which takes no note of recent (and potential) changes in Chomsky's methodology.

The related complaint is that Chomsky rests his case in recent work (sometimes? frequently?) on examples whose status is marginal or suspect: 'remote reaches of English', 'only the shakiest intuitions of well-formedness', 'no serious theory of language should have to rely on examples like this to make general points'. Such charges are far from new, are easily made, difficult to support, difficult to dismiss readily, and ultimately irrelevant to the basic issue of whether Chomskyan linguistics has anything to offer AI. Wilks' view is that the sort of examples Chomsky uses are judged well-formed precisely to the extent that they can be interpreted in context. Given Wilks' previously expressed view (e.g., Wilks, 1975) that it is not possible to make a distinction between *semantically* well-formed vs. semantically ill-formed (since it is the natural inclination of hearers to attempt to make sense of what others put their way), it is now clear that he is committed to a corresponding view concerning *syntactic* well-formedness—a view which is patently wrong: we may argue about *where* to draw the line between syntactic well-formedness and syntactic ill-formedness (and Chomsky's theory nicely anticipates such argument), but the line must be drawn. It must be drawn in AI just as much as in linguistics—unless, that is, one wants to ignore all of the clear and unequivocal judgments of native speakers, along with the 'shakiest intuitions'. It would indeed be useful to build into a natural language understanding system the ability to handle deviant syntactic input, just as we might well want our morphological analyzer to make an intelligent attempt at handling nonce-forms, but such a facility presupposes a grasp of the non-deviant and the non-nonce.

REFERENCE

Wilks, Y. (1975) 'Preference semantics', in Keenan, E. (Ed.), *Formal Semantics*, Cambridge, Cambridge University Press.

WILKS REPLIES TO BIGGS

There is little with which I want to disagree in Colin Biggs' contribution: we consider very much the same bodies of work and come to not dissimilar conclusions. The crucial matter that I take us both to have emphasized is that there is now a body of linguistic work (e.g., Gazdar, 1981) which is clearly within the fold of linguistic methodology, and yet which can carry on a fruitful dialogue with AI and other computationalists. That is proof, if it were needed, that linguisitic methodology is independent of the competence/performance issue, which is what, above all, has divided Chomsky from AI, but which has no place in the methodology of Gazdar and other linguists of like mind. Hence, that distinction and all that followed from it was always dispensable baggage, peculiarly Chomsky's and not any essential part of the discipline. For the first time in nearly thirty years the separation of the man and the discipline can be seen clearly, and the relief all round is enormous, just as in those fairy tales where the peasants rejoice and sow again after some brave young man has slain the giant on the hill who held them in thrall for so long. The question is, why the villagers allowed it to go on for so many years, since it was not for lack of informed advice on how to improve their lot.

If I must disagree with Biggs, it is over the list of 'responses in AI to this lack of fit [between the competence/performance distinction and process-based accounts of language]' (p. 189). The list seems to me both to misrepresent attitudes in AI in recent years, and to pay too much implicit respect to the distinction itself (CPD for short). The four responses he gives can be characterized as (1) AI is about *use* so the CPD is irrelevant; (2) CPD is irrelevant to AI because Chomsky's own particular grammar model is irrelevant to processing; (3) CPD applies equally well to processing itself and so may apply equally as well to AI as linguistics; (4) AI builds systems and has no time for the considerations that CPD expresses. Biggs' own view seems to be that (3) is the only basis for interaction between AI and linguistics, and that this will in the end reduce to AI's need 'for a sustaining meta-theory' (p. 194).

I cannot accept this account as giving a fair statement of AI views, even though researchers can be found to express each of (1) to (4). The last (and perhaps the first) are cheerful philistines, so let us leave them aside for, having no views on these abstract issues, they also do no harm.

My own understanding of current discussions between AI workers and the linguists I picked out above, using Gazdar as a prototype, is that they do not proceed on the basis of (3) at all, but on a tacit understanding that CPD is irrelevant to the details of the systems they want to discuss and implement and so need never come up. That, of course, is a view closer to (2) than to (3), and is consistent with my point in my original chapter that, unfair as it may be, the CPD is seen as inextricably linked with Chomsky's particular model of TGG, even though they are logically independent. Their independence is a point on which I could agree with Chomsky, but progress in academic disciplines, as in evolution itself, is ruthless and illogical, and the CPD is being thrown out with TGG (except perhaps in Italy and Holland, but I am generalizing about the heartland of the Empire and not remote European colonies).

As to (3), it is not a bridge between linguistics and AI, as Biggs suggests, because insofar as the CPD can be interpreted in computational terms, and some writers have sought to do so, both sides of the distinction are formally precise, and so none of the difficulties that have dogged its application to cognitive areas can ever arise. It is therefore not even the same distinction in the two areas, linguistics and computer science.

As to Biggs' plea about meta-theory, I think we must just disagree: 'For if AI needs an overall theoretical framework and sustaining meta-theory, then ... where is it to get these from?' (p. 191). If AI is a discipline, it will work up its own, and if it cannot, then it isn't. Although AI is a young field, it, like all fields, is defined by its methodology, and so the ongoing disputes[1] about AI methodology is are also disputes about what AI is. It will be obvious that linguists interested in computation tend, implicitly, to prefer the specify-implement-verify paradigm for AI, one where they do the specifying and the AI men in white coats do the implementing.

I reject not only Biggs' particular claims, but the much more general software engineering approach as a basis for AI, one which works for airline reservation systems but not, I suspect, for natural languages. But if AI *were* to take its paradigm from outside, it would certainly not be from the little field of linguistics but from the much more general one of software engineering!

My own hope and belief is that AI will develop its own methodology, and its own particular theories in the area of language: the omens are good for both, and that is the only outcome consistent with the cognitive science enterprise being a cooperative one and not a disguised take-over bid. But, again, this difference over theories, between AI workers and compatible linguists, is now well-conducted, with the possibility of different outcomes that settle issues, just as in science, and not at all the sort of ugly, rancorous and bullying affair of the bad old days of the giant on the hill.

NOTE

1 Between repeated implement-test-implement cycles (or trial-and-error, if you will), and those of a software engineering persuasion who want to assimilate AI to the specify-implement-verify paradigm, which looks more scientific (see Partridge, in press, for extended discussion), but is arguably inapplicable to the subject matter of the cognitive sciences.

REFERENCE

Partridge, D. (in press) *Artificial Intelligence and Software Engineering*, Chichester, Sussex, Ellis Horwood and Wiley.

IX: Part Five: Linguistics and Epistemology

16. Psychologism in Linguistics, and Its Alternatives

PHILIP CARR

CHOMSKY AND PSYCHOLOGISM

One of the principal issues in the philosophy of science is whether scientific theories should be given a realist or an instrumentalist interpretation. Instrumentalism has been defined by Popper (1956, 1983) as:

> the doctrine that a scientific theory such as Newton's, or Einstein's, or Schrödinger's, should be interpreted as an instrument, *and nothing but an instrument*, for the deduction of predictions of future events ... and more especially, that a scientific theory should not be interpreted as a genuine conjecture about the structure of the world, or as a genuine attempt to describe certain aspects of our world. (Vol. 1, pp. 111–12, emphasis in original)

The realist, on the other hand, claims that our theories *should* be taken to be attempted descriptions of aspects of our world, while not denying that they also serve as valuable tools for predicting and classifying the phenomena. While the realist/instrumentalist debate is much more complex than this brief characterization suggests, it is clear that, prior to Chomsky's exposition of a coherent conjectural realist philosophy of linguistics, the discipline had embraced a version of instrumentalism whereby our linguistic theories were taken to be mere taxonomic devices for classifying the phenomena, which were taken to be speech noises and marks on paper, etc. A central part of Chomsky's philosophy of linguistics is this conjectural realism, whereby the linguist is taken to be proposing falsifiable hypotheses which are attempts at characterizing a linguistic reality underlying the phenomena. This notion alone has resulted in a vast amount of progress in our understanding of linguistic structure, and underlies all the approaches to linguistic methodology discussed below.

However, as a consequence of the adoption of this view the realist linguist must also specify the ontological status of the object of inquiry. Chomsky's position on this has been the consistent claim that our object is a speaker-internal, psychological one; it is this thesis which I refer to as psychologism. A typical statement of it is as follows: 'The theory of language is simply that part of human psychology that is concerned with one particular "mental organ", human language.' And: '. . . language, after all, has no existence apart from its mental representation' (Chomsky, 1968, p. 81). This ontological claim is distinct from, and logically prior to, the 'innateness hypothesis', or claims about the 'psychological reality' of any particular linguistic analysis. While the innateness hypothesis is a central component of Chomsky's philosophical position, I will not be dealing directly with it here. Rather, I will examine two alternatives to psychologism and establish the outline for a third, which I think sheds considerable light on the nature of linguistic methodology and the status of the object of inquiry.

It should be clear from Chomsky's comments above that he rejects the possibility of an 'autonomous' theoretical linguistics, distinct from psychology, with an object and a methodology of its own. He maintains, rather, that ' . . . the theoretical psychologist (in this case, the linguist), the experimental psychologist, and the neurologist are engaged in a common enterprise . . . ' (Chomsky, 1976, p. 37).

One response to this view is that linguistic hypotheses should therefore be made amenable to falsification by experimental testing in psychology. Thus Derwing (1973, p. 322) argues that linguistic hypotheses, if they are about anything, must be about human storing, processing and production of language, and that 'the linguist seriously interested in establishing knowledge about human language processing must become familiar with those techniques which the experimental psychologist has developed, and try to adapt them to the investigation of natural language pheno-mena.' Furthermore, Derwing and Harris (1975, p. 312) claim that 'if linguists are not interested in these goals—in explaining language use and acquisition—then they might as well close up shop and declare bankruptcy.' I will argue that the first of these quotations is a valid comment on a psychologistically interpreted theoretical linguistics, and that the second is entirely mistaken.

Chomsky's response to the sort of claim made in the first of these passages, namely the requirement that, if the object of inquiry is psychological, then hypotheses about it should be amenable to psychological testing, is to claim that the relation between 'cognitive structure', as the object, and experimental data, is very indirect. Thus: ' . . . the relation of a cognitive structure to experience may be as remote and intricate as the relation of a non-trivial scientific theory to data; depending on the character of the "innateness hypothesis", the relation might even be partial and indirect' (Chomsky, 1976, pp. 38–9). Chomsky's analogy here with scientific theories is untenable. Non-trivial scientific theories do bear an intricate and remote relation to experience, it is true, but not so remote as to be unaffected by experimental testing. To take a random example, Einstein's work on the general theory of relativity was very abstract and speculative, but in order to be considered a scientific theory at all, it had to be specified in what way it would relate to experience, i.e., experimentally testable consequences had to be deducible from it. The first of these, that one would expect curvature of light rays by the gravitational field of the sun, led to an experiment which would potentially falsify the theory. The point about this is that Einstein could not shrug off experimental testing on the grounds that (a) he was a speculative theorist whose hypotheses were 'remote and intricate' in their relation to experience and (b) our knowledge of physical structure was insufficiently advanced to show the relationship between the theory and the object of investigation. The relation of Einstein's theory to experimental data was far from simple and direct, but it was *specified*, and had to be for the theory to have any validity. This, however, is clearly not the case with the relation between linguistic hypotheses and the putatively psychological object of inquiry.

This leaves us with two options: (i) retain psychologism and proceed as Derwing suggests (i.e., become psychologists of language) or (ii) abandon psychologism and adopt an autonomist view of linguistic inquiry, where the object is taken to be non-psychological in nature and theoretical linguistics to be distinct from cognitive psychology. I suggest we adopt the latter (certainly, very few linguists have, since Derwing's book first appeared, adopted the former). In what follows, I discuss a variety of reasons why we should, and consider answers to the question: 'if the object of inquiry is not psychological in nature, then what sort of thing is it?'

ITKONEN AND HERMENEUTICS

A very clearly worked out version of autonomism is that presented in the work of Esa Itkonen (cf. in particular, Itkonen, 1978). His proposals can be summarized as follows. He distinguishes between spatiotemporal *events*, which are not intentional in nature, and *actions*, which are, and are carried out by conscious agents. Both of these are in turn distinct from socially agreed upon *norms*, which are mutual rules constituting the basis for our actions. From this set of distinctions, Itkonen argues that grammatical inquiry is qualitatively distinct from physical inquiry. Physics has as its testing ground spatiotemporal events, whereas grammar has as its testing ground not spatiotemporal events but sets of forms (sentences, particular word forms) which are either well-formed or ill-formed, according to the intuitive judgments of the native speaker. These intuitive judgments involve accessing, via the act of intuition, our knowledge of the norms (or rules) which characterize the notion 'correct sentence'.

Defining empirical sciences as those which are falsifiable on the basis of spatiotemporal events, Itkonen argues that grammatical inquiry is non-empirical. This conclusion has generated a certain amount of disagreement and misunderstanding (cf. Dahl, 1975; Linell, 1976; Sampson, 1976 for criticisms, and Itkonen, 1976 for replies to these). The point to be stressed is that Itkonen is *not* claiming that grammatical hypotheses are unfalsifiable, but is making a claim about the manner in which they are falsified, which relates directly to the ontological status of the object under investigation. The issue here is not what we choose to convey by the term 'empirical'. Clearly, if 'empirical' simply means 'falsifiable', then for Itkonen grammatical hypotheses are empirical. But then the distinction between one method of falsification and another remains valid if it accurately characterizes what theorists actually *do*. And it is beyond doubt that theoretical linguists do not assemble a corpus of observations of spatiotemporal events in order to test their hypotheses against them. Rather, the data and evidence in grammatical arguments and analyses are simply a series of well-formed and ill-formed structures.

Itkonen notes that this method of falsification distinguishes theoretical linguistics from both the physical sciences such as physics, which are experimental, corpus-based sciences, and social sciences such as sociology and psychology, which are partly experimental, corpus-based disciplines, and partly make reference to the norm-based actions of conscious agents. Thus psycholinguistics and sociolinguistics are social sciences, and theoretical linguistics a 'hermeneutic' science dealing with the explication of our knowledge of mutually established norms.

Itkonen therefore characterizes linguistic structure in terms of linguistic norms, which it is the grammarian's task to describe. Thus, to take a simple example, the sentence *Eats Bill the mango*? is taken to be 'incorrect' in that it does not correspond to the notion 'correct sentence', which is established by our set of sentence-formation rules (where we take 'rule' to mean 'intersubjective norm'). In particular, it violates a specific norm for the formation of yes/no questions (I return to this example below: it raises problems for Itkonen's conception of rules as norms). The notion 'correctness' is not applicable, however, to spatiotemporal events, such as the curvature of light rays; and 'correctness', Itkonen claims, is a central feature of actions. Grammatical analyses will yield, according to Itkonen, a characterization of what are and are not correct sentences by stating the norms for their formation, which we know intuitively.

One might notice a parallel here between Chomsky's and Itkonen's proposals, in that both take the grammarian to be characterizing that which the native speaker/hearer intuitively knows, but it is important to bear in mind that Itkonen's rules-as-norms are necessarily *public* in nature. This follows from Itkonen's adoption of (a version of) the Wittgensteinian private language argument, where 'correctness', as the central notion in explicating actions, is taken to be definable only in an intersubjective manner (we cannot privately devise and then correctly follow a rule, since we can have no independent checks on whether we are in fact acting, i.e., following the rule, correctly).

It should be noted how strong Itkonen's claims are: norms are not only established socially, they are entirely *constituted* by their social context. 'Common knowledge literally constitutes concepts and rules as what they are, whereas their (social) existence is independent of the subjective knowledge of any individual person...' (Itkonen, 1978, p. 322, n. 67). Furthermore, Itkonen's view of linguistic rules is not only social, but also *functional*: rules exist in response to some social function. This is, I think, an untenable view of the nature of linguistic rules. To take the functional aspect first, it meets with the problem that we can never specify any *particular* social function to which a linguistic rule is a response. The rule alluded to above, that verbs like *eat* never invert with their subjects, could never be said to be a response to any particular social need or function. Even more telling is the fact that we cannot normally specify any *general* social function of linguistic rules. What, for instance, is achieved by the rule of subject-auxiliary inversion, in terms of social function? *Eats Bill the mango?*, were it the 'correct' form (rather than *Does Bill eat the mango?/Is Bill eating the mango?*) would be just as adequate a sentence, in terms of communicative function, as the correct yes/no question forms. The point is that there is something about yes/no questions in English that the grammarian wants to capture, and this thing has nothing to do with social function (cf. Lass, 1981 for detailed criticism of 'functional' explanation in (historical) phonology). It is difficult to take the notion of social function in language as anything other than a very general requirement that language functions as a means of interpersonal communication; but such a requirement has little, if any, relevance to the investigation of linguistic rules.

In addition, it is clear that Itkonen's conception of linguistic structure as a set of intersubjective norms, entirely constituted by their social context, is peculiarly ill-suited to what we know about linguistic structure. Itkonen rarely cites examples of linguistic rules other than the trivial, low-level sort such as '. . . in English, the definite article precedes the noun' (1978, p. 158). It is worth asking why this is such a poor linguistic statement. It mentions only lexical categories, and linear precedence. It does not mention the sorts of thing we have to mention to make coherent and interesting grammatical statements, namely hierarchical structure, modifier-head relationships, immediate dominance, etc. It is very difficult to see how these sorts of thing can be described in terms of norms as the basis for actions. Could we say, for instance, that it is a socially constituted norm that determiners are premodifiers of a category within NP? Is the head-modifier, or the governor-complement relationship a socially constituted norm? Itkonen's examples deal only with sequential order, presumably because we can relate this sort of notion to the spatiotemporal aspect of actions, whereby, for instance, one performs an act in uttering *the* before *mango*. My claim, then, is that linguistic entities and relationships are not describable in terms of norms and actions. At the very least, the onus is on Itkonen to show that they are; I suggest the following set of randomly selected linguistic notions as candidates for attempted description in terms of social norm: syllable, head, governor, non-finite clause, verb phrase, vowel harmony, reduplication, phrasal category.

My principal argument is that if such notions are not describable in terms of social norms, then under a realist philosophy of linguistics they are not social in nature. This is not surprising if one adopts the following anti-reductionist proposal: that, given an emergent entity, it is not possible to describe that entity in terms of the factors present during its emergence. That is, one would not expect to be able to characterize linguistic structure in terms of social, psychological and biological factors, even if these were the only three factors present during the emergence of language. However, this is to anticipate my outline of Interactionism. For the moment, we should conclude that, having rejected psychologism, we should also reject the notion that linguistic structure is social in nature. The question then arises: what ontological framework can be supplied which will adequately fit the nature of the object of inquiry? Platonism is an attempt to do that.

KATZ AND PLATONISM

A version of autonomous linguistics has recently been outlined by Jerrold Katz (Katz, 1981, and, from the same 'New York School of Platonism', Langendoen and Postal, 1984) whereby the object of inquiry is taken to be neither social nor psychological, but atemporal, aspatial, Platonic in nature. Specifically, both sentences and languages, as the objects of linguistic inquiry, are assumed to be 'abstract objects' of this Platonic sort. This raises the question whether particular languages, in addition to sentences, should be taken to be linguistic objects, rather than socio-politically defined, non-linguistic objects, as in the standard Chomskyan interpretation. Restrictions of space prevent my discussing this issue; instead, I will restrict my comments to the status of sentences as linguistic objects. Katz's arguments for their Platonic status are as follows.

Theoretical linguistics crucially involves acts of intuitive judgment; the objects of these acts are quite distinct from the objects of acts of perception or introspection; while the object of an act of introspection (e.g., remembering) is some internal, psychological state of affairs, this is not so of that to which we gain access via the act of intuition. A parallel situation can be found, Katz claims, in mathematical inquiry, where the numbers, and the relations between them, are not psychological in nature, but possess the properties they do regardless of the internal states of human beings. The objects of investigation in logic, i.e., logical relations, are held to be of this status too, namely non-spatiotemporal abstract objects which exist independently of the psychological states of human beings. (It is as well to note that, even if a psychologistic interpretation of logic and mathematics were shown to be the most appropriate, this would not necessarily render Katz's claims about sentences as abstract objects invalid; Katz's argument does not rest on the analogy with logic and mathematics.) Central to Katz's argument is the proposal that we distinguish that which we have knowledge of via intuition, and our internal representations of it; the former is not psychological in nature, but the latter is. Thus sentences (and for Katz particular languages) as the object of linguistic inquiry are abstract objects, and quite distinct from our internal representations of them, and facts about the way we store, process and produce internal representations of sentences are distinct from facts about sentences per se. Katz further argues that it is not possible to give an account of necessary truth in natural language if we take it (natural language) to be psychological in nature, since properties of human psychological make-up are entirely contingent in nature. It follows that theoretical linguistics is an autonomous discipline with regard to psychology (or sociology), with an object of inquiry quite distinct from that investigated by the psychologist.

Katz argues that the imposing of facts about the human processing, storing and production mechanism upon linguistic hypotheses would amount to imposing unnecessary restrictions upon them. The thought experiment Katz cites to support this claim is as follows: imagine a group of aliens, with a cognitive make-up entirely different from ours, learn one of our human languages, and are able to speak it fluently (or otherwise signal it), and judge ill-formedness and well-formedness of sentences. The psychologistic interpretation of linguistic structure forces us to claim that these aliens have not acquired the language in question. That is, since 'language has no existence outside of its mental representation', the representations within the aliens being distinct from ours, they do not possess the same linguistic entity that we possess. If the psychologistic linguist were to reply that in such a case the alien's and the human's mental representations of the grammar of the acquired language are like algorithms for the same function, then he literally collapses psychologism into autonomism, since that is precisely what the autonomist is claiming.

Thus far, in this necessarily brief characterization of Platonism, much of Katz's argument is parellel to Itkonen's, namely that theoretical linguistics is an intuition-based discipline, distinct from psychology, whose object of inquiry is not a speaker-internal psychological one. What differentiates them is Katz's insistence that linguistic objects are pre-existing Platonic objects which we do not bring into being. This conflicts with the notion, almost universally held, that language is a product of human activity which has emerged during the evolutionary process. This leads to the weakest part of Katz's framework, namely the epistemological problems involved in our coming to have internal representations of Platonic objects. Since Itkonen's object is produced by us, it does not run into the problem of how our contingent mental capacities should be able to gain access to an object which is not of our creation and is non-spatiotemporal.

Katz, well aware of this, attempts to deal with the problem as follows. He argues that a fault of past versions of Platonism is a tendency to extend, excessively, the similarity between intuition and perception, in an attempt to show how we could apprehend Platonic objects. That is, if perception involves causal interaction between perceiver and perceived, then intuition also involves some sort of direct contact between the subject and that to which he gains access. Katz argues that this view of intuition is mistaken, and should be replaced by a Kantian epistemology whereby intuitive awareness comes about, not by abstract objects acting causally upon us, but as the effect of an 'internal construction' (Katz, 1981, p. 202). According to this account of intuition, the act of constructing an object of intuitive apprehension produces, not a Platonic abstract object, but an 'internal representation' of an abstract object (p. 203). However, this still leaves us short of establishing a link between abstract objects and our internal representations of them. Katz fills this gap by proposing a version of nativism just like that proposed by Chomsky, except that what is innately specified is the following: the 'knowledge of' relation, and an innate idea of 'abstract object'. We end up with the following range of components in Katz's ontological framework: abstract objects themselves, aspatial, atemporal, not capable of entering into causal relations; the act of intuition; an innate idea of the 'knowledge of' relation; and an innate idea of 'abstract object'. The internal construction that Katz describes consists of these factors working in conjunction to create internal representations of abstract objects, without abstract objects themselves acting causally upon the mind.

This is obviously the weakest point in Katz's ontological framework. It looks dangerously likely to collapse into standard Chomskyan nativism, simply by means of an application of Occam's Razor, as Pateman (1983) points out. Furthermore, apart from the complexity and multiplication of entities it involves, it still remains a mystery just how such innate specifications as these could have come about: what possible factors could have led to the development of innate ideas of abstract objects, especially when these objects are unavailable to causal interactions?

The principal problem with Platonism, then, is its insistence that linguistic structure is not a product of human activity, and its inability to account for, in general terms, the emergence of language. Yet the arguments that both Katz and Itkonen propose regarding the non-corpus-based nature of grammatical inquiry and the role of intuition in theoretical linguistics accord well with the facts of linguistic practice. Not only do grammarians not formulate their hypotheses on the basis of a corpus of observations, but it would be completely redundant for them to do so. One need not seek spatiotemporal correlates for what one already intuitively knows to be the case, and if one did assemble a corpus of, say, yes/no questions in English, one would only end up applying one's intuitive knowledge to the corpus to eliminate those utterances which one knows not to correspond to well-formed sentences.

This aspect of the actual practice of theoretical linguistics is an important one, and contrasts markedly with the experimental, corpus-based nature of psycholinguistics and sociolinguistics. Furthermore, there is another very salient and important fact about the relationship between these disciplines which supports the metatheoretical claims of the autonomists. This is that one need not have any knowledge of psychology or sociology in order to formulate perfectly good grammatical hypotheses; allied to this is the equally important fact that it is absolutely essential to know something about linguistic structure in order to begin to make any headway in the psychology or sociology of language. This is hardly surprising if, as the autonomist claims, linguistic structure is distinct from social or psychological structure, but is a complete mystery if one rejects autonomism. Adopting Katz's and Itkonen's arguments in favour of autonomism, but rejecting the proposals that linguistic objects are Platonic objects, or are characterizable in terms of social norms,

I will argue that interactionism provides an ontological framework which accords well with the facts of linguistic practice and sheds light on the relationship between theoretical linguistics on the one hand, and both psycholinguistics and sociolinguistics on the other.

INTERACTIONISM

Popper (1972) has proposed that we distinguish the following three sorts of reality: (i) *physical* objects, states, functions, relationships (ii) *mental* states, processes, functions and (iii) *objective* contents of thoughts. To explain what is meant by (iii) it is as well to explain what the motivation for this tripartite distinction is. Popper argues that we ought to consider the content of a scientific theory to be distinct from any states of mind which lead to its formulation. In assessing a theory we want to check its claims against the evidence, as well as checking it for internal consistency, elegance, etc. None of these constitutes mental states: a theory is contradicted by experimental results or is internally contradictory regardless of the psychological state of its proponent. Furthermore, a theory may be internally inconsistent even if no-one knows it at the time, and may similarly turn out to be false even if on-one knew it when the theory was proposed. This suggests that these properties of theories are *objective* properties, independent of anyone's mental states or beliefs. This clearly involves an anti-psychologistic thesis of autonomism for scientific theories: objective problem situations and objective contents of theories have a largely autonomous existence relative to human mental states. This claim that theories may have properties (e.g., internal contradiction) even if no-one is aware of them is an important one for Popper: it means that we may later come to discover properties of theories and their relationships to problems, and that science progresses by means of an *interaction* between the scientist, the objective problem situation he is trying to solve, and the objective contents and properties of scientific theories. Popper (1972, p. 109) illustrates this with a quotation from Heyting concerning Brouwer's inventing the theory of the continuum: 'If recursive functions had been invented before, he [Brouwer] would perhaps not have formed the notion of a choice sequence, which, I think, would have been unlucky.' Popper points out that the act of forming the notion of a choice sequence is a subjective act, influenced in this case by the existence of a notion of 'recursive function' which is considered independently of any theorist's state of mind. The fact that recursive functions had been invented is, of course, also part of the objective problem situation which Brouwer was tackling. With Brouwer's devising of the theory of the continuum the objective situation is changed, with the content of that theory then available objectively to any other theorist working in the area. The interaction occurs between the products of our intellectual activity and the intellectual activity itself, where these are taken to be two entirely distinct things. Popper uses the terms 'world three' to refer to the ontological status of the products, and 'world two' to refer to the mental states and activities that are involved in their production. The term 'world one' is then reserved for purely physical states and entities, which may act upon our mental states (e.g., in the act of perception) and may be acted upon by us (e.g., in our manipulation of the physical world).

Popper couches all of this in a biological, evolutionary framework, whereby world three objects emerge through our interaction with objective problem situations relating to our survival, i.e., hypotheses are formulated in response to external problems. Thus the activity of the scientist is seen as an attempt by organism or species to solve problems about the world in which it lives.

I suggest we follow a suggestion originally made by Lass (1976) that we view linguistic structure in this 'world three object' way. Popper has argued that the emergence of language, with its descriptive and argumentative functions, was crucial in the emergence of the sorts of world three objects in which the philosopher of science is interested. If we argue that the internal structure of language itself is a largely autonomous product of human activity of the sort Popper describes, then we come up with a version of autonomism which accords well with what we know about linguistic practice, and suggests how theoretical linguistics might relate to neighbouring disciplines.

First, it is obvious why one should be able to study linguistic structure without any knowledge of psychological processes: for the same reason that one need not understand the psychology of scientists in order to understand the content of scientific theories, namely that its structure is largely independent of social or psychological factors.

Secondly, this autonomism can be related to a general anti-reductionist thesis regarding the products of evolutionary processes, namely that one cannot reduce them to lower level phenomena. Thus psychological and social factors, which no doubt were central to the emergence of language, will not prove sufficient to the characterization of linguistic structure per se as an evolutionary product. This is precisely what we find to be the case in, for example, Itkonen's view of linguistic structure as social reality.

Furthermore, unlike the Platonist, the interactionist can begin to outline a framework under which we can investigate the interrelationships between linguistic structure as an autonomous reality and psychological (as well as social) states and processes. These in turn can be investigated for their relationships to purely physical structure (neurological structure and function). Thus we retain Chomsky's goal of interdisciplinary investigation without mischaracterizing the nature of our object of inquiry.

That Popper's framework is of heuristic value in establishing a viable interdisciplinary research programme can be seen from his collaboration with neurophysiologist John Eccles. Thus in Popper and Eccles (1977) an attempt is made to correlate brain structure and function with mental states, and to correlate these in turn with world three objects. The consequence for language study is that we begin with a clear idea of the ontological status of neurological, psychological and linguistic factors, and can then attempt to fill in specific details about their exact interrelationships. And there are consequences internal to theoretical linguistics itself.

In the fields of phonetics and phonology, for instance, it follows from this framework that we are investigating three distinct, but interrelated, areas: (i) physical sounds, and their articulatory and acoustic properties, (ii) mental storage, perception and production of these, in addition to mental perception and storage of phonological structure, and finally, (iii) the structure and properties of phonological systems in and of themselves, taken largely independently of psychological facts about their storage or perception. A consequence of the adoption of the framework outlined here is that any reductionistic, 'concretist' interpretation of phonology is mistaken. That is, phonological structure is not reducible to phonetics: phonetic factors are necessary, but not sufficient, for the explication of phonological structure. Put another way, there are phonological generalizations which are not phonetic generalizations, and under the sort of realist methodology adopted here these generalizations refer to real entities and processes. Note that this interactionist approach to phonology rules out O'Hala's (1975) phonetic reductionism, where phonetic factors are both necessary and sufficient for the explication of phonological facts, and also Foley's (1977) non-interactionist view that such factors are neither necessary nor sufficient for this purpose. The sort of approach to phonological phenomena which this ontological framework supports is that outlined in Anderson (1981); restrictions on space prevent any further discussion of this, but the nature of phonological systems as discussed by Anderson is very much what one would expect if the suggestions made in this interactionist programme are along the right lines.

Regarding syntactic structure, it follows from this programme that discourse structure, involving as it does social and psychological factors, should be taken to be distinct from, if able to interact with, syntactic structure per se. One would not expect it to be possible successfully to reduce syntactic structure to discourse structure, nor would one expect it to be necessary to have a theory of discourse structure in order to analyze syntax; the reverse, however, ought to be the case, since syntactic phenomena necessarily enter into discourse. Furthermore, psychological processing of syntactic information will be held to be quite separable from syntactic structure itself under this methodological framework. Thus it would be quite possible, as in Katz's thought experiment, for a particular set of syntactic rules and representations to be processed in a variety of different ways by organisms with perhaps very different internal cognition processes; the investigation of how humans process them is the domain of the psycholinguist.

Restrictions of space have allowed only the briefest of outlines of the four ontological positions discussed here. I hope to have shown that the facts of the practice of theoretical linguistics should prompt us to reject psychologism, and to adopt a version of autonomism. I also hope to have shown that the version I have outlined fits rather well with what we know of the nature of linguistic reality, and has a variety of interesting consequences both internal to theoretical linguistics and in the area of its relationships with neighbouring disciplines. In adopting it we are still able to retain Chomsky's realist position, his view of language as a product of biological development, and his interdisciplinary goal.

REFERENCES

Anderson, S. R. (1981) 'Why phonology isn't natural', *Linguistic Inquiry*, **12,** pp. 494–553.

Chomsky, N. (1966) *Cartesian Linguistics*, London, Harper and Row.

Chomsky, N. (1968) *Language and Mind*, New York, Harcourt Brace Jovanovich.

Chomsky, N. (1976) *Reflections on Language*, London, Temple Smith.

Chomsky, N. (1980) *Rules and Representations*, New York, Columbia University Press.

Dahl, O. (1975) 'Is linguistics empirical? A critique of Esa Itkonen's Linguistics and Metascience', *Gothenburg Papers in Theoretical Linguistics*.

Derwing, B. L. (1973) *Transformational Grammar as a Theory of Language Acquisition*, Cambridge, Cambridge University Press.

Derwing, B. L. and Harris, P. R. (1975) 'What is a generative grammar?' in Koerner, E. F. K. (Ed.), *The Transformational Generative Paradigm and Modern Linguistic Theory* Amsterdam, Benjamins.

Foley, J. (1977) *Foundations of Theoretical Phonology* Cambridge, Cambridge University Press.

Heyting, A. (1962) 'After thirty years', in Nagel, E. *et al.* (Eds), *Logic, Methodology and Philosophy of Science*, Stanford, Stanford University Press.

Itkonen, E. (1974) *Linguistics and Metascience*, Studia Philosophica Turkuensia II.

Itkonen, E. (1976) 'Linguistics and empiricalness: Answers to criticisms', *Papers in Linguistics 4*, University of Helsinki Linguistics Department.

Itkonen, E. (1978) *Grammatical Theory and Metascience*, Amsterdam, Benjamins.

Katz, J. J. (1981) *Language and Other Abstract Objects*, Oxford, Blackwells.

Langendoen, D. T. and Postal, P. M. (1984) *The Vastness of Natural Languages*, Oxford, Blackwells.

Lass, R. (1976) *English Phonology and Phonological Theory*, Cambridge, Cambridge University Press.

Lass, R. (1981) *On Explaining Language Change*, Cambridge, Cambridge University Press.

Linell, P. (1976) 'Is linguistics an empirical science? Some notes on E. Itkonen's Linguistics and Metascience', *Studia Linguistica*, **30.**

Pateman, T. (1983) Review of Katz (1981), *Journal of Linguistics*, **19,** pp. 282–4.

Popper, K. R. (1956, 1983) *Realism and The Aim of Science*, Vol. 1 of the *Postscript to the Logic of Scientific Discovery*, New York, Rowan and Littlefield.

Popper, K. R. (1972) *Objective Knowledge*, Oxford, Clarendon Press.

Popper, K. R. and Eccles, J. C. (1977) *The Self and Its Brain*, Berlin, Springer.

Sampson, G. (1976) Review of Koerner (1975), *Language*, **52,** pp. 961–6.

17. Three Kinds of Question about Modularity

JAMES RUSSELL

Chomsky's claim that language competence exists as a 'mental organ' distinct from but 'interacting'[1] with other mental organs is, like much of Chomsky's theorizing, fascinating, provocative and deeply obscure. My aim in this chapter is not to elucidate its obscurity but to say, as it were, 'If this is what Chomsky means then he is wrong.' I will discuss the matter under three headings: processing, acquisition, scientific status.

PROCESSING

Comprehension

In his recent book on modular processes in human cognition Jerry Fodor (1983) distinguishes between 'input systems' and 'central systems'. Input systems are modular and central systems are holistic.[2] To be modular, according to Fodor, a mental process must have at least the following properties (there are nine properties in his complete list): non-conscious and unamenable to revelation in consciousness; very fast; mandatory; and informationally encapsulated. One of the clearest examples of an input system is vision: for no matter how intentionally we wish to regard vision there *are* visual mechanisms—computational processes if you will—that make visual experience possible. What of sentence parsing? For Fodor this is clearly a modular process: indeed he points out that his whole thesis was inspired by a remark of Merrill Garrett's to the effect that sentence parsing is a reflex—and of course the reflex is a paradigmatically modular process. How does this claim bear on Chomsky's thesis?

In Chomskyan theoretical psychology, when we hear a sentence *linguistic* mechanisms of enormous complexity spring into action to yield a syntactic decomposition of the sentence, a decomposition that is sufficiently predigested to be a fit nutrient for the 'conceptual' component—whatever that may be. This linguistic decomposition view of comprehension bears comparison with Donald Davidson's claim that comprehension involves a form of logical decomposition.[3] Now if we are to view Chomsky's claim as theoretical psychology (Davidson's is something different) I think it is fair to ask whether Fodor's criteria, assuming these to be good criteria, do indeed capture a kind of modular stage of comprehension. If they do not, we should then ask what are the prima facie advantages of regarding sentence parsing as a modular process—that is, despite the fact that it does not look any more modular than do general conceptual ('central'?) capacities.

We can contrast the decomposition view of parsing with an holistic view. A supporter of the holistic view would certainly not have to deny that the process of comprehension fulfils Fodor's conditions. On the holistic view sentence parsing is very fast because it is very *practised*. It is non-conscious in the sense that we cannot become conscious of the causal conditions of our conscious processes: for in addition to being a wild implausibility about performance the claim that we can leads to a regress into the purest Cartesian dualism. What of the mandatory nature of the process? Certainly, no serious theory would have it that we typically *decide* whether we should parse a sentence in one way or another or as grammatical or agrammatical; under normal circumstances the parsing just happens. But this fact does nothing to support the claim that the parsing consists of purely linguistic computations that 'interact' with a 'conceptual' component. Finally, on the holistic view, we can certainly regard parsing as informationally encapsulated in the sense that the parsing process is relatively unaffected by belief and knowledge states. For example, we will parse 'What's the capital of France?' as the question it is even if it is said by an intelligent and informed adult whom we would expect to know the answer. Similarly our current visual state is unlikely to influence the parsing of sentences we hear. But again, these facts do not suggest that the informational encapsulation is purely linguistic.

Therefore, we can accept that parsing is 'modular' on Fodor's criteria whilst at no point distinguishing between 'linguistic capacity' and 'conceptual capacity'; we assume that rational thinking is in a grammar and that to use language is to think. Of course the holistic view may be hopeless for any number of empirical or philosophical reasons, but we are for the moment considering its viability relative to the decomposition view. My point is, therefore, that there is nothing in the nature of sentence parsing that immediately recommends a modular view to us.

In further illustration, let us apply the criteria to another area of comprehension: spotting logical contradictions. In an adult of normal intelligence spotting that 'The black cat is white' is nonsense is surely non-conscious, very fast, mandatory and informationally encapsulated. For a *child* though it is none of these things.

I turn now to what prima facie advantages the modular or decomposition view may have over the holistic view. One apparent advantage is that it provides us with hypotheses about mechanisms, where the holistic view is non-committal. But in offering solutions to one problem it provides us with another that is far less tractable because it comes wrapped around with promissory, pseudo-scientific notions. The most promissory and pseudo-scientific notion is that of an 'interaction' that is supposed to happen between linguistic and conceptual components (see the next section).

How then are we to regard sentence parsing on the holistic view? Sentence parsing is something that creatures who know the meanings of the words in their language, who know rules of grammar, who have the requisite information-processing capacities, who have knowledge about the world, themselves and others are able to do 'without thinking about it'. Sentence parsing cannot be explained in isolation from the extra-linguistic conditions for it. This is not to deny that Chomskyan linguistics cannot make suggestions about the nature of its linguistic conditions. But in insisting that parsing exists in a linguistic module the role of parsing within comprehension is made more, not less, mysterious.

Production

Chomsky writes: 'The study of grammar raises problems that we have some hope of solving: the creative use of language is a mystery that eludes our intellectual grasp' (1980a, p. 222). Here, of course, he means creativity *qua* autonomy not *qua* the generative nature of the language system. Again we find a division which would not be made on the holistic view: between a preverbal something to say and its instantiation in grammar. At first blush the denial that there is such a bifurcation looks plain silly; but my point is not that no such distinction can ever be drawn but that drawing the distinction sharply between a wholly non-verbal, let us call it 'schema for judgment', and the spoken sentence leads to severe difficulties. We have to posit some kind of gradation between the schema and the sentence and thus some stage in which the schema is primitively verbal. We certainly have to abandon the idea that the schema → sentence transition is a modular process in the way that Fodor's input processes are. We do not want to say that sentences, that is *particular* sentences, happen to us.

Let us consider ways in which the schema → sentence transition could work on Chomsky's thesis. Here is a possible sequence: (1) information pick-up via input processes, (2) schema for judgment, (3) schema → sentence transition. As Hunter (1973) points out, the modular view of production (not his term) entails that the third stage in the process involves a 'talking machine' which converts non-verbal input into sentences. (Chomsky repudiates the talking machine analogy but not, I think, convincingly.[4]) Hunter is surely correct in insisting that, for Chomsky, what I am calling the schema must be completely non-verbal, certainly without the sketchiest linguistic organization—into subject and predicate, for example. Let us assume that the language production module or talking machine has representations that are exclusively linguistic; and this boils down to saying that they are formal in the sense of obeying Fodor's (1980) 'formality condition'.[5] Thus words are represented in terms of abstract phonetic categories, their syntactical roles, and their (what shall we say?) abstract semantic properties (dictionary entries? meaning postulates?). At its crudest but most fundamental this means that the representation of a word such as 'tree' in the production module is not in terms of reference:[6] it is not 'plugged in' to real world knowledge. So we are entitled to ask '*How then does the module do its job?*' How is it able to attach words to the corresponding elements in the preverbal schema? The problem is that for representations to be formal in just the way that Chomsky intends them to be they must have no written-in connection with reality and thus with things to say. Moreover, having something to say is not analyzable as a mental state which will result, all being well, in a sentence, in much the same way that a state of sexual arousal will result, all being well, in certain well-known bodily events. Imagine, in other words, that the schema → sentence transition were mandatory, then we might in the middle of a conversation about the population explosion suddenly opine that the rain in Spain falls mainly on the plain.' Or we would make utterances like, 'I think I want to ask you what time it is, but maybe what I want to know is what day of the week it is' (Hunter, 1973, p. 161).

All this is to suggest that talking involves the intentional framing of inputs into a grammatical shape. This is not to suggest that the framing is not very complex in the sense of involving the rapid manipulation of mental representations (whatever *they* may be), nor does it make mental operations any less non-conscious. It does though make a purely modular view of speech production look distinctly unappetizing.

Finally, a caveat: one thing that these broadly Wittgensteinian thoughts about the verbal nature of the schema does *not* justify is the claim—popular among the more 'Roundhead' of the Wittgensteinians[7]—that there is nothing to be explained about how we talk, that it is a pseudo-question. For to say that the explanation must be holistic is not to imply that processes cannot be pragmatically isolated and studied. In the area of speech production the work of Willem Levelt (1983) on self-correction and Brian Butterworth (1980) on pauses springs immediately to mind.

ACQUISITION

If the rules and representations that constitute the language capacity are *sui generis* then it is difficult to see how we should regard the sensorimotor apprenticeship that takes place prior to the onset of comprehension and speech. This difficulty forms a close parallel to the question I have just been discussing: how to relate preverbal schemas of something to say to language production modules.

There are two main kinds of view here. The Chomskyan view is that sensori-motor and social development in infancy is a kind of gearing up in preparation for the work of the innate language acquisition device (LAD). On this view there is nothing protolinguistic about sensorimotor development: *cognitive* foundations for *linguistic* abilities are laid down without these cognitive foundations having a linguistic character—except in some weak metaphorical sense. The opposing—broadly Piagetian—view is that interaction with the physical and the personal world (although Piaget virtually ignores the latter in infancy[8]) lays the foundations of thought, and the foundations of thought *are* the foundations of language. Obviously this view does not entail that each universal feature of language is directly traceable to a sensorimotor antecedent: it is rather that the linguistic system has a logic because successful action has to have a 'logic'. The problem with this view is that it is vague and unrealized; the problem with the modular view is that it is not at all clear that it even *could* be true.

On the modular view we are forced to distinguish as clearly between the structure of sensorimotor schemes and the grammar as between, say, the structure of the liver and of the circulatory system—separate but interacting. Thus the LAD contains information about what constitutes a sentence, about modification, about subject-verb-object relations, and so forth; but the information is computational in the sense of being formal and independent of experience. The LAD contains the apparatus for computing varieties of reference before the child has any notion of there being something out there to which to refer. Let us assume—as many would not—that such an innate mechanism is intelligible. During the course of early sensorimotor development infants become richly informed about reference, at least to the extent that they can separate and relate intentions (their own and others') and objects (including their own bodies); they can relate actions within superordinate goal-directed sequences; they can share attention to objects with other people; they may even be able to express linguistic functions such as greeting, requesting and refusing. The exact list is unimportant, but this one fact is all important: the prelinguistic infant knows something and wants a number of things and has, therefore, something to say. (This leads, of course, to the very strong empirical claim that the human infant has something to say in a way that the chimpanzee infant has not. Some attempts have been made by baby researchers to spell out what this is (e.g., Kaye, 1982, pp. 136-7). The spelling out will be difficult and controversial; but there are no philosophical arguments to the effect that there *cannot* be a significant gulf between ape and man in this regard.)

Given this, let us take an example of a rule that Chomsky takes as one of the *sui generis* linguistic rules, rather than something that the child could learn through 'inductive generalization': the rule that *wh*-clauses are units or 'islands' whose elements cannot be lifted free of the constituent clause when performing transformations of the sentence. More generally, this is an illustration of the hierarchical nature of language.[9] But action too is hierarchical, and the fact that it has to be hierarchical is a consideration in favour of the view that the roots of logic are sensorimotor. To illustrate: lifting the first occurrence of 'is' out of a *wh*-clause to form an interrogative creates gibberish: 'Is the car which late will leave first?' Similarly, releasing one's hand from the handle of a cup of hot coffee in order to position a saucer whilst returning the cup from the lips will create a nasty accident. It seems to be wrong to argue that structured schemes just *are* linguistic rules that are yet to be expressed verbally, that, for example, reaching plus turning to mother 'for help' is a 'request' that just happens not to be verbally instantiated. (Behaviour is open to interpretation in a way that verbalization is not.) But what mastery of such preverbal procedures can make possible is the *intelligibility* of linguistic rules to the learner. That is, the *wh*-clause 'island' rule is not a deep *linguistic* rule: it is deep in the sense that it forms part of our mental scaffolding,[10] the part which ensures that things that belong together stay together. 'Which is late' belongs with 'car'; a hand belongs on the handle of a lifted cup.

Banal as this may appear, it does at least enable us to escape from what may be called the Chomsky-Fodor paradox.[11] This states that linguistic rules are of such a nature that they could not be acquired unless something substantial were already known about their general nature. Ergo, knowledge of the basic grammatical rules must be innate. This is true on the modular construal of linguistic rules as *sui generis*—as formal, contentless, computational entities waiting around to be mapped onto the child's model of reality. Indeed, the child *does* have to know something about the nature of linguistic rules to acquire them, but this something need not itself be linguistic.

Predictably, this brings me once more to my *motif*: formal rules (obeying, that is, the formality condition) cannot by their very nature map onto pre- or non-verbal knowledge. This is so because such rules, in *addition* to being individuated by their computational 'shapes', would have to contain some kind of mapping rules to reality. But if they are to have mapping rules to reality then they are not formal; they are contentful and thus no longer modular in Chomsky's sense.

Let me broaden my case just a little with consideration of the property that is constitutive of all symbol systems: intensionality. Intensionality arises from the fact that reference can be achieved in more than one way (note that intensional contexts are created by the possibility of substituting co-referential terms). Thus the child is sooner or later going to have to appreciate that, for example, the family cat can be referred to as 'Ginger', 'it', 'you', 'puss', 'the cat' and so on,[12] and he is going to have to be *prepared* for this. On the Chomsky-Fodor paradox no child could understand co-reference and thus intensionality unless such a principle were represented in his nervous system prior to experience. To dispel this paradox all we need to do is to attend to the blinding truth that the preverbal child's mental life is awash with behavioural (e.g., reach to where the object was hidden) and interpersonal (mother-infant interaction studies *passim*) co-reference.

This is not to deny that there is a lot of specifically linguistic knowledge (specific to the native tongue and to language itself) that the child has to learn. But he learns this once he has entered the language system as a junior member, once the use of language in communication and representation has become intelligible to him. Chomsky says that we should be impressed by how 'fast' language acquisition is. Maybe. But what is far more significant than the speed is the fact that we never find children saying things like (to use one of Chomsky's examples), 'What book did we say that John gave to Bill?' without having first served an apprenticeship saying much simpler things. My concern in this section has been with how the child gets to the stage of being an apprentice.

SCIENTIFIC STATUS

Chomsky (1980, pp. 189–92) regards his linguistics as strongly analogous to theoretical physics, in particular to the kind of physics that has to be done in the absence of 'direct' experimentation (e.g., solar physics). This is a very poor analogy indeed. It is not simply that the analogy with physics is unworthy of serious consideration (see Bunge, 1984): theoretical linguistics as practised by Chomsky hardly even qualifies as an empirical enterprise. This is because—I shall argue—Chomskyan linguistics exists in a kind of hermeneutical circle. It is itself a *module*.

Let me begin with what I think we can regard as a defining feature of scientific theories. I will call it 'the distance principle' and illustrate it with the following example. The theory of reincarnation states that one self can exist at different historical periods. But it appears to be a necessary condition of being a self that there be a thread of transitive memory (Parfit (1971) calls it 'psychological continuity') running from life to life. The notion that only Smith's *characteristics* existed in mediaeval Italy is too weak for the theory. For there to be one self there must be memory. But there *are* such memories say the reincarnationists. This is the problem: to say that there are memories is to state at once a condition for the intelligibility of the theory and the evidence for it. In this way the division principle is flouted because there is insufficient distance between the hypothesis and the evidence. To become empirical the reincarnation hypothesis has to move beyond memory evidence to evidence for the validity of memories; it has to move outside its own circle.

What bearing does this have on Chomsky? Chomsky's hypotheses concern the nature of the rule system by which we comprehend and produce language. They are not supposed to be merely helpful descriptions because the whole theory is billed as an empirical account of the mental rules and representations that constitute linguistic competence. The theory is built up from consideration of the kind of sentences that we do and the kind of sentences that we do not judge to be grammatical. Its intelligibility is grounded in agreement between the theorist and the community to which the theory is addressed about what constitutes an admissible word string. But in what sense is the theory answerable to evidence? It is answerable to (i.e., its deep rules have to explain without undue anomaly) new examples of sentences that will be assessed by these same intuitions. For this reason I think we are justified in claiming that there is insufficient distance between the content of the theory and the evidence for it. As theoretical linguistics perhaps this is fine. But as theoretical psychology (which Chomsky says he is doing) this is a case of plain old circularity. As we found with the reincarnation hypothesis, to become an empirical hypothesis—that is, psychology rather than theoretical linguistics—we need evidence for the 'evidence' to break out of the circle. In this case we need evidence about how we are able to deploy the linguistic intuitions that we do deploy in assessment (and in language use). This 'how' may be developmental, neurological, performance, social, or otherwise, but it must be non-linguistic. In being non-linguistic it can certainly support or undermine claims about competence that spring from purely linguistic considerations; we need have no quarrel with *that*.

My point is not merely that there is no sharp boundary between grammatical and ungrammatical sentences (which, of course, there is not; and this, *pace* Chomsky, breeds a host of methodological problems[13]). For even if there were such a sharp boundary and even if linguistic intuitions were as secure as mathematical intuitions, the problems posed by the division principle would still loom. Theoretical linguistics in the Chomskyan style is not intelligible without the deployment of the very intuitions that are supposed to test it. Evidence is only 'outside' the hypothesis in the sense that new examples of sentences come to be considered. It is as if the reincarnationists cited more and more cases of memories before birth as evidence for their theory (which in fact they do: but we should be able to do better than this in theoretical psychology!). Nothing could be more different in physics because physicists' theories entail predictions about phenomena that are theory-neutral. Brute facts are of course never 100 per cent brute, but they are physical facts, and to deny that such facts can be regarded as theory-neutral is to deny the objectivity of physics. Perhaps a sentence too is a kind of physical fact; but a 'grammatical sentence' is a fact fused with a judgment, a fusion which keeps linguistic evidence within the module of linguistic theory.

Consider now the failure of one of Chomsky's physics/linguistics analogies (Chomsky, 1980a, pp. 189–92). Astrophysicists who try to determine the nature of thermonuclear reactions that take place deep within the sun have, for obvious reasons, to content themselves with evidence collected 'at the periphery'—evidence about light emission. This evidence is indirect. But this does not, Chomsky points out, devalue it as evidence about hidden physical processes. More direct evidence (e.g., gleaned from a study of the neutrinos released by these reactions) is only more evidence: and no piece or kind of evidence is ever conclusive. So in the kind of theoretical psychology that Chomsky takes himself to be doing—as a linguist he deals with data 'at the periphery' about language use and evaluations from which he constructs competence models of the mental representations responsible for the performance 'at the periphery'. A linguist's proposals have no less 'psychological reality' here than the proposals of an astrophysicist have 'physical reality'. But this analogy breaks down, not necessarily because developing theories of mental representation 'within the brain' from examining language use is a fundamentally different kind of enterprise to that of the astrophysicist in the example. Admittedly there is a loose, though not every interesting, kind of parallel. The analogy breaks down by virtue of the practice of Chomskyan theoretical psychology, not its structure.[14] For Chomsky as a theoretical psychologist is not open to data in the way in which an astrophysicist is open to data. A 'Chomskyan astrophysicist', when presented with data about neutrinos or *per impossibile* with data collected directly from the heart of the sun would ignore it—just as Chomsky ignores (though see below) data from neurology, experimental psychology, and so forth. The Chomskyan astrophysicist would insist that there is absolutely no need to consider any other data than that gleaned from studies of light emission. For if we look at what Chomsky does rather than what he says about the status of what he does, we see that his theoretical psychology is conducted in splendid isolation from psychology and specifically (in view of the implied sun-brain analogy) from physiological psychology.

Why does Chomsky feel able to do this? Because: 'I think that principles based on evidence derived from informant judgment have proved to be deeper and more revealing than those based on evidence derived from experiments on processing and the like, although the future may be different in this regard' (1980a, p. 200). If by 'informant judgment' Chomsky means grouped data about how people judge grammaticality, then this is just a false generalization. But if he means the intuitions of himself as representative of the linguistic intuitions of humankind, then we have an example of flouting the division principle. The *existence* of such intuitions is what has to be explained and their detailed nature forms the stuff out of which the hypotheses of this particular kind of theoretical psychology are made; but they are not evidence for such hypotheses.

And yet ... Chomsky does sometimes consider developmental evidence (one is tempted to add: 'when it suits him'), but as before we must attend closely to how it is done not to the fact that it is done at all. Looking at how acquisition takes place, Chomsky suggests (1980b), must convince us that the child is like a scientist with a theory rather than a Baconian induction-generator. The evidence for this claim is broadly that children's early utterances actually make sense. But this fact can only appear remarkable to somebody in the grip of a modular conception of language as a computational entity. Given that very young children know a good deal about the physical and the personal world, and that they have been exposed to regularities of word meaning and word order, what else should we expect? The fact that young children 'obey' the *wh*-clause island constraint and do not come out with questions like, 'Was the teddy which lost has been found yet?' is no more remarkable than the fact that novice tennis players do not try to hit the bat with the ball. The 'making sense' that children do is not evidence for a theory, any more than adults' ability to make sense is evidence for any theory of how they are able to do so.

POSTSCRIPT

These negative remarks are supposed to be directed against the *purism* of Chomsky's theoretical psychology: against the conception of processing, acquisition and data collection as purely linguistic processes. I suspect that, were this purism to be abandoned, most of the substance of Chomsky's theorizing would remain. It would still be tremendously original and adventurous theoretical psychology.

However, I believe that Chomsky's influence on theoretical psychology has not been through his detailed proposals about linguistic competence. It has been made through his championship of the computation theory of the mind—the view that mental processes are radically independent of our mental orientations to an objective world. In this respect he has become, as Auden wrote of Freud, 'a whole climate of opinion'.[15]

NOTES

1   See, for example, Chomsky (1980a, p. 55): in fact Chomsky has used the term 'interact' in this context for a number of years.
2   The terms used by Fodor are 'isotropic' and 'Quinean'.
3   See Davidson (1967) and Strawson (1976) for a criticism of this approach that can be extended to that of Chomsky.
4   It is wrong, he says, to argue that linguistic theory either 'explains the creative aspects of language use or it explains nothing' (1980a, p. 78). True, but in his defence against Hunter he seems to be using 'creative' in the sense of '*what* to say'—in the autonomy rather than the generative sense. Surely Chomsky wants his theory to have implications for the kinds of rules and representations that make production possible—the 'how to say it'. If he does, then the notion of a language production module or 'talking machine' fits perfectly well with his position.
5   'Formal operations are the ones that are specified without reference to such semantic properties of representations as, for example, truth, reference, and meaning .... Formal operations apply in terms of the, as it were, "shapes" of the objects in their domain .... The computational theory of the mind requires that two thoughts can be distinct in content only if they can be identified with relations to formally distinct representations. More generally: fix the subject and the relation and then mental states can be (type) distinct only if the representations which constitute their objects are formally distinct' (Fodor, 1980, p. 64).
6   See Evans (1982) for a defence of what he calls 'Russell's principle': that for the subject to refer to an object in thought he must be able to individuate that object. The implication is that there can be no such thing as purely formal individuation (see note 5). Evans' book contains a briefly made case against Fodor's formality condition.
7   I am thinking principally of Norman Malcolm here; but also Hunter himself and the kind of Wittgensteinian approach set out in Baker and Hacker (1984).
8   Some would claim that this is a disastrous omission on Piaget's part. But equally disastrous is the view that some quite specific form of preverbal parental interaction and interpretation (see, e.g., Kaye, 1982) is necessary for acquisition. I suspect that, were the kinds of interactions described by such workers really necessary, very few children would ever acquire language!
9   Geoffrey Sampson (1980) has argued that the existence of linguistic universals does not need to be explained in terms of innate linguistic structures, but may be due to the fact that the genetic process is necessarily hierarchical (in ontogeny and phylogeny) given that complex systems will always be built up from smaller units that have a degree of independence and autonomy (Simon, 1962).
10 I have in mind here Wittgenstein's (1969) remarks about 'scaffolding'.
11 See Fodor (1975); for good recent criticism of this see Blackburn (1984).
12 For further elaboration see Russell (1984a).
13 See Ney (1975), and for Chomsky's response see Chomsky (1980a, p. 198).
14 Much the same can be said in the case of Freud: see Cioffi (1970).

REFERENCES

Baker, G. P. and Hacker, P. M. S. (1984) *Language, Sense, and Nonsense*, Oxford, Basil Blackwell.
Blackburn S. (1984) *Spreading the Word: Groundings in the Philosophy of Language*, Oxford, Clarendon Press.

Bunge, M. (1984) 'Philosophical problems in linguistics', *Erkenntniss*, **21**, pp. 107–73.

Butterworth, B. (1980) 'Evidence from pauses', in Butterworth, B. (Ed.), *Language Production*, Vol. 1, London, Academic Press.

Chomsky, A. N. (1980a) *Rules and Representations*, Oxford, Basil Blackwell.

Chomsky, A. N. (1980b) 'On cognitive structures and their development', in Piattelli-Palmarini, M. (Ed.), *Language and Learning: The Debate Between Jean Piaget and Noam Chomsky*, London, Routledge and Kegan Paul.

Cioffi, F. (1970) 'Freud and the idea of a pseudo-science', in Borger, R. and Cioffi, F. (Ed.), *Explanation in the Behavioural Sciences*, Cambridge, Cambridge University Press.

Davidson, D. (1967) 'The logical form of action sentences', in Rescher, N. (Ed.), *The Logic of Decision and Action*, Pittsburg, Pa., University of Pittsburg Press.

Evans, G. (1982) *The Varieties of Reference*, Oxford, Clarendon Press.

Fodor, J. A. (1975) *The Language of Thought*, Hassocks, Harvester Press.

Fodor, J. A. (1980) 'Methodological solipsism considered as a research strategy in cognitive psychology', *The Behavioural and Brain Sciences*, **3**, pp. 69–109.

Fodor, J. A. (1983) *The Modularity of Mind: An Essay in Faculty Psychology*, Cambridge, Mass., MIT Press.

Hunter, J. F. M. (1973) 'On how we talk', in *Essays after Wittgenstein*, London, George Allen and Unwin.

Kaye, K. (1982) *The Mental and Social Life of Babies*, London, Methuen.

Levelt, W. (1983) 'Monitoring and self-repair in speech', *Cognition*, **14**, pp. 41–104.

Ney, J. W. (1975) 'A decade of private knowledge', *Historiographia Linguistica*, **2, 2**, pp. 143–56.

Parfit, D. (1971) 'Personal identity', *Philosophical Review*, **80**, pp. 3–27.

Russell, J. (1984a) 'The subject-object division in language acquisition and ego development', *New Ideas in Psychology*, **2**, pp. 57–74.

Russell, J. (1984b) *Explaining Mental Life: Some Philosophical Issues in Psychology*, London, Macmillan.

Sampson, G. (1980) *Making Sense*, Oxford, Oxford University Press.

Simon, H. (1962) 'The architecture of complexity', *Proceedings of the American Philosophical Society*, **106**, pp. 467–82.

Strawson, P. F. (1976) 'On understanding one's own language', in Evans, G. and McDowell, J. (Eds), *Truth and Meaning: Essays in Semantics*, Oxford, Clarendon Press.

Wittgenstein, L. (1969) *On Certainty*, Oxford, Basil Blackwell.

Interchange

CARR REPLIES TO RUSSELL

Most of the points of apparent disagreement between Russell and myself stem from the fact that we are concerned with two quite distinct areas of interest: he with the philosophy and methodology of theoretical psychology and I with the method and philosophy of theoretical linguistics. It is hardly surprising that he should wish to assess Chomsky's work in relation to theoretical psychology, since that is the discipline in which Chomsky claims to be working. Russell and I agree that there is a discrepancy between what Chomsky does and what he says he is doing; we agree that, whatever it is, it is not theoretical psychology. My principal point is that it is a mistake in the first place to take theoretical linguistics to constitute theoretical psychology, and that, as an autonomous activity, theoretical linguistics is a perfectly valid area of scientific inquiry, with an object and a methodology quite distinct from that of theoretical psychology.

Having said that, there are a couple of points on which Russell and I are clearly in disagreement. One of them is his claim that theoretical linguistics (as represented by Chomskyan linguistics) is not a scientific enterprise, and the other concerns the status of 'holism' as opposed to 'interaction' (between modules, specifically).

Regarding the scientific status of Chomskyan linguistics: I am not certain why Russell chooses to devise his own criterion of demarcation between scientific and non-scientific theories, when there is an abundance of literature already in existence on the topic, within the philosophy of science. His 'distance principle' is not, I think, very workable as such a criterion. My aim was to utilize a fairly standard demarcation criterion used by philosophers of science: that of falsifiability (cf. Popper, 1959, 1972, and Lakatos, 1970, 1974, for the development of the notion). I then went on to look at *modes* of falsification within a realist interpretation of scientific theories. I concluded that hypotheses in theoretical linguistics are falsifiable, but not in the same way as those in either theoretical physics or theoretical psychology. I ended up adopting something along the lines of Itkonen's (1978) view of the status of these three disciplines, whereby each differs from the others with respect to the ontological status of its object of inquiry and the mode of falsification it employs, Russell's remarks on the distance principle parallel Itkonen's on observer's knowledge: such knowledge is that which is arrived at when the distance principle applies (when the data are 'outside of' the observer). But Russell is mistaken, I believe, in assuming that such knowledge alone constitutes scientific knowledge. While the distance principle alone is sufficient to characterize the sort of knowledge gained in physics, it is arguable that in the psychology of language observer's knowledge alone is insufficient for the success of

233

the enterprise. Unless one already has a conception of what counts as grammatical and what does not, plus some sort of structured account of what it means to say that a structure is well-formed (and this is agent's knowledge, arrived at in violation of the distance principle), then one cannot proceed in the investigation of the processing, storage and acquisition of linguistic structure (this is abundantly evident from Russell's remarks on what he calls *wh*-clauses—see below). The upshot of this is that theoretical psychology itself, in relation to language at least, requires a theoretical component which violates the distance principle. But if this principle is to be our criterion of demarcation, then theoretical psychology must be taken to be only partly scientific in nature. I suggest we abandon the distance principle as a demarcation criterion, and rely on falsifiability, in line with much current thinking in the philosophy of science. Theories in physics, psychology and linguistics are therefore scientific if they are falsifiable; I argued that this is the case for all three disciplines.

I have a few remarks on holism as opposed to modularism, with its concomitant notion 'interaction' (the eponymous notion in the sort of research programme I wish to adopt for theoretical linguistics). Russell feels that the very notion of an interaction between modules is 'promissory and pseudo-scientific'. This may or may not be the case when the notion is applied to psychology (at any rate, I think we can ignore the term 'pseudo-scientific', since Russell's account of what it means for a theory to be scientific seems unworkable and uninformed by any reference to the literature on the subject). It is probably best to assess the applicability of his remarks with regard to linguistics by simply considering his alternative, holism. Lack of space allows me only to discuss one of his examples of the holistic view. He suggests that 'action is hierarchical' in the same way that grammatical structure is, and that 'lifting the first occurrence of "is" out of a *wh*-clause to form an interrogative creates gibberish', in the same way that 'releasing one's hand from the handle of a cup of hot coffee in order to position a saucer while returning the cup from the lips will create a nasty accident'; that 'which is late' belongs with 'car' just as a hand belongs on the handle of a lifted cup.

If this example, and the analogy drawn within it, is an example of holistic investigation of linguistic structure, it is sadly lacking in explanatory force. I take it that by the expression, 'the things that belong together stay together', Russell is making some sort of reference to constituency, given that he explicitly refers to the hierarchical structure of linguistic expressions in his comments on why certain elements cannot be moved. If so, what has he said about the nature of *wh*-clauses that makes them different from other constituents whose elements *can* be moved? The auxiliary *will* in his example equally well belongs in its place in the hierarchical structure of the sentence, so why should it be moveable? What is Russell to make of the cases where elements can be moved from where they 'belong'? How do his remarks account for pairs like *He could never have been successful* and *Successful he could never have been*? Doesn't *successful* 'belong with' *have been*, and if not, why not?

Russell's remarks do not go any way towards explicating the nature of constituency or answering questions as to what elements can and cannot be moved. His remarks about 'things belonging together staying together' are pre-theoretical and barely state the problem, never mind give a systematic answer to it. Chomskyan linguistics, on the other hand, poses the problem clearly and attempts a clearly structured account of what elements can be moved, where to, and why. Given that this is the case, one wonders whether it is holism that is 'promissory and pseudo-scientific'.

REFERENCES

Itkonen, E. (1978) *Grammatical Theory and Metascience*, Amsterdam, Benjamins.
Lakatos, I. (1970) 'Falsification and the methodology of scientific research programmes', Lakatos, I. and Musgrave (Eds), *Criticism and the Growth of Knowledge*, Cambridge, Cambridge University Press.
Lakatos, I. (1974) 'Popper on demarcation and induction', in. Worrall, J. and Currie, G. (Eds.) *The Methodology of Scientific Research Programmes*, Cambridge, Cambridge University Press.
Popper, K. R. (1959) *The Logic of Scientific Discovery*, London, Hutchinson.
Popper, K. R. (1972) *Objective Knowledge*, Oxford, Oxford University Press.

RUSSELL REPLIES TO CARR

The principal point of interest in Chomsky's linguistic theory resides in the claim that theories of linguistic structure suggest strong hypotheses about the psychological processes of mental representation and of language acquisition. My scepticism about Chomsky's programme, as expressed in the final third of my paper, did not concern this claim itself—which I wholeheartedly support—but concerned the way it is treated by Chomsky. If you move from the linguistic to the psychological, then you must face empirical refutation of your linguistic claims. I argued that Chomsky is not only reluctant to accept such empirical vulnerability but that he has, as it were, built this reluctance into his theory.

How does this relate to the Platonic or 'realist' construal of linguistics that Carr discusses? I find it difficult to understand how one can make any substantial *rapprochement* between the Chomskyan and Katzian positions. Although, as Gleitman and Wanner (1982) have pointed out, Katz's argument against Chomsky's psycholinguistic view of grammar 'formally parallels Chomsky's arguments against the Bloomfieldian physicalistic interpretation of grammar' (p. 43), linguistic realism is thoroughly incompatible with that which makes Chomsky's theory interesting to psychologists and philosophers. Quite rightly, Chomsky tells us that linguistic reality is welded to psychological reality by virtue of the fact that human grammar must be learnable. There must be something about linguistic structures that renders them accessible to young humans with such-and-such psychological capacities. We have, therefore, to do *two* things: (1) study the cognitive capacities available, (2) examine the structure of the language for implications about learnability. This is not, of course, to deny that Chomsky could turn out to be substantially wrong here: maybe the contribution of general learning capacities to language acquisition is far greater than Chomsky supposed (this is what I argued in the second part of my paper), in which case 'learnability theory' would come to be of diminishing interest. But the importance of learnability theory is an empirical question; whereas Katzian realism seems to assume a priori that language is acquired by general problem-solving mechanisms. Which leads me to what is good and salutary about realism relative to Chomskyan theory. One is ever being pulled by the Chomskyan analysis into the assumption that any linguistic rule of any language must be explained by reference to specifically linguistic knowledge that is independent of general learning capacities. At least a whiff of linguistic realism stops us being embarrassed about saying that the rules which underlie our desire to accept (say) 'He painted the chair red' and to reject 'He painted the chair pretty' may tell us nothing at all about the intellectual structures which we require to learn language.

I want to raise another, not unrelated, difficulty with Platonism in linguistics. It is a problem that is shared with Platonism in logic. Propositions of the kind 'All *a* are *a*' would seem to express necessary truths. What about 'All bachelors are bachelors'? But all unmarried men are not holders of the first academic degree. The point is that autonomous symbol relations do not constitute necessary relations because necessity is conferred in terms of the intensions under which the symbols are held. It seems to be the case that 'holding under an intension' is a quintessentially psychological state of affairs. If so, the same form of argument could be used against any Platonic notion of being 'grammatically acceptable'. This fact has implications for how we judge ungrammaticality and non-standard English.

REFERENCE

Gleitman, L. R. and Wanner, E. (1982) 'Language acquistion: The state of the art', in Gleitman, L. R. and Wanner, E. (Eds), *Language Acquisition: The State of the Art*, Cambridge, Cambridge University Press.

X: Part Six: Anthropological Linguistics

18. Systems of Kinship: The Historical Construction of Moral Orders

THOMAS DE ZENGOTITA

Kant's *Critique of Pure Reason* once established the limits of natural science and provided eighteenth and nineteenth century cultural and historical studies with an opportunity to justify themselves philosophically on their own terms. Chomskyan linguistics, in setting the substantive and methodological standard for sciences of human nature, now provides a similar opportunity. Post-Chomskyan human sciences must follow the example of generative grammar; they must be logically explicit theories of naturally definable domains of cognition, perception and behaviour which are uniquely characteristic of our species, and they must entail empirical consequences for testing in that domain.

This situation confronts anthropologists with a clear choice. Their traditional subject matter cannot meet the substantive standard set by Chomskyan linguistics. Method cannot produce a science when its object does not exist. Politics, religion and kinship are not faculties of our nature like language and vision. They are aspects of a total social performance constituted by all the human faculties in particular historical contexts. If there can be no science of language performance, we cannot expect a science of social performance. Anthropologists wishing to be scientists should give up their traditional subject matter for the study of brain organization. Anthropologists wishing to retain that subject matter should find an appropriate way to approach it.

This need not mean that all hope of generality is lost. Many critics of structural functionalism's natural science approach to kinship have been too easily discouraged. They have announced a crisis in social anthropology, saying that there is no such thing as kinship in a universal sense. Descriptive studies on a case-by-case basis are the order of the day.[1] But ideographic historiography was not the only product of neo-Kantian culture history; phenomenology was another. The term 'theory' can refer to a discipline of the imagination, a way of reconstructing subjective positions and experiences—more or less generally specified and necessarily incomplete. What follows is a sketch for such a theory, a theory of an essential aspect of social performance which accommodates the nature of its object.

Kinship and marriage have always been 'to anthropology what logic is to philosophy and the nude is to art ... the basic discipline of the subject.'[2] These terms refer, in some vague and pretheoretical way, to the most obviously significant and most necessarily social of universal customs. At the heart of these customs, in all their variety, lies an incest taboo. General theories of kinship, of whatever type, must begin here.

THE PROHIBITION OF INCEST AND THE ORIGIN OF CONSCIOUSNESS

A fundamental fact about performance deserves closer attention than it usually gets. All instances of performance, including novel instances, are necessarily historical. They must occur—as the writing and reading of this sentence occur. The first conscious thoughts of *homo sapiens*, like the first conscious thoughts of a child, must be conceived as occurring in the same way—it makes no difference if we are ignorant of the details; it makes no difference how elaborate and specific the underlying physiology. An account of performance depends upon an acknowledgement of its historical nature.

Partly as a result of that acknowledgement, the speculations to follow resemble the kind of 'conjectural history' we associate with the Scottish Enlightenment and nineteenth century evolutionism. Another justification for reviving so discredited a method should be mentioned. This imaginary reconstruction of the origin of consciousness is not a factual hypothesis. It is only the most natural way to describe certain conditions on the existence of consciousness. The argument goes on to show how the incest taboo in its universal form embodies just those conditions, and how plausible modifications of those conditions correspond to the major types of kinship systems known to anthropology. The claim is not that consciousness first occurred in the events described but only that it must have arisen in events *like* those described,[3] and that the main forms of exogamy institutionalize the basic characteristics of such events.

In the Beginning

As an accidental consequence of the mutation underlying the capacity for syntactic organization the sensorimotor moment of animal awareness exploded. This unitary, non-conscious state was shattered by the arbitrariness which syntactic alternatives introduced. The realm of symbols, the concrete imagination, was built by social action out of sensorimotor debris.

In the beginning, as the ancient stories tell, was chaos. There was the innate capacity for language but no actual languages, the innate capacity for thought but no actual thoughts. There was, in effect, the capacity for conscious, representational being but no *established representation*. The flow of sensorimotor fragments simply proceeded, a sequence of randomly related and mingled images. That sequence was, in itself, determined by laws of brain chemistry and by instinctive and conditioned organism/environment relations. But notice: such laws and relations are as indifferent to the phenomenological structures and objects of consciousness as the laws of chromosome chemistry are to the phenotypic consequences of mutation. The chemical accidents which produced the opposable thumb were not caused by and did not anticipate the tool. The brain events which produced the first potential objects of consciousness were not caused by and did not anticipate their established meanings and values.[4]

Before imagining the sort of event which might produce established representations and consciousness of them, their essential characteristics and certain conditions on their existence must be described.

Displacement.[5] Consciousness requires, at a minimum, that a conscious being possess an established representation of itself. It follows that the conscious subject is somehow divided, for it cannot entirely be what it regards.

Let the term *displacement* refer to a relation between a subject-in-context and the same subject in some possible, represented, context. All displacements can be described in the three dimensions of a pure Kantian intuition: subject/space/time. The actual self-in-context is I/here/now and the possible self-in-context is I/there/then. The form of all displacements is:

I/here/now ↔ I/there/then

The form does not exist; only actual displacements exist and only in individual subjects occupying specific spaces populated by particular things or images at particular times. Displacements are historical events which constitute conscious entities.

This account can be checked against experience. When you act with reference to the past or future you demonstrate its accuracy. You/here/now check your change before leaving the house to board a bus. In some sense you exist in an image of you/there/then, you-getting-on-the-bus. But that is not all: as a representational being your existence as you/here/now, you-checking-your-change, depends upon your being in you-getting-on-the-bus. When you displace to a you/there/then, you/here/now become, from *that* point the view, a representation as well. You are never (consciously) entirely here/now; that is animal awareness. Consciousness is a relation between instances of awareness. The indivisible core of subjectivity, the point which always regards and cannot be regarded, is the way we experience the set of relations between a series of actual and a penumbra of possible self-in-context moments.

There are two *modes of displacement* in the realm of the concrete. I/here/now 'gets to' I/there/then by means of two basic types of assoication. They are resemblance and contiguity.[6]

A set of displacements is indeterminate. That is, nothing is the perfect cause of I/there/then images in themselves, in their meaning and value. Similarly, nothing is the perfect cause of the acts which convert I/there/thens into I/here/nows. Instead of representing you-getting-on-a-bus at a given actual moment, you might have represented something else and, once outside, you might decide to walk. We experience this indeterminacy as freedom.

Although nothing determines displacements, they could not exist as coherent sets without powerful constraints. Such constraints are established representations, the cultural and social conditions of our mental being. To ask about the origins of consciousness is to ask about the most essential of such social and cultural conditions, about some core class of established and establishing representations.

Reciprocal Displacements. These are the primordial displacements. They brought order to the original debris and established the first conscious representations. Like all displacements, reciprocal displacements can only be actual acts but their form may be given as:

This form means that consciousness originally depends upon some 'other' as an analogue of the self. The form says that each can become analogue of the other only simultaneously. That is the first of five 'appropriateness conditions' on the emergence of consciousness in a reciprocal displacement.

The second appropriateness condition says that both modes of displacement are essential to a consciousness constituting reciprocal displacement. Both resemblance and contiguity must be involved.

The third appropriateness condition says that resemblance and contiguity relations must be 'balanced' in a consciousness constituting reciprocal displacement. They must be equally involved.

The fourth appropriateness condition says that the phenomenological characteristics of the subjects involved in a reciprocal displacement must 'fit' the modes. They must have features sufficiently alike and sufficiently contiguous to make the act feasible.

The fifth appropriateness condition says that the features involved in a consciousness constituting reciprocal displacement must be 'interesting'. Sex and food are interesting.[7]

Reciprocal displacements establish consciousness by 'recognizing' analogues through an exchange of contiguous substances which resemble each other.[8]

A Just-So Story. One afternoon, millions of years ago, under some particular tree upon some primeval plain, two preconscious but fully 'wired' hominid females sit opposite each other with their respective infants at their sides. The two infants begin to cry. By accident (the same kind of accident that can lead a man who is smoking and writing at the same time to take a puff of his pen), the two mothers exchange babies. Arcs of conditioned reflexes move each mother to put the other's baby to her breast while watching her own at the other's breast. Each sees her own (contiguous substance) baby acting in its nursing way at the other's (analogous) breast while feeding the other's (analogous) baby (contiguously) at her own. The my-infant visual stimulus 'infects' the other-breast visual stimulus with my-breast nursing sensations. The mothers see each other inhabited, feature by analogous feature, with their own sensational space—but their own sensational space also remains in them. They 'divide.' Their eyes meet. They realize their consciousness simultaneously and recognize the realization in themselves through, as well as in, the eyes of the other. Both are here/now and there/now.[9]

Coherent acts of displacement as ongoing states depend upon ongoing social acts of reciprocity which sustain the fundamental relation 'I am because I could be you.' Societies and cultures, once established in the representations which channel sets of displacements, will allow a great deal more latitude in the structures of such acts than was possible at first. To become and remain a conscious being in a group of already conscious beings is a very different matter from arriving at consciousness to begin with. Nevertheless, a moment's consideration of the etiquette of gifts, invitations and even greetings on the street will suggest how fundamental to our existence the simplest structures of reciprocity remain. If universals of morality exist, they are here.

Forms of Exogamy

Systems of exchange—and especially of reciprocal exchange—are now widely recognized as dominant features of the world's ethnographies. But for reasons which go behond the scope of this chapter, explanations of such systems have generally been functionalist in kind. Even those accounts which are explicitly conceived as critical of functionalism tend to appeal to unintended adaptive effects as the ultimate 'reason' for the existence of these activities.[10] The emphasis here is very different. While such effects unquestionably exist and are of great practical importance, unless they are intended objectives, they are accidental by-products of systems of kinship conceived as historical, moral constructions. Exchanges of food, artifacts, services, even of gestures and words—and certainly of kin—all have adaptive consequences. But our attention is on their human nature, their subjective significance. People exchange their concrete parts and, in the process, these parts become embodiments of mind. If a culture is a way of ritualizing nature, people are animals arranging themselves ritually. The animal characteristics of human sex and reproduction and the appropriateness conditions on a recriprocal displacement combine to produce the major forms of exogamy.

I The Universal Form. All allowable systems of marriage express sets of reciprocal displacement in which contiguous substance is exchanged to create analogous substance.

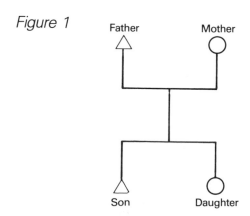

Figure 1

Father   Mother

Son   Daughter

With these conditions:

1   People become contiguous substance by birth, by sexual congress and by extended coresidence and commensality.
2   Analogues must be of the same sex and generation and they must stand in the same contiguous relation (R_1) to the substance given and the same contiguous relation (R_2) (where $R_1 \neq R_2$) to the substance received.

Under the universal form and its conditions, marriage within the 'nuclear family' cannot be allowed. In effect, the taboo prohibits overloading contiguous relations. It suggests that, if sexual connections are added to connections of birth and propinquity, the incorporative blending of individual identities becomes overwhelming. Individuals are enabled to represent themselves because the incest taboo enforces a separation of parts within the family body and a connection of parts, a powerful and persistent connection, with another, similar family body.[11]

Figure II

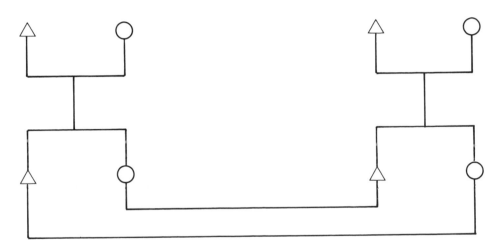

The most elementary—and common—type of exogamous connection under the universal form is referred to as 'sister exchange'. It occurs in societies of all three major kinds—matrilineal, patrilineal and cognatic or bilateral—though the nuclear families shown in Figure 2 are most appropriate to bilateral systems like our own. Notice that, from the point of view taken here, this structure might well be called son, daughter or brother exchange; it effects a reciprocal displacement for each member of both families.

II The Unilineal Form. These conditions are added to the universal form:

1   Contiguities of birth substance with incestuous value extend undiluted through links with one sex and not at all through the other.
2   Any two contiguously related persons who stand in the same relation to all contiguologues and all analogues involved in an allowable exchange are regarded as identical.[12]

These yield 'Iroquois' systems of patrilineal and matrilineal lineages and clans practising bilateral 'cross-cousin' marriages (a man marries a woman whom he calls what he calls his mother's brother's and his father's sister's daughter). Specifiable

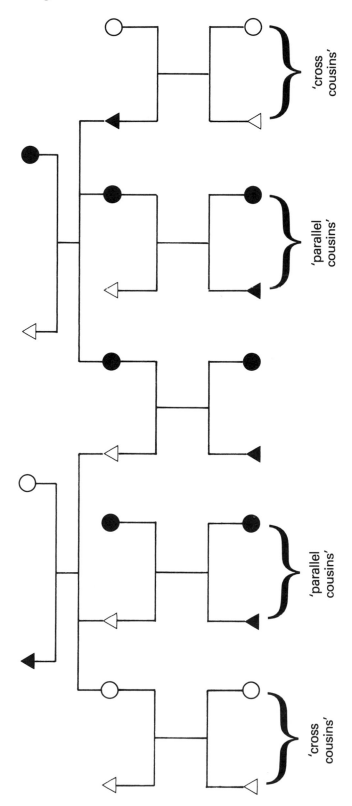

Figure III: Contiguities of birth substance with incestuous value extending through women only. Two matrilineal clans connected by marriage are the simplest result.

interpretations of the phrase 'same relation' in condition (2) prohibit 'parallel cousin' marriage for the same reason that the universal form prohibits nuclear sibling marriage. A man's mother's sister's daughter and father's brother's daughter are 'identical' with his sister. They are all sisters of one clan substance.

Because social anthropology is so jurally oriented (see Note 10), societies with unilineal status and property relations are usually grouped with societies described as unilineal here. Women and offspring become objects of 'rights', and marriage a 'contract' between lineage 'corporations'. But many such societies recognize incestuously-valued birth substance through links of both sexes, through a 'complementary filiation'. Some even favour parallel cousin marriage. There have been many more or less ad hoc efforts to accommodate these facts. Here is a principled reason for regarding such societies as cognatic with respect to incest and exogamy.[13]

III The Cognatic Form. This condition is added to the universal form:

1   Contiguities of birth substance with incestuous value extend in dilutable ways through links of both sexes.

The way to grouping 'unilineal' societies having incestuously valued complementary filiation with cognatic and bilateral societies, as traditionally defined, has been well prepared. Societies with 'ambilineal' descent groups and societies which regularly recruit members to unilineal groups through bilateral and even affinal links have been used to attack the applicability of the unilineal model to the societies which originally inspired it.[14] We are now in a position to hope for a general account of this variety. Many problems not raised in this space may admit of general solutions along the lines outlined in this sketch—most notably unilateral marriage rules and non-incestuous forms of prohibited sex.[15] Ultimately, only a case-by-case description will tell us exactly how contiguous and analogous human substance is deployed in a given social group; that uniqueness is essential to historical human performance. But all these descriptions express a set of general conditions on human performance as they are realized in relations which, more than any other, are used by human beings to define their natures.

It is too early to declare that kinship does not exist. The notion of kinship can be confined to contiguous and analogous relations between human subjects as core embodiments of their representational being. When this definition is grasped it becomes apparent that, while it is highly appropriate to distribute property and status relations in patterns determined by kinship relations, it is certainly not necessary. If human embodiments in other, non-human, bodies are distributed in ways of their own and distinguish other sorts of common and analogous substance, this seems quite understandable. If various societies at similar levels of 'primitivity' vary along these lines, this seems perfectly reasonable. If some societies use property embodiments as a means of 'incorporating' members into groups of contiguous and therefore, over time, common substance, this seems very natural. 'They are like brothers', people say, 'They have shared the same food, the same places, the same experiences for so long.'

But nowhere in the world does one say, 'We are like teammates age mates, platoon or classmates, exchange co-contributors, racial or religious brethren, etc., because we are born of the same womb.' The contiguities and analogies of kinship and marriage may vary, but they retain their representational priority in human consciousness. In that sense, there is such a thing as kinship and, with that sense understood, there can be such a thing as kinship theory.

NOTES

1   Needham, R. (1971) *Rethinking Kinship and Marriage*, London, Tavistock, p. 5; Schneider, D. (1972) 'What is kinship all about?', in Reining, P. (Ed.), *Kinship Studies in the Morgan Centennial Year*, Washington, D. C., The Anthropological Society, p. 59.

2   Fox, R. (1967) *Kinship and Marriage*, Harmondsworth, Penguin, p. 10.

3   The problem of imagining consciousness developing by degrees is not treated at all in this chapter.

4   See de Zengotita, T. (1983) 'Après Jonestown', *Le Genre Humain*, 6, pp. 55–71 for a discussion of the implications of this fact.

5   This term is used in various ways in discussion of mental phenomena. The usage here is closest to that of C. Hockett (1964) in 'The problem of universals in language', in Greenberg, J. (Ed.), *Universals of Language*, Cambridge, Mass., MIT Press.

6   The 'modes of displacement' are simply empiricism's principles of association revived once again. The persistence of these principles in studies of symbolic meaning is remarkable. Freud's processes of dream work are reducible to these principles; so are Frazer's 'Laws of Thought'; so are Levi-Strauss' 'metaphor and metonym'.

7   If one asks of the appropriateness conditions, 'Why are they thus and not otherwise?' there is no answer. One does not ask why the laws of gravity are thus and not otherwise. The question is whether the conditions cover the facts (in their own, interpretive, way). The conditions define a domain. The word 'appropriate' was chosen with its aesthetic, moral and etiquette connotations in mind.

8   Readers familiar with the work of Marcel Mauss and Claude Levi-Strauss will recognize influences too numerous to mention.

9   The first 'there/then' is, therefore, a 'there/now'. Representation of the past and future may not be as problematic as it has seemed. It may simply be a matter of tense marking alternative 'nows'. The real problem seems to be to account for the representation of alternative selves in represented contexts.

10   For a discussion of the predominance—often unconscious—of functionalism, see de Zengotita, T. (1984) 'The functional reduction of kinship in the social thought of John Locke', in Stocking, G. (Ed.), *Functionalism Historicized; Essays on British Social Anthropology*, Madison, Wisc., University of Wisconsin Press. Even critics of functionalism in anthropology routinely admit its fundamental assumptions to their arguments. Levi-Strauss described exogamous institutions as mechanisms which 'pump women' through the social system. Leach and Needham and their followers thought to attack structural-functionalism by destroying the 'geneological' basis of kinship theory. They have argued that kinship was 'purely social'—by which they meant jural. But 'jurality' is a product of Western social and political history, a conceptual aspect of consciously constituted societies which were *designed* to function. Jurality is the foundation of social functionalism. Levi-Strauss, C. (1969) *The Elementary Structures of Kinship*, Boston, Mass., Beacon Press; Needham, R. (1971) *Rethinking Kinship and Marriage*, London, Tavistock, pp. 3–5; Leach, E. (1961) *Rethinking Anthropology*, London, Athlone Press, pp. 105–8.

11   We might ask of clinical psychologists: are victims of long-term sexual abuse by a parent impaired in their self-image in some characteristic way which involves a failure to separate in the absence of an analogue? Of course, the failure would be only partial since an 'as-if' identity could be structured on an axis involving normal families as images. The overwhelming incorporative quality of incest only emerges if we imagine it as a regular feature of social life. In any event, children are clearly involved in extended comparisons of themselves with their peers, comparisons which involve constant exchanges of clothes, toys, invitations, insults, compliments, etc. Parents become very involved in the details of these comparisons in analogy-sustaining ways. In effect, the child who says: 'So-and-so's mommy reads him *two* goodnight stories' is forming an image of *himself* and *his* mommy as separate entities.

12   This condition refers Radcliffe-Brown's descent-based principle of sibling group solidarity directly to marital appropriateness. This is one of many ways in which the notion of reciprocal displacement transcends longstanding disputes over the relative 'priority' of descent and marriage. Contiguous and analogous relations are equally essential to self-representation.

13   Space does not permit a full discussion but this account also gives a principled reason for assigning priority to kinship relations over property and power relations. The direction of influence in anthropology, which runs from jural concepts to concepts of kinship and marriage, must be reversed—if it is to parallel the direction of influence of concepts in primitive cultures. Fortes' notion of 'complementary filiation' is basically a way to preserve the overall taxonomic 'unilineality' of societies with largely unilineal estates but bilateral ties of kinship substance. Critics of this taxonomic imperialism see the error in Fortes' insistence on genealogical criteria. They seem not to

appreciate the enormous difference between saying, wrongly, that a single set of genealogical concepts underlies all kinship systems and saying, rightly, that genealogical concepts of some sort underlie all kinship systems. See Forest, M. (1959) 'Descent, filiation and affinity: A rejoinder to Dr. Leach', *Man*, 59.

14   Firth, R. (1957) 'A note on descent groups in Polynesia', *Man*, 57, pp. 4–8; Keesing, R. (1975) *Kin Group and Social Structure*, New York, Holt, Rinehart and Winston; Sahlins, M. (1965) 'On the ideology and composition of descent groups', *Man*, 65, pp. 104–7.

15   The variety of cases in which no flesh and blood contiguity is ascribed to the relation between a child and one of the parents may still involve other sorts of contiguities powerful enough to make sexual congress identity threatening. The most famous of such cases, the Trobriand father, for example, is said to 'mould' the child into his likeness by sexual contact with the pregnant mother and his constant feeding and caretaking of the growing child. Masturbation, homosexuality and adultery may also involve more or less serious mixing and overloading of contiguous and analogous relations in particular cultural contexts.

19. Folkbiological Universals as Common Sense

SCOTT ATRAN

Imagine a scientist, henceforth S, who is unencumbered by the ideological baggage that forms part of our intellectual tradition and is thus prepared to study humans as organisms in the natural world . . . .

S might begin with the observation that people seem to act in systematic ways with respect to the objects around them and that they use and respond to expressions in organized ways . . . .

Suppose that S succeeds in developing a tentative theory of learning for common sense and language. If my guess is right, these would . . . involve fixed and highly restrictive schemata which come into operation under limited conditions of exposure to data, determine the interpretation of these data as experience, and lead to the selection of systems of rules (grammar, common sense) which are put to use in human action and interaction. (Noam Chomsky, *Reflections on Language*, 1975, pp. 139, 154)

FOLKTAXONOMY

Lay taxonomy, it appears, is universally and primarily composed of two ranks: generic-specieme and life-form (Atran, 1985b; cf. Berlin *et al.*, 1973). The generic-specieme level is logically subordinate but psychologically prior. Ideally it is constituted as a *fundamentum relationis*, that is, an exhaustive and mutually exclusive partitioning of the local flora and fauna into well-bounded morpho-behavioural gestalts. To a significant extent, taxa at this level correspond to the 'non-dimensional' sympatric species of the field biologist, at least for those organisms which are manifest, including most vertebrates and flowering plants. Since the frontiers of a cultural group do not always correspond to the boundaries of a set of sympatric species, the partitioning can fall short of the ideal: e.g., migrating birds may be only intermittently or vaguely represented. Insofar as the scientific distinction between genus and species is largely irrelevant in any local area, this basic folk kind also generally conforms to the modern genus, being immediately recognizable both morphologically and ecologically.[1]

The life-form level further assembles folkgenerics into larger exclusive groups (tree, grass, moss, quadruped, bird, fish, insect, etc.). Life-forms appear to partition plants and animals into a contrastive lexical field. This comprises a pretheoretical *fundamentum divisionis* into positive features which are opposed along one or more perceptible dimensions (size, stem habit, mode of locomotion, skin covering, etc.). By and large plant life-forms do not correspond to scientific taxa, whereas animal life-forms approximate modern classes, excepting the phenomenally 'residual' invertebrate groupings (bug, worm, etc.) (Atran, 1986).

Folktaxonomic structure for living kinds may be characterized thus:

1   Every natural object is either a living kind or not.
2   Every living kind is either a plant or an animal.
3   Each plant or animal belongs to one and only one generic taxon, *G*.
4   No two generic taxa share all of their characteristic phenomenal properties; that is, for all G_i and for any G_j, G_j lacks at least one readily perceptible feature which is characteristic of G_i.
5   Every generic taxon, *G*, belongs to only one life-form taxon, *LF*.
6   For every LF_i there is at least one phenomenal property, D_i which is characteristic and diagnostic; that is, for all LF_j, D_i is not characteristic.

The hierarchical ranking of living kinds is apparently unique to that domain. Thus the field structure for artifacts, which is often confounded with that of living kinds, is in fact quite different. For one thing, that taxa of the same category are disjoint precludes the possibility of artifact groupings entering into ranked taxonomies. Not only can artifacts belong to more than one 'taxon' within an inclusion series (a wheel-chair as both 'furniture' and 'vehicle', a piano as both 'musical instrument' and 'furniture'), but a given item may belong to different inclusion series (the same item as a crate used for packing furniture or as a table used as a piece of furniture). Further considerations also exclude artifacts from entering into non-ranked taxonomies;[2] for taxonomic inclusion, whether considered simply in terms of class inclusion or ranked orderings, requires transitivity in judgment. As Hampton (1982) has shown, however, artifactual judgment may be non-transitive (e.g., 'car-seats' may be judged varieties of 'chair', but not of 'furniture', even though 'chair' is normally thought of as a type of 'furniture').[3]

NATURE AND NECESSITY

According to Rosch (1973, p. 111): 'Some colors to which English speakers apply the word "red" are "redder" than others. Some breeds of "dog" (such as the retriever) are more representative of the "meaning" of dog (than a Pekinese).' But the analogy with colour is untenable. If a Pekinese is not properly, or only peripherally, a dog, what other kind could it be confused with? It may be difficult to decide where 'red' ends and 'orange' starts, or where 'cup' leaves off and 'bowl' begins (cf. Kempton, 1978), but it is most certainly not so for 'dog', 'oak' or any other such living kind. Perhaps there is a lesser degree of confidence in the judgment (especially the child's judgment) that a Pekinese or Boston terrier is a dog and not another basic kind such as a cat, than in the judgment that a retriever or German shepherd is a dog rather than a cat. But Pekinese and Boston terriers cannot *be* anything but dogs.[4] The reason this is so is because members of a living kind, but not an artifactual kind, are presumed to have essential underlying natures which operate in a causally identical manner regardless of the extent to which (because of circumstances beyond control) those members actually differ in physical appearance. It is this which underpins the taxonomic stability of ordinary living kind terms despite variation among individuals of a kind.

Still, there seems to be an obvious objection to positing *logically* necessary features which uniquely characterize a living kind, since a given exemplar may always lack one or more of these typical features. In line with this objection, Ziff (1960, p. 184) claims that any attempt to define, say, 'tiger' in terms of such characteristic features as 'being striped' or 'quadrupedal' would lead to the absurd conclusion that a three-legged tiger which had lost its stripes is a *contradictio in adjecto*. As Fodor (1977, p. 148) remarks, cows differ:

> from horses and dogs and camels in some quite familiar ways, but it is no part of the MEANING of *cow* that cows say 'moo', and give milk, and look thus-and-so. These are not NECESSARY truths about cows; a cow that did not say 'moo' would still be a cow, and so would one that did not give milk or was purple . . . .

If these objections hold, it would appear that only a 'family resemblance' of perceptible features can cover the full extension of many living kind terms, and that for such terms all perceptible features are merely contingent (Mervis and Rosch, 1981). The 'ness' (or linguistic equivalent in other languages) which seem to attach to ordinary living kinds would then appear to denote only the prototypical 'configuration by which members of the category . . . are recognized' (Hunn, 1976, p. 514). Instead of definitions there could only be 'default values' (Miller and Johnson-Laird, 1976). But consider this anthropological observation as to why, e.g., a bean bag chair hasn't 'its' legs though a legless tiger has 'its'.

> If an animal does not actually possess a feature ascribed to it by its definition, then it possesses it virtually: not in its appearance but in its nature. In such conditions it would be hard for empirical evidence to contradict the definitions of folk taxonomies. These definitions are not falsifiable theories of natural species and their conformation with the empirical world need not engender anomalies (Sperber, 1975, p. 22).

Thus a plucked bird still has its feathers 'by nature' just as a coneless pine 'by nature' has its cones. Similarly, although for American folk being taller than a person and having a perennial stem seems to be criterial for being a tree (since non-woody palms and banana plants are classed as trees), bonsais are still trees because they are 'by nature larger than a person'. If, in order to predict entailments in the lexical field of living kinds, the abstract property 'by nature larger than a person' proves to be criterial for marking a 'tree', then the fact that a given referential token (exemplar) of the semantic type (the concept TREE) lacks the perceptual correlate of such a property is a contingent fact of the world and extrinsic to the semantic logic of living kinds.

Yet, how comes it there is no anomaly? How can, say, 'quadrupedal' ever be truthfully predicated of a tiger which never has four legs? Knowing the meaning of a living kind term must at least put us on the right track in search of an answer. For, if not, then what in the world can meaning conceivably be about? Since an object may fail to manifest all aspects of the meaning of the term under which it falls, to consider such aspects as conditions that must hold for the object to be seems counter-intuitive. The problem is not simply one of a three-legged tiger losing or growing back a defining property, but of perhaps never having it in fact.

The knowledge problem for ordinary living kind terms thus appears to require at least this for its resolution: grasping the meaning of the term involves knowing that, in principle (if not how, in fact), instances which fall within the true extension of the term necessarily *would* manifest the attributes, whenever normal conditions obtain. This requires explication. In line with Aristotle let us first make the following rough distinctions. Of the whole set of synthetic attributes of a given living kind, there is a subset which is intrinsic to that kind and a subset which is incidental to it. For example, if it were true that tigers are large, striped felines seen only on Tuesdays, then being a feline and being large and striped would be among the intrinsic attributes of tigers and being seen on Tuesdays would be incidental to tigers. Thus, the counterfactual (7) is true:

7   'It would not be a tiger, unless it were feline'

And (8) is false:

8   *'It would not be a tiger, unless it were seen on Tuesdays'

But what of (9)?

9   (?) 'It would not be a tiger, unless it were striped'

To answer, we are first obliged to note that the intrinsic attributes of a living kind appear to come in two grades, one more essential, but less well-known, than the other. The essential trait, or nature, (e.g., the peculiar felinity of tigers) 'underlies' the better-known perceptible features (e.g., being large and striped); that is, the perceptible features of a kind are *presumed* to be natural consequences of, or to be *naturally caused* by, the essential nature of that kind, even if the essential nature is largely unknown and perhaps effectively unknowable.

Now, being a natural consequence is dependent on a 'normality' clause. When an exemplar possesses a trait essentially, e.g., when Tio the tiger has its peculiar felinity essentially, then when normal conditions obtain, it will necessarily manifest the perceptible features of its kind. But it is possible to envisage situations where such conditions do not obtain and some external event has broken the putative natural chain which physically links Tio's having a particular essential nature and Tio's being large and having stripes. Shaving Tio, or Tio being a naturally deformed dwarf, would be examples of such interference. We ordinarily cope with such situations by distinguishing semantic properties of the kind from the perceptible features of particulars. We say of the shaven Tio that it has no stripes, but that it is 'striped by nature'. Hence (9), now suitably modified as (10) by an implicit normality clause, is true:

10   'It would not be a tiger, unless it were striped by nature'

In other words, it is in virtue of the essential nature of the tiger that the tiger is endowed with the *propensity to manifest* four legs, and would so manifest them in fact whenever normal conditions obtain. In effect, it is to propensities (e.g., inherently quadrupedal) that semantic properties advert, not to manifest features as such (e.g. actually four-legged): what it *means* to be an entity of one kind rather than another is to have the nature and propensities of that kind. For we presume every individual of a kind has a causal nature with propensities that normally lead the individual to mature in accordance with the morphological type of its kind.[5] Despite obvious token variation among exemplars of a given (folk) biological kind, then, phenomenally prototypical and atypical individuals invariably instantiate the kind *just the same*.

Manifest features per se are not essential to members of a natural kind; rather if, and when, they do occur, then we say that they 'necessarily occur by nature'. This commonsense notion of natural necessity is a conditional necessity: it will be necessary that if a natural feature is manifested, then if the organism has the propensity to manifest the feature as a constituent of its essential nature, and all is normal, then indeed the feature is manifested. So, if *p* is a natural feature, and *P* the corresponding propensity:

11 Nec [$P(x)$ and normal conditions obtain → $p(x)$]

This natural necessity accompanies a (non-Humean) conditional causality. Suppose the stripes of a tiger to be a natural feature of tigers. It is not the stripes as such which cause tigers to manifest stripes; rather, it is the fact of having a propensity to manifest stripes that is the cause of tigers' manifesting stripes if and when tigers actually do manifest stripes. Thus, the phenomenal features being-striped or being-four-legged are not natural kinds, or natures, nor are they even 'in' a nature. They are merely produced 'by nature'. Only the corresponding propensities are in a nature, not distinctly, but as integral components of the complex whole which constitutes the nature of the kind of organism it is.[6] That is why we believe it *natural* for tigers to be four-legged: this is what we *expect* to happen unless something *hinders* their normal maturation (cf. Aristotle, 1980, p. 179).

The commonsense locution 'by nature', when fully analyzed, thus yields the ontological relation *because of*. To discover the physical nature of individuals of a kind, then, is to find out *what it is* for those individuals to have the necessary features they should have. It follows that two generics, which cannot share all their natural features, cannot have (and cannot be discovered to have) natures of a kind. Generics do, however, equally partake of the nature of their common life-form. But this does not mean that to class an organism under a life-form is simply to presume that it has the nature of that life-form; rather, it is to predicate of the organism membership of one or the other of the generics which has as part of its nature the nature of its life-form. So, for instance, as Theophrastus (1916, pp. 25–6) stresses, when mallow, which is normally not like a tree, grows tall like a tree it departs from its 'essential nature' (*physis*). In this case mallow is said to be merely 'tree-like' (*apodendroumeni*), and not a tree 'by nature' (*physei*). Similarly for American folk, although pussy willows may not always look like trees, the fact that they are considered willows, and that willows are considered trees, entails that pussy willows are nonetheless trees.

Among the Tobelo of Indonesia: any young uncultivated 'tree' may be called *o rurubu* in this word's sense of 'weed' [i.e. herb] ... one often hears of a particular small sapling, *o rurubu nenanga o gota* 'this weed (*o rurubu*) is a tree (*o gota*)' (non contrastive sense of *o rurubu*); or of the same sapling, *nenanga o rurubuua o gota ho* 'this is not a (member of the) herbaceous weed class, it is a tree' (*o rurubu* here contrasts with *o gota*) (Taylor, 1978/1979, p. 224).

The cross-cultural disposition (and perhaps innate predisposition) to formulate such views of the organic world is perhaps explained by the empirical adequacy presumptions of essence afford human beings in dealing with a local biota. Knowledge of biological species *qua* biological species, and knowledge that organic individuals naturally fall into groups within groups, is a knowledge humankind shares, whether bushman, layman or scientist. Such knowledge determines the way we see the world and regulates our inductions about what we do not see.

In brief, living kind terms are conceived as 'natural kinds' whose intrinsic nature, or (to use Locke's notion) 'real essence', is presumed, even if unknown. The essential role of possibly unknown underlying structure is to permit variation, and even change, in reference without a change in the corresponding phenomenal type classed in the dictionary. By incorporating auxiliary empirical knowledge (e.g., on metamorphosis, courtship behaviour, genetic structure, niche sharing, etc.) into encyclopedic theories of underlying traits, one may thus come to include, e.g., the caterpillar under the concept BUTTERFLY and the tadpole under that of FROG, despite the fact that caterpillars and tadpoles share few, if any, perceptible attributes with normal frogs and butterflies. Our theories of underlying traits may also facilitate acceptance of mutants, ecological variants and so on. As a result, we are able to accommodate unusual and novel aspects of the physical world to our conceptual system without compromising our basic stock of ordinary knowledge about everyday matters.

Usual variation requires little more than mere presumption of an underlying nature and knowledge of the local ecology. However, when exotic organisms are reported or actually introduced into the local scene on a large scale (as among certain sections of Western society after the Renaissance) a more elaborate notion of underlying natures and their origins is required in order to accommodate the new to the old without destroying the local taxonomic scheme. This elaboration may be partially, but it cannot be wholly, deferred to science inasmuch as science often rides rough-shod over the local order. It is the overriding concern with maintaining the integrity of our ordinary knowledge about the living world which distinguishes terms used by both sophisticated and uninformed folk from those employed in fields of scientific expertise.

SCIENCE AND COMMON SENSE

The epistemic priority of phenomenal properties for ordinary kinds precludes analyzing the natural locution 'because of' as a nomic relation. So, ordinary 'natural necessity' differs from metaphysical 'nomological necessity' with which it has been recently confused by an ever-increasing number of psychologists, linguists and philosophers. Consistent with the first notion is the idea that the archetypical properties attached to living kind terms, when construed 'by nature', are logically necessary for determining what the referents are. In regard to the second, all typical properties, though *useful* for the purposes of communication between laymen uninitiated in the secrets of science, are neither sufficient *nor* logically necessary.

On this view, known as 'the causal theory' or 'the theory of historico-scientific determinism', the term's (unknown and possibly unknowable) nomic extension (as determined by a true scientific theory) establishes its (unknown and possibly unknowable) true meaning. Whatever advantage this latter view may have over 'conventionalist' accounts of expert understanding for the *non-phenomenal* terms of science, it is clearly *not* right that since 'the expert's ideal of understanding is the layman's, though the layman may make less use of it', it follows that ordinary 'in the head' meanings which the layman attaches to living kind terms provide no necessary truth conditions (Macnamara, 1982, pp. 204ff.). Nor is it the case that, commonsensi-cally, 'there is no meaning dimension' in the case of living kind terms; that is, 'the only dimension is empirical' in the sense that 'we should not expect to discover the necessary characteristics' of a living kind by analyzing the ordinary use of the term for that kind (Schwartz, 1979, p. 304).

In Putnam's (1975, pp. 141–2) version of the causal theory, 'natural kind' terms, such as 'tiger', can be given by an 'ostensive definition' with the following empirical presupposition: that the creature pointed to bears a certain sameness relation (say, *x is the same creature as y*) to most of the things which speakers in the linguistic community have on other occasions labelled 'tiger'. Leaving aside the historical fiction of baptism, the interesting claim is that this nomological relation of sameness may be 'operationally' determined by a conceptual stereotype.

Although Putnam offers no explicit account of how stereotypes operate, one which does ample justice to his proposal is as follows: first, select a sampling of exemplars as distinct from one another as is compatible with the taxon's stereotype. For maximum generality, foils chosen from other taxa could serve to demarcate limits of compatability. One would then seek the most specific nomic relation that holds between every pair of exemplars and which cannot be extended to pairs containing a foil. Failing that, one would look for the nomic relation covering the widest variety of pairs in the sampling. Thus, assuming that whales were at one time ordinarily included under 'fish' and bats under 'bird', then no nomic relation would have been available for all and only those pairs of exemplars falling under 'fish' or 'bird'. For example, if one of the exemplars of a fish-pair were a whale, then the most specific nomic relation applicable to all fish-pairs would extend to the mammals. So, rather than obliterate the distinction in 'meaning' between 'mammal' and 'fish', here the preferred strategy would be to accept the nomic relation with the greatest partial scope, viz., that which characterizes fish exclusive of whales.

There are problems, however. Consider 'sparrow'. If scientific taxonomy is indicative of nomic relationship, then 'sparrow' as commonly perceived does not have a nomic extension: it is ordinarily taken to denote only species of plain-coloured birds in the finch family and birds of the genus *Passer* in the weaver family. To accord with science, ordinary users of 'sparrow' would not likely restrict the term to plain-coloured finches, since the most specific sameness relation applicable to plain-coloured finches also applies to goldfinches and canaries (which are normally perceived as foils to 'sparrow'). Moreover, the restriction excludes birds usually accepted as sparrows by Americans (e.g., the house sparrow), and typically viewed as such by the English. The alternative is to limit the term to the widest (i.e., highest ranked) grouping wholly included within the common extension of 'sparrow', such as the genus of weavers (as opposed to any one of the heterogeneous collection of plain-coloured finch species). But this would mean that our most typically American sparrows (e.g., the chirping sparrow) are not really sparrows at all, and that is plainly counter-intuitive.

Kripke (1972, p. 315) argues that such considerations 'may make some people think right away that there are really two concepts . . . operating here, a phenomenological one and a scientific one which then replaces it. This I reject.' His point is that the customary term must ultimately either prove co-extensive with some nomic kind, or simply cease to denote a natural kind. Kripke fails to appreciate that the 'phenomenological concept' may persist *as an underlying trait term* regardless of what science has to say on the matter. 'Hawk' and 'sparrow' persist as underlying trait terms because their usual denotations are readily perceived to be components of local nature; the Tzeltal Maya, for instance, recognize similar taxa morphologically and ecologically (Hunn, 1977, pp. 143, 190). The traits underlying commonsense kinds need not be (or even include) nomic traits, though they may.

With prescientific folk there is usually, and with modern sophisticated folk seemingly always, a presumption of historical continuity between commonsense traits, or natures, to the effect that 'like begets like'. But this presumption of historical continuity does not, as with science, necessarily imply descent from a common ancestor: sparrows do beget sparrows yet do not form a phyletic line. Additionally, with modern sophisticated folk there is usually, and with prescientific folk seemingly always, a presumption that it is in the nature of a kind to bind its members together into an interactive ecological community (cf. Bulmer, 1974, p. 12). Thus, genealogical and ecological criteria largely figure in the determination of the nature of a commonsense kind. Functional criteria, however, do not (Atran, 1985a). Indeed, if ordinary living kinds did become functional, Kripke would be justified in implying that they thus cease to be natural kind terms; but nothing of the sort happens.

'Tree' and 'grass' are cases in point. These were once perfectly respectable taxonomic terms that have now disappeared from systematics; however, unlike countless ill-fated terms for microscopic and extinct organisms which have since gone the way of phlogiston and the ether, they have not also vanished from common parlance. This is because trees and grasses are phenomenally, though not nomically, natural kinds. Supposing evolutionary taxonomy the best available representation of the true structural history of plants and animals, then trees and grasses are not central historical subjects. This is not to deny the ecologist's legitimate interest in the 'objective' correlates of their phenomenal properties, any more than it would be to deny the physicist's circumstantial concern with colour phenomena. But to extrapolate from Quine (1969, p. 127), cosmologically, trees and grasses would no more qualify as kinds than would colours. That there is a definite anthropocentric bias in these pretheoretical divisions cannot be gainsaid. But such (possibly even innate) bias can in no way be construed as a variant of some utilitarian or cultural viewpoint: 'tree' is no more derived from a functional preoccupation with wood than 'green' is derived from a cultural preoccupation with plants in general.

The layman's stubborn adherence to the (phenomenal) validity of his everyday kind terms thus markedly contrasts his lack of prior commitment to the (non-phenomenal) terms of science.[7] Take 'animalcule' which first arose in the scientific and popular literature of the late seventeenth century as a natural kind term for all microscopic organisms (including spermatozoa). By the end of the following century this term had ceased to denote a natural kind. Although today the term barely lingers as a qualifier to a heterogeneous collection of micro-organisms (barrel animalcule, wheel animalcule, etc.), 'animalcule' is no more considered a natural kind term by scientist *or* layman than is 'caloric'.

This is not to ignore that scientific developments can effectively alter our commonsense appreciation of the phenomenal world. It is only to disclaim that a theory of ordinary meaning is directly related to scientific reference, and that one is consequently justified in levelling the distinction between the terms of common sense and those of science. Accommodation to science at the life-form level occurs most readily with generics whose phenomenal affiliations with their respective life-forms are only marginal; although from a strictly logical standpoint there is no *taxonomic* anomaly. Most frequently, folk views on the extension of zoological life-forms differ from scientifically construed extensions of the corresponding classes in regard to what, from the folk standpoint, are admittedly rather peculiar cases (and for natural history traditionally the most problematic ones): ostrich, bat, whale, etc. Indeed, as often as not these marginal groupings assume a separate life-form status of their own; hence they are treated as monogeneric life-forms. As such, they differ from the other life-forms in being minimally polytypic and in having a restricted, rather than wide-ranging, role in the overall local economy of nature. In view of the tenuous phenomenal associations which such groups thus bear to other groups in respect of life-form, modern folk are amenable to a shift in the life-form status of such marginal cases which would be in conformity with scientific opinion.

At the folkgeneric level of classification ethnobiologists appear to be largely in agreement that considerations other than morpho-ecologic affinity are rather peripheral. Apart from bugs and cryptogams, when disagreement between science and common sense occurs at the generic level, it is usually because the strict reproductive (descent) criteria of the scientist conflict with the morpho-ecologic criteria of the layman. Most often these two sets of criteria overlap for biological species and folkgenerics, but when they do not ordinary folk generally refrain from acceding to scientific opinion. In regard to most insects and non-flowering plants, since these are not phenomenally salient species-wise, they are often lumped together in residual taxa. But the residual character is phenomenally compelling enough to resist scientific pressure to restrict, say, 'moss' to the bryophytes or 'worm' to the annelids.

In sum, lay taxonomy differs significantly in structure from scientific taxonomy, and is logically independent of it. So far as I can see, there is no scientific advance which would *necessarily* lead to a restructuring of lay taxonomy. Moreover, we need not, and normally do not, seek to reconcile the fact that, e.g., 'tree', 'bug', 'thistle', 'butterfly', 'hawk', etc. have no biologically valid extensions. When it does happen that some commonsense taxon falls within the extension of a scientific taxon, then the layman *may* come to accept a modification of the commonsense taxon so that it corresponds more closely to the scientific taxon (e.g., including whales with the mammals and excluding bats from the birds). But this is only possible if the scientific notion can be given a phenomenal expression,[8] and if expert opinion is not incompatible with everyday commonsense realism. In short, neither the relation between meaning and reference, nor that between common sense and science, can be reduced to identity.

NOTES

1 Species are more often than not isolated from their congeners. So in any given locale species and genus are usually equivalent perceptually and extensionally. When species do have congeners within the range of a single language community, they are apt to have distinct names if they manifest distinct morphologies and ecological strategies. Generally congeneric species are given separate mononomial labels if the local family which contains them is monogeneric or minimally polytypic (Atran, forthcoming).

2 'Taxonomy' is often defined in the cognitive literature as: 'a system by which categories are related by class inclusion' (Rosch, 1978, p. 30; Frake, 1961; Conklin, 1962; Kay, 1971). But such notions of 'category' and 'taxonomy' fit neither folkbiology nor the Linnaean system. In biological classification 'category' denotes a hierarchical *rank* and not the taxonomic grouping, or taxon, itself. Thus, disjoint taxa are termed higher and lower with respect to one another not because they stand in any inclusion relations, but because they are members of different categories: e.g., 'robin', 'pike' and 'gnat' are taxonomically related to 'cat' by reason of common generic rank (the same class of classes), and not by reason of inclusion within some shared superordinate taxon (class). Categories and taxa thus represent different logical types.

Taxonomy conceived as class inclusion precludes ranking. This leads the above authors to the erroneous conclusion that there is no systematic relation of folk to scientific taxonomy; for, without ranking monogeneric life-forms are indistinguishable from generics, and monospecific generics (which need not have social import) are confused with folkspecifics or varietals (which are generally deemed socially noxious or beneficial). Talk of 'levels of abstraction' or 'contrast' is equally illusory. For instance, the 'terminal level of contrast' or the 'lowest level of abstraction' is a purely linguistic artifice of the ethnosemanticist negatively defined as that level containing only terms which have no subordinates. As such this level includes an admixture of monogeneric life-forms, monospecific generics, and so forth. If one tried to analyze the Linnaean system in terms of levels of abstraction and terminal contrast, one would wind up with an equally odd collection of taxa (e.g., with monospecific families and orders placed at the same level as monospecific genera and species).

Note also that ranked hierarchies may be imposed artificially, Procrustean style, on other domains. Biological taxonomy historically served as a model for chemical substances; and social—even artifactual—types are occasionally rigidly ranked in some cultures. Humans, it seems, are apt to use natural means of ordering as expedients even where the means do not spontaneously apply. But such contrived uses are generally intermittent or incomplete, except in specially delimited ritual circumstances.

3   Unfortunately, as in many studies in 'semantic memory', Hampton attempts to generalize these findings from artifacts to living kinds; e.g., as with Smith, Shoben and Rips (1974), he confounds vegetables and fruits, which are artifactual concepts, with living kinds *per se* (see also McCloskey and Glucksberg, 1978; Loftus, 1977). In general, when living kinds enter the space of concern with human function and use, such as eating, gardening (weeds and flowers), farming (beasts of burden), entertainment (pets, circus and fair animals), they cease to be of taxonomic importance. Hampton further cites Randall's (1976) study of non-transitivity in folkbotany; however, many of Randall's examples evince the same kind of confusion, and those which do pertain to living kinds seem to confound classificatory judgments with identification strategies (see Atran, 1985a).

That results for artifactual terms are extended without warrant to living kind terms (and vice versa) is by no means peculiar to recent work in cognitive studies (see also Anglin, 1977; Smith and Medin, 1981). Reputable philosophers and biologists (Gilmour and Walters, 1964; Sneath and Sokal, 1973) also argue against inherent differences between the logical and conceptual processes that determine the taxonomic ordering of living kinds and those governing the classing of artifacts. As a result, interesting findings for one domain risk being trivialized by being inconsiderately applied to another. Meaning should be assumed a motley, and not a monolith, until independently assessed semantic domains can be *shown* similar.

4   This does not deny that prototypicality judgments are crucial to mnemonic processing strategies and perceptual verification procedures. It denies that they always necessarily pertain to the 'meaning' of terms. For example, although the numbers one, two and three are doubtlessly prototypically prime, they are no more nor less perfectly 'prime' than any other unfactorable numbers (cf. Armstrong *et al.*, 1983). Similarly, Rosch's prototype indicator, 'perches on trees', no more defines 'bird', than, say, 'wears a white smock' comprises the sense of 'nurse'.

5   Speaking of the nature of a kind is ambiguous. In many, if not most or all, prescientific cultures kinds are taken as individuals of a higher order: 'Thus, for Rofaifo [New Guinea Highlanders] species share an essence which . . . immediately renders the idea, species, intelligible in a natural (biological) sense' (Dwyer, 1976, p. 433). But whether the educated layman of modern society considers the kind itself, with *its* nature, as a distinct being rather than simply as the kind of (lawful tendency in the) organism that organism is remains moot. Either of these alternatives is compatible with experience at the commonsense macroscopic level.

6   Propensities may pertain to behavioral dispositions (for a dog to bark) or developmental capacities (for a tiger to be large). The former resemble Lockean dispositions, but are not required to have particular molecular and geometrical loci. The latter are akin to Aristotelian potentials, without requiring the developed being to be ontologically distinct from the undeveloped being. Realization of a developmental capacity for, say, mature tigers to be large causally requires tiger cubs to be small. A cub's smallness is just as conditionally necessary to being a tiger (to tiger-ness) as the largeness of mature tigers. Both derive their necessity from the nature and propensities of a tiger.

7   Of course, if there is no prior phenomenal concern to stand in the way, the layman may extend his ontological commitment by proxy to non-phenomenal terms ('cancer virus', 'electricity', etc.), and be willing to defer to any scientifically motivated decisions about the meaning (or meaninglessness) and reference (or null extension) of such terms.

8   In such cases the lay concept may yet differ from the scientist's. The layman may regard 'mammal' as an 'air-breathing, warm-blooded, milk-giving' creature, whereas the scientist views 'Mammalia' as a portion of the genealogical nexus of evolution—a term for a logical *individual* and not, as with the layman, a term for a class (Ghiselin, 1981). Scientists *cannot* impute essential natures to things that evolve, while ordinary folk *do* regard living kindhood essentially and *sub specie aeternitatis*.

REFERENCES

Anglin, J. (1977) *Word, Object, and Conceptual Development*, New York, Norton.

Aristotle (1980) *Physics*. Trans. P. Wicksteed, Cambridge, Mass., Harvard University Press.

Armstrong, S., Gleitman, L. and Gleitman, H. (1983) 'What some concepts might not be', *Cognition*, **13**, pp. 263–308.

Atran, S. (1985a) 'The nature of folkbotanical life-forms', *American Antropologist*, **87**, pp. 298–315.

Atran, S. (1985b) 'Pre-theoretical aspects of Aristotelian definition and classification of animals', *Studies in History and Philosophy of Science*, **16**, pp. 113–63.

Atran, S. (1986) *Fondements de l'histoire naturelle. Pour une anthropologie de la science*, Brussels, Editions Complexe.

Atran, S. (forthcoming) 'Origins of the species and genus concepts', *Journal of the History of Biology*.

Berlin, B., Breedlove, D. and Raven, P. (1973) 'General principles of classification and nomenclature in folk biology', *American Anthropologist*, **75**, pp. 214–42.

Bulmer, R. (1974) 'Folk biology in the New Guinea Highlands', *Social Science Information*, **13**, pp. 19–28.

Conklin, H. (1962) 'Lexicographical treatment of folk taxonomies', in Householder, F. and Saporta, S. *Problems in Lexicography*, Report of the Conference on Lexicography, 11–12 November 1960, Indiana University, pp. 119–41.

Dwyer, P. (1976) 'An analysis of Rofaifo mammal taxonomy', *American Ethnologist*, **3**, pp. 425–45.

Fodor, J. D. (1977) *Semantics: Theories of Meaning in Generative Grammar*, New York, Crowell.

Frake, C. (1961) 'The diagnosis of disease among the Subanun of Mindanao', *American Anthropologist*, **63**, pp. 113–32.

Ghiselin, M. (1981) 'Categories, life, and thinking', *The Behavioral and Brain Sciences*, **4**, pp. 269–313.

Gilmour, J. and Walters, S. (1964) 'Philosophy and classification', in Turrill, W. (Ed.), *Vistas in Botany*, Vol. 4: *Recent Researches in Plant Taxonomy*, Oxford, Pergamon, pp. 1–22.

Hampton, J., (1982) 'A demonstration of intransitivity in natural categories', *Cognition*, **12**, pp. 151–64.

Hunn, E. (1976) 'Toward a perceptual model of folk biological classification', *American Ethnologist*, **3**, pp. 508–24.

Hunn, E. (1977) *Tzeltal Folk Zoology: The Classification of Discontinuities in Nature*, London & New York, Academic Press.

Kay, P. (1971) 'On taxonomy and semantic contrast', *Language*, **47**, pp. 866–87.

Kempton, W. (1978) 'Category grading and taxonomic relations: A mug is a sort of cup', *American Ethnologist*, **5**, pp. 44–65.

Kripke, S. (1972) 'Naming and necessity', in Davidson, D. and Harman, G. (Eds), *Semantics of Natural Language*, Holland, Reidel, pp. 253–355.

Loftus, E. (1977) 'How to catch a zebra in semantic memory', in Shaw, R. and Bransford, J. (Eds), *Perceiving, Acting and Knowing*, New York, Erlbaum, pp. 393–411.

McCloskey, M. and Glucksberg, S. (1978) 'Natural categories: Welldefined or fuzzy set?', *Memory and Cognition*, **6**, pp. 462–72.

Macnamara, J. (1982) *Names for Things: A Study of Human Learning*, Cambridge, Mass., MIT Press.

Mervis, C. and Rosch, E. (1981) 'Categorization of natural objects', *Annual Review of Psychology*, **32**, pp. 89–115.

Miller, G. and Johnson-Laird, P. (1976) *Language and Perception*, Cambridge, Mass., Harvard University Press.

Putnam, H. (1975) 'The meaning of "meaning"', in Gunderson, K. (Ed.), *Language, Mind and Knowledge*, University of Minnesota, pp. 131–93.

Quine, W. (1969) 'Natural kinds', in Quine W. (Ed.), *Ontological Relativity and Other Essays*, Columbia, pp. 114–38.

Randall, R. (1976) 'How tall is a taxonomic tree? Some evidence for dwarfism', *American Ethnologist*, **3**, pp. 541–57.

Rosch, E. (1973) 'On the internal structure of perceptual and semantic categories', in Moore, T. (Ed.), *Cognitive Development and the Acquisition of Language*, New York, Academic, pp. 1–20.

Rosch, E. (1978) 'Principles of categorization', in Rosch, E. and Lloyd, B. (Eds), *Cognition and Categorization*, New York., Erlbaum, pp. 27–48.

Schwartz, S. (1979) 'Natural kind terms', *Cognition*, **7**, pp. 301–15.

Smith, E. and Medin, D. (1981) *Categories and Concepts*, Cambridge, Mass., Harvard University Press.

Smith, E., Shoben, E. and Rips, L. (1974) 'Structure and process in semantic memory', *Psychological Review*, **81**, pp. 214–41.

Sneath, P. and Sokal, R. (1973) *Numerical Taxonomy*, San Francisco, Freeman.

Sperber, D. (1975) 'Pourquoi les animaux parfaits, les hybrides et les monstres sont-ils bons a penser symboliquement?' *L'Homme*, **15**, pp. 3–34.

Taylor, P. (1978–1979) 'Preliminary report on the ethnobiology of the Tobelorese of Hamalhera, North Moluccas', *Majalah Ilmu-ilmu Sastra Indonesia*, **8**, pp. 215–29.

Theophrastus (1916) *Enquiry into Plants*, Trans. A. Hort, London, Heinemann.

Ziff, P. (1960) *Semantic Analysis*, Ithaca, N.Y., Cornell University Press.

20. Chomsky in Anthropology

CLIVE CRIPER

The direct influence of Chomsky in the field of anthropology has been slight. Such a statement is so broad and sweeping that it invites either an equally sweeping counter-attack or a series of mitigations to reduce the target for such an attack. I would prefer to do the latter without basically revoking my thesis.

Perhaps the first explanation for my opening sentence is my own background. As a social anthropologist, and a British one at that, there would be good reason for viewing any statement from me as suspect. Social anthropologists have been trained for many years or rather generations to recognize the importance of language for their studies of the social institutions and social relations of the groups amongst whom they have lived. Yet this 'recognition' has been rather odd.

In the first place, unlike the American tradition, the study of language per se by anthropologists is rare. The attitude towards language has been to regard it as a tool—a tool for communication and a tool for the explication of social meaning. In the first case the fieldwork ideology has required the anthropologist, often an apprentice, to lay claim to learning the language so well that he or she is able not only to participate at the level of daily social interaction but also to discuss matters of a complex and abstract or even philosophical nature. Reality is rather different from ideology. Few anthropologists are born language learners and imitators able to pick up and use a quite strange language, often unrelated to their own mother tongue, within a few months. The collection of texts, both oral or written, may be an occupation in which we spend a lot of time but that in itself does not provide any true measure of the mastery of a language at the basic level which we would require of even a quite ordinary translator or interpreter. 'Immersion' in the society and culture we are studying is an odd concept in the light of our general lack of competence to participate in the day-to-day exchanges that make up social life. As any teacher of a foreign language will attest, it is one thing to teach a learner a set of exchanges either of a ritualized kind or of a transactional nature. It is quite another to develop an appropriate discourse or to understand a discourse involving a subtle interplay of

259

roles or monologues on abstract beliefs and ideas. Lengths of fieldwork undertaken by anthropologists have, even in the past, been short, particularly for North American though also for British social anthropologists. Today periods have become shorter and the likelihood of an anthropologist having enough time to acquire fluency and the ability to comprehend fully is even smaller.

The anthropologist's attitude and treatment of language as a tool for the explication of social meaning is even more inexplicit. The difference in attitude of British and American anthopologists to the study of language has been quite marked. Very few British anthropologists have attempted to study systematically the structure of the language they have been using as a vehicle to master the culture or social organization that they have been studying. Much more attention has been paid to such studies by at least a section of the American profession. There has been a tradition of anthropological linguists and linguistic anthropologists way back to Sapir, Kroeber and beyond. But here our perception of what is needed to 'describe' a language has been altered by Chomsky's work. The phonological and syntactic descriptions based on informants' utterances have given way to a greater emphasis on the intuition and knowledge about the language known only to the native speaker. The 'stranger anthropologist' therefore suffers a major disadvantage if he/she is having to approach a group whose language is not well described. Of course, what anthropologists are interested in as the prime area of their professional concern is 'meaning'.

To say this is to recognize the shift that has taken place in social anthropology away from a primary interest and concern with function. The purpose of investigation in this context was to lay bare for inspection the machinery or structures within which members of the society under investigation operated and by which they were constrained. The analogy was a biological or mechanical one and gave rise to undue deterministic explanations. The emphasis was on studies of kinship, political systems, micro-economic systems and the like, all of which were designed to show the extent that individual acts were patterned and influenced, if not controlled, by the social structure. Not all social anthropolgists either followed this line or restricted themselves and their enquiries as this might infer. Anthropologists such as Evans Pritchard placed a strong emphasis on language, for example, in the attention he paid to the explication of Zande texts, to problems of the translation (both linguistic and cultural) of concepts and to the detailed study of belief systems in their own right and not solely as systems of legal or political control.

One direction that the change from functionalism took was towards structuralism. Lévi-Strauss published his *Anthropologie Structurale* in 1958 just one year after *Syntactic Structures* but independent of it. In it and in the next decade Lévi-Strauss was concerned with developing a model of the 'fundamental structure of the human mind'. Chomsky likewise was concerned with a model of linguistic competence. The areas which the models were designed to cover were myth and all its variations and grammar and all well-formed utterances. Lévi-Strauss' rather crude borrowing of linguistic categories turned into something more explicitly anthropological. His model was certainly more obscure, less explicit and less formal than that of Chomsky, but the underlying aims seem parallel.

At the time Lévi-Strauss' endorsement of the parallelism between language and other aspects of human behaviour implied in his early crude reliance on the Prague School structuralist phonology led to many analyses based on this assumption of parallelism. Treating a society as a linguistic system meant that first 'opposition' as used in describing the formal properties of phonemic systems and consequently, following Chomsky, 'deep', 'surface', 'transformations' all became part of the anthropological analytic terminology for a short period. The attempts were aimed at laying bare the underlying structure of society, or myth, in much the same way, though using a quite different analogy from that of the functionalists. The excitement and interest at the time derived from the attempts at formal modelling and the interest in universal characteristics. Chomsky himself has always been quite categoric in maintaining the uniqueness of language and the improbability of the language system being a model which can be used for the description and analysis of a social system. 'Transformation' in Lévi-Strauss' usage and in Chomsky's has a different status which the common term hides. Perhaps of more importance, however, is the fact that attempting to show that society operated like language has not in itself provided stimulating insights. The straight linguistic concepts do not fit the anthropologist's intuitions about the ethnographic facts or any 'structure' underlying them.

Currently anthropology is experiencing its own movement to parallel the ethnomethodological trends in sociology. A traditional acceptance of the anthropologist as (impartial) observer of either structures or relations between signs is questioned by those who argue for more self-awareness of the role and practice of the anthropologist in 'translating' one culture experience to another. It is also questioned by those who wish to emphasize man's ability to define and interpret meaning and not receive it as automata.

Parallelisms between the directions being taken by anthropology and the directions being taken by linguistics are clear but the specific influences are less clear. Chomsky's direct influence on anthropology seems very limited. As I have pointed out, his own claims do not take him to attempt to examine the way in which the outside environment triggers and shapes the way in which language grows in the mind. He clearly does not deny the effect of the environment—children grow up speaking different languages and that is clearly not due to any genetically determined factor. Indeed he acknowledges that he has underplayed these environmental factors, which are of particular interest to the anthropologist. His emphasis on universal grammar derives from his interest in the intrinsic genetically determined factor in language growth. The reasons for the anthropologist's comparative lack of interest in Chomsky's work derive from their major preoccupation with differences shaped by environmental (social) factors. At the cognitive level anthropologists are interested in questions of whether the utterances that occur as a result of environmental factors are associated with different conceptual structures. To this question, so fundamental to the anthropologist's study of systems of classification, Chomsky has nothing to say other than that the answer is not known.

Atran's chapter attempts to look at the similarities of folk classifications of animals and plants, 'living kinds' in his terminology. His point is that the cross-cultural uniformities in the structure of such classifications are so striking that they must be attributed to some universal, though 'domain-specific', process of human cognition. His basic point is that all classification systems of plants and animals operate differently from classification systems of artifacts or other non-living things. Colour systems allow for 'more' or 'less' questions to be asked—is this colour more red than that one? Or to take a different example: is a particular object more like a cup or a bowl? Animal and plant classifications operate differently, he argues. In those systems there can be no more/less questions. An animal either belongs to one category or it does not. His example of a Pekinese illustrates the argument: a Pekinese may seem to some to be a distortion of what a real dog should be, but if it is not a dog, what is it? It obviously cannot be a rat or a rabbit. He goes on to argue that animals and plants are conceived as having an intrinsic nature which would allow, in his example, a legless tiger still to be classified with animals considered to be quadrupeds 'by nature'.

In all classification systems it is the boundaries and the anomalies that interest the anthropologist. I am not clear that the distinction Atran makes between living and non-living classifications is as clearcut as he makes out. If one goes back to his opening argument about the impossibility of something being more or less 'dog' on the grounds that a particular specimen either *is* or *isn't* a dog, how far does this apply to the classification of whales and bat that he mentions, and the many others that he does not? Is a penguin a bird or a mammal? Is an emu or a cassowary a bird? If it is, is it not less of a 'bird' than other birds? Coming nearer to home can we always say that the classification of human is clearcut? Genetically deviant examples have in the past been displayed in fairs and it is not at all clear that they have been thought of and hence treated as humans. Double-headed 'monsters' are precisely examples of living beings which have not fitted in with folk classifications or rather have been fitted in with the classification of monster/devil or equivalent. The advent of the first white human beings to New Guinea caused consternation (literally) because they did not fit in with the existing classification of 'human' and were therefore judged to be some form of non-human, i.e., spirit. Later familiarity enabled the 'nature' of human to be redefined to include the new animals.

Aside from animals the same difficulty of classification occurs in any changing environment with the introduction of new species—modern plant genetic engineering has led to the introduction of fruit which no longer fits our original classification. At this lower level the initial introduction of the nectarine certainly gave rise to questions of 'is it a peach or a plum?' Variations along the continuum of cucumber through sweet cucumber to melon occur and different groups make the cut at different points, e.g., English and Burmese.

The point is that the rate of introduction of new things requiring to be fitted in to existing classifications is far greater for non-living things at present. But this is unusual in historical and ethnographic terms. Where convention is strong in the use of particular artifacts or even forms of art or expression, then it is perhaps maintained precisely because there is thought to be something which defines the 'nature' of the set of objects. A chalice remains a chalice notwithstanding irregularities of form. Once irregularity of form and substance becomes the norm we arrive at cup, bowl, beaker, mug and a dozen others and the 'nature' which we knew has disappeared. Fear of this dislocation in the classification of animals and humans underlies our resistance to current experimentation in genetics.

I think that Atran is presenting this opposition between living forms and non-living forms as an illustration of the interest in anthropological work of 'universals', i.e., a cross-cultural similarity in human cognitive behaviour, and that this derives from the influence of Chomsky, though not in any direct form. While I applaud the search for universals of this sort, I remain somewhat sceptical that the environmental factors, as Chomsky puts it, are as absent as is implied.

If one is trying to assess the influence of Chomsky's work on anthropology, I think one is faced with the recognition either that similar intellectual influences have been at work both in linguistics and in anthropology or that, as is likely, his influence on anthropology has come through his influence on this general intellectual climate. His direct contribution or influence is minimal and he would, I think, be the first to say so. His position has always been that human linguistic knowledge is different in kind from other types of knowledge requiring special programming and special principles. So it does not seem profitable to expect that the study of the non-linguistic systems constructed and used by humans can be carried out in the same way that we study structures and transformations; semantic rules are not likely to illuminate our study of social institutions or even other aspects of cognition.

Interchange

ATRAN REPLIES TO CRIPER

Criper makes a brief but convincing case for Chomsky's lack of influence in British social anthropology. The chief reasons for this, though, are perhaps other than those suggested. One specific claim is that 'in all classification systems it is the boundaries and anomalies that interest the anthropologist.' Although my own contribution made no mention of such problems, here I will argue that any reasonable understanding of the role of social convention in delimiting the boundaries of folkbiological taxa and of the symbolic construal of such taxa is logically and psychologically posterior to a comprehension of universal folktaxonomical schema. In any given culture, the rather straightforward exercise of transcultural and domain-specific basic commonsense dispositions is a necessary, if not sufficient, condition for any social or symbolic elaboration of them. Direct attempts at a psychologically adequate evaluation of the whole socio-symbolic 'world-view' of a society (or even a part of it) are, I believe, misconceived. They lead either to speculations about 'formal universals' of the sort proposed by the structuralist current of (originally French) anthropology, or to relativistic interpretations of cultural representation of the kind proffered by the (largely American) hermeneutical school that has people doing more or less 'their own kind of thing'.

Virtually all introductory courses and texts in anthropology begin by emphatically declaring the psychic unity of man, but straightway proceed only to assort humankind's varieties. Having so long combatted the colonial and ethnocentric view of Western thought as innate or inevitable, anthropology, it seems, has come to renounce all appeal to nativism as ideologically pernicious. This is surely one important factor in the refusal of many of my colleagues to consider people's thinking as being inherently and specifically rule-bound. For the most part, Chomsky's larger philosophical conception of innate rules that allow freedom in *directing* choice, and the relation of this conception to the moral foundations of our discipline, has passed unnoticed.

Another reason for the absence of any serious consideration of Chomsky in our field owes to its curious epistemological bias. In the past anthropologists assumed (along with psychologists, historians and philosophers of science) that symbolic cognitions associated with mythico-religious thought were psychologically primary, historically and ontogenetically primitive, and prerational. In the beginning—went the story—the intuitive, imagistic and undirected thought of savages (common folk and children) produced magical adumbrations as to the state of the world. This stone age metaphysics gradually yielded to a neolithic common sense born of civilized endeavour. As long as the neolithic mind restricted itself to a science of the concrete it proved logically and practically efficient. But this primitive 'tact', or practical sense of everyday experience, was incapable of creating consistent systems of relations

264

overarching and connecting the concrete categories of experience, or of rationally absorbing new experiences. Relation and extension could only be pursued atavistically, by reverting to symbolism's evocative power. Science emerged by purging systematizing thought of vague, sentient images and overhasty associations, substituting studied observation or experiment that could empirically verify or falsify direct logical inferences.

Unfortunately, today's anthropological theorists have done little to dispel the tale. Although many shy from the conclusion that knowledge must be scientific to be worthy, few forsake the assumption that inextricably binds the cognitive foundations of local knowledge to social ceremony. There are two apparently conflicting major approaches to this 'world-view' way of thinking about culture. In the 'univeralist' account there is acceptance of an overly vague or impossibly simplistic notion of a general 'intelligence' or 'mental structure' to all of cognition. According to Claude Lévi-Strauss, for instance, there is an 'all embracing dynamic taxonomy' that encompasses artifactual, biological and social classifications (*The Savage Mind*, 1966, p. 139). Thus, totemic myth supposedly:

> confirms . . . first that the 'system of women' is, as it were, a middle term between the system of (natural) living creatures and the system of (manufactured) objects and secondly that each system is apprehended as a transformation within a single group . . . the logical rigor of oppositions can be unequally manifested without thereby implying any difference of kind . . . only the semantic level adopted to signify the system changes (p. 128).

But consider the matter of the 'binary system' allegedly identical in form, if not content, for all domains of 'taxonomic' thought. What exactly this 'logic of oppositions' is intended to express is logically inscrutable. Mathematical analogies are given, ranging from lattice-theory to group-theory to category-theory. But the supposed social manifestations of these mathematical notions lack all formal power, invariably contain principles in contradiction to mathematical axioms and are equivocal. As for the alleged binary 'code', the contention that it is both symbolic and semantic renders the very idea of a code unintelligible. To be a semantic code is to be a function that assigns, correlates and fixes linguistic expressions to designata. Yet Lévi-Strauss concedes: 'it is pointless to try to discover in myths certain semantic levels that are thought to be more important than others' (*The Raw and the Cooked*, 1969, p. 342).

Basic commonsense dispositions are universal aspects of *propositional* (i.e., truth-valuable) understanding of the everyday environment. They lead to the construction of mental representations of what is always taken to be manifest empirical fact. This includes people's assertions pertaining to what are likely, innately grounded, and species-specific, apprehensions of the spatiotemporal, geometrical, chromatic, chemical and organic world in which we, and all other human beings, live their usual lives. Considered in this way, common sense does not preclude, but neither does it include, any magical, mythico-religious, metaphorical or other 'symbolic' elaborations of the empirical world. Such symbolic elaboration is by nature non-propositional; for it can be assigned no fixed meaning (not even a context-relative one) that can be appraised for its logically consistent entailments; neither can it be ascribed a determinate factual content with verifiable consequences that experience may either readily confirm or disconfirm. Symbolic cognition consists, as Kant would have it, of semi-schematized, quasi-propositional representations for which no definite 'intuition commensurate with them can be given.'

From a 'relativist' view, there are no transcultural truth-values, only truth-values *in a language*. What appears logically fickle to us could prove logically coherent to the native. Magic, for instance, may simply be the most intellectually convenient way of importing known causes into hitherto causally opaque situations. From this view-point, magic and science are equally propositional. They respectively differ only in their practical, 'commonsense' value relative to the whole culture. The unified world-view of a given society owes not to any overall logic of the mind, but to what Clifford Geertz deems 'common sense as a cultural system':

> There is little doubt that the consensus in the field now supports the Lévi-Strauss point of view ... 'primitives' are interested in all kinds of things of use neither to their schemes or to their stomachs. But ... they are not classifying all those plants, distinguishing all those snakes, or sorting out all those bats out of some overwhelming cognitive passion rising out of innate structures at the bottom of the mind either. In an environment populated with conifers, or snakes, or leaf-eating bats, it is practical to know a good deal about conifers, snakes, or leaf-eating bats, whether or not what one knows is in any strict sense materially useful, because it is of such knowledge that 'practicalness' is there composed (*Local Knowledge*, 1983, p. 88).

People, it seems, tend to classify trees because wood is materially beneficial, and poison ivy because it is noxious. But they appear just as disposed to categorize useless herbage because it aids us in knowing the habits of various kinds of insects that are, in turn, directly beneficial or harmful, or simply suggestive of other sorts of knowledge.

This view of things confounds basic commonsense dispositions with practical sense, or the *sensus communis* of the Roman orators; that is, the mental capacity for exemplifying proper judgment, as when we say of a wise man that he shows good common sense in his choices, or of a handy man that he knows his ass from his elbow. That kind of pragmatic judgment *is* culturally relative. What is not relative, however, is humankind's evolutionary disposition to know, e.g., a hawk from a handsaw, an artifact from a living kind. Put simply, humankind is universally disposed to believe, or know to be true, that the world of everyday experience is composed of artifacts that exist by reason of the functions humans give them, and of natural chemical and biological kinds that exist in virtue of their physically given causal natures. *Inter alia*, these are the universally perceived facts. To the contrary, animism, for instance, may well be a convenient and widespread metaphysical fiction to which many folk are religiously devoted, but it can never be manifestly presented as fact. Even when taken in the context of a particular language and culture, assertions pertaining to animism have no definite propositional content. They are believed on authority or as a matter of faith.

Whether because of universalist or relativist positions, claims for the existence of highly articulated, transcultural, and domain-specific cognitive principles are largely denied by anthropologists. For example, the claim for taxonomic principles restricted to the cognitive domain, or region of object-giving intuitions, that concerns living kinds is either generalized to other cognitive domains (artifacts, diseases, kinship, eskimo ice classification, etc.), or rejected and implicitly attributed to the rigid ordering eccentricities of the theorist rather than the native. Criper's remarks incline towards rejection.

Consider the case of boundaries. In a widely cited paper on 'Why is the cassowary not a bird?' (*Man*, 2, 1967), Ralph Bulmer opines that questions of 'cultural cosmology' must be considered in regard to the special status of isolated generic-speciemes, that is, basic taxa not included under any of the more extensive higher-order taxa. With respect to the Karam (New Guinea) taxon *kobt* (cassowary), Bulmer notes that its referents are indeed aberrant creatures by perceptible-ecological standards: it is an exclusively terrestrial bird that has no wings and does not fly; it also has heavy, strong and very human-like leg bones, and a large bony casque on the top of its skull; and its behaviour is correspondingly odd. Nonetheless, such factors do not purportedly suffice to explain its distinct status in Karam taxonomy. Why not? The reasons given are two: the cassowary is clearly a specieme (folkgeneric), yet it is isolated linguistically from the other speciemes and often contrasted with the larger (life-form) groupings such as the flying vertebrates (bats and birds); and it has a privileged place in Karam ritual and mythology.

Should the Karam be presented with an emu or ostrich, they would, I imagine, be as likely to group them with the cassowary as would Australian aborigines (who value the emu) and African tribesmen (who put a symbolic premium on the ostrich). Logically there is no anomaly. The cassowary is simply a monogeneric life-form with but one known representative specieme, much as the aardvark is the only known species of the monospecific scientific order Tubulidentata. Monogeneric life-forms are exceptions that prove the rule. Nor must the undeniable socio-symbolic import of a taxon be considered in ascertaining a taxonomy's logical or substantive nature. Perceptual aberrance often serves to focus symbolic evocation. Inasmuch as symbolic evocation is more or less diffuse (because never completely propositional) it is best grounded in easily memorizable and striking commonsense features of the world. Symbolism cannot arise without common sense. This, however, has nothing to do with *per se* understanding of common sense in general, or folkbiological taxonomy in particular.

The claim for universal principles of folkbiological taxonomy is not for the universal status of particular *taxa*, only for taxonomic *categories*. Taxa are particular groups of organisms (e.g., dogs, trees). Categories are ranked classes of taxa (i.e., generic, life-form). Taxa and categories thus comprise different logical types. The categories of generic-specieme and life-form are universal. The delimitation and placement of particular taxa are not. When applied to a local biota, universal taxonomic principles (including presumptions of underlying causal natures) tend to yield basic-level groupings that correspond to biological species, at least for the phenomenally salient vertebrates and flowering plants. Unlike the conceptual boundaries of generic-speciemes, those drawn at the life-form level seem conventionally manipulated. These conventional boundaries are delineated so as to reconcile formal constraints on taxonomic reasoning with the actual array of the whole flora and fauna in a given locale.

Formal taxonomic constraints are deductive and inductive. The deductive constraint requires transitive inference as to group adherence: if one discovers a new kind of oak, then one knows it to be a tree. The inductive constraint allows for inferences as to the general distribution of taxonomic (and ancillary morpho-ecological) features throughout the local flora and fauna: if one discovers two organisms to possess a feature, then one may infer that the feature belongs to all organisms in the lowest ranked taxon housing the two. The inductive aspect of life-forms pertains primarily to the ecological and morphological relationships among species. Some cultures classify bats with birds, others place bats with quadrupeds, still others accord bats their own (monogeneric) life-form status, depending upon the bat's perceived relationships with the totality of the local fauna (and flora). Since the distribution of ecological boundaries and morphological characters varies from one locale to another, so may life-form boundaries. Whatever the case, universal taxonomic principles operate just the same.

Classification below the folkgeneric, at the level of the folkspecific and varietal, are culturally idiosyncratic in a way that folkgenerics and life-forms are not. In fact, it was this realization that led to the discovery of universal folktaxonomic principles. In the early work on folk classification, the notion of 'lexical contrast', rather than rank, served the anthropologist to assemble and distinguish folk taxa. For example, the level of terminal contrast, that is, the level at which there is no further lexical categorization, was thought to indicate the bottom, or basic, level of folk thinking about the world. But this purely ethno-linguistic notion indiscriminately mixed monogeneric life-forms (cactus), monospecific generics (redwood), mono-varietal specifics (red maple) and folkvarietals (spotted white oak). Using such data, Lévi-Strauss, Rosch and others incorrectly concluded there was no systematic correspondence between biological and folkbiological taxa. An important element in their reasoning was facts, such as Criper rightly notes: e.g., that 'variations along the continuum of cucumber through sweet cucumber to melon occur and different groups make the cut at different points.' Even within a culture, classification at the level at which cultivars and cultigens are introduced is notoriously unstable over time. Introduction of genetically engineered varieties into a culture has even less to do with taxonomy considered as a cognitive scheme for accessing the phenomenal world of living kinds that *nature* presents to us. True, we may make mistakes about what nature manifests. Thus New Guinea natives may have thought initially of the airplane as a silver bird. But after having found it to be an artifact, they could no longer take 'silver bird' literally.

Finally, talk of 'taxonomies' and 'natures' of artifacts is idle. Artifacts are not unequivocally *ranked* into categories; there are no general rules of transitive reasoning spanning the artifact domain; and it would be absurd to think that artifact classifications are designed to support inductions as to underlying nature (e.g., from the fact that tables are usually observed to have four legs to the conclusion that tables are by nature quadrupedal). This is not to deny that anthropologists and psychologists might one day discover that different cognitive domains share interesting organizational principles. But such a discovery would constitute a significant (and surprising) advance only if those principles were first detailed independently for each separate domain. Chomsky's significance for anthropology, as elsewhere, stems not so much from the particulars of his method of linguistic analysis as from a general philosophical attitude to the cognitive unity of humankind. The rigorous quest for that unity, it appears, is best approached piecemeal and without prejudice, rather than given over to global flights of speculation or abandoned to all socially peculiar manner of interpretation.

CRIPER REPLIES TO ATRAN

[Criper incorporates his reply to Atran in his chapter.]

XI: Part Seven: Chomsky and Politics

21. The Mandarin and the Commissar: The Political Thought of Noam Chomsky

CHRISTOPHER COKER

As a political polemicist Noam Chomsky has helped to shape the sensibilities of a generation of American political scientists; as a polemical essayist he is one of the radical left's most powerful voices. He has shown an impressive ability to bring to life the most banal and the most disturbing elements of American foreign policy and to go further: to look at the damaging effects it has had upon post-war attitudes and values in the United States itself.

His corpus of work—some half a dozen books, many of them collections of essays—is impressive as a literary experience, as a way of combining massive scholarship with a telling command of literary technique. At heart Chomsky is an advocate, more than a philosopher, a writer whose political philosophy is much more elusive than his political journalism. His voluminous books present a case which is so telling that it frequently rolls over any misgivings which might arise over the nature of its melodramatic appeal. Although the story of American policy in the Third World, Chomsky's main theme, is a familiar one, its familiarity does not matter since we are impressed by the nature of the telling. The scope of the theme is touched by special pleading, of course, and often a highly selective use of evidence, but it depends on both for its impact. His writing is of such a massive explicitness that one is at the same time overawed and alienated. When his books succeed they do so on such a large scale that all doubts are dispelled; but equally when he strikes a false note it lasts as long in the memory as other people's books.

In this chapter I shall be concerned not with Chomsky's career as a self-publicist, drawing the attention of an indifferent public to the 'crimes' which he ascribes to the United States, but with the essential philosophical underpinning of his work.

LANGUAGE AND FREEDOM

Most of Chomsky's professional life has been devoted to the study of language. Although the abuse of language runs as a theme through most of his political essays, in only one of his books, *For Reasons of State*, does he use the study of linguistics as a starting point for his political arguments. Chomsky commends to the reader Rousseau's *Discourse on Inequality*, in which civil society is tellingly portrayed as hardly more than a conspiracy by the rich to guarantee their plunder, a society based on a system of laws which, as Anatole France was to say, 'in their majesty deny to rich and poor alike the right to sleep under a bridge at night'. If freedom is the basis of man's actions, and if his consciousness of freedom distinguishes him from 'the beast machine', it is the use of language which confirms the distinction. To the Cartesians each man possesses a mind, a substance whose essence is thought, and it is the use of language which reflects man's freedom of thought. Of course, Rousseau went on to discuss the faculty of self-perception in terms not discussed by the Cartesians at all. Chomsky goes on to discuss it in terms which go far beyond the *Discourse on Inequality*. Like Wilhelm von Humboldt he believes that language is not taught but 'awakened' in the mind, a phenomenon which he likens to the 'awakening' of political consciousness of the Central American peasants, the transformations of the masses into conscious and critical masters of their own fate.[1].

Chomsky goes on to argue that Western man has fallen into the slavery of the market. Like Fourier he looks forward to 'the third and last emancipatory phase of history' which will eliminate the 'commodity character' of labour and transform the proletariat into free men by eliminating wage slavery. In this process language will play a central role. Social action for Chomsky must be animated by a vision of future society and by explicit judgments of value concerning its character. We must all discover through a study of language, in Humboldtian terms, its generative grammar rooted in the innate properties of the mind, that man is not a malleable plastic being with no innate structures of mind or intrinsic social needs, but a being who cannot be subsumed into an autocratic state such as the Soviet Union or the militarized state capitalism that the United States represents, or the 'bureaucratized, centralized welfare state societies' of Western Europe. Only in 'libertarian socialism' is man likely to find his true freedom.

Chomsky's view of the ideal society stems from a peculiar blend of socialism and anarchism. At the conclusion of this chapter I will say something more about it; but to the extent that his work is more descriptive than prescriptive I shall first turn to his description of American policy, the behaviour of a militarized capitalist state.

THE SEMANTICS OF TERROR

For Chomsky a foreign policy reflects the nature of the society which sustains it; it follows that if the state is a form of organized violence its policies must be violent too. At the beginning of *For Reasons of State* he cites a trenchant comment by Bakunin:

> The state is the organised authority, domination and power of the possessing classes over the masses . . . . The most flagrant, the most cynical and the most complete negation of humanity. It shatters the universal solidarity of all men on earth and brings some of them into association only for the purpose of destroying, conquering and enslaving all of the rest.

It is Chomsky's contention that United States writers have totally disregarded the long-term violence inherent in the oppressive social structures thrown up by capitalism, that the United States as a 'violent' state has sustained Third World societies cast in its own image, and that in so doing it has practised terror on a wide scale not only against the people of the developing world, but also against its own citizens, most recently in the form of the draft.

For Chomsky free institutions offer no guarantee against repression. The common belief that internal freedom makes for humane and moral international behaviour is supported neither by historical evidence nor by reason. Like Kurt Vonnegut in *Slaughterhouse Five* he is strongly of the opinion that the strategic bombing of Germany by the democracies was an even greater crime than the Holocaust. Most recently he has blamed the 'democratic' government of the United States for the rise of 'neo-fascist state terror' and repression which is now common in the Third World.

In most of his essays Chomsky has tried to illustrate why freedom is perfectly consistent with exporting war, or intervening to prop up 'fascist' dictatorships, or even displacing democratic regimes in pursuit of a totalitarian order.[2] Just as slavery and institutionalized racism, he contends, could be rationalized and reconciled with the idea of the United States as a land of liberty and equality of opportunity, so the 'Washington connection', the links of terror between the United States and its Third World clients, can be reconciled with America's recent enthusiasm for human rights. 'Brainwashing under pressure' is Chomsky's description of the ability of the system to reconstruct and shape the perspective of history according to its own pressing interests.[3]

In this conspiracy Chomsky finds particularly unredeeming the role of the intellectuals—the *traison des clercs*, in particular their contribution to American 'imperialism' and the ideology sustaining it. In one of his most recent works, a massive two-volume *Political Economy of Human Rights*, he dismisses the intellectual fraternity as a 'herd of independent minds':

> When the herd stampedes in a different direction for one reason or another, and service to some favoured foreign state no longer has its earlier appeal, we enter the 'God that failed' phase which at one time had a certain validity and integrity but now has become, all too often, a pose for those who adopt the more typical stance of the intelligentsia—namely service to the propaganda system of their own state.[4]

The charge Chomsky levels at the intellectuals is a grave one: they have betrayed their own profession; while they have taken care to present their arguments as an objective critique of American policy and are often highly critical of government policies, in practice they have helped to underwrite an ideology of repression. Chomsky believes that America's 'new mandarins' have been particularly receptive to 'imperialism' because they have been more conscious than most other people of the shrinking moral status of the United States in the world at large, and the extent to which its international reputation has long ceased to be commensurate with its economic and military power.

Over the years Chomsky has investigated the network of foundation grants, research programmes and special academic lobbies which have contributed to what Hans Morgenthau once called America's 'conformist subservience to those in power'. The 'counter-revolutionary' subordination of the intellectuals for Chomsky represents as much a threat to independent thinking in a non-revolutionary society as revolutionary subordination does in a revolutionary state. The principal theme of his most popular book, *American Power and the New Mandarins*, is the extent to which society has been maimed through the systematic corruption of its intelligentsia.

The cause of the problem he traces to a highly restrictive ideology on the one hand, and the inherent dynamics of professionalization on the other, as the intellectuals have moved closer to the centre of power, or at least been absorbed more fully into the decision-making structure.[5]

With regard to the first, he is especially critical of America's *mission civilisatrice*, the post-war delusion that the United States can use its economic resources to build new nations, or refashion the old, to undertake social engineering programmes of the kind which were pursued in Vietnam. In *The New Mandarins* Chomsky is at his best in exposing the self-serving (or self-deceiving) nature of this argument, which explained why the American academic community challenged the use of military force in Vietnam without challenging America's right to intervene in the first place. He rightly maintains that social engineering can be as destructive as military intervention, and that the mentality behind both is much the same. 'When we strip away the terminology of the behavioural sciences we see revealed the mentality ... of the colonial civil servant persuaded of the benevolence of the mother country and the correctness of its vision of world order.'[6] In the Russell lectures he cites with evident approval the remarks of Peter Berger (*Invitation to Sociology*) that 'as the physicists are busy engineering the world's annihilation, the social scientists can be entrusted with the smaller mission of engineering the world's consent.'[7]

As to the second part of the equation, it is Chomsky's contention that the scholar-experts have supplanted the free-floating intellectuals of the past. In the universities they have constructed a 'value-free' technology for the solution of technical problems that arise in contemporary society. He goes on to argue that the popularity of the behavioural sciences lies in the ease with which they can be refashioned as a new coercive ideology. Welfare state democracy, he concludes, has thrown up an intelligentsia that claims to possess the technique and understanding to manage social change whether in the 'post-industrial societies' of the West or the pre-industrial societies of the Third World. The danger exists insofar as the claim to knowledge is real as well as insofar as it is fraudulent. Insofar as the technique of management exists, it can be used to consolidate the authority of those who exercise it.

In *The Political Economy of Human Rights* he returns to this theme, focusing less on the intelligentsia than the media and its 'engineering of consent', a technique of control that is substituted for the use of force in democratic societies. Indeed, Chomsky commends the democratic system of thought control as more effective than its totalitarian counterpart. Because it sets limits to the public debate rather than imposing beliefs the debate as such presents no threat; the more lively and vigorous it is, the better the propaganda system is served.[8]

Although it is not always clear whether he is attacking bad journalism or selective reporting, or both, Chomsky maintains that the media are to blame for distorting political discussion in three ways. First, they tend to suggest through their style of reporting that government terror in countries such as Uruguay and Guatemala is merely a response, albeit a regrettable one, to left-wing guerilla terrorism and that the killings on either side are in some kind of rough equivalence. Chomsky blames the media for suppressing information and for presenting America's clients in a better light than they deserve by drawing attention to elections and other forms of 'fascist tokenism'. Secondly, he accuses the media of portraying the United

States as an innocent and disinterested bystander rather than as a participant in the Third World's misery, a leading sponsor of 'client fascism'. Finally, he blames the media for 'atrocity management', for minimizing American abuses and exaggerating those perpetrated by communist regimes. For Chomsky this last practice is final confirmation that if the dominant interests of a supposedly free society call for a policy of foreign aggression the mass media will voluntarily mobilize the population as effectively as under a fully censored system.

It must be said, however, that Chomsky's preoccupation with the 'semantics of terror' raises troubling questions. The problem stems not from his concern, but from the fact that he draws implications from his analysis that many people, including many on the radical left, find unpersuasive or overdrawn. It is true, for example, that he has created a political economy of human rights, an impressive achievement. It is more rigorous than most of the arguments put forward by other human rights advocates, but is it rigorous enough? Can all the terror of the Third World be laid entirely at the door of the United States? Is he right to argue that torture, which has begun to decline in Eastern Europe, is on the increase in the free world? One can reach this conclusion only by ignoring the more subtle psychological abuses in the East which say much about the nature of Soviet society. Chomsky also ignores the new pattern of human rights violations in Latin America that have turned statistics of political prisoners into statistics of 'disappeared people', a pattern which is to be explained much less by reference to the United States than by reference to the high inflation rates in most Latin American societies. Recognizing that human rights abuses differ in Latin America from elsewhere less in the scope than the form of the problem, the OAS has recently established its own human rights committee. Because Chomsky does not address these points in his overwhelming preoccupation with the 'Washington connection' his analysis fails to carry all before it.[9]

There is also a particular lack of rigour in the assertion that the violence of the United States is of an entirely different moral order from that of other participants in the Vietnam War because it was foreign in origin. 'How would we respond to the claim that discussion of the acts of the fascist aggressors in World War 2 must be "balanced" by an account of the terrorism of the resistance in occupied countries?'[10] In fact, the terrorism of the resistance, whether of non-communists against communists in the Macquis, or communists against communists of the kind that Tito displayed against Mihailovic, is a much discussed historical theme as well as a valid one. Even self-defence brutalizes the defenders, which is one argument for trying to 'socialize' the invading force, for applying the positive sanction of cooperation as opposed to the negative sanction of resistance, for offering not to act as an occupied power at all, a course proposed by Johann Galtung among others.[11]

The other problem with Chomsky's case is one of degree. At one point in *For Reasons of State* he argues that the scale of violence applied by the United States in Indo-China was greater than anything attributable to the indigenous participants: 'Its terroristic attack on the people of South Vietnam long preceded and also always outweighed by a considerable margin the terrorism of its Vietnamese antagonists.'[12] What Chomsky objects to is the use of napalm, phosphorus and fragmentation bombs, the steady use of technology in counter-insurgency warfare, which he takes to be further evidence of the scant regard shown by the Pentagon for the so-called primary value of 'the sacredness of the individual'.

The problem is that the indiscriminate treatment of the Vietnamese people discriminated in favour of drafted American combat troops. Looked at systematically, it was a product of conserving American casualties at the expense of the civilian population, of fighting a war of high fire power and carpet bombing to minimize the impact on American troops, one reason why, but for 1971, desertion rates in the United States army were well below those of the Second World War.

Of course, Chomsky's basic argument against limited war still holds. It is not limited for the people to whom it applies. But perhaps, more to the point, one which Chomsky does not address, it invariably produces far more casualties than an intensive conflict in which the rules of war are not applied at all. In a word, the United States fought a protracted war in Vietnam (or so it can be argued) because it chose to fight with less than the force at its disposal. Its respect for international conventions (insofar as they were respected), the issues raised by My Lai, even Washington's reluctance to push Saigon into more extensive political reforms for fear of conveying the impression that the latter really was what the Vietcong claimed, a My-Viet or puppet government, produced more casualties than it saved.

This point is made most tellingly in Tolstoy's *War and Peace*, itself a brilliant indictment of the folly of governments for failing to ask themselves important questions about the necessity of war, still less about its justification. The passage which describes Prince Andrei's feelings on the eve of the battle of Borodino is a long diatribe against the illusion of 'civilized conduct' on the field of battle. 'If there was none of this magnanimity business in warfare, we should never go to war except for something worth facing certain death for . . . (and then) it would be war . . . . Our attitude towards the fearful necessity of war ought to be stern and serious. It boils down to this, we should have done with humbug and let war be war and not a game.' Tolstoy is not suggesting that war should be taken seriously in the most literal sense: that the combatants on both sides should be willing to die. Nor is the passage to be construed less literally as meaning that the only justifiable wars are those in which men know there are no alternatives between victory and certain death—countless men, after all, have gone into battle on this understanding and died bravely for the very worst causes. What Tolstoy is really saying is that if the rules had not applied, Hessian and Westphalian soldiers would never have invaded Russia with Napoleon's army, and Russian troops would never have invaded Austria and Prussia without knowing why they were fighting.[13] Ultimately, in Vietnam the American public and American troops in the field did not know why the United States was there, or why South Vietnam was worth defending.

Unlike Tolstoy, Chomsky does not take this view, largely, one suspects, because he refuses to enter the mind of the main participant. In *The New Mandarins* he tells us why. Once, he writes, reading a study of Nazi policy in the occupied territories of Eastern Europe, he found to his disbelief that by entering the arena of argument and counter-argument, in discussing the technical feasibility of the Holocaust and its tactics, he came near to losing his humanity. The scholar who enters into the debate about whether the United States should have been in Vietnam runs a similar risk:

> He degrades himself and insults beyond measure the victims of our violence and own moral blindness. There may have been a time when American policy was a debatable matter. This time is long past. It is no more debatable than the Italian war in Abyssinia or the Russian suppression of Hungarian freedom. The war is simply an obscenity, a depraved act by weak and miserable men . . . .[14]

This line of reasoning unfortunately led inevitably to his equivocal attitude to events in Cambodia after 1975. Moral relativism that excuses (because it comprehends) indigenous crimes but deplores foreign intervention offers no profound moral insight into the systemic nature of international violence. It is all very well to adopt an anarchistic view which deplores great power politics, but it is of little solace to its victims who are expected to endure terror by their own side, but not by external parties.

Like Chomsky, William Shawcross also attributes much of what happened in Cambodia and the brutalization of the Khmer Rouge to the bombing of 1969–71, and the intensive bombing of the population three years later in a twelfth-hour attempt to avert the collapse of the Lol Nol government. Both men are critical of the United States media's scant interest in the fate of the Cambodian people as the bombs and napalm rained down upon them compared with the preoccupation with their fate after the fall of Phnom Penn. But Shawcross departs from Chomsky in refusing to argue that the bombing of Cambodia alone accounts for the genocide that followed. History is never so simple; monocausal explanations rarely ring true.[15].

If Chomsky's stand in the 1960s outraged the American right, for their part many left-wing writers were dismayed over his lack of moral indignation over the Cambodian tragedy. Chomsky simply ignored the highly charged emotional reference points of the American debate over Cambodia and remained far too attached emotionally to his old position. As a result he found himself defending the indefensible. Together with William Kunstler and Dave Dellinger, he was part of a small group of writers who refused to accept the reports coming out of Indo-China in the late 1970s. Ironically, in speaking of their 'extreme unreliability', his own accounts were found to be unreliable as well. Chomsky, whose pieces on the war had been a major feature of the *New York Review*, quietly disappeared from its pages.[16]

AN ANARCHIST'S CRITIQUE

Since the early 1960s Chomsky has written countless political essays, most of them dealing with the United States in an uncompromisingly critical way. He has been criticized frequently for his polemicism and identification with the causes about which he writes. Yet to complain that Chomsky exaggerates is like saying that he has somehow mislaid his central theme.

It is Chomsky's merit to have spelled out the logic of superpower status more thoroughly and effectively than most of his contemporaries. He has also helped us to think about the impact of this status on the United States, and given that the latter is so crucial to an understanding of American behaviour, this means that he has helped us to understand our times. His painfully accurate description of the political landscape still rings true. We are still confronted with some or all of its melancholy features: America's support for dictatorships which are either drifting or collapsing into a shambles of post-colonial repression; societies created in the image of their cold-war patrons; countries trapped between a dependence they cannot endure and an independence they cannot achieve, uncertain which of these frustrations they resent the most.

Yet for all this Chomsky still fails to convince. It is absurdly naive to dismiss right-wing or left-wing governments in the Third World as being ruled by monsters, imbeciles or madmen, grotesque in temperament, devoid of all imagination, un- worthy of being treated as civilized men. Such descriptions appeal to history to support the distinction between 'civilized' behaviour and the stigma reserved for countries on the margins of the civilized community, or even as outcasts from it. If the history of recent years has not made us any better disposed to the Third World's post-colonial past, neither should it make us better disposed to our own. Chomsky's description of 'fascist client regimes' imports criteria that have little relevance to Third World conditions; his anarchist critique is still that of a Western intellectual tradition whose application to non-Western societies is highly questionable.

Chomsky may be right to detest the stupidity and violence of Somoza's Nicaragua and Mobutu's Zaire, but he does so in a way that would erroneously lead us to expect much better behaviour of their left-wing successors. The historical record in this respect is, alas, not very encouraging. Like Burckhardt the United States may well be guilty of shedding tears over the 'silenced moans' of the victims of progress 'who as a rule want nothing else but *parta tueri*', while remaining silent about the victims of *ancien regimes* who as a rule have 'nothing to preserve',[17] but to ignore the victims of revolutionary regimes whether in Indo-China or Central America is to come perilously close to special pleading, which is in itself equally patronising to the societies in question.

In the end everything turns on his own anarchistic critique. Ultimately, the problem with his work is that he offers no advice, and establishes no guidelines. As an anarchist the problem of freeing man from his economic enslavement is one of time. At every stage of history the anarchist's concern must be to dismantle those forms of authority and oppression that survive from an era when they might have been justified in terms of the need for security or survival, but which now contribute to rather than alleviate man's material deficit.[18]

It follows that anarchism cannot be prescriptive, only descriptive, that it can offer only a social critique not a social programme. If Chomsky is correct to argue that there can be no doctrine of social change fixed for the present or the future, not even necessarily a specific and unchanged concept of goals towards which social change should tend, then the anarchist can only communicate to the people their own predicament, recognizing that once he has done so his purpose is exhausted.

Unfortunately even his philosophy—a mixture of socialism and anarchism lacks the rigour of Marxist analysis; indeed it was only recently that he went back to Locke to find a more enduring case on which to build his critique of the liberal democratic system. We will find no fully developed theory of capitalist development or American 'imperialism' such as is in the works of authors such as Gabriel Kolko and Harry Magdoff. It is largely as a metaphor that Chomsky's political works must be judged.

We will also find no realizable vision of the future. In the lectures he delivered in memory of Bertrand Russell he came closest to defining his ideal society—one which enshrines the democratic control of production (workers' councils, etc.) in place of the autocratic control of production by private capital, or central planning. But he sees little hope of any profound changes, or any significant challenge to the present political system in the United States, the 'elective dictatorship' which he feels is not all that far removed from Jefferson's early fears of an 'elective despotism'.

Chomsky is a pessimist, not an optimistic prophet. He feels that a mass reform movement, or organized resistance to the state which in *The New Mandarins* he wrote was a duty, might now merely absorb some of the energies that could be devoted to more radical social change. At the end of the lectures he admits that the future holds out little hope—that it is the problem of survival not revolution that obsesses us all—

the survival of the victims of Western imperialism, the survival above all of mankind itself 'as the state risks total destruction to ensure its prestige and dominance.'[19]

Chomsky's anarchism is, of course, less acceptable today than it was fifteen years ago. Far from embracing the new left revisionist message, liberal opinion has embraced many of the tenets of neo-conservatism. The cold-war ideology, far from becoming eroded as Chomsky believed it might at the height of the peace movement in 1971,[20] has gained new life with the coming of the Second Cold War. As a 'technique of social control' it remains as effective as ever. Like most other writers of the radical left Chomsky finds himself on the defensive at a time when many liberals have lost faith in their beliefs and many conservatives are developing unaccustomed confidence in their own.

This is all the more ironical since Chomsky's message is perhaps more relevant (if not necessarily more right) than ever. As the United States begins to lose confidence in its ability to live with change in the international system (an inevitable concomitant of declining power), so it will probably continue the course Reagan has set: of becoming an imperialist rather than an imperial power, a distinction first drawn by Raymond Aron (*Imperial Republic*) to explain the difference between a power like the United States that did not need to intervene to prop up its imperial system, and a power such as the Soviet Union that did. Today that distinction is becoming rather blurred.

American 'imperialism' since 1981 has taken many forms, but where the United States has not intervened directly it has worked increasingly through proxies, in particular South Africa and Israel, with implications for the latter which Chomsky deeply regrets. In one of his most recent works he deplores the fact that Israel has chosen a more adventurist course under pressures which have strongly influenced that course, especially the pressures imposed by Washington. 'Repeatedly, alternative paths have been blocked by "support" that has been the despair of Israelis who had a different vision of what their society might become.'[21]

In the face of such developments the left most obviously needs to produce a consistent and coherent programme which goes beyond unqualified support for small-power politics and unrelenting antipathy to the neo-realist tradition. In the past it was able to get away without such an approach simply by defining its opposition to Vietnam and the 'Vietnam syndrome' in which very few Americans now believe. If the left is to be heard it will have to stop acting as if its only settled principle were hostility to the United States playing a role in contemporary history. It is one thing to argue the legitimacy of the anarchist approach, one's own perhaps recondite understanding of libertarian socialism; it is quite another to insist that it is the only understanding possible. In the final analysis, Chomsky's approach is too polemical, too restrictive and in its use of such concepts as the 'CIA-Pentagon Gulag' and 'atrocity management' simply too chic.

All this is not to suggest that his analysis holds no message or utility for the American people. The examples of Third World violence and state terror still have unusual validity. His analysis of the political economy of human rights still serves as a valuable check on America's mindless cultural chauvinism, its continuing incomprehension of the complexities of social and economic life in the developing world, complexities which because they are often unseen are not suspected to exist. Chomsky may have no prescriptive advice to offer, but the fact that he is published in the United States and still maintains a following is important in itself. The United States as a society is still far more open to self-enlightenment than the Soviet Union. When all is said and done the mandarin is still preferable to the commissar.

NOTES

1   Chomsky, N. (1973) *For Reasons of State*, London, Fontana, pp. 167–86.
2   Chomsky, N., Gittings, J. and Steele, J. (1982) *Superpowers in Collusion: The New Cold War*, London, Penguin, pp. 21–42.
3   Chomsky, N. and Herman, E. (1979) *The Political Economy of Human Rights*, Vol. 1: *The Washington Connection and Third World Fascism*, Nottingham; Spokesman, p. 67.
4   Chomsky, N. and Herman, E. (1979) *The Political Economy of Human Rights*, Vol. 2: *After the Cataclysm: Post-War Indochina and the Reconstruction of Imperial Ideology*, Nottingham, Spokesman, p. 24.
5   Chomsky, N. (1969) *American Power and the New Mandarins*, London, Penguin, p. 26.
6   *Ibid.*, p. 37.
7   Chomsky, N. (1971) *Problems of Knowledge and Freedom*, New York, Vintage Books, p. 73.
8   Chomsky and Herman (1979), Vol. 1, *op. cit.*, p. 30.
9   See, for example Kaufman, E. (1981) 'Human rights in Latin America: A watershed', *The World Today*, February.
10   Chomsky (1973) *op. cit.*, p. 35.
11   Galtung, J. (1965) 'On the meaning of non-violence', *Journal of Peace Research*, 2, pp. 247–9.
12   Chomsky (1973) *op. cit.*,
13   Gallie, W. B. (1978) *Philosophers of Peace and War*, Cambridge, Cambridge University Press: pp. 117–19.
14   Chomsky (1969) *op. cit.*, p. 12.
15   William Shawcross (1979) *Sideshow*, London.
16   For an attack on Chomsky's stand on Cambodia see Labedtz, L. (1980) 'Revisiting Chomsky', *Encounter*, June.
17   Burckhardt, J. (1959) *Judgments on History and Historians*, London, Allen and Unwin, p. 85.
18   Chomsky (1973) *op. cit.*, p. 152.
19   Chomsky (1971) *op. cit.*, p. 110.
20   *Ibid.*, p. 83.
21   Chomsky, N. (1983) *The Fateful Triangle: The United States, Israel and the Palestinians*, London, Pluto Press, p. 442.

XII: Part Eight: Conclusion

22. Tabulated Summary

SOHAN AND CELIA MODGIL

NEUROBIOLOGY

Negative Orientation	Positive Response to Negative Orientation	Positive Orientation	Negative Response to Positive Orientation
— Marshall considers the extent to which Chomsky's work can be responsible for the changes in approach to infant's language as revealed in the changing terminology: language *learning*, language *acquisition* and language *growth*. The hypothesis that language is learned, in the sense that it is taught by pedagogically' adult users has fared badly in recent years. Further, attempts to account for the course of language acquisition in terms of environmental contingencies that an all-purpose learning device could respond to have not met with much success — Marshall concludes that if the development of current linguistic theory succeeds in explaining the course of language growth, it will reveal wider areas of ignorance about how to relate 'abstract conditions' to their biological realization *Marshall*	— Danchin finds that the distance between his and Marshall's orientation is not large and that there is a correspondence with the current attitudes of Chomsky himself — it seems therefore more appropriate for Danchin to add a few comments to the hypothesis he made in his article than to start an argument with Marshall on points that would be, finally, of minor importance. *Danchin Replies to Marshall*	— a series of neuroanatomical, psychophysiological and genetical data, in parallel with linguistic analysis, suggests the existence of an innate neuronal structure underlying language acquisition — it can be concluded with the MIT Group (1976) that the linguistic structuration of the cultural environment is a *consequence* of the brain organization of humans rather than the *cause* of their capacity for language — the link between meaning and structure: that abstract structure must be the carrier of a meaning, receives emphasis — it is thought unreasonable to support the Chomskyan view of inborn brain structures underlying universal syntactic structures without giving some hint about a neuronal organization that would explain at least some of the language features — the model proposed is far from explaining all of the syntactic structures and cannot easily be reconciled with the formal properties of transformation grammar	— Marshall is in agreement with Danchin's focus on the importance of understanding the 'actual roots' of language universals within neurobiology — there remains however, the central problem of linking linguistic descriptions with their neuronal (and ultimately, genetic) substrate — Chomsky's notion of generative grammar has set the problem of language growth firmly within a biological framework; it has inspired others to the realization that formal theories of generation appropriate to a wide range of neurobiological problems after a quotation from Niel Jerne's Nobel Prize Address of 1984: 'biologically speaking, this hypothesis of an inheritable capability to learn any language means that it must somehow be encoded in the DNA of our chromosomes. Should this hypothesis one day be verified, then linguistics would become a branch of biology', Marshall concludes 'I agree: but the route from neurons to noun phrases is tortuous enough; how much more so, the route from

genes to generative syntax!'
Marshall Replies to Danchin

— the model can show a path for investigating neuronal structures and it demonstrates that it is not absurd to conceive the question of language related neuronal circuitry in the terms proposed by Chomsky; it also demonstrates the difficulties inherent in neurolinguistic research

— 'syntactic structures are therefore universals, but tongue and culture are brought into the centre of brain organization of perception.'

Danchin

UNIVERSALS AND TYPOLOGY

— in the study both of universals and of typology, Chomsky's work has been controversial as a result of his ability to force us to rethink our assumptions about the nature of linguistics in general, largely on the basis of the development of novel kinds of argumentation and his resolution of the tension between description and explanation in terms of a theory of *parametric variation*

— *parametric variation* involves the attempt within generative grammar to account for differences among languages on the basis of the choice of particular values for universally determined variables

— different instantiations of the universal principle of Subjacency are illustrated by reference to English and the Philippine language Hiligaynon

Smith Replies to Kilby

— Smith adopts the common rhetorical device of using the terms 'linguistic theory' only in relation to work in a Chomskyan vein

— he makes some 'quite astoundingly optimistic claims', e.g., that 'the only (sort of explanation for linguistic universals) which is particularly well-motivated empirically is the innatist variety'; Kilby knows of no such empirical motivation

— the substance of Smith's argument amounts to four points:

(a) that 'traditional' typological generalizations are invariably wrong

(b) that even if right they would need an innateness-based explanation

(c) that 'parametric typology' avoids these traps

(d) that where it goes wrong, we

— despite making a number of positive points Kilby fails to characterize Chomsky's programme accurately, drawing negative conclusions which do not follow from his arguments

— the radical effect of Chomsky's work on the study of universals and typology is overlooked

— such an oversight reflects Kilby's deeper misapprehension about the nature of explanatory theories in general and of typological ones in particular

— it is because of Chomsky and his work on universals and typology that our position *vis-à-vis* the learning child is not even worse.

Smith Replies to Kilby

— a contrast is made between the essentially comparative work on language universals in the Greenberg tradition and the Chomskyan approach to universals where they are interpreted psychologically and are argued for on the basis of just a small range of languages

— just as the Greenbergian tradition has found it more fruitful to move in the direction of implicational universals and typology, so in recent years has the Chomskyan trend moved towards typology

— it is argued that the general orientation of the Chomskyan tradition tends to ensure that typology in that framework is inadequate and that inconvenient data can be disposed of with too many special considerations: the notion of 'markedness' is singled

Negative Orientation	Positive Response to Negative Orientation	Positive Orientation	Negative Response to Positive Orientation
	UNIVERSALS AND TYPOLOGY		

out
— much of the criticism is based on the 'Pro-drop' phenomenon in a range of languages.
    Kilby
		— a plea is made for the 'cessation of hostilities between traditional typology and generative theory so that each can benefit from the insights of the other.'
		    Smith
			should not abandon the theory, but wait for a better one
			— Kilby counter-argues:
			(a) many typologic generalizations are wrong but then so are many generative ones—recent work on hierarchies of implicational word order universals by Hawkins (1984) causes the empirical basis of subjacency to pale in comparison
			(b) non-nativist explanations can be explored and contrasted; nativist explanations are take-it-or-leave-it affairs with no internal structure and are a last resort for many linguists
			(c) parametric typology has severe problems of significance
			(d) it can be seen that someone who quite reasonably regards languages as ill-defined objects, and therefore does not recognize the possibility of a 'grammar' in the formal sense, is quite outside Chomsky's range of vision. Chomsky would seem in

danger of cutting himself off from the mainstream of linguistics

— non-Chomskyan typologists have made great progress of late in making their typologies more powerful and explicit in increasing the sophistication of different types of explanation and in linking diverse phenomena under a simple explanation, together with expanding the number of languages on which there are typological data.

Kilby Replies to Smith

PIDGINS AND CREOLES

— Chomsky's view of language universals is somewhat narrow; his emphasis on their biological necessity leads to the conclusion that language structure is arbitrary and unmotivated

— it is argued that 'functional' or 'external' explanations are at least as important and interesting as 'internal' or 'innatist' ones: it is possible that a number of principles of universal grammar fall out naturally because they are the most likely solution to a particular set of problems

— this can be illustrated by looking at pidginist creoles; these are simpler than full languages, yet utilize similar linguistic processes

— they therefore provide a microcosm for studying the 'natural' developmental course of language

— both are agreed that language universals may be accounted for in both psycho-biological and functional terms

— Deuchar focused in her chapter on phenomena particularly amenable to explanation in psycho-biological terms, though she recognized the possibility of functional explanations as an alternative

— in reply Deuchar concentrates with Aitchison on functional explanations, but Deuchar's analysis of Aitchison's data will lead to a different conclusion as to what phenomena should be accounted for and to a different kind of functional explanation from that proposed by her

— Aitchison argues that focusing of constituents in Tok Pisin is achieved by leftward rather than

— it is in accounting for similarities among historically unrelated languages (including pidgins and creoles) that Chomsky's notion of language universals is of considerable benefit

— a set of grammatical characteristics appears to be shared both by creoles and sign languages, despite the different media in which they are realized

— it can be suggested that the recognition that sign languages might be creoles, combined with a language universals approach to pidgins and creoles, has led to new possibilities of explanation in the field of sign language research

— sign language research has provided empirical support for Chomsky's view of the relation between universal grammar and language

— Aitchison has argued in her chapter that Chomsky's innatist view of language universals is valid and interesting but that he over-emphasized this approach

— instead of being innate Aitchison argues that a number of seemingly arbitrary universals or near universals might be the most probable response to certain communicative needs and might therefore fall out naturally in a particular set of circumstances

— given certain basic propensities for coping with language (such as an ability to sequence and to use structure dependent operations) speakers of different languages might rediscover the same solutions repeatedly and independently of one another

— Deuchar suggests that the

Negative Orientation	Positive Response to Negative Orientation	Positive Orientation	Negative Response to Positive Orientation
		PIDGINS AND CREOLES	
— an examination of focusing devices used in the early stages of Tok Pisin (Papua New Guinea) leads to the conclusion that leftward movement rules are considerably more likely to develop than rightward movement ones. This in turn may shed some light on the fact that in languages in general leftward movement rules tend to be unbounded, whereas rightward ones are severely constrained. *Aitchison*	rightward movement rules and that this fact can be accounted for in terms of the functional consideration of parsability. Deuchar illustrates that what appears to be focusing may in fact be topic marking; and that the prevalence of topic marking constructions in pidgin/creole data can be accounted for in terms of the functional consideration of ease of processing in a situation of communicative stress — such predictions could be supported by reanalysis of Aitchison's data and the collection of further data. *Deuchar Replies to Aitchison*	learning, by providing a unique test case for the 'poverty of the stimulus' argument — research in sign language development produces a different kind of evidence from that adduced by Chomsky, in that it shows what child grammars include when deprived of input data rather than what they exclude when exposed to limited data. While Chomsky's work so far might be said to be oriented towards determining the limits of boundaries of universal grammar, the sign language evidence could be said to give support to the idea that there *is* a universal grammar, as well as some concrete indications of what it minimally might contain. *Deuchar*	characteristics shared by pidgins, creoles and sign language are likely to be genetically programmed. Aitchison suggests that the particular features selected for comment fit well into the scenario Aitchison has proposed, they are the inevitable or most likely solution to a particular set of communicational problems — the typical, though not inevitable, relative positions of temporal and aspectual markers in pidgins, creoles and sign language can be explained as the most obvious response to a set of communicative needs. *Aitchison Replies to Deuchar*
		DISTINCTION BETWEEN CORE GRAMMAR AND PERIPHERY	
— three central characteristics of Chomsky's mentalistic linguistics are the autonomy thesis, the distinction between language and grammar and the view that language is a joint product of a number of mental faculties, of	— Gil argues persuasively that a wide variety of data conform to the small-precedes-large principle; furthermore, Gil is surely right that the principle applies to many different domains, not just natural language; there are, however,	— the distinction between core grammar and periphery plays a central part in Chomsky's recent work — the chapter argues that the distinction is a virtually inevitable consequence of Chomsky's basic	— the two chapters complement each other in that Gil argues that it is necessary to choose between a grammatical account and an account in terms of other mental faculties and Salkie's suggests that within grammar one must choose

which grammar is but one

— it is suggested that these three characteristics when followed through to their logical conclusions lead to a theory of grammar substantially different from most current models; a theory of considerably narrower scope

— a wide variety of phenomena in language and elsewhere is shown to instantiate a general principle of linearization whereby small precedes large; this principle is accounted for within a theory of man's prosodic faculty

— the linguistic phenomena upholding this principle—pertaining *inter alia* to syllable structure, case and agreement morphology and word order—are consequently argued to fall outside the scope of grammatical theory

— the methodological moral is that the study of grammar can only proceed hand in hand with the study of other mental faculties such as prosody, vision and mathematical reasoning

Gil

counter-examples

— Gil's work is not considered to be a direct challenge to the generative enterprise

— if Gil had taken some of the rules and principles proposed in Government Binding Theory and argued that his principle could handle the same data, then that would have cast doubt on Chomsky's approach

— Gil uses 'case marking morphology' as an example of a phenomenon which is generally considered to be 'hard-core grammatical' but which in his view is part of a theory of prosody

— the theory of case in core grammar is not concerned with morphological case; what the theory says is that every NP must have abstract case and that Case in this sense is assigned according to certain structural principles; Gil's work is concerned with an entirely different issue

— this comment applies to almost all the linguistic data that Gil discusses (except word order)

— Gil offers an alternative to Chomsky's approach rather than a challenge to it—he is not saying that Chomsky can achieve his goals in a different way, but that one should have different goals; Chomsky has always been single-minded in his pursuit of depth; people with the same cast of mind will continue to follow Chomsky;

aim in studying languages; to apply the approach of the natural sciences to the study of language

— the distinction is one of a number of idealizations and simplifications which Chomsky says are necessary if language is to be studied in this way; aspects of competence which in Chomsky's view are not amenable to explanation are called the periphery

— the theory of core grammar can be evaluated in two ways: it can be assumed that Chomsky's basic aim in the study of language is a valid one and notions like core and periphery can be assessed in terms of whether they contribute to that basic aim; the kind of work that core grammar advocates have produced can be looked at and consideration given to whether this is what linguists should be spending their time on

— with reference to the first approach, there is little doubt that the core-periphery distinction has enabled Chomsky and his co-workers to propose interesting hypotheses about language which have a considerable amount of depth; the notion of parameters of core grammar has led to many interesting attempts to reduce apparently unrelated differences between languages to one underlying difference; Chomsky and others are now able to assume a set of rules and conditions on rules

between a core-grammar account and an account in terms of rules and principles belonging to the periphery of grammatical theory

— Gil sheds serious doubt on Salkie's claim that the emphatic use of reflexes belongs to the periphery of grammar

— assuming as Gil has that language is a joint product of grammar and a number of other autonomous mental faculties, then the possibility clearly exists that linguistic phenomena not amenable to explanation within core grammar can be accounted for in terms of alternative theories pertaining to these other mental faculties; in other words there is no longer any need for a periphery

— however, the question is not one of need but of empirical fact; whether or not there exists a periphery within grammar is a question of substance about the way the mind, in particular the faculty of grammar, is structured

— two logically possible alternatives exist: that grammar contains a core grammar plus a periphery, and that grammar consists wholly of an undifferentiated core

— at present we are still far from being able to adjudicate between these two alternatives

— adopting a Galilean mode of inquiry it is therefore eminently reasonable for us to posit a periphery in which we may locate

Negative Orientation	Positive Response to Negative Orientation	Positive Orientation	Negative Response to Positive Orientation
DISTINCTION BETWEEN CORE GRAMMAR AND PERIPHERY			
	people who are interested in broader concerns will look for principles common to many faculties; for linguists of this kind, Gil's paper is a useful contribution. *Salkie Replies to Gil*	which are tightly integrated so that a small change in one area of the grammar can have large consequences — in a broader perspective, even if Chomsky is beginning to succeed in his aim, the question must be whether the notion of core grammar is just one more way of removing Chomsky's work from reality; it remains for the theory of universal grammar and empirical work on language acquisition to interact in fruitful ways. *Salkie*	linguistic phenomena that do not appear amenable to explanation within state-of-the-art theories of core grammar and of other mental faculties — ultimately, however, the choice between these two alternatives will depend on whether such theories succeed in accounting for the entirety of phenomena attributed during previous stages of research to the periphery. *Gil Replies to Salkie*
INNATISM VS CONSTRUCTIVISM			
— Chomsky's impact on philosophy and psychology is strong and salutary and Sinclair acknowledges the insights his work has afforded her personally — Chomsky's anti-empiricist views are shared but not his modular view of the human mind nor his genetic determinism of language — it is not believed that no real ontological development of important cognitive structures takes place; Piaget's theory is accepted	— Roeper asks if Sinclair's conclusions are about language or grammar; her approach might be on the right track in describing the growth of language; is it appropriate for the explanation of grammar? The terms 'grammar' and 'language' refer to vastly different phenomena in current linguistic theory; the term 'language' refers to the interaction of grammar with knowledge of the world; the term 'grammar' refers only to the deductive principles	— in general most theories in their internal structure cannot readily be compared; comparison of theories is not the goal of science; if a comparison must occur it should occur at another level, typical for biology; are the theories equally robust and do they both offer a subtle *fit* between theory and fact? — impressionistically, Piagetian theory seems programmatic and unable to address subtle features of human language; linguistic research	— on the whole Sinclair sees more convergence than conflict between Roeper's position and her own; she agrees that as yet there is no proper theory of language acquisition; it is, in Roeper's words, 'a complex process which we do not yet understand' — Sinclair is in agreement with what she sees as a purely constructivist Piagetian proposal that semantic factors interact with syntactic factors in a complex way and that

that especially human genetic endowment does not determine development in any direct way; 'between the level of hereditary characteristics and that of the acquisitions due to environmental factors, there is a level of self-regulation or equilibration which plays a vital role in development. This does not oblige or even authorize us to think of everything which is not due to exogenous learning as innate.' These epigenetic self-regulations become self-constructive mechanisms,

— Sinclair cannot see language competence in the form of universal grammar with the particular properties Chomsky bestows on it as a separate unit (not even if one accepted a modular view of the human mind); language is seen as a tool constructed by the human mind (on the basis of its innate capacities) in the service of representation and communication; even in a modular conception of human cognition, universal grammar cannot be seen as a primary, independent unit; it is believed that basic language competence is constructed by the child subsequent to and on the model of the child's fundamental achievements during the pre-verbal practical intelligence period

— Chomsky starts from facts about adults' knowledge, performs a highly technical analysis on certain common to all languages

— Piaget's work is open to the interpretation that local cognitive coherence, mapped directly onto neurological descriptions may, eventually, reveal that 'general cognition' or 'general psychological mechanisms' are a collection of epi-phenomena

— instead of 'psychology' we have modular systems which have individual neurological roots; sometimes modules reproduce the same knowledge in different domains (like stereoscopic eyes and ears), sometimes they interact mechanically (like the heart and lungs) and sometimes they interact in unsystematic ways producing the bewildering array of behaviour that typically occurs on any day in the life of a human being.

Roeper Replies to Sinclair

the acquisition process itself might lead to this pattern

— Sinclair finds a difference in relation to studying child grammar; she prefers to start with the study of child grammar to avoid an adult-centred bias rather than asking important questions about UG from the adult grammar working backwards to the child grammar; however, there is no reason why there might not be a meeting point in the middle of itineraries: a combination of both approaches would be promising

— with reference to the empirical challenge cited by Roeper to show how a child knows that certain sentences are disallowed or ungrammatical: how can a child avoid use of structures and forms which are *not* found in human language? Sinclair finds this most difficult to comment upon and a challenge for constructivist theory in general

— Sinclair elaborates Piaget's solution to this question but comments that it is only just beginning to be seen how this constructivist principle could be applied to language acquisition

— Sinclair's 'constructivist heart is delighted' with Roeper's hypothesis that 'what appears rather arbitrary in the adult language is rendered quite sensible when the problem of acquisition is included.'

Sinclair Replies to Roeper

constantly discovers new data which shift the centre of research and our view of what a theory must explain

— it is often asserted that children of 5 have mastered English grammar; yet most of the structures currently under scrutiny in linguistic theory have never undergone acquisition research; there is a vast descriptive deficit in acquisition work and a huge bias toward simple syntactic forms

— with reference to the roles of UG, the hunch is that the way to approach the question is from the adult grammar working backwards to the child grammar

— part of the problem lies in allegiance to the methods of the psychologist and not to the methods of the field linguist; we need first a rough sense obtainable by informal conversation of what lies in children's grammar and then a refined sense of how each step is taken; the distinctions are subtle and sharp enough that any consistent difference in interpretation (in virtually any experimental context) will be significant

— this is where Chomsky and Piaget may meet; Piaget's interview techniques resemble the methods of the field linguist and they become more and more relevant as the sophistication of linguistic theory grows.

Roeper

INNATISM VS CONSTRUCTIVISM

Negative Orientation	Positive Response to Negative Orientation	Positive Orientation	Negative Response to Positive Orientation
sentences, brings the system of rules he has uncovered back to a universal principle, and concludes it is implausible that this principle and thus the more specific rules could have been induced by native speakers from the evidence they dispose of — a constructivist psycholinguist starts from the facts about children's behaviour in experimental situations, analyzes the facts in a psycholinguistic manner and concludes that it is implausible that the developmental line uncovered could be the result of an unfolding innate competence. — Sinclair considers both methods justifiable and that neither is more 'scientific' nor 'explicit' than the other. *Sinclair*			

ARTIFICIAL INTELLIGENCE

Negative Orientation	Positive Response to Negative Orientation	Positive Orientation	Negative Response to Positive Orientation
— it is argued that Chomsky's adoption of a range of inappropriate metaphors, with which he has tried to support a particular view of linguistic methodology opposed to all	— Biggs originally anticipated in his communication with the editors that his views would emerge as occupying a fairly central position. It is therefore not surprising that Wilks and Biggs both accept that	— the extent of the possibility of establishing theoretical links between the work of Chomsky in theoretical linguistics and the field of Artificial Intelligence is	— both have emphasized the body of linguistic work, clearly within linguistic methodology, which can carry on a fruitful dialogue with AI and other computationalists

— considered

— it is concluded that Chomsky's influence on AI has been considerably less than his influence on other areas identified in this volume

— however, there is a clear sense in which AI can now benefit in practical and theoretical ways by drawing more on the work of linguists and (in particular) by incorporating the methodological insights and explanatory goals of current competence-based grammatical theories

— Chomsky's central tenet of the competence/performance distinction is of importance; four responses to this distinction are identified in the AI literature:

  1 The competence/performance distinction is only half relevant to AI, since AI is concerned with the way language is *used* and that is a matter of performance

  2 an acceptance (often implicit of the competence/performance distinction as such, but a rejection of the particular model of competence Chomsky offers, as made explicit in the grammar, as being fundamentally irrelevant to the needs of a discipline concerned, centrally, with processing

  3 a rejection of the first response in favour of a competence/performance distinction which

— that is proof that linguistic methodology is independent of the competence/performance issue, which is what, above all, has divided Chomsky from AI

— the competence/performance distinction and all that followed from it was peculiarly Chomsky's and not any essential part of the discipline

— if there is disagreement with Biggs, it is over the list of responses in AI to this lack of fit (between the competence-performance distinction and process-based accounts of language); the list seems both to misrepresent attitudes in AI in recent years, and still to pay too much implicit respect to the distinction itself (CPD)

— the four responses he gives can be characterized as:

  1 AI is about *use* so the CPD is irrelevant

  2 CPD is irrelevant to AI because Chomsky's own particular grammar model is irrelevant to processing

  3 CPD applies equally well to processing itself and so may apply equally as well to AI as linguistics

  4 AI builds systems and has no time for the considerations that CPD expresses

— Biggs' own view seems to be that (3) is the only basis for interaction between AI and linguistics, and that this will in the end reduce to AI's

— contact and influence in relation to Chomsky's work and Artificial Intelligence have so far been minimal

— however, there is disagreement concerning the respective perceptions of the essential characteristics of Chomskyan linguistics, which are elaborated by Biggs.

Biggs Replies to Wilks

— empirical concerns, has been at the heart of the controversies and misunderstandings between artificial intelligence workers and Chomsky and his supporters

— recent developments in linguistics, free of the competence/performance distinction, show that there are at bottom no insuperable barriers between the two disciplines

— both AI and TGG emerged as representational studies from predecessors that were in a strong sense anti-representational (cybernetics and structural linguistics)

— early AI work on the analysis and understanding of general natural language was much preoccupied by what its practitioners saw as the wrongheadedness of Chomsky's preoccupation with syntax and the need for semantics-based methods to understand language

— in doing so they may well have overlooked much that was of value in Chomsky's system; but on balance they were right for TGG itself has changed to give a far greater role to logic semantics and surface considerations than was then the case

— a key matter at issue between Chomsky and much of AI, as it is between certain groups of AI workers, is the modularity of knowledge and whether there is, in any useful sense, a language faculty

— the question can be thrown into

Negative Orientation	Positive Response to Negative Orientation	Positive Orientation	Negative Response to Positive Orientation
		ARTIFICIAL INTELLIGENCE	

Negative Response to Positive Orientation

need 'for a sustaining meta-theory'; Wilks cannot accept this account as giving a fair statement of AI views, even though researchers can be found to express each

— Wilks' understanding of current discussions between AI workers and linguists is that they do not proceed on the basis of (3) at all, but on a tacit understanding that CPD is irrelevant to the details of the systems they want to discuss and implement

— (3) is not a bridge between linguistics and AI because the distinction is not the same in the two areas of linguistics and computer science

— as to the plea about meta-theory, AI is a discipline and will work up its own

— Wilks' hope and belief is that AI will develop its own methodology and its own particular theories in the area of a language.

Wilks Replies to Biggs

Positive Orientation

applies *across* the domain of processing; on this view a theory of competence should hook up with processing phenomena (in some way not typically very clearly articulated) although it is accepted that some aspects of processing will need to be covered by a theory of performance

4 there is no time for self-indulgent philosophizing.

— it is clear that for fruitful contact between Chomskyan linguistics and AI, the third response, or a minor variant on it, has to be the accepted one

— it is argued that AI is, for both theoretical and practical reasons, in need of a sustaining meta-theory; Chomsky's recent discussion in *Rules and Representations* suggests that a (new-style) competence-based theory might well be developed to serve that function; which grammar will turn out in the end to be more user-friendly to the computer, government and Binding or Generalized Phrase Structure grammar, or one of the other alternatives, is a matter for debate

Negative Orientation

sharper relief by an extreme position held in AI: that language is merely one among many alternative ways of achieving human ends and often no more than a side effect of other processes

— Chomsky responds in terms of unsuitable metaphors and false inferences, however recent writings qualify that: 'we should not exclude the possibility that what we now think of as language might consist of quite disparate cognitive systems that interweave'; if that quotation really represents Chomsky's considered position then there may be no serious dispute

— in conclusion Wilks declares his personal interest in the procedural explication of language mechanisms and the relationship of meaning and language; he believes that there must be distinctive representations and characterizations for the language phenomenon and that these cannot be replaced by side-effect explanations or by general word-knowledge mechanisms

— most of the evidence is known to Chomsky but his assertions are not based on testable evidence and are

— not contributing to the endeavour.
Wilks

— reciprocal interaction between AI and linguistics would seem beneficial.
Biggs

EPISTEMOLOGY

— Chomsky's claim that language competence exists as a 'mental organ' distinct from but 'interacting' with other mental organs is, like much of Chomsky's theorizing, fascinating, provocative and deeply obscure

— it is argued that Chomsky's insistence that linguistic competence consists in *sui generis* linguistic rules and representations makes speech production, comprehension and acquisition very difficult to conceptualize

— the basic problem is how an 'interaction' is supposed to take place between a conceptual and a formal-computational component this difficulty carries over into the way in which Chomsky regards the scientific status of this theoretical psychology

— Chomsky feels able to justify paying scant attention to the extra-linguistic determinants of language competence

— the aim in this chapter is not to elucidate the obscurity of Chomsky's theorizing but to say, as it were, 'if this is what Chomsky means then he is wrong.'
Russell

— argues that Russell is concerned with the philosophy and methodology of theoretical psychology and Carr with the method and philosophy of theoretical linguistics

— both Russell and Carr argue that there is a discrepancy between what Chomsky does and what he says he is doing, both agree that whatever it is, it is not theoretical psychology

— Carr's principal point is 'that it is a mistake in the first place to take theoretical linguistics to constitute theoretical psychology, and that, as an autonomous activity, theoretical linguistics is a perfectly valid area of scientific inquiry, with an object and a methodology quite distinct from that of theoretical psychology.'

— there are a couple of points on which Russell and Carr are in disagreement. One of them is Russell's claim that theoretical linguistics (as represented by Chomskyan linguistics) is not a scientific enterprise, and the other concerns the status of 'holism' as opposed to 'interaction' (between modules, specifically)
Carr Replies to Russell

— a fundamental assumption in Chomsky's work is that the object of linguistic inquiry should be taken to be a speaker—internal, psychological entity

— this assumption has been fairly widely accepted in the past, and with it the view that linguistics is therefore a branch of cognitive psychology

— however, this conception of the ontological status of linguistic structure has been challenged over the years by those in the field of philosophy of linguistics and within theoretical linguistics itself

— principal among these are Itkonen and Katz, both of whom take the object of linguistic inquiry to be non-psychological, and both of whom establish a philosophical basis for an autonomous theoretical linguistics, distinct from either psycholinguistics or sociolinguistics

— Katz's and Itkonen's arguments in favour of autonomism are adopted, but proposals that linguistic objects are Platonic objects or are characterizable in terms of social norms are rejected

— interactionism is suggested as an alternative which acts as the basis

— Russell finds it difficult to understand how any substantial *rapprochement* between the Chomskyan and Katzian positions can be made

— linguistic realism is thoroughly incompatible with that which makes Chomsky's theory interesting to psychologists and philosophers

— Chomsky tells us that linguistic reality is welded to psychological reality by virtue of the fact that human grammar must be learnable there must be something about linguistic structures that renders them accessible to young humans with such-and-such psychological capacities

— the importance of learnability theory is an empirical question; whereas Katzian realism seems to assume *a priori* that language is acquired by general problem-solving mechanisms

— a further problem with Platonism in linguistics is shared with Platonism in logic; autonomous symbol relations do not constitute necessary relations because necessity is conferred in terms of the intentions under which the symbols are held

Negative Orientation	Positive Response to Negative Orientation	Positive Orientation	Negative Response to Positive Orientation
EPISTEMOLOGY			
		for an autonomous theoretical linguistics, but which nonetheless allows for fruitful interdisciplinary work on the relationship between, on the one hand, linguistic structure per se, and on the other, social, psychological and neurological factors — this allows the retention of Chomsky's realist position, his view of language as a product of biological development and his interdisciplinary goal. *Carr*	— it seems to be the case that 'holding under an intention' is a quintessentially psychological state of affairs; if so, the same form of argument could be used against any Platonic notion of being 'grammatically acceptable' — this fact has implications for how we judge ungrammaticality and non-standard English. *Russell Replies to Carr*
ANTHROPOLOGICAL LINGUISTICS			
— the direct influence of Chomsky in the field of anthropology has been slight — a series of mitigations to reduce the target for counter-attack is presented, without basically revoking the above thesis — the study of language *per se* by anthropologists is rare; it is regarded as a tool for communication and for the explication of social meaning — the influence of structuralism led to attempts to lay bare the underlying	— Atran proposes other reasons for Chomsky's lack of influence in British social anthropology — anthropology has come to renounce all appeal to nativism as ideologically pernicious — another reason pertains to the epistemological bias in anthropology — the practical sense of everyday experience was considered incapable of creating consistent systems of relations connecting the concrete categories of experience or of	— there are striking cross-cultural uniformities in the structure of folkbiological classification — it is argued that such uniform taxonomic knowledge, under sociocultural learning situations so diverse, results from certain regular and domain-specific processes of human cognition, though local circumstances undoubtedly trigger and condition the stable forms of knowledge attained — meaning for living kind terms is analyzed as essentially distinct from	— Atran's chapter attempts to look at the similarities of folk classifications of animals and plants, i.e., 'living kinds' in his terminology; his point is that the cross-cultural uniformities in the structure of such classifications is so striking that it must be attributed to some universal, though 'domain-specific', process of human cognition — his basic point is that all classification systems of plants and animals operate differently from classification systems of artifacts or

other non-living things
— Criper is not clear that the distinction Atran makes between living and non-living classifications is as clearcut
— there are many difficulties in classification, particularly in the changing environment with the introduction of new species;
— variations along the continuum occur and different groups make cuts at different points
— the rate of introduction of new things requiring to be fitted into existing classifications is far greater for non-living things at present
— Atran presents this opposition between living forms and non-living forms as an illustration of the interest in anthropological work of 'universals', i.e., a cross-cultural similarity in human cognitive behaviour; this derives from the influence of Chomsky, though not in any direct form; while the search for universals of this sort is to be applauded, Criper remains somewhat sceptical that the environmental factors are as absent as is implied.

Criper Replies to Atran

the semantics of other object domains (e.g., artifacts)
— a living kind being is conceived as a physical sort whose intrinsic 'nature' is presumed, even if unknown; that is, the semantically typical properties which the definition of a living kind term describes are necessary
— not merely possible—by virtue of the presumed underlying nature of that kind; that is why, e.g., a legless tiger can still be classed with animals considered to be quadrupeds 'by nature'
— it is this presumption of underlying nature which underpins the taxonomic stability of such phenomenal kinds
— also our ordinary commitment to phenomenally typical properties precludes construing the bond between a phenomenal type and its underlying nature simply as a causal tie between a provisionally useful stereotype and some nomic essence which experts tell us our stereotype must really stand for (or, barring likely discovery of a nomic essence, stand for nothing at all)
— commonsense meaning may thus be logically independent of scientific reference: e.g., trees and sparrows remain American folk kinds, with presumed natures, even though they are not scientific (phyletic) kinds.

Atran

absorbing new experiences
— anthropologists do not forsake the assumption that inextricably binds the cognitive foundations of local knowledge to social ceremony
— basic commonsense dispositions are universal aspects of propositional (i.e., truth-valuable) understanding of the everyday environment
— humankind is universally disposed to believe or know to be true that the world of everyday experience is composed of artifacts that exist by reason of the functions humans give them, and of natural chemical and biological kinds that exist by virtue of their physically given causal natures; *inter alia* these are the universally perceived facts
— whether because of universalist or relativist positions, claims for the existence of highly articulated, transcultural and domain-specific cognitive principles are largely denied by anthropologists
— Chomsky's significance for anthropology, as elsewhere, stems not so much from the particulars of his method of linguistic analysis as from a general philosophical attitude to the cognitive unity of mankind.

Atran Replies to Criper

structure of society
— Chomsky himself has always been quite categoric in maintaining the uniqueness of language and the improbability of the language system being a model which can be used for the description and analysis of a social system attempting to show that society operated like language has not in itself provided stimulating insights; the straight linguistic concepts do not fit the anthropologist's intuitions about the ethnographic facts or any 'structure' underlying them
— current anthropology is experiencing its own movement to parallel the ethmomethodological trends in sociology; a traditional acceptance of the anthropologist as (impartial) observer of either structures or relations between signs is questioned by those who argue for more self-awareness of the role and practice of the anthropologist in 'translating' one cultural experience to another; it is also questioned by those who wish to emphasize man's ability to define and interpret meaning and not receive it as automata
— Chomsky's claims do not take him to attempt to examine the way in which the outside environment triggers and shapes the way in which language grows in the mind he clearly does not deny the effect of the environment—children grow

Negative Orientation	Positive Response to Negative Orientation	Positive Orientation	Negative Response to Positive Orientation

ANTHROPOLOGICAL LINGUISTICS

up speaking different languages and that is clearly not due to any genetically determined factor

— the anthropologist's comparative lack of interest in Chomsky's work derives from a preoccupation with differences shaped by environmental (social) factors

— at the cognitive level anthropologists are interested in whether the utterances that occur as a result of environmental factors are associated with different conceptual structures

— to this question, so fundamental to the anthropologist's study of systems of classification, Chomsky has nothing to say other than that the answer is not known.

Criper

Author Index

Subject Index